CULTURAL HISTORIES OF CINEMA

This new book series examines the relationship between cinema and culture. It will feature interdisciplinary scholarship that focuses on the national and transnational trajectories of cinema as a network of institutions, representations, practices and technologies. Of primary concern is analysing cinema's expansive role in the complex social, economic and political dynamics of the twentieth and twenty-first centuries.

SERIES EDITORS
Lee Grieveson and Haidee Wasson

FORTHCOMING
Subcinema: Mapping Informal Film Distribution, *Ramon Lobato*

Empire and Film

Edited by **Lee Grieveson and Colin MacCabe**

●

A BFI book published by Palgrave Macmillan

Contents

COLONIALISM AND THE REPRESENTATION OF SPACE

AFRICAN EXPERIMENTS

Contributors

SCOTT ANTHONY is a Leverhulme Fellow at Christ's College, Cambridge. He is the author of *Public Relations and the Making of Modern Britain* (2011), the BFI Film Classics volume on *Nightmail* (2007) and co-editor of *The Projection of England: A History of the GPO Film Unit* (2011).

JAMES BURNS teaches African history at Clemson University. He is the author of *Flickering Shadows: Cinema and Identity in Colonial Zimbabwe* (2002), and co-author (with Robert O. Collins) of *A History of Sub-Saharan Africa* (2007). He is currently writing a history of cinemagoing in the British Empire before World War II.

IAN CHRISTIE is a film critic, broadcaster and historian, with special interests in British and European cinema, and in the impact of new technologies on audiovisual spectacle. His work on early cinema began with *The Last Machine* (1995), a BBC television series and accompanying book, which he wrote. A study of Robert Paul and the origins of the British film business is in preparation. He is Professor of Film and Media History at Birkbeck College, University of London, a Fellow of the British Academy and vice-president of Europa Cinemas.

JULIE CODELL is Professor in Art History at Arizona State University, and affiliate in Film and Media Studies, English, Gender and Women's Studies, and at the Center for Asian Research. She wrote *The Victorian Artist* (2003) and *Images of an Idyllic Past: Edward Curtis's Photographs* (1988); edited *The Art of Transculturation* (2012), *Photography and the Imperial Durbars of British India* (2011), *The Political Economy of Art* (2008), *Genre, Gender, Race, World Cinema* (2007) and *Imperial Co-histories* (2003) and co-edited *Encounters in the Victorian Press* (2004) and *Orientalism Transposed* (1998), now translated into Japanese (2011). She teaches courses on South Asian film, artists' biopics, empire film and world film. She has received fellowships from the American Institute of Indian Studies, Getty Foundation, National Endowment for the Humanities, Yale British Art Center, Harry Ransom Humanities Center and Huntington Library.

FRANCIS GOODING is a writer and researcher, whose research interests include colonial history, art history and music. His publications include a book on modernist painting, *Black Light*, and he has written widely on art and music. He worked as a member of the postdoctoral research team on the 'Colonial Film: Moving Images of the British Empire' project, and he teaches at Birkbeck College and the London Consortium.

LEE GRIEVESON is Reader in Film Studies and Director of the Graduate Programme in Film Studies at University College London. He is author of *Policing Cinema: Movies and Censorship in Early-Twentieth-century America* (2004), and co-editor of various volumes, including *The Silent Cinema Reader* (2004), with Peter Krämer, and *Inventing Film Studies* (2008), with Haidee Wasson. Grieveson was co-principal investigator, with Colin MacCabe, of the 'Colonial Film: Moving Images of the British Empire' project, which aimed to digitally archive British colonial cinema spanning the twentieth century and to organise scholarly gatherings to investigate these materials. The project's website is <www.colonialfilm.org.uk>.

TOBY HAGGITH is a historian who joined the Imperial War Museum's Film Department in 1988. In 2000 he took charge of non-commercial access to the film and video collection and became responsible for devising the daily public film show programme. He is now a Senior Curator in the Department of Research and is in overall charge of the museum's annual film festival, which has been running since November 2001. He has a PhD in Social History from the University of Warwick and has published various essays on film and history. He is the co-editor, with Joanna Newman, of *Holocaust and the Moving Image: Representations in Film and Television since 1933* (2005), which is based on a conference held at the museum in April 2001. In 2007 he was a Visiting Research Fellow at the Humanities Research Centre, College of Arts and Social Sciences, Australian National University, Canberra. His research topic was titled 'The Heirs of Uncle Toby Shandy: Military Re-enactment in British Society and Culture'.

PRIYA JAIKUMAR is Associate Professor at the University of Southern California's School of Cinematic Arts, Department of Critical Studies. Her research interests include colonial histories of European cinemas, transformations in film policy and film form in India and spatial politics in film. Her book *Cinema at the End of Empire: A Politics of Transition in Britain and India* (2006) detailed the intertwined histories of British and Indian cinema from 1927–47. Other writings on cultural regulation, feminism, transnationalism and film appear in *Cinema Journal*, *The Moving Image*, *Post Script*, *Screen*, *World Literature Today*, *Velvet Light Trap*, anthologies like *Hollywood Abroad*, *Transnational Feminism in Film and Media*, *Outsider Films* and the forthcoming *Border Crossing*. Currently, she is working on a book called *On Location: India and the Problem of Space in Cinema*, and co-editing an anthology on the cultural turn in the study of state power.

COLIN MacCABE is Distinguished Professor of English and Film at the University of Pittsburgh and Associate Director of the London Consortium. He has taught at Cambridge, Strathclyde, Exeter and Birkbeck College, University of London. Between 1985 and 1998 he worked for the British Film Institute. His publications include *James Joyce and the Revolution of the Word*, *Godard: A Portrait of the Artist at 70*, *T. S. Eliot*, *The Butcher Boy* and the co-edited *True to the Spirit: Film Adaptation and the Question of Fidelity*.

CHARLES MUSSER is a Professor of Film Studies and Theater Studies at Yale University where he teaches courses in documentary film-making and critical studies. His books on silent film include *Oscar Micheaux and His Circle: African American Filmmaking and Race Cinema of the Silent Era* (2001, co-edited with Pearl Bowser and Jane Gaines). He recently completed the documentary *Errol Morris: A Lightning Sketch* (2011) with Carina Tautu.

TOM RICE is a Lecturer in Film Studies at the University of St Andrews. Prior to this appointment, he was the senior researcher for three years on the 'Colonial Film' project. As part of this work, he wrote more than 200 historical essays, focused primarily on Africa and the Caribbean, which are published online at <www. colonialfilm.org.uk>. He has also written on Malaya and on Indian newsreels, and has undertaken extensive research on the colonial film units. His dissertation at UCL was on the racial politics of silent cinema, and he is currently developing this as a manuscript.

ABOUBAKAR SANOGO is an Assistant Professor in Film Studies at Carleton University. His research interests include African cinema and culture, documentary, world cinema, colonial cinema and the relationship between film form, history and theory.

RICHARD SMITH teaches in the Department of Media and Communications, Goldsmiths University of London. He specialises in the race and gender implications of military service and has written widely on the experience of West Indians and black Britons in World War I. His book *Jamaican Volunteers in the First World War* (2004) has recently been reissued and he is currently researching the role of the media in the British West Indies from World War I to the labour rebellions of the 1930s.

DAVID TROTTER is King Edward VII Professor of English Literature at the University of Cambridge. He was co-founder of the Cambridge Screen Media Group and first Director of the university's MPhil in Screen Media and Cultures. His most recent publications are *Cinema and Modernism* (2007) and *The Uses of Phobia: Essays on Literature and Film* (2010).

AARON WINDEL writes on themes related to the history of development, media, empire and modern enclosure movements. He is currently a Visiting Lecturer of European History at the University of Massachusetts Amherst.

Acknowledgments

Empire and Film grows like its companion volume *Film and the End of Empire* out of an Arts and Humanities Research Council Major Resource Enhancement research project entitled 'Colonial Film: Moving Images of the British Empire', which ran from October 2007 to September 2010. The project produced a catalogue for the 6,200 films representing British colonies housed in the British Film Institute (BFI), the Imperial War Museum (IWM) and the British Empire and Commonwealth Museum. That catalogue, with over thirty hours of digitised films and various writings about the films and other institutions, can be visited at <colonialfilm.org.uk>.

The initial idea for the project came from Heather Stewart at the BFI, who asked Colin MacCabe, then at the University of Exeter, to lead the bid. While Colin MacCabe was preparing this initial bid with Patrick Russell, Senior Curator of Non-fiction at the BFI National Archive, and Kay Gladstone of the IWM, Emma Sandon of Birkbeck College alerted him to a complementary bid being prepared by Anna Maria Motrescu of the British Empire and Commonwealth Museum and she joined the team, which submitted a bid that also included the Bill Douglas Centre at the University of Exeter. This bid was turned down in 2006. A new bid was submitted later that year, which was prepared by Colin MacCabe, now based at Birkbeck, and Lee Grieveson of University College London (UCL), who became Co-director. The project was led by MacCabe and Grieveson, with a research team including Russell, Gladstone, Sandon and Nigel Algar, Senior Curator of Fiction at the BFI National Archive.

The research team started work in October 2007 with Tom Rice and Anna Maria Motrescu as postdoctoral researchers. Anna Maria left the project to work in Cambridge in 2009 and was replaced by Francis Gooding. Before that, with funds provided by the London Consortium, Richard Osborne had been recruited as a third researcher. In May 2009 Filipa César joined the team to prepare her film and installation *Black Balance*. The team held regular seminars throughout the three years: thanks to Stuart Hall, Paul Gilroy, Priya Jaikumar, Tom Gunning, Stephen Frears, Laura Mulvey, Patrick Manning and David Trotter. The seminars led to two conferences, one held in London in July 2010 and one held in Pittsburgh in September 2010.

The project was administered through Birkbeck College with particular efficiency by Liz Francis. We benefited greatly from support from both the London Consortium and the University of Pittsburgh. The London Consortium contributed considerable financial support and two of the postdoctoral researchers. The Director of the London Consortium, Steve Connor, was particularly helpful in ensuring that the project had a real multidisciplinary base. The conference in London was supported with help from the Faculty of Arts and Humanities at UCL (special thanks to Henry Woudhuysen), and the Department of English and Humanities at Birkbeck (special thanks to Sue Wiseman). In Pittsburgh, John Cooper, Dean of Arts and Sciences, and Lucy Fischer, Director of Film Studies, pledged very considerable financial support to the project and their funds were supplemented by the Program in Global Studies (special thanks to Pat Manning and Nancy Condee), the Faculty Research Support Program (special thanks to Nicole Constable), the Humanities Center (special thanks to Jonathan Arac), the Department of English (special thanks to Johnny Twyning) and the Program in Cultural Studies (special thanks to Gissepina Mecchia). Neepa Majundrar and Shalini Puri helped to plan the Pittsburgh conference with administrative support from Carol Myselwiec. Sarah Joshi organised both conferences with exemplary efficiency. We would like to thank also Lora Brill, Lauren and Riley Martin-Grieveson, Rebecca Barden and Sophia Contento at BFI Publishing, and our contributors to these two books.

Lee Grieveson and Colin MacCabe, London and Pittsburgh, March 2011

'To take ship to India and see a naked man spearing fish in blue water': Watching Films to Mourn the End of Empire

Colin MacCabe

I might have called this introductory essay 'Never Apologise, Never Explain'. That was the advice offered by the late nineteenth-century Master of Balliol, Benjamin Jowett, to the young men whose education he oversaw, when the time came for them to leave the college and sally forth to rule the empire.[1] I must confess to a sneaking regard for the maxim. In an era where apologetic confession has become a dominant genre across domestic and public life, I prefer as a virtue the Stoic recognition of error. And as for explanation, there is so much of our lives to which T. S. Eliot's words about the impossibility of explanation apply: 'I can't tell you, not because I don't want to but because I cannot find the words to express it.'[2] And yet if it is possible to construe Jowett's maxim in positive fashion, it must also be admitted there is no more concise summary of the certainty that is perhaps the most seductive of imperialism's pleasures – to always be right, to be transported to a realm in which doubt is impossible. However, that pleasure should always be trumped by the even greater intellectual pleasure of getting it wrong, by the tremendously exciting possibility of failure. No intellectual inquiry is of much interest if its outcome is known in advance.

The research project of which this book *Empire and Film* and its companion volume *Film and the End of Empire* are a part risked failure at three very different levels. The initial task was to provide a catalogue for the films representing British colonies held in three different institutions: the British Film Institute, the Imperial War Museum and the British and Empire Commonwealth Museum. This catalogue was dependent on getting academics and archivists to work together. This, at least in principle, is about as advisable as throwing a set of cats into a sack. Archivists famously hate academics and academics despise archivists. Academics tend to regard archivists as dim troglodytes difficult to tempt from the underground dungeons in which they hoard treasures that they do not fully appreciate. Archivists tend to regard academics as arrogant ignoramuses; parochial in their intellectual interests, and incapable of understanding the long-term value of the material they are studying. It has to be said that both are, of course, right. Archivists conserve material so that future generations can find in it meanings which are not yet apparent to us, academics are concerned to interpret that material in terms of the meanings that are pressingly evident to them. My decade as Head of Research at the British Film Institute from 1989 to 1998 had given me a good understanding of both perspectives and I felt that it was of importance for the future of film studies to show that genuine collaboration between these two fundamentally different approaches was possible. June Givanni's work at the BFI for Africa 95 had also made me aware of a rich corpus of colonial films that had not been fully catalogued and whose very existence was known to only a handful of scholars. When it became possible to add the complementary holdings of the Imperial War Museum and the British Empire and Commonwealth Museum, it seemed clear that we had a perfect example of a corpus that needed collaboration between academics and archivists to make it available for wider study both by academics and by a more general public.

The primary task was to prepare a catalogue and one thing that a catalogue promises is completeness. Let us be clear that such completeness is always misleading for it promises a sufficiency that it cannot deliver. You probably don't have to be a pupil of Derrida or of Godel to appreciate the theoretical point. If one promises a catalogue *raisonnée* of Picasso, and it should be said that just such an art-historical genre was one of the models that the research team considered at the beginning of its work, one is assuming an importance for the individual artist that may be very misleading. Would a catalogue *raisonnée* of Picasso, Matisse and Braque 1906–14 not be more complete, or one that linked Picasso's work to the African art that was so powerful an influence and so on literally, if we talk theoretically, to infinity.

However, in committing itself to a catalogue the project had to opt for the vernacular of empiricism and to eschew the more complex questions of theoretical tongues. If we were to compile a catalogue then our first job was to establish a corpus. Our initial parameter was given by the holdings of the three archives with which we were working. First, the British Film Institute, which held many of the state-funded policy and educational films shot in the colonies. Then the Imperial War Museum with its unparalleled holdings in the field of conflict. These included, most importantly, footage from World War I that ruined for ever any claims of the superiority of European civilisation and World War II when the empire rallied to the anti-fascist flag on the explicit understanding that it was assisting at the end of empire. But it also included a wealth of material from, to take merely two examples, Palestine at the time of the mandate and Malaya during the Emergency, which illustrated the centrality of conflict to the empire throughout the twentieth century. Finally, the holdings of the British Empire and Commonwealth Museum completed these largely public holdings with some 800 home movies shot by those who administered Britain's colonies – a domestic record of empire.

The first definition of the corpus was thus given institutionally – we were looking at films held in these three institutions as the research project started at the beginning of October 2007. The institutions were determined by funding. It would of course make much more sense for this project to have been an international one. But, despite what the papers tell you, globalisation is not a recent event. It begins more than 500 years ago with Da Gama's rounding of the Cape and Columbus's crossing of the Atlantic. Indeed my dear dead colleague Paul Hirst used to argue that the international capital flows in the period leading up to World War I were a much more significant form of financial globalisation than more recent developments.[3] Certainly the distribution of film was much more globalised in this decade than at any time later in the twentieth century.[4] Hirst also argued very persuasively that the power of national governments has not been significantly weakened by the most recent wave of globalisations. What is certain is that our research was funded nationally and the most important definition of the corpus was determined by the national institutions that were our partners in the bid. It should be stressed that at every stage we were more than conscious of the international dimensions of our work and that we made every effort that we could to internationalise the perspectives on our research. Indeed, the two concluding conferences in London and Pittsburgh in July and September 2010 represented a major element in this effort. Even more crucial to that effort is the publication of the proceedings of those conferences. However, it is important to stress the national nature of our funding and the extent to which that determined our corpus. To develop fully the work begun with the catalogue and website will require the full participation of former colonies. The fact that the primary outcome of this research will be a globally available website, one with access to thirty hours of digitised film, removes some if not all of the material obstacles to such participation and one can hope it will stimulate interest across the full range of the former colonies. From another perspective the research would benefit from complementary work with the other former European empires. The Portuguese, the Dutch, the French, the Belgian, the German (I cite them in chronological order) all have similar archives and a comparative study would, I think, prove both fascinating and illuminating. But if the national nature of the corpus was given, there were further choices that were, more consciously, ours.

The two most important deliberate choices were the following: 1) to limit ourselves to celluloid rather than video; and 2) to opt for a juridical definition of the colonies in the definition of the films that we would catalogue. The choice of film rather than television was centrally governed by the research time at our disposal. Almost all significant colonies had achieved independence by 1965 and the video record was meagre. Both the war over the Malvinas/Falklands in 1982 and Hong Kong in the period leading up to China's resumption of sovereignty in 1997 had left a huge video archive that was beyond our resources to catalogue properly. Second was the vexed question of whether we should include the Dominions within our corpus. The decision against was again partly dictated by available resources, but just as the post-65 colonies fell outside the clear period of colonialism and de-colonisation, so the Dominions with their very different relations both to Britain and their own indigenous populations seemed to constitute a different set of political and cultural relations.

If these two axes of selection combined economic necessity and cultural analysis, two further choices seem much less justified. By opting for a juridical definition of a colony, we excluded all of South America apart from Guyana and yet on both economic and cultural grounds, it might be argued that a country like Argentina was just as closely bound to Britain as colonies in other parts of the globe. Perhaps even more serious: why accept the formal achievement of independence as a crucial break in the filmic record? Surely it is just as interesting to see what transformations attend these political changes. Here, most importantly, resources and funding were determining: our designated archives held almost no post-independence films and with only two postdoctoral researchers and effectively no travel budget we felt that this research would be dependent on inter-archival co-operation. When we started we had optimistic views of similar research projects running concurrently with our own. These hopes proved unrealistic but it cannot be stressed too strongly that our project marks only the first stage of what must be an international process if it is to achieve its most ambitious intellectual goals. The establishment of the website and the publication of these volumes is simply the first stage in a work that must involve the archives of the former colonies and further reflection from former colonies if it is to achieve genuine fruition.

These conscious decisions did produce the first requirement of a catalogue, that is a defined corpus: more than 6,200 films from over fifty colonies with 2,900 titles at the IWM, including a large number of rushes, 2,500 at the British Film Institute and 800 at the British Empire and Commonwealth Museum. The corpus constituted, we now had to fulfil our most precise intellectual aim and here I quote from the original Arts and Humanities Research Council (AHRC) bid: 'to offer a model of collaboration between archives and universities integrating international standards of cataloguing with production of academic knowledge at the highest level'. It is worth noting, in this context, that it was a conscious aim of the project to recruit researchers who were not only versed in film studies but who had qualifications and competences across the range of the humanities and social sciences: history, anthropology, art history, cultural studies, music studies and more.

The decisions on the constitution of the corpus occupied some two weeks, but it took us a further three months to settle on the form of the catalogue. In addition to the basic cataloguing that was intended for all titles, we wished to produce a form of enhanced catalogue entry that would guide any future researchers or teachers and that would open up a relatively closed and specialised collection to much wider audiences.

We did not aim to provide enhanced entries for all titles both because of the labour involved and because the archivists, who at that stage knew the collection better than anyone, felt that there was a great deal of repetition of date, region and genre. It was decided initially that we would attempt to produce enhanced entries for 10 per cent of the collection that we then calculated at 6,000 films. In fact, as we began to explore the corpus, we discovered that it was slightly larger than we thought but more repetitive. It also became clear that there were a number of institutions that warranted completely separate and much longer entries (the Colonial Film Unit and the multiple national film units that it spawned; the Empire Marketing Board and the Central Office of Information would be three such examples). We therefore in the second year, in consultation with the AHRC, revised our target of enhanced entries to 5 per cent or 350 (in fact, the figure is slightly higher) and added some twenty plus topic entries to our targets.

It should be said that these enhanced entries remain the core of the research project and it is probably worth saying something about their structure. Each film has, in addition to the basic cataloguing information, a 1,000-word entry, the length determined both by the time and labour of writing and the time and labour of reading. The entry is divided into two parts: context and analysis. The context section is itself divided into two; the first providing an account of the film's context in terms of the film institutions that produced it; and the second concentrating on the political, social and historical backdrop. The analysis that follows focuses on the film's form and genre to produce a preliminary reading of the film. Theoretically, of course, such divisions are suspect. It is an axiom of film theory that the frame is an integral part of the image and thus to divorce the context from the analysis is already to operate a spurious distinction. Further to attempt to divide the specifics of film history from the wider industrial, economic, political and ideological history of capitalism is to misunderstand how film is woven into the fabric of imperialism. From the Hays Code to the Blum Byrnes agreement – what might seem discrete events in an industrial history rapidly reveal themselves, on any serious inspection, as key moments in wider social, political and economic developments.[5] Notwithstanding these arguments, we felt that, to make the catalogue of more practical use, a division should be observed between discrete industrial history and wider historical processes, which future users could deconstruct in more complex analyses. While perhaps even more conscious of the provisionality of the line between context and text, we felt again, within the limits of the catalogue, that it was valuable to include a discrete analysis of each chosen film although we were well aware that the analysis section was of necessity more personal than the context. That is one of the reasons all entries have initials to identify their author. Let me take one such film, *District Officer* (1945), and consider its entry both as example and to lead us into more complex arguments about the value of this collection and to consider more difficult questions of success and failure.[6]

CONTEXT

District Officer was produced in 1945 by Information Films of India (IFI), and distributed throughout the British Empire by the Central Film Library, Imperial Institute (London). The IFI was a state-funded body producing war propaganda and the Indian News Parade with largely Indian personnel. Ezra Mir, the producer of this film, worked both for IFI and its predecessor the Film Advisory Board from 1940–6 (IFI was established in 1943). In this period Mir produced over 170 films, both short documentaries (of 1,000 ft) and 'quickies' (of 250 ft), working alongside Bhaskar Rao and B. Mitra. IFI produced material in English, Bengali, Hindi, Tamil and Telagu versions.

IFI initially focused on wartime propaganda under the direction of the information and broadcasting department However, over time IFI shifted towards more social, economic and ethnographic topics with titles like 1944's *Tree of Wealth* and *Kisan*, *Rural Bengal*, *All India Radio*, *Child Welfare* and *Country Craft*, all produced in the immediate post-war period. In 1948, IFI was reconfigured into the new Indian state with the remit of producing 'films for public information, education, motivation and for institutional and cultural purposes', to be distributed by Documentary Films of India. Mir left IFI in 1946 and went on to become a crucial figure in the post-independence film industry.

District officers were a crucial element of the British administration in India. Recruitment had been extended to Indians from late Victorian times but their numbers grew particularly after Britain's declared aim of self-government for the Raj in 1917. By 1929, there were 367 Indian civil servants to 894 Europeans and by the end of the war (the time of this film), there were 510 Indians to 429 Europeans. In part this was due to an ever-increasing difficulty in recruiting Europeans.

By the end of the war and with the independence that had been promised in response to the Quit India campaign at hand, these Indian district officers began to make political alliances to carry them into the future. On 11 December 1946, Lord

Wavell, Viceroy of India announced to the cabinet of India's committee that the Indian Indian Civil Service (ICS) officers 'could no longer be relied upon to carry out a firm policy'.

ANALYSIS

District Officer shows the work of an Indian district officer, who is part of the Indian Civil Service, as he mediates local disputes and manages local affairs in the district of Bengal. The film has a conventional two-part form: the first section, which lasts nearly three minutes, portraying the setting and moving from a map and statistics to generalised shots of the region. The second, longer section of nine minutes focuses on the individual who lives within this setting. The film relies on an authoritative British male voiceover throughout to structure the scenes and it also promises to divulge particulars of both an unknown place and its inhabitants. The ideology of the film is best described as liberal imperialism at the end of empire. The general narrative is one of progress in which the historical reclamation of land from the sea that signals man's triumph over nature blends seamlessly into the new forms of transport and communication, particularly railways and telephones. Thus the historical facts of British conquest and domination are transformed into a natural progression. The film was made two years after the disastrous Bengal Famine, caused not by shortage of food but by maladministration.[7] The film never mentions the famine but it portrays a picture of an efficient and humane administration that would never let another such disaster happen.

Within this general narrative of progress we are introduced to the district officer, who administers the affairs of 3 million people, and then in a flashback we look at him arriving for his first job. Both the initial shot of the district officer appearing in a court and the flashback which shows him alighting from a train, have him emerging from an unknown and solitary space into a crowded social one. The implication from the beginning is that the district officer is a man apart – one who through hard work and study is able to exercise judgment. He is a man without family or background – that is to say, he is a man outside any history except that of progress. This progress is signified by the usual tropes of medicine and clean water rescuing the natives from a dangerous primitivism.

What is interesting about this particular film is how it portrays the liberal imperialist dream of India ruling itself without any British direction but in a completely British manner. Only two Europeans appear in the film: the police chief, who is shown as a subordinate of the district officer and one of the army officers with whom the district officer is on an equal standing. Perhaps the most evident marker of this absence comes when the district officer goes to Calcutta to report to his superior. We do not, however, see this superior – at this moment the film anticipates independence still more than two years away.

However, perhaps the most striking feature of this film is what it does not contain – any explicit discussion of independence. We know that it is exactly in this period that the district officers began to prepare for independence by establishing political alliances with both the Congress Party and other local centres of power. Not, however, in this film, which represents an imaginary self-government completely dominated by British norms and independent of any local context or contacts.

Perhaps the most enigmatic sequence of all comes at the end when for the first time we see the district officer in an informal setting with his friends, a group judiciously made up of a Hindu, a Muslim and a fellow Westernised Indian. The scene coming just after the district officer's visit to Calcutta would exactly suggest a political discussion – but of that discussion we hear nothing.

In some ways this film could serve as an example of what we do not see in this or any other film in this collection. Sandwiched between the calamities just passed of the devastating 1943 famine and the almost worse calamities to come of Partition, the film produces an imaginary space in which such events are not just incredible but impossible.

●

Anybody who dips into recent histories of the British Empire needs an exceptionally strong stomach. The images of dead men and starving women and children haunt one's dreams long after the books have been cast aside. There is of course an argument, still perhaps dominant, that all this is one accident after another, the result of a temporary excess here, a misguided policy there, an unfortunate sequence of events in yet another place. In these films even accident, excess and misfortune have no place. Very, very occasionally in the amateur footage, particularly that held by the Imperial War Museum, the more brutal realities of empire, the realities of violent death and deportation are captured on the screen. One striking example comes from Malaya during the Communist insurgency. The aim of the Briggs strategy, adopted after 1950, was to relocate the Chinese living on the edge of the jungle into new villages that would separate them from the guerrillas.[8] If you look at official films produced by the Malayan Film Unit, one example would be the film entitled *A New Life* (1951), they stress how this movement is to separate the villagers from Communist terrorists, the collocation that all government propaganda used to describe the Malayan Races Liberation Army, the armed wing of the Malayan Communist Party, an almost entirely Chinese organisation. In these official films the Communist terrorists are depicted as an alien and mysterious force.

We do in this case have another perspective. The Imperial War Museum has for some decades now not simply collected amateur footage shot by British servicemen but tracked those servicemen down to provide commentaries on the films. Footage shot by Major Rhodes shows one of the operations in which villages were cleared and the villagers moved to another area. One interesting feature of this film is that it was shot in 1949 before Briggs had elaborated his strategy and thus shows that the tactics were already in place. Rhodes's footage and commentary make quite evident the amount of violence and force involved. He is explicit that the operation is a 'reprisal' for a previous ambush and he is also clear that the Communist terrorists are not some mysterious alien force but the able-bodied young men of the villages that are being relocated.

One of the most notable commentators to argue that violence and bloodshed, the recourse to emergency laws and the practice of judicial murder are not exceptional within the colonies is Paul Gilroy. Further, Gilroy contends that these practices are not horrors unknown to the mother country. Rather, he argues that we can only understand the practices of rendition and the suspension of immigrants' civil rights as the continuation of divisions and differences that are fundamental to the British state.[9] Gilroy's argument draws on many intellectual traditions but perhaps the single most important text is Hannah Arendt's *The Origins of Totalitarianism*, in which she reasons that the Nazis' concentration camps and the death camps of the Judeocide used bureaucratic procedures and practices first elaborated in the hell of the Namib Desert as the Germans attempted to eradicate the entire Herero race in the first decade of the twentieth century.[10]

If you believe, as Gilroy does, that in order to finish with empire we must first remember the reality of the violence that underpinned it, then these films are of little worth. You could systematically go through them and demonstrate, as I have with *District Officer*, that they constitute themselves in disavowal but there would be little point in unearthing hitherto unwatched films to argue that the only point in watching them is to appreciate what they do not show.

I said at the beginning of this chapter that the research team faced the risk of failure at three different levels. The first was to combine the skills and knowledge of the archivists with the skills and knowledge of the academic research team to produce a catalogue that would serve as a model for further collaboration between archives and academics. It will be for others to judge the ultimate success of this model but it is worth noting that, by the end of the first three months, we had established protocols acceptable to both archivists and academics and, at the end of the three years, we felt that we had accomplished our stated aim.

The second ambition was to establish a focus for a concerted attempt to sketch out the history of colonial film in the first six decades of the twentieth century. It would be simple arrogance to think that this was uncharted territory. Rachael Low's seven-volume *The History of the British Cinema* (1977) does cover some aspects of colonial film, although it does not foreground it and an array of scholars from Andrew Roberts and Rosaleen Smyth, on African cinema, John MacKenzie on imperial propaganda and Jeffrey Richards[11] on imperial fictions of the 30s have all done invaluable work in this area. More recently, a host of scholars, many represented in these volumes, have begun to work on this neglected area. By and large, however, all the work either past or current focuses on specific areas of the empire and it could be argued that there are no histories of British cinema that recognise the fact that for more than the first six decades of its existence British cinema was part of an empire and Commonwealth. This blindness is not of course specific to cinema. Much of the last forty years in both history and literary criticism has been concerned to weave into what had hitherto been genuinely insular histories, the complex weave that bound the British Isles to its colonies from the seventeenth to the twentieth centuries.

The aim of these two volumes was to use our work on the catalogue and website to bring together existing work, and to stimulate new scholarship, to provide such a general account of film and empire. Of course, there is still much work to be done and if these conferences succeeded in internationalising the scholarly perspective with contributions from Africa, the Caribbean, India and Malaysia, there is no doubt that still more research is needed for the full picture of the interrelations of cinema and empire to be understood. Ian Christie's contribution to this volume on the representations of empire in very early cinema offers us not only a number of astonishingly rich and complex vignettes but suggests that cinema may be an underrated element in the account of how Europe after nearly 100 years of unbroken peace, if we exclude the Crimea, rushed like sheep to shambles in August 1914. It seems possible to speculate, on the basis of Christie's account of the extreme reactions of cinema crowds to representations of imperial victory, that the cinema was a considerable factor in encouraging the incredible chauvinism that led to social democratic parties across Europe not simply failing, as they had pledged for over two decades, to stop imperialist war, but actively rushing to the flag of battle.

It is the imperial nature of that battle that is addressed in Toby Haggith and Richard Smith's account of the Imperial War Museum's holdings of World War I footage of non-white troops. Haggith and Smith make the point well that this footage was considered a key part of the British propaganda campaign and that the relatively small proportion of such footage (under 10 per cent) is probably more to do with the fact that the majority of cameras were located on the Western Front while the majority of non-British imperial troops were deployed in different theatres. Even so, the importance of this material, and its much richer counterpart in World War II, should not be underestimated as a resource for a much fuller account of the global conflicts that convulsed the world in 1914–18 and 1939–45.

One of the tangled skeins that runs through these histories, and particularly in the material from the Pacific theatre of World War II, is not simply the decline of the British Empire but the rise of the American empire that would replace it. An interesting precursor of this complicated rivalry can be read in James Burns's fascinating account of the way in which two of the most famous American foundations, the Rockefeller and the Carnegie, participate in the very birth of British colonial cinema. Burns also draws attention to the ambivalent attitude to American power and movie-making that runs through every aspect of the Anglo-American alliance throughout the twentieth century.

More central to this first volume and a crucial element in understanding the role of film in the 20s and 30s is the Empire Marketing Board. Lee Grieveson's magisterial essay makes clear how this initiative was not some incidental, one-off moment of imperial policy but indeed an integral part of a concerted attempt to rethink both empire and politics that placed cinema as a central method by which the passage from empire to Commonwealth could be represented. Tom Rice's, Scott Anthony's and David Trotter's essays can all be read as further elaborations of these themes with regard to the more specific histories of the Imperial Airways films (Anthony), British Instructional Films (Rice) and representations of Ceylon (Trotter). Together these essays make a powerful argument that the very form of the documentary can only be understood in relation to the complex legacy of imperialism.

The post-World War I Conservative view of empire depended on an autonomous economic block in which the colonies functioned as the producers of primary materials (and indeed colonies were identified with these primary materials) and the markets for Britain's manufactured goods. The history of the Empire Marketing Board and its affiliates is the history of the attempt to represent this economic and political world order. There is, however, a corresponding history in Africa itself. Aaron Windel's and Aboubakar Sanogo's complementary essays on the Bantu Educational Kinema Experiment (BEKE) analyse the attempt to produce film for Africans in British East and Central Africa in the period 1935–7. The fundamental economic strategy was to produce a 'modernised' African peasant farmer, one who would have absorbed sufficient 'modernity' to produce cash crops for an international market but not so much that he would leave both land and traditional ways of life. The two essays show how this experiment brought together missionary and imperialist ideology together with funding by the Carnegie Foundation and the British state to produce what Sanogo shows to be a textbook example of the relation between film and colonialism.

Francis Gooding's essay takes a wider perspective on the intertwining of missionary and imperial ideology to show how the BEKE represents merely one instance of the missionary use of cinema. These films, Gooding argues, may tell us little of the reality of colonial rule or even of the reality of missionary life but they do 'hold up a faithful mirror to the expectations and prejudices of this audience, and to that extent they are documents which shed light on a different dark and poorly understood place, the imaginary Empire of the metropole'.

If the majority of the films that the research project catalogued were documentaries and documentaries linked to this politico-economic vision of a global family of nations, it is also the case that empire and its colonies played a significant role in the fictional representations of the 30s. Perhaps the two most famous are *The Four Feathers* (1939) and *Sanders of the River* (1935) but the genre spawned a host of films from *The Lives of a Bengal Lancer* (1935) to *The Sun Never Sets* (1939). It is this last film that Julie Codell chooses to analyse with *The Four Feathers* because, unlike most of the genre, the narratives of both films are divided between colony and homeland. The majority of films of this genre subscribe to the development of empire to Commonwealth narrative that is the dominant imperialist ideology of this period. They accomplish this narrative work with plots set entirely in the colonies and which pitch 'good' against 'bad' natives. 'Good' here is equivalent to the moderated modernising proposed by the colonial metropole and 'bad' is the attachment to primitive and savage traditions. *The Four Feathers* and *The Sun Never Sets* eschew these narrative tropes in order to pit the delights of home against the horrors of the colonies. Codell suggests that these films represent a conservative anti-imperialist ideology in which the colonies constitute a dangerous distraction from European realities. It should perhaps go without saying that the one aspect of the colonies that finds no cinematic representation in fact or fiction is the growing anti-imperialist movement in both Africa and the Caribbean, which join the already powerful demand for Indian independence and which punctuate the 30s with strikes and demonstrations. If, by and large, these movements will rally to the anti-fascist flag in 1939, it will be on the clear understanding that Hitler's defeat will be followed by decolonisation. Of all this the film record provides neither sound nor image.

And yet that is not quite true. Several of these 'empire' films starred Paul Robeson, probably the most visible example of a black man committed to both the civil rights of African Americans in the United States and to decolonisation throughout the British Empire. Indeed, Robeson was an honorary member of the West African Students' Union in the 30s and friends with both Kwame Nkrumah and Jomo Kenyatta.[12] He also played Toussaint L'Ouverture in C. L. R. James's play of the same name. One of the curiosities of Robeson's career is how someone whose political beliefs were so markedly anti-imperialist could appear in a film like *Sanders of the River*, which seems little more than the most tawdry and banal imperialist propaganda. Charles Musser's fascinating essay reveals how much more complicated is the full story of Robeson's acting choices. On the one hand, Robeson was always very consciously building a career and the opportunity offered by Korda was a real one. Perhaps even more importantly, Musser shows, by going back to the Edgar Wallace source stories, that Robeson signed up for a much more complex and interesting character than emerged from Korda's final shooting and editing.

The consideration of Robeson offers a tantalising series of 'might have beens' as well as the actuality of Robeson's one-reel introduction to *My Song Goes Forth* (1937). However, the overwhelming reality of the film record analysed here is of a coincidence between cinema and empire. The essays collected here and in the companion volume *Film and the End of Empire* bring the second stage of the colonial film research project to an end. In addition to the website and catalogue produced entirely by the research team, these two collections of essays growing out of the seminars and conferences that the research team organised offer a new perspective on the history of British cinema. First, and most importantly, the adjective 'British' itself becomes a fiction because it is clear that the history of British cinema cannot be told separately from that of its empire or its colonies. Economically, politically, aesthetically – at every level from Grierson to Korda, from Balcon to Samuelson, the history of British cinema is the history of empire. If the essays collected in these two volumes will inevitably require correction and expansion, reworking and inflection, they constitute a serious contribution to a fresh understanding of the institutions of British cinema, like so much else of British life in the first half of the twentieth century, inseparable from the quarter of the globe ruled from Whitehall.

The catalogue and website on the one hand and the conferences and books on the other fulfil two of the ambitions that the research team set itself when embarking on the research project. There was, however, a third ambition for which this scholarship and research was only preliminary work. Paul Gilroy's book *After Empire: Multiculture or Postcolonial Melancholia?* (2004) argues that it is the loss of empire that is the central social, political and cultural fact of current British society and it is the inability to mourn that loss that prevents the elaboration of a more joyful present, in which the post-imperial reality that we inhabit could be embraced for what it is and in which race would, in a Utopian moment, cease to have any meaning. For its meanings are produced by the unfinished business of empire, by the division of the world that empire assumed and elaborated.

Gilroy's analysis of Britain as a society suffering from melancholia is inspired by Freud's analysis in which the melancholic, instead of mourning a lost object, identifies with it and thus, as it were, carries it around internally in a continuous process of loathing for an incomplete self. At least one possible cure that Freud considers is the process by which that identification is unmade and the love for the object is re-experienced in order to be renounced. Gilroy gives many hints but no explicit suggestions as to what such love is. Here it seems our corpus of films might be of real use in the present. And this constitutes the third risk of the research, for it was Gilroy's theses that underpinned the entire elaboration of the research project and it is as a contribution to Gilroy's conviviality that the project will finally succeed or fail.

At the end of Virginia's Woolf's *The Waves*, the central character Bernard reflects on his life as it draws to an end and regrets what he has not accomplished: 'to take ship to India and see a naked man spearing fish in blue water'.[13] This fantasy of empire as naked bodies diving into water is enacted again and again in the corpus, perhaps most remarkably in the spectacular *Dynamite Fishing in the Solomon Islands* (1909). It is perhaps worth noting here that one might venture the hypothesis that the innocence of this film's pleasure in the exoticism of empire is a feature of those films in the collection shot before World War I and that the corpus is significantly divided between pre- and post-World War I films. The innocence of European superiority simply could not survive 1914–18 and the first instalment of what Keynes called the European Civil War. Culturally because the carnage on the Western Front revealed barbarity on a scale unparalleled in human history; ideologically because the formation of the Third International took as its explicit aim colonialism and the freeing of subject peoples; and politically because from Gandhi down it destroyed what faith in empire those subject peoples had.

If this exotic confrontation between civilisation and nature is woven deeply into the web of empire it is not, for Woolf, central – it is the passing fantasy, replete with sexual undertones, of an ageing man. But empire is central to *The Waves*. In some ways this is not surprising. Virginia Stephen was the granddaughter of Sir James Stephen, who was the Permanent Undersecretary at the Colonial Office from 1836–47 and one of the most important colonial administrators in the whole history of the British Empire. She was married to Leonard Woolf, who was for seven years a district officer in Ceylon and who was to write both a novel and memoirs about his experience.[14] Famously on his return to London in 1911, and after much hesitation, Leonard resigned from the Colonial Service, married Virginia and went on to spend much of the rest of his life fighting colonialism.

Surely then, if Virginia Woolf were to put empire into her novels, it would be as the inhuman and unjust political exploitation that she knew it to be and against which she had devoted so much of her time and energy alongside her husband. But that is not how empire features. *The Waves* is the story of six childhood friends: three men, Louis, Bernard and Neville and three women, Ginny, Rhoda and Susan. We meet them as children and then twice more – once in their twenties and once in middle age. There is a final section where Bernard speaks alone but speaks for them all. The novel functions as a symphony in which every movement enters the minds of one of the characters. There is, however, a seventh character, whose mind we never enter but who nevertheless constitutes the centre of the book. His name is Percival and the friends have known him since school. When they meet in their twenties it is to bid him goodbye as he sets off for a career in the empire. At the middle-aged gathering, we discover that Percival is dead: killed falling from a galloping horse in India. His death becomes one of the major motifs of the final sequences of Woolf's novel. It should be said that Percival is not a hugely sympathetic character. He is effortlessly superior as only a public schoolboy of that time and place could be. His good looks, urbanity and social confidence are vaguely repulsive although almost all the characters are in love with him, particularly Neville.

Why does Virginia Woolf place such a character, one might think the kind of person she was least drawn to, at the centre of her greatest book? To find the answer I think that we must descend into the Underworld for the greatest ideological justification of empire comes in Book 6 of *The Aeneid* when Aeneas goes down to Hades to speak with his dead father. Patriarchal is a term that has perhaps been used too easily and inexactly over the past decades but Virgil's text demands that description. Briefly one could indicate the lines (45–50) when the Sibyl is divinely possessed and the frenzied body of the woman is made to speak in the measured tones of the male god. To develop this analysis fully would require an examination of Book 4 and Aeneas's rejection of Dido. In this sacrificing of desire for duty, *The Aeneid* makes clear that the masculine identity of Rome cannot be contaminated by the feminine body of Carthage. This rejection is replayed in Book 6 when Aeneas encounters Dido, who turns away from her former lover in one of the most powerful rejection scenes in Western literature (ll: 469–71). *The Aeneid* is not only patriarchal but explicitly imperialist, accomplishing an extraordinarily complicated ideological move that has Rome, as it asserts its political and ideological dominance, adopting Greece as the superior tutor culture, nowhere more clearly than in the form of *The Aeneid* itself.

These brief comments on *The Aeneid* give us some perspective on those lines of prophecy that all of Jowett's pupils and almost the entire administrative class of empire must have known by heart:

tu regere imperio populos, Romane, memento;
hae tibi erunt artes; pacisque imponere morem,
parcere subiectis, et debellare superbos.

Remember, Roman, it is for you to rule the nations with your power, (that will be your skill) to crown peace with law, to spare the conquered, and subdue the proud. (ll 850–3)

The lines conclude a very long account that presents the history of Rome as culminating in the fratricidal strife that had opposed Caesar to Pompey. It was these wars that Octavian had brought to an end with the defeat of Mark Anthony at Actium and Octavian's assumption of the name Augustus inaugurated the definitive shift from republic to empire.

It is important to remember that the fundamental justification of the empire is the promise of harmony. The imperium will usher in an unprecedented era of peace. The Romans, however, were pagan and Virgil died two decades before Christ was born. There was no hypocrisy about this peace. The fundamental meaning of *imperium* in Latin is power and the ruthless use of power was what guaranteed peace.

However many times one tells the story of how Latin Europe progressed from its Dark Ages, when beside the great shining lights of Byzantium and Baghdad it seemed indeed a region plunged in obscurity, to a position no more than five centuries later when it ruled the globe, no single explanation seems to suffice. Protestantism, capitalism, improvements in agriculture, improvements in navigation, a much greater centrality for chronological time. All these seem both persuasive and inadequate. But one of the peculiarities of the West was that it had no legal category of slavery. For Marx and others the development of the British economy in the sixteenth and seventeenth centuries is the story of the shift in the extraction of surplus from the political and ideological forms of feudalism to the economic form of capitalism. However, the historical work of the last forty years, which has stressed the globalised nature of the British economy, makes one speculate that Marx's analysis is too narrow, failing to take account of the way that race operated as a crucial economic category in the new world economic order.

'Race' is one of those very few words in the history of the language that suddenly appears without any previous etymology. It emerges in the sixteenth and seventeenth centuries (borrowed in English from French and Italian where it is similarly without etymological antecedents).[15] A full analysis of the complicated history of this word is beyond the confines of the present essay. However, one can say that slavery had to be racialised in the New World to make the cotton and sugar plantations economically viable, and it was that economic viability that licensed the horrors of the Middle Passage. It can also be said that it was race, not power, which provided the ideological justification for the exploitation visited on India and other colonies in the East.

Thus race and empire come together in the image of the civilised Englishman who will colonise and improve the territories under his control until self-determination is possible. If all that the Romans needed to justify the harmony of empire was power, Christian Britain found the justification of its ideological certainty, its claim to empire, in the superiority of race. For the Roman citizen we substitute an English gentleman, his race the guarantee of his imperial virtue and his right to economic surplus.

This is Percival and, if Virginia Woolf placed him at the centre of her novel devoted to telling the story of her generation of the English upper middle class, this was because the claims of realism were much greater for her than any parroting of politically correct wish fulfilments. It was this fantasy of the English gentleman, born to rule, which lived still in her age and one of the things *The Waves* performs is an end to that fantasy as Bernard, her other selves and the wave of her own generation crash on the beach and die:

> And in me too the wave rises. It swells; it arches its back. I am aware once more of a new desire, something rising beneath me like the proud horse whose rider first spurs and then pulls him back. What enemy do we now perceive advancing against us, you whom I ride now, as we stand pawing this stretch of pavement? It is death. Death is the enemy. It is death against whom I ride with my spear couched and my hair flying back like a young man's, like Percival's, when he galloped in India. I strike spurs into my horse. Against you I will fling myself, unvanquished and unyielding, O Death![16]

Had Virginia lived to see Percival live on in the diminished and grotesque figure of Tony Blair, she would I am sure have been more than horrified but when she wrote *The Waves* in the late 20s, it would have been difficult to predict how powerful liberal imperialism would become as an ideology. Indeed in that period, it might have been easy to argue that liberal imperialism, that hybrid of Gladstone's morality and Disraeli's interest, was on the wane. Churchill, the greatest liberal imperialist of them all, was beginning his long period of political isolation not least because he continued to hold to the necessity of maintaining India in imperial subjugation.[17] But when Churchill took office in June 1940 liberal imperialism took centre stage. Churchill's political genius was to make of the struggle with Germany both England's last great imperial war and a global anti-fascist struggle. It is the difficulty of disentangling these two ideological strands that explains both their efficacy in the past and their continuing importance in the present. Let us take Blair's Chicago speech of 1999 in which he argued for armed intervention across the world. Blair's certainty that 'Now our actions are guided by a more subtle blend of mutual self interest and moral purpose in defending the values we cherish. In the end values and interests merge',[18] is the certainty of liberal imperialism.

It is here that the archive may prove of great value because it articulates time and time again the fantasy of liberal imperialism embodied in a superior white race that demonstrates beneficent rule in its very whiteness. Likewise, these collections of films and essays demonstrate that political decolonisation was not accompanied by any of the work of ideological unmaking. It is here that these films may well prove useful in allowing us to finally mourn the lost object of imperial rule and the automatic certainty that it vouchsafed to those born white and British.

It is these reflections that ensure that, as we end our project with the 6,200 entries on our website and our thirty hours of digitised film, with the two volumes produced from the two conferences, we are also only now beginning. If we want these films to yield a better understanding of the reality of the British Empire and the continuing consequences of colonialism both in the former colonies and at the heart of the British state, then they must have a very substantial afterlife. I want to end by suggesting two ways in which this might, hopefully, happen.

Cultures change and develop with an infinite set of determinations, which are by that very definition unknowable in their entirety. But good Marxist empiricists have to start somewhere and it is now time for scholars across the humanities and social sciences to call for a common history curriculum, from play school to GCSE, which focuses on the British Empire. This curriculum should not be heavily coercive and should, in the best traditions of English education, allow a great deal of local determination. It will need, however, to start on 30 January 1649 with an event of world-historical importance, when a people executed their king with an attempt at the due process of law. It would then follow Cromwell's terror campaign in Ireland and the destruction of the Scots as an independent nation at Dunbar before the Chairman of the Council of State turned to the business of commerce and drafted the Navigation Acts of 1651, which furnished the legal basis for the British Empire. By uniting the most important event in English political history with the military and legal basis of empire, we might begin to teach all the children in this country how they come to be sitting together in their classrooms. It should be stressed that such a curriculum would have nothing to do with either triumphalist or apologetic accounts of empire. If such a focus on the complex and variable history of the British Empire were to enter our classrooms, then this collection of colonial film might become a very valuable resource. This emphasis is why the website includes lesson plans developed with Greycoats Hospital School and it is crucial, if this research project is to achieve its most ambitious goals, that these images should circulate in schools.

However, those images can circulate in more than one way. While it is essential to register these films within an already established historical order, they can also serve another function, perhaps as important in promoting that conviviality promised by Gilroy as an alternative to melancholia. Priya Jaikumar touches on this in her acute essay on geography and empire when she writes

Such perspectives are available to us now, not only because it is possible to situate the geographical films in their contexts, but also because we can see them in relation to alternative and actively anti-imperial ways of knowing, recording and ordering colonial space. This, for me, is in large part the attraction of the new digital film catalogue. Inspired by the greater availability of colonial films on digital archives, our sifting through the material offers us a rare opportunity to reorder the matrices of comprehension through which colonial space was grasped at a previous time of imperial filming, screening and archiving.

In the concluding remarks to his chapter in *Film and the End of Empire*, Isaac Julien remarks that the first methodological principle of his work in these archives is to remove the soundtrack.[19] It is remarkable how little is lost by such a procedure. For the soundtrack of these films is in its fullest sense monotonous. Almost all these films, documentary and newsreel, industrial or missionary, are overlaid with a male voice speaking a form of Received Pronunciation, which, if it is comic in its over-enunciated vowels, is horrific in its assumption of superiority and knowledge. And it is a voice that has only one message, endlessly repeated, of British superiority and colonial backwardness. That voice removed, the images take on a very different life of their own. That they were framed and edited from the same perspective as the monotonous voiceover is without question but, as Bazin constantly reminds us, the reality of the image always exceeds the intention of the film-maker. The reality before the camera cannot be mastered by the discourse of the film-maker, however skilful the cinematography or editing. These films constitute, at their most simple and banal level, images from across the world of the British Empire in every decade of the twentieth century, images that enable us to see much more than the film-makers who captured them. It is this surplus of the image that enabled Filipa César to make the film and installation *Black Balance* (2010) a crucial element in the research project, serving as an example of necessary work for the future. Her words can perhaps best capture our hopes for this project into that future:

> The images in the corpus are strongly manipulative and the camera is used with enormous power to subdue its African subjects. But there is always something in these images that resists the film-makers' colonisation, a disobedience which is both rebellion and dignity.[20]

NOTES

1. The phrase has long been attributed to Jowett although the first textual citation is in a novel, *Peace and Quiet: A Novel* by Edwin Milton Royle (New York: Harper and Brothers, 1916). The phrase is also used by John Wayne in *She Wore a Yellow Ribbon* (1949).
2. Lyndall Gordon, *T. S. Eliot: An Imperfect Life* (New York: Norton, 1999), p. 118.
3. Paul Hirst and Graeme Thompson, *Globalisation in Question*, 2nd edn (Cambridge: Polity Press, 1999).
4. Tom Gunning, 'Early Cinema as Global Cinema: The Encyclopedic Ambition', in Richard Abel, Giorgio Bertellini and Rob King (eds), *Early Cinema and the "National"* (Bloomington: Indiana University Press, 2008), pp. 11–16.

5. Richard Maltby, 'The Genesis of the Production Code', *Quarterly Review of Film and Video* vol. 15 no. 4 (1995), pp. 5–32.
6. This film is available on the project's website at <http://www.colonialfilm.org.uk/node/1331>.
7. Amartya Sen, *Poverty and Famines* (Oxford: Clarendon Press, 1981), pp. 52–83.
8. T. N. Harper, *The End of Empire and the Making of Malaya* (Cambridge: Cambridge University Press, 1999) and Kumar Ramakrishna, *Emergency Propaganda: The Winning of Malayan Hearts and Minds 1948–1958* (Richmond: Curzon Press, 2002).
9. Paul Gilroy, *After Empire: Multiculture or Postcolonial Melancholia?* (London: Routledge, 2004).
10. Hannah Arendt, *The Origins of Totalitarianism* (New York: Harcourt, Brace & Co., 1951).
11. Rosaleen Smyth, 'The Development of British Colonial Film Policy, 1927–1939, with Special Reference to East and Central Africa', *Journal of African History* vol. 20 no. 3 (1979), pp. 437–50; Jeffrey Richards, *The Age of the Dream Palace* (London: Routledge and Kegan Paul, 1984), pp. 286–8; John M. MacKenzie, *Propaganda and Empire* (Manchester: Manchester University Press, 1984).
12. Martin Bauml Duberman, *Paul Robeson* (New York: Knopf, 1988), p. 171.
13. Virginia Woolf, *The Waves*, annotated and with an introduction by Molly Hite (New York: Harcourt, 2006), p. 220.
14. Ibid.
15. See Raymond Williams, *Keywords* (London: Fontana, 2010).
16. Woolf, *The Waves*, p. 220.
17. For the extent of Churchill's isolation on the India question, see Richard Toye, *Churchill's Empire* (New York: Henry Holt, 2010) pp. 181–8.
18. See <http://keeptonyblairforpm.wordpress.com/blair-speech-transcripts-from-1997-2007/>.
19. Isaac Julien, 'Undoing the Colonial Archive', in Lee Grieveson and Colin MacCabe (eds), *Film and the End of Empire* (London: BFI, 2011).
20. Filipa César, 'Notes on the Making of *Black Balance*: An Ongoing Film Essay on the Colonial Archive', in Grieveson and MacCabe (eds), *Film and the End of Empire*.

EARLY CINEMATIC ENCOUNTERS WITH EMPIRE

●

2

'The captains and the kings depart': Imperial Departure and Arrival in Early Cinema

Ian Christie

The tumult and the shouting dies;
  The captains and the kings depart:
Still stands Thine ancient sacrifice,
  An humble and a contrite heart.
Lord God of Hosts, be with us yet,
Lest we forget – lest we forget!

(Rudyard Kipling, *Recessional*, 1897)

Historians of empire, both on the left and the right, have been slow to recognise the early impact of 'animated photographs' picturing scenes associated with imperial events.[1] Even while film screening was still a novelty, little more than two years after its first public appearance in London, there is evidence that music-hall audiences were alert to the imperial implications of an image such as that of General Kitchener's troops returning after the defeat of the Mahdist army at the Battle of Omdurman in September 1898. A month later, the *Era* reported audience reaction at the Palace Theatre:

> The American Biograph can accomplish wonders. For on Thursday night a picture was thrown on the screen at the Palace showing the Guards, home from the Soudan, marching just a few hours before to Wellington Barracks … . The photograph was taken shortly after 2.00 pm, and by 10.30 was being shown to prolonged applause … . The enthusiasm was, of course, uproarious, breaking out as soon as the tablet announced 'See the conquering heroes come! Welcome home'.[2]

At this time, Kitchener held the rank of Sirdar, or commander in chief of the Egyptian army, and all contemporary coverage of his triumphs, including this report of another Biograph show a month later, refers to him as 'the Sirdar'.

> The Biograph at the Palace Theatre has out-biographed itself. Last night, through the medium of this wonderful invention, Londoners were able to look upon the idolised Sirdar, if not in the flesh, at least in the animated photographic representation of it. The strangeness of it all lay in the fact that the pictures shown were reproductions of scenes taken in France as recently as yesterday afternoon, and in England a few hours later. In the first instance the Palace audience saw the conqueror of the Soudan at Calais. They saw six feet odd of hard, wiry

humanity, framed in an ordinary lounging suit of grey, alert and smiling. They saw him exchange a hearty shake of the hand with the steamer's skipper – and they rose to a man, aye, and to a woman – cheering loud and long. And when the cheers had died away, they were succeeded by volley after volley of vociferous and unmistakably genuine British 'hurrahs', which spread from floor to ceiling, from pit to gallery, from the back of the stage even into the fashionable areas of the tiers of boxes. The demonstration was renewed when the second scene was presented – representing the reception of the Sirdar, hat in hand, walking down the Admiralty Pier to meet the Mayor of Dover.[3]

The fact that this was quoted in a Biograph Company promotional brochure suggests that it was recognised as an exceptionally vivid account of the impact of two of the company's films. But there is little reason to doubt its accuracy, in view of the extraordinary lionisation of Kitchener. Robert Paul, the English film pioneer, would record a later stage of his triumphal progress in *The Sirdar's Reception at the Guildhall* (1898): a distant figure seen arriving at the Guildhall, when he was given the freedom of the City of London, and no doubt equally capable of provoking patriotic sentiment.[4]

Referring to Kitchener as 'the Sirdar' invoked an imperial code – he was the warrior-leader of an exotic army that had become part of the British imperial forces – and the 'Sirdar's Return' films evoke a history of Britain's humiliation, when the Mahdist army took Khartoum and killed General Gordon in 1885, now avenged by decisive (and brutal) victory. Kitchener may be merely shaking hands, or appear small on screen to our modern eyes, but by witnessing his reception, audiences are participating in a ritual of imperial acknowledgment. Yet, within a year, the warning against hubris that Kipling had sounded in his 1897 poem *Recessional* – 'lest we forget' – would be put to the test as Britain faced the challenge of the Boer settlers of Transvaal at the end of 1899, with film now playing an established part in showing the departures and arrivals of that conflict.

There are a number of intersecting issues to elucidate around this pattern within early cinema: the tradition of the departure/arrival genre in other arts, and how this became integral to the new medium's astonishing growth. And in view of the quantity of such films at the turn of the century, I want to argue that they must have played a significant part in communicating the *experience* of empire, otherwise they would not have been so popular. But first, why should such activities be thought of as a genre? I suggest that a departure or arrival, when staged for display or recording, becomes a form of ritual, perhaps best described as a 'performative act'. (I am here adapting J. L. Austin's famous concept of 'performative utterance', which refers to statements that are also actions, or performances, as in betting, swearing or apologising).[5] Departing or arriving is, of course, already an action or a movement of some kind; but to be considered 'performative' it would be one that is recognised by actor and audience as having symbolic significance. Thus, Columbus's departure in search of a new route to India, or Prince Charles Edward Stuart's arrival in Scotland in 1745, both announced intentions, like Caesar crossing the Rubicon. Such celebrated departures and arrivals have long been recorded in paintings and illustrations that strive to condense their significance into a static image. Mantegna's late-fifteenth-century series of paintings *The Triumphs of Julius Caesar*, long resident in Britain, have been credited with inspiring a revival of interest in the traditions of

Roman imperial ritual.[6] And the nineteenth century saw a rising level of public display that owed something to this tradition. After Nelson's unprecedented state funeral of 1806, the funeral of the Duke of Wellington in 1852 was planned on an even grander scale, with the design of his massive funeral car apparently modelled on Mantegna's victory carriage.[7]

In addition to the images of monarchs and national heroes, by the mid-century there was also a turn towards commemorating the departures and arrivals of ordinary, anonymous people: the emigrants setting off for a new life in Ford Madox Brown's painting *The Last of England* (1855); the shipwrecked sailor who eventually returns in Tennyson's narrative poem *Enoch Arden* (1864); and in Russia, a political prisoner's arrival home in Ilya Repin's *The Unexpected Return* (1888).[8] The first and last of these are elaborate tableaux that evoke the emotions surrounding emigration and political imprisonment, focused in the moment of departure and return. Film would eventually take up this narrative tradition, creating extended portrayals of such emotion-charged departures and arrivals.

But coming and going emerged very early as ideal subjects for 'animated photography'. Among its pioneers, Louis Lumière, co-inventor of the Cinématographe, was unusually well versed in the aesthetics of instantaneous 'still' photography, and seemed to know instinctively the kind of diagonal movement towards the camera that would produce a strong sense of 'nature caught in the act'.[9] The first subject he took in 1894 showed his own workers leaving the family photographic supplies factory, which produced a varied cavalcade of 'ordinary citizens', discreetly marshalled to make their entry onto the new stage of cinematography.[10] Another early Lumière subject in 1895, *Photographic Congress Disembarking*, allowed a succession of fellow professionals to present themselves before the new apparatus as they came ashore from a boat. With these two distinctly democratic films of 1895, which were included in almost every early demonstration of the Cinématographe, the Lumières inaugurated one of the most common genres of the new medium.[11] These films of between one and three minutes, recording little more than the moment of departure or arrival, are so short that they are difficult for us to 'read', or to give due weight to. We are in danger of assuming that contemporary audiences might have considered them 'primitive' or fragmentary, although of course they stood for the exact opposite, demonstrating a miraculous new technology and immediacy. Consider, for instance, Robert Paul's Animatograph show at the Alhambra music hall in Leicester Square in August 1896, a rival attraction to the Lumière Cinématographe at the nearby Empire. Among the twenty 'animated photographs', one showed Princess Maud's wedding procession leaving Marlborough House. This is probably explained by the fact that Paul had discovered two months earlier how popular royal association could be, when his film of the Derby, won by the Prince of Wales's horse Persimmon, was cheered to the roof of the Alhambra and encored both there and at other music halls. Audiences seemed to have learned quickly how to focus on a film lasting less than a minute, and to associate its contents – however indistinct to our eyes – with contextual information. At a time before printed captions appeared on screen, they were often helped by a 'lecturer' identifying what they were seeing.[12] And they were very far from a passive audience: music halls were noted for the lively interaction between stage and audience, especially those in the upper gallery.

The Alhambra, in particular, had been the scene of frequent demonstrations and riots, often sparked by patriotic issues.

How might the short film of Princess Maud's wedding procession have been received? Maud was the daughter of the popular Prince of Wales (whose Derby win was still on the same Alhambra programme), and she married Prince Charles of Denmark on 22 July, at the height of a heatwave, with London gaily decorated and crowds out to see the procession. The *Illustrated London News* had already carried a double-page engraving of the wedding party, stiffly posed, and Paul's 'animated photograph' would have offered a livelier, less formal image, and almost certainly a closer view of the princess than those lining the procession route had.[13] Maud's wedding may have been the first such informal royal film to be shown widely in Britain, but it was by no means the only departure or arrival on this Alhambra programme. There were passengers disembarking at Rothesay Pier and a ship leaving the same; more passengers landing from a small boat on Brighton beach; the Paris Express arriving at Calais, and Gordon Highlanders leaving their barracks in Glasgow.

How can we gain insight into what the viewers might have made of these films as they saw them in the music halls, in fairgrounds and at a growing number of improvised venues? Raphael Samuel offered a striking demonstration of ways to connect individual experience with the overarching edifice of 'empire' in his unfinished essay 'Empire Stories: The Imperial and the Domestic'.[14] Noting that, *contra* Edward Said (or at least *contra* the wholesale generalisation of Said's thesis in his influential book *Orientalism*), '"Orientalism" was by no means necessarily a pathological affair', Samuel quotes a number of texts that convey the 'non-pathological' fascination of India for Victorians of many kinds.[15] One of these is from Mrs Gaskell's novel *Cranford* (1851), and is the parenthetical story of an army wife who leaves her husband stationed in India to undertake a perilous journey home in order to save their latest baby from early death. He suggests that, 'in recounting the odyssey ... Mrs Gaskell takes us to India itself'.[16]

We have few ways of knowing if or how early films 'transported' their audiences to the remote places they portrayed. But one text from the period offers an imaginative insight into how an early encounter with film might have worked upon the individual psyche. Rudyard Kipling's story 'Mrs Bathurst' appeared in 1904 and turns upon the obsessive fascination that a film image can create. The narrator is invited by a warrant officer, Vickery, to accompany him to a film show in Cape Town, described as 'a new turn of a scientific nature called "Home and Friends for a Tickey"'. Another character in the conversation, Hooper, is already an initiate:

> 'Oh, you mean the cinematograph – the pictures of prize-fights and steamers. I've seen 'em upcountry.'
> 'Biograph or cinematograph was what I was alludin' to. London Bridge with the omnibuses – a troopship goin' to the war – marines on parade at Portsmouth, an' the Plymouth Express arrivin' at Paddin'ton.'
> 'Seen 'em all. Seen 'em all,' said Hooper impatiently.

Vickery forces the narrator to return night after night to the show, convinced that a woman on screen, seen arriving in Paddington station, is the Mrs Bathurst he previously knew in Auckland. She appears

quite slowly, from be'ind two porters – carryin' a little reticule an' lookin' from side to side –
comes out Mrs. Bathurst. There was no mistakin' the walk in a hundred thousand. She come
forward – right forward – she looked out straight at us with that blindish look which Pritch
alluded to. She walked on and on till she melted out of the picture – like – like a shadow
jumpin' over a candle, an' as she went I 'eard Dawson in the tickey seats be'ind sing out:
"Christ! there's Mrs. B.!"'

The ambiguities of this story continue to perplex Kipling critics, many of whom
consider the film show as incidental to the central theme of Vickery's obsession with
'Mrs B'.[17] But what strikes a film historian is that this appears to be the first fictional
account by a major writer to describe the perceptual and psychological impact of the
film image, which Kipling uses as the trigger for, or token of, Vickery's descent into
madness and eventual death.

Inevitably we wonder: where and when had Kipling seen a film show, and what
had he seen? There seems to be no definitive answer, except that he could have
seen a show either on board a ship travelling to or from South Africa, in 1898 or
1900, or possibly in South Africa during one of his annual visits after 1900.[18] What
matters is that he clearly *had* seen a typical show of the period, with its London
scenes, troops embarking and a train arriving at a station. As in another of his
stories, 'Wireless', which appeared in the same collection as 'Mrs Bathurst', Kipling
was quick to see the eeriness and poetic potential of new technology.[19] Whatever
the sources of his intuition about film, 'Mrs Bathurst' vividly conveys not only the
psychological impact of the film image – 'the real thing – alive an' movin'', as one of
the characters says – but its emerging potential to connect the far-flung nodes of
the empire with affective imagery of 'home and friends'. Vickery's vision in 'Mrs
Bathurst' connects three continents, strongly suggesting what might have been the
appeal of a film show for the seafarers who travelled to the remote outposts of the
empire.

'Mrs Bathurst' belongs to the 'rather brief period', as Samuel describes it, between
about 1883 and the outbreak of the Great War, when

> Empire appeared in our school textbooks as a kind of ultimate fulfilment of our country's
> historic mission, and earlier periods were reinterpreted in the light of it. England was, quite
> simply, the greatest nation in the world.[20]

A key event had helped shape that belief, and perhaps gave it visual, dynamic form.
Queen Victoria's Diamond Jubilee celebration in June 1897 provided an unprecedented spectacle in the heart of the empire's capital that became moving pictures'
first great international subject. This event was promoted by the dynamic Colonial
Secretary Joseph Chamberlain as a 'festival of the British Empire', and instead of
Europe's crowned heads, the governors and heads of state of all Dominions and
colonies were invited to take part in a great circular procession, which took the queen
from Buckingham Palace to St Paul's, where a brief service took place in the open
air at the bottom of the steps (to avoid the elderly queen having to ascend them).
Detachments of exotically costumed servicemen, on horseback and on foot,
accompanied the royal party and dignitaries, all in open carriages.

The result, helped by excellent weather, was an entirely outdoor spectacle, ideal for filming. Series of films were made by up to a dozen film companies, and subsequently shown throughout the UK and worldwide. The Lumière coverage, by its cameraman Alexandre Promio, began with two typical 'arrival' films, taken on Sunday 20 June, as Victoria arrived at Paddington from Windsor and her cortege was followed by crowds.[21] Two days later, the jubilee procession was covered by cameramen stationed at many points along the route, among crowds that were estimated to total 3 million. A journalist, G. W. Steevens, saw clearly what Chamberlain and the organisers had achieved in this procession:

> Up they came, more and more, new types, new realms at every couple of yards, an anthropological museum – a living gazetteer of the British Empire. With them came their English officers, whom they obey and follow like children. And you begin to understand, as never before, what the Empire amounts to. Not only that we possess all these remote outlandish places ... but also that these people are working, not simply under us, but with us.[22]

Other contemporary commentators understood that film would carry this spectacle to wider audiences. The *Era* urged:

> Those loyal subjects of her Majesty who did not witness the glorious pageant of the Queen's progress through the streets of London ... should not miss the opportunity of seeing the wonderful series of pictures at the Empire, giving a complete representation of the Jubilee procession ... by the invention of the Cinématographe ... our descendants will be able to learn how the completion of the sixtieth year of Queen Victoria's reign was celebrated ... .[23]

A writer who interviewed Robert Paul about his filming of the jubilee introduced his article in *Cassell's Family Magazine* with a similar eye on the future:

> This automatic spectator, who is destined to play an important part in life and literature by treasuring up the 'fleeting shows' of the world for the delight of thousands in distant countries and in future ages.[24]

The processions had indeed been organised like a pageant or 'gazetteer' of the empire, with highly recognisable figures from the Dominions and detachments of their armed forces. What would the far-flung audiences make of this quintessentially imperial spectacle?

The jubilee films appear to have been popular and commercially successful in their new 'secondary markets'. Six weeks after the jubilee, the Melbourne showman Harry Rickards, who had first presented animated photographs a year earlier, advertised on Friday 13 August that 'an enormous attraction will be announced tomorrow'. Monday's edition of the Melbourne *Herald* recorded

> one of the most thrilling spectacles ever witnessed, the appearance of Her Most Gracious Majesty on the Royal Carriage, drawn by six cream ponies, causing a perfect blizzard of LOYAL and Acclaimative ENTHUSIASM, the vast audience rising EN MASSE, cheering incessantly until the picture was reproduced.[25]

In Canada, the Dominion's first premier of French ancestry, Sir Wilfred Laurier, was appreciatively recognised by local audiences, who would also have known that he had been knighted on the morning of the jubilee procession. And in Melbourne, 'the waving arm of Sir George Turner', the Australian prime minister, was reported to be 'loudly applauded every evening'.[26]

The Diamond Jubilee had been staged to assert Victoria's and Britain's imperial power, and especially to display – visually and logistically – the extent and diversity of the empire. In this, its organisers were able to draw on experience that had been accumulating since the success of the Great Exhibition of 1851, closely followed by the state funeral of the Duke of Wellington. For the latter, Prince Albert had asked that the design of the funeral car should be 'symbolic of England's strength and statesmanship, and also an expression of all the efforts of Victorian art'.[27] The result, although impressive, was also considered vulgar by many and backward-looking in its overloaded classicism. During the intervening years, lessons had been learned, and in place of any misguided attempt at creating a symbolic vehicle, the focus in the jubilee procession was on a diversity of peoples united by the overarching concept of empire. It marked the beginning of what David Cannadine has described as

> These new-old, royal-cum-imperial extravaganzas, which pulsed outward towards the localities of the imperial periphery, where they further strengthened and reinforced the community-based festivities from which they simultaneously drew their own inspiration and legitimacy. By these interconnected pageants and mutually reinforcing ceremonials, the British Empire put itself on display, and represented itself to itself.[28]

Cannadine is even more sceptical than Samuel of Said's 'orientalism', maintaining that 'the British empire was not exclusively (or even preponderantly) concerned with the creation of "otherness"', but was at least as much concerned with 'the construction of affinities'.[29] His riposte to postcolonial historiography argues that the 'ornamental' aspects of the British Empire were in considerable part its substance – or at least the visible expression of its connecting ideology.

Cannadine's subtitle, 'How the British Saw Their Empire', refers to the deliberate process of creating an elaborate system of honours and rituals that would confer rank on all those who formed part of the imperial 'family', and record their place in its hierarchy. Although many would question Cannadine's insistence that status mattered more than race in the empire's 'system', his analysis of how its honours, costumes and rituals worked to bind together diverse peoples and to 'domesticate the exotic' is persuasive. Cannadine typically does not refer to film at all, but the photographs that illustrate *Ornamentalism* are eloquent evidence of how important image-making was. And the examples of enthusiastic reception of Diamond Jubilee films quoted above confirm how the new medium of film allowed a greater degree of participation in collective imperial emotion.

Jubilees, funerals and coronations provided full-dress occasions when the 'gazetteer' of empire was explicitly laid out. But what of the more mudane rituals of departure and arrival, and what I have termed their 'performative' dimension? The fact that these figure extensively in early film-company catalogues is already evidence of their appeal, but further testimony about their reception is inevitably sparse.

The outbreak of the Anglo-Boer War triggered a wave of departures and arrivals, and films of these doubtless played a part in fostering a sense of imperial unity in the face of widespread international hostility to Britain's war against the Boer settlers. Films of the City Imperial Volunteers departing and returning showed Britain's business elite joining in the struggle against the Boers. *Troops Boarding the Braemar Castle* (October 1899) is described in the Warwick Trading Company catalogue as 'an inspiring film'; and the kilted Gordon Highlanders clearly symbolise Britain's military determination, as in *The Gordons Arriving at the Cape* (1899):

> The arrival of the Gordon Highlanders was quite an event at the Cape, as it ensured lively action and daring deeds of these heroic troops at the front. A contingent of these stalwart Highlanders is seen marching down the street accompanied by the Pipers and Cycle Corps, all in the picturesque native uniform. They are lustily cheered and welcomed by the spectators lining the route.[30]

Paul's 1901 catalogue included a section entitled 'Railway, Shipping and Marine Subjects. Arrival and Departure of Generals and Troops', which features both named figures and regiments that are associated with particular events of the war, such as *The Return of the Naval Brigade Which Saved Ladysmith* (1900). As it wore on, with Britain's early reverses overcome under the command of Kitchener, the South African war would encourage film producers to innovate and produce many different kinds of war-related films, including patriotic tableaux and staged 'reproductions' of battlefield action.[31] By the end of the conflict in 1902, after months of stalemate, there was little enthusiasm to record more war-related traffic, other than the arrival of Boer generals in Britain after the peace treaty had been signed.

Two 1903 films, however, demonstrate the ideological significance attaching to imperial departures and arrivals, even if not by 'captains and kings'. The catalogues of the period often refer to 'close' views and describe moments of informality, as statesmen enter or leave trains, wait on the quayside, they become briefly visible as travellers, sharing something of the experience of their ordinary viewers. As Joseph Chamberlain set off on a post-war visit to South Africa, Hepworth's *The Departure of Mr Chamberlain for South Africa* showed Mr and Mrs Chamberlain 'smilingly acknowledge the reception accorded to them', after which 'a close animated portrait is secured while the Colonial Secretary stands chatting to his friends' before boarding the ship. Much recent history is condensed into this brief scene; and in the liminal space of embarkation, the Chamberlains are revealed in a new, somewhat democratic, light. Several months later, Paul's *The Return Home of the Rt. Hon. Joseph Chamberlain* shows 'four different views of the reception accorded to ... Chamberlain after his tour in South Africa'. During two hectic months, Chamberlain had done much to reconcile former enemies and lay the foundations for political progress in South Africa; and the film ends with what sounds like an effective filmic flourish:

> the fourth view finishing with the departure of his train [from Southampton] for London. On the front of the decorated engine is seen a photograph of 'the Man of the Hour', which gets gradually larger as the engine approaches the camera until the front of the engine fills the whole of the picture, and Mr Chamberlain's photo forms a fine conclusion of a fine series.[32]

With the war concluded and reconciliation under way, the imperial spotlight began to shift from South Africa to India.

India was always an exception to generalisations about the empire, being in many ways the cradle of a concept of empire. After the Mutiny of 1857, British policy turned away from replacing existing rulers and states towards supporting and guiding them; and Indian ritual played a growing part in the development of imperial spectacle, as monarchs from Victoria onwards were crowned its empresses and emperors. After Victoria's death, her son Edward was due to travel to India to be anointed emperor, but he refused to go, despite the two years of elaborate preparation that Viscount Curzon had put into organising a coronation durbar. His place was taken by the Duke of Connaught, Victoria's third son, who had previously served in India as an army officer. Curzon's chosen theme was 'joint Anglo-Indian sovereignty', and special prominence was given to the princely rulers and their retinues, who afforded an exotic display of Cannadine's 'ornamentalism'.[33] Paul's catalogue entry for his series of durbar films emphasised spectacle, with 210 elephants 'of which a large number appear in the picture, each decked with chains of precious metals, and elaborately worked cloth-of-gold'.[34] The Duke and Duchess of Connaught were duly filmed returning from the event, with the now-familiar ritual of scenes onboard ship, followed by a transfer to the London train in Southampton. Paul's catalogue suggests showing this film 'in conjunction with films of the Delhi Durbar', indicating the trend that now existed towards linking separate 80 and 100 ft films into travelogue-like narrative sequences, as tours of far-flung territories were 'bracketed' by quayside scenes, providing a metonymic allusion to the spaces and connecting trajectories of empire.

We might wonder how these now routinely filmed subjects regarded their screen appearances. Members of royalty were certainly aware of the impact of film at an early stage, and were able to view their results 'by command'. Even officials seem to have been aware of being filmed from a relatively early date. One instance appears in the 1910 memoir of a former senior member of the Bengal Civil Service, J. H. Rivett-Carnac.[35] As an aide-de-camp to Queen Victoria, Rivett-Carnac was on duty at the coronation of Edward in 1903, and had been given a new charger to ride in the procession. He remembered rehearsing a dozen times 'to see how the horse would behave in a crowd and amidst traffic'.[36] But on the day, a pipe band suddenly struck up nearby, so that 'the good horse stood straight up on his hind legs and it was quite as much as I could do to keep my seat'. Rivett-Carnac recalled 'the expectant crowd' waiting to see 'an old gentleman a-comin' off his 'orse', but he managed to hold on. Then comes a surprising observation to end the anecdote:

> although it was interesting enough to see oneself and show oneself to one's friends in the 'living pictures' riding along in the procession, one did not want to be handed down to posterity coming off one's horse in an undignified attitude.

This aside from an old India hand delivers a rare glimpse into the attitudes of both rulers and subjects: Rivett-Carnac's intense awareness of the crowd gleefully anticipating his fall; and the unexpected implication that he would take his friends to see his appearance in films of the coronation. But this genre of the parade and procession was now being supplemented, and would soon be eclipsed, by the informality of the Chamberlain departure – seeming to allow viewers to eavesdrop on private conversations – and the similarly informal quayside scene at the Duke and Duchess of Connaught's return.

By the end of Edward's reign, there could be little doubt that film was playing a major role in amplifying imperial spectacle. When the newly crowned George V and his wife travelled to India in 1911, fulfilling the ambition that Curzon had in 1903 for a second coronation, Charles Urban's Kinemacolor process had developed to the point where it, too, needed an epic subject. The Delhi Durbar at which the king and queen were created emperor and empress of India furnished a fitting subject for Urban's full-length documentary, which enjoyed wide commercial success.[37] It would prove to be the climax of what Samuel characterises as the period of empire seen as Britain's manifest destiny, which did not survive the trauma of the war.[38] During the interwar years, Britain's commitment to empire was no less profound; indeed, the empire reached its greatest geographical extent in the 1920s and was celebrated in the massive British Empire Exhibition of 1924. But it had taken a new direction, more focused on trading relations, and on modernisation. The interwar years saw the rapid development of air travel and of radio, both powerful media for shrinking distance and maintaining closer imperial connections, alongside the instrumentalisation of film as 'documentary' – with empire a major theme of this new form.

These developments have been well studied, and are often seen as the main arena in which British film played its part in raising imperial consciousness. Historians of empire have been slow, or reluctant, to recognise the early contribution that film made to popularising imperial sentiment in its first decade after 1896. I have tried to show that empire was present from the outset in film's attraction for turn-of-the-century audiences. The colonial wars and conquests of the late nineteenth century predisposed them to read imperial significance in the first fleeting films – a glimpse of Kitchener or Chamberlain could spark emotional outpourings. And even before films were expected to have diegetic structure, the short arrival-and-departure films created condensed signifiers of empire as a matrix of *movement*.

Is it possible to go beyond noting a coincident relationship between the growth of the popular audience for film and the growth of imperial confidence in the early years of the twentieth century? One way of theorising this relationship might be through the relatively neglected work of Harold Innis, the pioneer Canadian historian of communication technology. Innis sought to relate the rise and fall of empires throughout history to their command of new media technologies.[39] Media, he argued, offered ways of mastering time and space, and the success of empires relies on a balance being struck between those that emphasise time, which favour decentralisation, and those that emphasise space, encouraging centralisation.[40] Innis's most famous disciple was Marshall McLuhan, who would go on to analyse media according to what Innis called their 'bias'. Without wanting to accept uncritically McLuhan's often simplistic labelling of media, we can perhaps see that film, as a new medium around 1900 and one in which the leading imperial power, Britain, had an important early stake, offered a striking new spatiotemporal experience – as when a past moment of departure or arrival was re-presented to the Alhambra or the Palace audience, and to countless other audiences around the empire's variety theatres.[41] Did this new mastery of space-time in endlessly repeated microcosm contribute to changing their sense of place in the world? We cannot know, except by proxy, as in Kipling's story, and by trying to interpret the surviving records of imperial performances by captains, kings and many others that make up what P. D. Morgan has described as 'an entire interactive system, one vast interconnected world'.[42]

NOTES

1. As far as I am aware, no historian of empire, from Eric Hobsbawm to David Cannadine or Niall Ferguson, has attached any importance to film in the period between 1895 and 1914. Even John MacKenzie, in his studies of popular culture and empire, has ignored early cinema: there is, for example, no mention of film in Penny Summerfield, 'Patriotism and Empire: Music Hall Entertainment 1870–1914', in John M. MacKenzie (ed.), *Imperialism and Popular Culture* (Manchester: Manchester University Press, 1986). See also my essay, '"As in England": The Imperial Dialogue in Early Film', in Francois Amy de la Brèteque (ed.), *Domitor 2008* (Perpignan: Presses Universitaires de Perpignan, 2010), pp. 223–30.

2. *Era*, 18 October 1898, p. 19a; quoted in John Barnes, *Pioneers of the British Film*, vol. 3 of *The Beginnings of the Cinema in England, 1894–1900* (London: Bishopsgate Press, 1983), p. 157.

3. *Morning Leader*, 28 October 1898, originally quoted in *The Mutoscope: A Money Maker* (New York: American Mutoscope Co., 1898), p. 8; quoted in Richard Brown and Barry Anthony, *A Victorian Film Enterprise: The History of the British Mutoscope and Biograph Company, 1897–1915* (Trowbridge: Flicks Books, 1999), p. 51. The American Mutoscope and Biograph Company was incorporated in December 1895, and would develop its highly successful 70mm format as a rival to Edison's and all the other pioneers' 35mm standard. Its British offshoot was launched in 1897, and made a long-term exclusive arrangement with the Palace Theatre, Cambridge Circus, to show a selection of between fifteen and twenty short films as an item within the Palace variety programme (ibid., p. 48).

4. Announced in the *Era*, 4 November 1898; cited in Barnes, *Pioneers of the British Film*, p. 185. This film is extant, and appears on the DVD *R. W. Paul: The Collected Films 1895–1908*, curated by the author for the British Film Institute, 2006.

5. J. L. Austin, 'Performative Utterances', in Austin, *Philosophical Papers* (Oxford: Oxford University Press, 1961).

6. Mantegna's nine paintings date from the last decades of the fifteenth century, and were brought to Britain in 1629 by King Charles and hung at Hampton Court, where they have remained ever since.

7. Peter W. Sinnema, *The Wake of Wellington: Englishness in 1852* (Athens: Ohio University Press, 2006), pp. 75–6.

8. *The Last of England* exists in two versions, in Birmingham Museum and Art Gallery and the Fitzwilliam Museum, Cambridge. Tennyson's *Enoch Arden* has served as the basis of many films, beginning with D. W. Griffith's 1911 version. Ilya Repin's *They Did Not Expect Him* (1884–8), is in the Tretyakov Gallery, Moscow.

9. '*La nature prise sur le fait*': the phrase used by several early viewers of the Cinématographe.

10. *La Sortie des usines* (1895). Although Louis Lumière insisted that he filmed only one version of this, there appear to have been at least two, possibly three, indicating that it was carefully 'composed'. See Georges Sadoul, *Lumière et Méliès* (Paris: L'Herminier, 1985), p. 123.

11. Showing a cross-section of society was a feature of the Lumière 'brand': their earliest illustrated advertisement for the Cinématographe features a 'family' audience watching the *Gardener Watered* (1895) comedy.
12. Robert Paul introduced titling, first on slides, then printed onto the film around 1900. A reference to a 'lecturer' being optional in 1900–1 (to present his recruiting film series *Army Life*) indicates that this was still common practice, as it would continue to be until around 1909. However, it is not clear if lecturers were common in music halls.
13. See an eyewitness account of the wedding procession in Mary H. Krout, *A Looker-on in London* (New York: Dodd, Mead, 1899), ch. XV, at <www.victorianlondon.org>, <www.victorianlondon.org/publications2/lookeron.htm>.
14. Raphael Samuel, 'Empire Stories: The Imperial and the Domestic', in Alison Light (ed.), *Island Stories*, vol. II of *Theatres of Memory* (London: Verso, 1998), pp. 74–97.
15. Samuel, 'Empire Stories', p. 76.
16. Ibid., p. 74.
17. 'Mrs Bathurst' perplexed many of Kipling's readers, and continues to do so. It has been described as his first 'Modernist' work, even as 'the first modernist text in English', by Harry Ricketts, *The Unforgiving Minute: A Life of Rudyard Kipling* (London: Chatto & Windus, 1999), p. 288.
18. Paul advertised several films taken on board ships bound for South Africa between 1898 and 1900, which suggests there could also have been screenings during these voyages. In the case of Kipling's story 'Wireless' (1903), it is known that he witnessed early wireless telegraphy experiments while on a navy ship in 1898. See Lord Birkenhead, *Rudyard Kipling* (London: Weidenfeld and Nicolson, 1978), p. 241.
19. After their magazine appearances, both stories were collected in Rudyard Kipling, *Traffics and Discoveries* (New York: Charles Scribner's Sons, 1904).
20. Samuel, 'Empire Stories', p. 84.
21. Luke McKernan, 'Queen Victoria's Diamond Jubilee', text of 1997 presentation, referenced at <www.lukemckernan.com/victoria_flyer.pdf>.
22. G. W. Steevens, *Daily Mail*, quoted by McKernan, 'Queen Victoria's Diamond Jubilee'.
23. *Era*, June 1897, quoted by McKernan, 'Queen Victoria's Diamond Jubilee'.
24. John Munro, 'Living Photographs of the Queen', *Cassell's Family Magazine*, July 1897, p. 327.
25. Opera House advertisement, *Herald* (Melbourne), 14 August 1897 (State Library of Victoria, Melbourne).
26. *Sun*, Melbourne, 27 August 1897, p. 5.
27. Leopold Erdiger, 'The Duke of Wellington's Funeral Car', *Journal of the Warburg and Courtauld Institutes*, vol. 3 (1939); quoted in Sinnema, *The Wake of Wellington*, pp. 76, 144.
28. David Cannadine, *Ornamentalism: How the British Saw Their Empire* (London: Allen Lane, 2001), p. 111.
29. Ibid., p. xix.
30. Warwick catalogue, quoted by John Barnes, *Filming the Boer War*, vol. 4 of *The Beginnings of the Cinema in England* (London: Bishopsgate Press, 1992), pp. 288–9.
31. See my essay, 'The Boer War in North London: A Micro Study', in Laraine Porter and Bryony Dixon (eds), *Picture Perfect: Landscape, Place and Travel in British Cinema before 1930* (Exeter: Exeter Press, 2007), pp. 82–91.
32. The film is lost. Description from *Paul's Films, Supplementary List*, April 1903, BFI Special Collections.

33. Cannadine illustrates 'The Procession of the Princes' at the 1903 durbar, *Ornamentalism*, p. 47.
34. Only fragmentary and degraded material survives from Paul's 1903 series; this is included on the *Collected Films* DVD.
35. J. H. Rivett-Carnac, *Many Memories of Life in India, at Home and Abroad* (London: Blackwood, 1910).
36. Ibid., p. 410.
37. Urban's durbar film ran two hours thirty minutes, and attracted vast audiences, both at the Scala in London and around the UK. See Luke McKernan, 'The Eighth Wonder of the World' (chapter from unpublished PhD), at <www.charlesurban.com/color.htm>.
38. Samuel, 'Empire Stories', p. 82.
39. Harold Innis, *Empire and Communications* (Oxford: Oxford University Press, 1950). Harold Innis (1894–1952) was primarily a political economist, who came to regard communications media as crucial to political change and power.
40. For a recent discussion of Innis's theories, see Megan Mullen, 'Space Bias/Time Bias: Harold Innis, *Empire and Communications*', *Technology and Culture* vol. 50 no. 1 (2009), at <etc.technologyandculture.net/2009/02/space-biastime-bias-harold-innis-empire-and-communications/>.
41. Although Britain would soon cede its place in the forefront of the developing film industry – to France and to the United States – between 1896–c. 1903, British producers and distributors had a significant share of the global film business, with imperial trade relationships underpinning this.
42. P. D. Morgan, 'Encounters between British and "Indigenous" Peoples, c. 1500–c. 1800', in M. J. Daunton and R. Hapern (eds), *Empire and Others: British Encounters with Indigenous Peoples 1600–1850* (Philadelphia: University of Pennsylvania Press, 1999), p. 68; quoted as an epigraph in Cannadine, *Ornamentalism*, p. vi.

3

Sons of Our Empire: Shifting Ideas of 'Race' and the Cinematic Representation of Imperial Troops in World War I

Toby Haggith and Richard Smith

During Queen Victoria's Diamond Jubilee in 1897, the *Illustrated London News* observed the 'curious medley of soldiery representing various races of men, African, Asian, Polynesian, Australasian, and American' from all over the British Empire, gathered at Chelsea barracks to take part in the ceremonies.[1] At the height of the imperial era the British Empire was recruiting on five continents to fill the ranks of local militias, garrison troops and expeditionary armies. The multiethnic composition of the British army was inextricably linked to colonialism and the imperial project. Prior to colonial expansion, Ireland, Scotland and Wales had been traditional recruiting grounds. From the 1650s African slaves and free blacks were deployed during the conflicts with France and Spain in the Caribbean. By the mid-eighteenth century, the East India Company had established local recruitment to fill the ranks of its armies in the three presidencies. At the turn of the twentieth century, the Royal West Africa Frontier Force and the King's African Rifles helped to garrison and police Britain's African possessions. World War I underlined the dependence of the empire on the Indian Army and other non-white units and was clearly an imperial, rather than simply a British effort. For example, over 550,000 members of the Indian Army served overseas, the campaigns in Africa drew on the service of over 1 million carriers during the course of the war and territories as far flung as Fiji and the Bahamas provided contingents.[2]

The British Army remains a multiethnic force today, although British-born minority ethnic groups are underrepresented in the ranks. In 2002, one in six combatant troops was not born in Britain, many hailing from the Commonwealth.[3] In 2006 3,000 Nepalese, 2,000 Fijians, 975 Jamaicans, 720 South Africans, 565 Zimbabweans, 280 Vincentians and 225 St Lucians were enlisted. Data from the Ministry of Defence suggest the reliance on overseas recruits is likely to continue, particularly in the context of the UK's commitments in Iraq and Afghanistan.[4] However, the sacrifices of non-white troops who have helped to sustain British military campaigns, both past and present, often go unrecognised. The collection of films in the Imperial War Museum (IWM) that records the contribution of imperial troops is an invaluable, if currently underused, resource in helping to redress this historical omission. These film texts also offer researchers insight into the complexities of military service within an imperial context. During World War I, as the examples below demonstrate, imperial categories of race and masculinity were being increasingly called into question. Film-makers reflected the ambiguities of this moment as they attempted to project conventional racial hierarchies, while presenting the vision of a united empire and acknowledging the martial capacities of non-white troops.

Interest in the wartime experiences and contribution of black and Asian troops has increased steadily over the past four decades, inspired by 'history from below', subaltern studies and 'the new imperial history'. Several other significant influences in the burgeoning of this field of research may be observed, including the assertion of new national identities in the post-imperial era; the imagining of an imperial heyday of paternalism and co-operation; and the affirmation of citizenship by diasporic communities in Great Britain through the ancestral sacrifice of imperial subjects in the World Wars. The rehabilitation and reworking of war memory is not therefore limited to a narrow association with a single nation-state. Jamaican subjects, for example, ostensibly volunteered to defend the British Empire, but subsequently within the popular imagination also served the cause of pan-Africanism, the independent Jamaican nation and its diaspora. The rediscovered participation of black and Asian troops in the World Wars can play a significant part in asserting contemporary claims to citizenship and social inclusion.[5] But the recovery of such historical memories is not unproblematic. Discourses of national belonging and citizenship may come to depend on a post-imperial nostalgia that privileges military service, especially front-line duty and the imagining of heroic hand-to-hand combat.[6]

Archive film footage can play an important part in the recovery of war memory and, where footage is relatively scarce, film fragments can in themselves become emblematic or objects of antiquarian curiosity. It is important therefore to retain a sense of historical context and to measure film evidence against existing documentary sources. This paper therefore discusses the provenance of the collection and the institutional, historical and practical issues that have contributed to the neglect of this field by curators, historians, teachers and television researchers. It then provides an overview and contextualisation of some of the key items of World War I film relating to non-white forces held by the Imperial War Museum to assess the importance these may play in the historical memory.

PROVENANCE AND SCOPE OF THE IWM COLLECTION

There are 1,235 films listed in the museum's catalogue for the World War I period. The majority were acquired between 1919 and 1921 when the museum became the custodian of all 'official war films' commissioned by the War Office, Admiralty, Air Ministry and Tanks Corps and which recorded British and imperial military forces in all theatres of armed conflict. The museum also received government-funded information and propaganda films about and for the home front, a near complete series of the wartime newsreel *Topical Budget* (taken over by the War Office in 1917) and eighty-two issues of *Annales de la guerre* (from May 1917 to December 1918), acquired from the French government. During the interwar period this core collection was supplemented with material from the commercial newsreel companies, including 'documentary' histories of the war, such as *The World's Greatest Story* (1919) and *Our Empire's Fight for Freedom* (1918) and official films produced by other combatant powers – Germany, Russia and the US. The museum also made agreements to exchange films with Australia, Canada and New Zealand.

India and members of the Indian forces are referred to in over eighty films produced during the World War I era. Sixteen of these were shot on the Western Front (France and Belgium), twenty-six cover Indian forces in Palestine and seventeen in Mesopotamia. Indian troops also appear in one film shot in Egypt, three filmed in London, one in Paris and a couple in the Balkans. Black Africans serving in World War I are covered in nine titles[7] with men of the British West Indies Regiment (BWIR) appearing in a further three (West Indian agricultural workers also feature in a section on sugar production in Trinidad in the British official film *Feeding a Nation* of 1918).[8] The appearance of West Indians in two additional films is to be confirmed.[9] Researchers working in this field may be familiar with *South African Native Labour Contingent: Somewhere in France* (November 1917), discussed in more detail below, but will not know of an *Egyptian Labour Contingent* (December 1917), which follows this unit from its recruitment and training in Egypt to its arrival in France, with its treatment of native uniformed labourers bearing similarities with that of the South Africans in the earlier film.[10]

Researchers are also directed to *Chinese Labour Contingent* (November 1917), held at the IWM in a Spanish version, which is one of ten films covering this unit in France.[11] Four films in the collection include scenes of Māori soldiers; the first shows a group recuperating in England after seeing action at Gallipoli and the remainder Māoris serving with the New Zealand Division on the Western Front.[12] There is also film of Edward Prince of Wales meeting Māori veterans at Rotorua, during his world tour in 1920.[13] There are eight films of the Arab horsemen and soldiers who were supported by the British and French in their uprising against the Turks in Arabia.[14] A number of films show locally recruited native peoples working for the British military forces as non-uniformed labourers in various overseas war zones (e.g. women refugees in Mesopotamia).[15] Non-white troops are also found in films produced by the French and Americans. For example, native troops from French African colonial possessions (Algerians, Annamites, Moroccans, Senegalese and Spahis) are found in ten films, all but one being from the *Annales de la guerre* newsreel series produced by the Section Cinématographique de l'Armée Française. African American soldiers appear in seven films, four produced by the US Signal Corps, two British official titles and one issue of *Annales de la guerre*.[16] An African prisoner of war (POW) in a German-run camp in Belgium even appears in an issue of the German wartime newsreel *Messter Woche* (1915).[17]

Compared with the overall size of the IWM's World War I holdings, the number of films featuring non-white colonial forces is small. However, one should not assume this was due to deliberate or unconscious attempts to disregard the contribution made by colonial forces to the Allied war effort. As discussed below, British propagandists made much of the colonial contribution. The support of potentially millions of soldiers from the empire was a valuable way of boosting civilian morale in a beleaguered and isolated Britain. This is well exemplified in Lancelot Speed's animated cartoon, *Britain's Effort* (1918), in which John Bull is joined by nations of the empire represented by animal mascots – Canada (moose), Australia (kangaroo) and India (elephant). Furthermore, and again exemplified by this cartoon, the British cause was morally strengthened when it could be demonstrated that men from scattered, remote colonies and Dominions were willing to volunteer to fight for the mother country.

One of the main reasons for the relative lack of coverage of colonial troops is that for most of the war they were not serving in the theatres of conflict where official filming was best organised – the Western Front. Even here the first two cameramen did not arrive in France until the beginning of November 1915 and there were never more than three operating at any one time. Elsewhere, film coverage was patchy. There was one official cameraman on the Salonika Front for about a month in the spring of 1917, a cameraman in Mesopotamia from July 1917 to June 1918, a cameraman in Egypt and Palestine with the Egyptian Expeditionary Force from May 1917 to October 1918, and a cameraman in Italy from December 1917 to January 1918 and again in June 1918. By the end of 1915, most of the Indian Corps apart from two Divisions of the Indian Cavalry Corps had been withdrawn from the Western Front to serve in Mesopotamia, Egypt, Palestine and the Balkans. African troops mainly fought in Africa itself and, although battalions of the BWIR did serve on the Western Front, they were routinely switched to depots in Palestine, Egypt and Italy during the winter months.

On reflection, given the small number of colonial troops on the Western Front after the beginning of 1916 and the poor film coverage of British military forces in other theatres, colonial troops are perhaps reasonably well represented in the film record. This is not to argue that the treatment of colonial forces in these films is on a par with the representation of white British and imperial troops. As discussed below, the portrayal of colonial forces is often problematic, in many cases reflecting the racialised perceptions that ranked colonial peoples according to ascribed martial characteristics.

SHOOTING AND PRODUCTION OF OFFICIAL FILMS

Until July 1915 filming was forbidden on the Western Front, but gradually camera-men were given access. In November 1915, two cine cameramen, William Tong and Geoffrey Malins were appointed to cover the British Army and its Allies on the Western Front. Filming was overseen by a War Office committee of leading commercial newsreel and documentary companies. The committee was given the right to film on the Western Front in exchange for agreeing to share film-rental profits with War Office charities. The cameramen sent to film in France were commercial newsreel cameramen. William Tong had been a cameraman with Jury's Imperial Pictures, Geoffrey Malins was working for Gaumont Graphic at the start of the war and J. B. McDowell had been employed by the British and Colonial Kinematograph Company. F. W. Engleholm, appointed by the Admiralty to cover the Royal Navy's wartime exploits, had been working with *Topical Budget*.

Once appointed, the War Office ensured that these cameramen were controlled by and fully inculcated into the ethos of the British Army. They were issued with officers' uniforms, billeted and fed at general headquarters (GHQ), and salaried at £1 per day. The cameramen were transported by military vehicle and assisted by a soldier who helped carry their equipment. They were always escorted by a conducting officer, most usually Captain Faunthorpe, the military director of kinematographic operations, who told them where and what they could film.

The exposed films were returned to England for processing, editing and titling, the latter task being controlled and undertaken by the War Office, which in practice meant that the titles were written by Captain Faunthorpe. A rough cut of the film was then passed to the War Office for approval, with this version then being sent to GHQ in France for further censorship, before being finally returned to England for printing and distribution to the cinema trade.

Although the British obtained film from all war zones, beyond the Western Front the War Office often relied on independent commercial cinematographers to provide coverage or supplement the output of individual official cameramen. Footage of British forces in Mesopotamia was obtained by a deal with the American Ariel Vargas of International Film Services. Another American, Lowell Thomas, supplied footage of Palestine, notably of the Arabian forces partly established through the efforts of T. E. Lawrence. There were no official cameramen in East Africa or Gallipoli and the only coverage of these campaigns was supplied by the unofficial amateur cameramen Cherry Kearton (*Operations of the British Expeditionary Forces in East Africa*, 1916) and Ellis Ashmead Bartlett (*Heroes of Gallipoli*, 1920).

INSTITUTIONAL AND PRACTICAL ISSUES CONTRIBUTING TO THE NEGLECT OF FILM OF IMPERIAL TROOPS

Despite the importance and richness of the IWM collection, it has been neglected by historians of race and empire. With the exception of a couple of episodes from the 1964 BBC *Great War* series, archive film covering Britain's imperial forces was rarely seen until the late 1990s. Between 1970 and 2010, the IWM's Film and Video Archive supplied footage to three television productions about non-white troops during World War I – *Mutiny* (1999), about the BWIR and *Unknown Soldiers* (2000), about the contribution of African, Asian and West Indian British Empire servicemen to World Wars I and II, and *Black Flash* (2006), about colonial troops in the trenches. By contrast for the Battle of the Somme, there are fifty-nine production files for programmes on this topic. Until recently, there was also little scholarly research into the films covering non-white members of the British armed forces, and few people visited the museum to view these films.[18]

This neglect may be attributed to a number of factors. Despite being the world's first film archive, this is still a collection that is not widely known beyond specialist military historians and professional film researchers. Much of the footage, particularly from the World War I era, consists of films presented in a form far removed from the modern concept of the moving image – black and white, mute and unedited. Finding footage covering non-white imperial troops can be difficult due to the range of nomenclature for non-white people in the catalogues, including pejorative or idiomatic terms such as 'native', 'colonial', 'coloured' or 'negro' where these words have been used in the original film intertitles. Military units and individuals have not been identified on the basis of ethnicity, unless ethnicity was specifically referred to in the actual name of a unit, such as the South African Native Labour Corps (SANLC) or the British West Indies Regiment.

Moreover, cataloguers have tended not to identify a non-white soldier among a unit of white troops. For example, in *Topical Budget 272-2* (11 November 1916), an item titled 'The Armies of the Allies. An Interesting Group of Nationalities Fighting the Central Powers in the Balkans. British, French, Russian, Italian, Serbian, Indian, Cretan, Senegalese, Greek and Annamite Type of Soldier', featured a range of ethnicities, including two black Africans from Senegal and an Indian Sikh. The last item in the same issue of *Topical Budget* presents a more striking example of this problem. It records the visit of the King of Belgium's military band to the UK and, among the group of uniformed Belgians, is a black soldier, presumably a man originating from the Belgian Congo. However, the cataloguer did not mention this individual, even though he was one of two men inspected by Viscount French.

Apart from these practical factors that have hindered access to the collection, there is also the historical neglect of this whole topic by British society, reflected in the lack of scholarly interest in this part of the IWM collection and the fact that few films and television programmes were made on the subject. British society's comparative indifference to the history of Britain's non-white colonial allies and comrades has also been reflected in the IWM's exhibitions and public programmes. The current permanent gallery narrating World War I, opened in 1989, gives little coverage to the involvement of non-white troops. Indian troops, whose numerical contribution to the empire forces was second only to Britain's, receive scant attention. There is reference to Indian troops in the Mesopotamian campaign, but no account of their crucial role on the Western Front in 1914/15 or the Indian Brigade in Gallipoli; the two divisions that fought in Palestine are only covered in the interactive video. There were also few attempts to promote parts of the collection recording this history through loans and educational work. It was not until 1990 that the museum's film and video loan scheme for higher education included titles covering non-white colonial forces. Only from September 2003 did such films feature in the daily cinema screening programme for school parties.[19]

Some IWM historians and curators felt that the contribution made by non-white colonial forces was (perhaps with the exception of the Indian forces) marginal to the military histories of both World Wars. There was also an argument, born out of the spirit of both World Wars, but especially World War II, that to identify members of the armed forces on the basis of their ethnicity and relate the history of the wars on this basis undermined the spirit of common endeavour that had united the peoples of the British Empire against a fundamentally racist and undemocratic regime. Another institutional factor that contributed to this marginalising of the history of non-white troops, and therefore the films that recorded it, may be explained by the fact that white people did and still do dominate the curatorial staff of the IWM, as is the case in most museums and cultural institutions in the UK. Since the late 1990s, there has been an active effort on the part of the museum to reverse this attitude, and since 2005, this new thinking has been enshrined in the institution's policy:

> To review collections, research, exhibitions, public and learning programmes and budgets on a continuing basis with the aim of achieving greater diversity in their use. To also ensure that exhibitions and public learning programmes with a diversity facet are funded and embedded over the long term rather than relying on project funding.[20]

Long before this change in IWM policy, and the recent efforts of the Arts and Humanities Research Council 'Colonial Film' project to document the non-white histories in the collections, attitudes were changing behind the scenes. A new generation of historians joined the museum, who reflected a more progressive attitude to race in British society. In the 1980s cataloguers, recruited primarily for their historical expertise rather than as librarians or for their knowledge of film theory, began to systematically catalogue the film collection. An informal policy was adopted, which identified non-white people in the catalogue notes who had not been mentioned in the original titles. This is particularly noticeable in the catalogue for the World War I collection. On a number of occasions film cataloguers diligently recorded the appearance of black or Asian subjects. For example, in 1983 the cataloguer Stephen Badsey pointed out in the notes to *War Office Topical Budget 353-1* (IWM 675b, 27 May 1918), which recorded a visit by Lloyd George to Edinburgh, that two Africans or West Indians (possibly students) appeared in the crowd greeting the prime minister. Similarly, in another issue of the *War Office Topical Budget 367-1* (2 September 1918), which recorded the king decorating servicemen at Buckingham Palace, Badsey mentioned that Indian troops were among those receiving medals.[21] Ironically, this effort to identify non-white troops reflects an awareness of the IWM's historical obligations to the legacy of the British Empire that derive in part from its name, a title that many now feel is anachronistic.

THE WESTERN FRONT

The Indian Division

We now turn to a discussion of some of the most significant pieces of footage in the IWM collection. The importance of colonial troops to the British cause may be indicated by the fact that the first official film of the Western Front released to British audiences was *With the Indian Troops at the Front* (January 1916).[22] From the beginning of the war, Indian troops featured regularly in commercial newsreels of the war, receiving coverage in at least seven issues released in Britain prior to the release of *With the Indian Troops*. Footage included the Indian Corps arriving at Marseilles in September 1914; Indian troops at Arras in the winter of 1914/15, returning 'for rest after weeks of hard fighting'; and an item subtitled, 'Our Gallant Indians Cured of Their Wounds Returning to the Front', which recorded troops from various units (Sikhs, Gurkhas, etc.) marching along a rural English road, lined with waving civilians before entraining at a station.[23] A Canadian, Hilton de Witt Girdwood, was appointed official photographer to the Indian Army. He filmed Indian troops in a semi-official manner during the Flanders fighting of July 1915, although his film, *With the Empire's Fighters* (September 1916), has not survived.

    With the Indian Troops, which portrays the Indian Division on the Western Front in late 1915, may have underlined the increasing remoteness of the war to metropolitan audiences, perhaps highlighting the gulf between civilian and military experiences identified by Paul Fussell in many literary responses to the war.[24] However, the validity of such a divide has subsequently been called into question by critics of Fussell, who highlight the impact of total war, particularly in terms of the changes in gender identity, and the privileging of white male literary voices. It is equally important to recognise that, while the Indian population in Britain during this period could perhaps only be numbered in the hundreds, India occupied a central place in the British imagination, not only in terms of the colonial products that had become everyday items in British life but also the images of Indian military traditions and spectacles. In the two decades before World War I, colonial and imperial troops had marched through London on several occasions. As well as Queen Victoria's Diamond Jubilee, non-white troops were also present at the coronations of Edward VII in 1902 and George V in June 1911. All three events were filmed and screened to public audiences.[25]

In February 1912, Charles Urban's lavish two-and-a-half-hour Kinemacolor film of the Delhi Durbar – the coronation of George V as emperor of India – was shown at the Scala Theatre in Charlotte Street. The commercial success of the production highlighted the central role of royalty, empire and military spectacle in the development of a mass audience for cinema.[26] From December 1914 to January 1916, the Indian presence in Britain became increasingly visible when the Brighton Pavilion was converted to a military hospital for Indian soldiers wounded on the Western Front. Partly as a propaganda exercise to present the benevolent face of empire, thousands of postcard images were circulated showing the newly converted facilities, which included prayer rooms and other facilities to cater for the needs of Muslim, Sikh and Hindu soldiers.[27]

Rather than signalling the war as an alien and remote experience, *With the Indian Troops* continued this tradition of signalling the war as a common imperial effort, linking the British home front with colonial possessions and the troops serving on the Western Front. This issue became particularly important once war had been declared on Turkey in November 1914 and both the military and the India Office became increasingly concerned to preserve the loyalty of the subcontinent's Muslim population.[28] Racialised difference is to a limited extent elided. The Indian soldier becomes domestic and familiar, a long cry from the potentially mutinous and murderous sepoy of 1857. This is underlined in the sequences of Indian soldiers engaged in everyday tasks, then commonplace in both civilian and military life – digging, carpentry, cutting timber, caring for horses. Here is the image of an empire united in adversity, an 'Empire in arms against German tyranny' in the words of a military padre working with West Indian troops.[29] These concerns and representations of a less hierarchical empire were underlined when, with voluntary enlistment drying up, King George V issued his 'Appeal for Men', which was distributed throughout the empire in October 1915 as the sequences of *With the Indian Troops* were being filmed:

At this moment in the struggle between my people and a highly organised enemy ... I appeal to you.

I rejoice in my empire's efforts, and feel pride in the voluntary response from my Subjects all over the world who have sacrificed home, fortune and life itself, in order that another many not inherit the free Empire which their ancestors and mine have built.

I ask you to make good these Sacrifices ... I ask you, men of all classes, to come forward voluntarily and take your share in the fight.

In freely responding to my appeal, you will be giving your support to our brothers who, for long months, have nobly upheld Britain's past traditions, and the glory of her Arms.[30]

With the Indian Troops at the Front (1916). Courtesy of the Imperial War Museum (IWM FLM 4211)

The focus on imperial subjects can result in the white British soldiers taking almost a subsidiary or auxiliary role. This is underlined when, in a brief sequence Indian soldiers light-heartedly jostle white soldiers who are endeavouring to enter the frame (to the left of still above). Alongside the Indian troops in domestic and familiar poses, there is also a reminder of Indian military prowess. We see the rituals associated with military tradition – Sikhs offering the blades of bayonets for the officer to touch, Gurkhas sharpening their traditional kukri swords. The juxtaposing of Sikh and Muslim troops with Scottish Seaforth Highlanders suggests an attempt to present a popular version of martial race theory to a mass audience. Martial race taxonomies were developed by the British and Indian Armies in an attempt to demarcate the recruiting grounds in South Asia, Africa and the Celtic periphery.[31] Martial race theories were increasingly significant in the wake of the Indian Mutiny of 1857. Up until this point, the British had recruited with little discrimination and much pragmatism in order to sustain military campaigns and policing operations. But in the wake of 1857, non-whites were increasingly caricatured as unreliable and potentially traitorous, as well as falling short of British ideals of heroism, military élan and steadfastness. The black presence in the army as a whole declined and racial theories were elaborated that attempted to dictate the racial groups from which colonial armies could be recruited.[32] Closely aligned with scientific racism, martial race theories held that some races possessed predetermined fighting qualities, which were in turn influenced by cultural practices and climate. After 1857, the main recruitment grounds for the Indian Army were redefined, the northern states replacing the south and east. Tropical climates were believed to dissipate manliness and so hill-dwellers from cooler climes, such as Nepal, were preferred over the plainsmen of southern India. The so-called Aryan races of north India were also regarded as superior as it was believed they shared a common Euro-Indian heritage. Often however, martial theories were pragmatically adapted to meet recruiting targets.[33]

Recruitment policy in imperial Africa from the 1880s was also informed by martial race thinking. Men from remote, impoverished regions were preferred as they were held to be able to survive on irregular food supplies and to have natural scouting skills. Groups who had previously resisted colonial rule, such as the Nandi of Kenya, were also favoured.[34] But, in all cases, it was believed that martial capability could only be fully realised under white leadership.

Whatever concessions to non-white races were encompassed within martial race theory, white predominance could never be brought into question. As the nineteenth century progressed, the model of white military masculinity upholding ideals of self-control and rationality became more entrenched. Wherever non-white units were raised in the empire, they were led by white officers. Non-whites were only able to rise to the rank of non-commissioned officer (NCO) in the 'native regiments' as they came to be designated.[35] The one exception was the Indian Army, where Indian officers could receive commissions from the viceroy. Their main purpose was to advise white officers, particularly on cultural matters. However, Indian officers remained subordinate to their white counterparts regardless of rank, as the latter held the king's commission. Furthermore, the proportion of Indian officers in relation to whites declined as the war approached. By 1914, each unit contained matching numbers of white and Indian officers, reflecting the feeling of the military establishment that units officered solely by Indians would not act decisively in the front line.[36]

So while simultaneously presenting the image of a united empire, there is also a suggestion in these films that racialised difference and hierarchy must be preserved. So while images of Indian troops, for example, may have a familiar immediacy, the films retain a sense of otherness. In this respect they represented recognisable 'types' in a way that was also visible in educational texts, children's storybooks and anthropological studies during this period, which frequently identified peoples by rituals or customs, whether these be Indian soldiers engaged in traditional wrestling or Scottish Highlanders breaking into impromptu reels.[37]

When we watch *With the Indian Troops*, it is important to consider the impact that the presence of Indian troops in Europe had elsewhere in the empire. Many men in the West Indies, for example, were inspired to volunteer when they saw pictures and reports about the Indian contribution on the Western Front in West Indian newspapers.[38] Although after two winters in France, the morale of the Indian soldiers was beginning to falter, partly due to high casualty rates among officers, but also because Indian customs of military service were not recognised.

The British West Indies Regiment

The Battle of the Ancre marked the final stage of the Somme campaign in autumn 1916. In terms of commercial and popular success, *The Battle of the Ancre and the Advance of the Tanks* (1917) was second only to *The Battle of the Somme* (1916).[39] The film contains in a brief ten-second fragment one of the very few moving images of troops from the BWIR, who are seen rolling shells towards light railway wagons near the front line. The fleeting glimpse of the BWIR has escaped the notice of the intertitle writer, despite the slightly clumsy editing at this point. Formed in November 1915 for the duration of the war only, the BWIR comprised twelve battalions and recruited over 16,000 men from the West Indies, British Honduras, the Bahamas and Bermuda. Like many other non-white units in the European theatres of war, the BWIR was restricted to labour battalion duties, even though the regiment had been established as an infantry unit. The Army Council, the army's supreme authority, declared that 'coolness, courage and initiative are at a premium [in the front line] – qualities of which the ordinary coloured labourer is deficient'. But these attitudes contrasted with those white men who had seen the West Indian soldier in action. Alfred Burdon Ellis, officer and historian of the West India Regiment, believed black West Indian troops were superior to whites in harsh tropical conditions. He claimed black troops could march two to three times the distance of white comrades and could match European troops even when on half rations. According to Ellis, 'the principal difficulty with [the West Indian soldier] in action is to hold him back, so anxious is he to close with his enemy'.[40]

In reality, as this brief scene shows, the division between front-line and support troops was a semantic one and the BWIR suffered many casualties during artillery attacks. Given the pressing need for personnel, prejudice alone does not explain the British reluctance to deploy black soldiers on front-line action in Europe. Rather, there was an underlying fear that black soldiers might outperform their white counterparts, with deep implications for the hierarchy of empire. Ideas of white masculine prowess, characterised by heroic endeavour, stoicism and self-control, had been brought into question by the epidemic of psychiatric disorders afflicting the British Army.[41] Ideals of white masculinity were also undermined by the poor physique of many recruits who were assigned to the labour battalions or home garrison duty.[42]

To preserve imperial racial hierarchies on the Western Front, West Indian soldiers were routinely excluded from social facilities, such as camp cinemas and *estaminets* (soldiers' cafés). Men requiring medical services were regularly treated in the 'native' hospitals reserved for South African, Chinese, Egyptian and Indian labour contingents, where treatment and accommodation fell below the standard applied to German prisoners of war. Deaths from disease were disproportionately high as a result. The BWIR was also excluded from the pay increases awarded to other regiments and it was not until mid-1919, after vigorous protest, that the matter was finally redressed. This discrimination in pay and conditions, and a sense among many volunteers that they had been denied an equal place in the firing line, culminated in a mutiny of BWIR battalions stationed at the port of Taranto, a key logistical base in Italy.[43]

The South African Native Labour Contingent

Between November 1916 and January 1918, 25,000 black South Africans were recruited to serve as labour battalions in France, as supplies of European labour dried up. A further 35,000 black South Africans supported the campaigns in German West Africa (Namibia). Like the West Indian troops on the Western Front, black South Africans, despite their longstanding military tradition, were not deployed as front-line troops. There were particularly strong concerns in South Africa that white supremacy would be called into question should black soldiers defeat a white opponent and there were protests in the Dominion when Indian troops were deployed on the Western Front. Even the use of black South Africans in labour battalions was viewed as problematic in case the local labour supply was disrupted, especially as members of the SANLC were paid 10 per cent more than the average South African wage. Many black South Africans were also reluctant to volunteer as they feared their lands might be confiscated in their absence under the Native Land Act introduced the year before the war. The military and colonial authorities were also keen to ensure the segregationist policies maintained in South Africa would be enforced in France. The SANLC was therefore deployed on forestry and quarrying work, to ensure a degree of separation from white civilians. Segregation was underpinned by the cantonment of the SANLC in camps.

The SANLC was filmed in November 1917 by the Topical Film Company.[44] Like the footage of the Indian Division in France, these images of South Africans engaged in everyday tasks – tree-felling, road digging and uploading supplies – rather than military manoeuvres, convey a certain domestic familiarity. At the same time a racialised division of labour is clearly upheld. White soldiers carry out technical tasks such as operating mechanical saws, while black soldiers carry out the manual labour. In early 1917, War Office officials suggested that the replacement of white Royal Engineers 'by coloured men would ... be most dangerous to the efficiency ... of the armies in France'.[45] The scenes of South Africans digging roads and breaking stones are particularly telling with the association of colonial penal labour and public works schemes for the rural unemployed.

Despite allusions to their status among fellow black South Africans, 'native chief' NCOs are presented as inferior to the white officers in the footage. Indeed, 'native' was a designation routinely used by the War Office to pay black units, such as the West India Regiment and the BWIR at a lower rate, even though they were line regiments of the British Army. The Indian Army had made longstanding use of indigenous officers as intermediaries, but Indian officers holding a viceroy's commission could never wield authority over a white Indian Army officer holding the king's commission.[46] There is clear anticipation here of the indirect-rule policies advocated by Lord Lugard in the 1920s in which imperial authority was retained behind the smokescreen of local authority figures.[47]

An early sequence in this newsreel appears to show members of the BWIR unloading supplies from railway wagons. The West Indian troops can be identified by the wearing of regular-issue uniforms and caps with badges. Under General Routine Orders, SANLC soldiers were issued with the navy corduroy trousers and jackets, blue greatcoats and Gurkha-pattern hats, evident in the remainder of the film. A clearer

Sons of Our Empire (1917). Courtesy of the Imperial War Museum (IWM FLM 4213)

mis-cataloguing of the BWIR occurs in *Sons of Our Empire* (Episode 3).[48] Here the intertitle erroneously identifies a group of West Indians unloading shells as 'West Africans of the Labour Corps' (see above). No West African troops or labourers were deployed by the British Army on the Western Front. Such misidentification raises a number of issues. Film-makers did not automatically engage with preoccupations with racial-type evidence in much imperial thinking. Where it served a narrative purpose, taxonomies of race were much in evidence. In more pragmatic terms, a shortage of stock footage or editorial effect could lead to the blurring of racialised categories as evident in *South African Native Labour Contingent Somewhere in France.*

The Māori Pioneer Battalions

The first Māori contingents were raised in early 1915 and fought at Gallipoli. After Gallipoli, they were reformed as the Māori Pioneer Battalions comprising around 2,200 Māori and 500 Pacific islanders after campaigns by Peter Buck (Te Rangi Hiroa) a politician, doctor and anthropologist of Māori heritage. It is hard to understand why the Māori battalions were regrouped as labour battalions, given their strong martial tradition. It seems most likely that this was a way of ensuring they did not step outside their place in the imperial racial hierarchy. Many Māori did enlist in the other New Zealand infantry regiments.[49] Despite the Māori contribution, the Anzac legend of 'mateship' and the stoical 'digger' centred on the Gallipoli campaign has tended to be a largely white affair.[50]

The Māori Pioneer Battalions were stationed in France from April 1916 until the end of the war. They were filmed during a visit by New Zealand premier William Massey and his deputy Sir Joseph Ward to the Western Front in 1918.[51] Massey and Ward are seen reviewing the Māori troops in a characteristically jovial and informal fashion. In one section cigars are shared with the troops. More significantly, the film captures how, despite the whiteness of the Anzac myth and the exclusion of Māori troops from the front line, elements of Māori culture have become incorporated into New Zealand national identity. The most notable example is perhaps the *haka*, which the Māori troops demonstrate in this footage. In frontier societies, such as New Zealand, racial identities had the potential to become blurred, particularly where white settlers perceived martial qualities that could be admired in, or even appropriated from, local peoples. Such qualities perceived in a subject race, which were usually regarded as innate, rather than acquired and complex, could be deployed to underpin a vigorous settler identity, which was often cast in opposition to purported metropolitan enfeeblement and enervation.[52]

BEYOND THE WESTERN FRONT

The campaigns in both East and West Africa are often overlooked. In these campaigns both the Allies and the Germans were heavily reliant on locally recruited troops. There was also a marked dependence on locally recruited carriers and other auxiliary labour to maintain the troops in the field, which were notable for improvised and guerrilla war tactics.[53] To both the British and the Germans, the advantage of using local troops and labour reduced the dependency on lengthy and resource-heavy supply routes. But the semi-enforced enlistment of black soldiers and labourers and the heavy depletion of local resources for the war effort had disastrous long-term consequences for local African economies.[54]

The role of African troops and labourers is captured in film shot by the naturalist and wildlife film-maker Cherry Kearton in *Operations of the British Expeditionary Forces in East Africa: Our Grip on the Huns* (1916).[55] Men of the King's African Rifles, formed in 1902 and recruited in Nyasaland, Kenya, Uganda and Somalia are seen on patrol and the reliance on local canoes to maintain supply routes is highlighted.[56] Kearton was serving in East Africa with the 25th Royal Fusiliers (Legion of Frontiersmen), a battalion raised by the Boer War veteran Colonel Daniel Patrick Driscoll. The Frontiersmen battalion was an eccentric group of big-game hunters, explorers, showmen and artists, lured by the promise of adventure and the chance to test their masculinity on the margins of empire. Kearton's freelance footage, which was also shown alongside official films, captures the spirit of the battalion, which prided itself on improvisation and backwoodsmanship. The footage includes the casting of a primitive trench mortar in the field and the construction of bivouacs and improvised field kitchens. Kearton's first preoccupation is with the landscape and environment. The opening sequence is captioned 'Midst the Wild Beasts … A Glimpse of the German East African Country', which reflects an interest in the picturesque, but nevertheless menacing landscape, rather than the human presence. Kearton's published account of his wartime service is similarly interspersed with such interludes, including a menacing encounter with lions at a watering hole.[57] The usual hardware associated with the industrialised slaughter of the Western Front is little in evidence, apart from brief footage of a reconnaissance plane and a heavy field gun that appears to be deployed to subdue the landscape, as much as to defeat the German forces. Any heavy equipment was carried over long distances by African carriers, many of whom found themselves forcibly enlisted by both sides.[58] Kearton himself was carried by two porters after being injured.[59]

A fleeting sequence of the British West Indies Regiment on the march during the Middle East campaigns can be seen in footage shot by the Topical Film Company at Deir El Belah, Gaza.[60] Three battalions of the BWIR were engaged against the Turkish Army in Palestine and Jordan from the summer of 1917 to the end of the war. In July 1917, the machine-gun section of the first battalion took part in several raids on the Turkish trenches at Umbrella Hill on the Gaza-Beersheba line.[61] Allenby, commander-in-chief of the Egyptian Expeditionary Force, was sufficiently impressed to state in a dispatch to the Jamaican governor,

> I have great pleasure in informing you of the excellent conduct of the Machine Gun Section … . All ranks behaved with great gallantry under heavy rifle fire and shell fire, and contributed in no small measure to the success of the operations.[62]

CONCLUSION

This essay has highlighted the relative neglect of moving-image resources portraying the involvement of black and Asian imperial subjects in World War I. Although often fragmentary, these moving images of black and Asian soldiers and military labourers add texture and further insight to the other documentary sources in the field of new imperial history. These images, however fleeting, also provide a tangible link with the past for post-imperial nations and diasporic communities in the United Kingdom and yield powerful visual symbols to support the recovery of historic memory and claims to nationhood and citizenship.

Imperial attitudes to race and military service clearly impacted on cinematic representations of black and Asian troops. However, it is also clear that film-makers went to some lengths to emphasise the role played by imperial troops, recognising the importance a collective imperial effort had on national morale, the success of the imperial project and the legitimacy of the Allied cause. Wartime film-makers worked in strictly controlled environments and with limited access to imperial troops. This was especially so beyond the Western Front where the majority of black and Asian troops served. Nevertheless, effective use was made of the relatively small amount of footage taken. The subsequent neglect of this element of the IWM collection can be linked to a collective forgetting process within the British war memory that occurred with the realignment of British national identity during the era of colonial independence and mass migration from former imperial possessions.

Much of the IWM footage portrays black and Asian troops within the roles determined by imperial military ideology and the empire's division of labour: as martial races or domesticated, often emasculated labourers. However, the pragmatic considerations of both film-makers and military officials on the ground meant that some representations of imperial troops step outside these limited categories. Racialised identities are blurred and white martial supremacy is brought into question. These moving images of black and Asian troops assert claims for their wartime sacrifices and experiences to be recognised on equal terms with white imperial troops and to be fully integrated into the post-imperial war memory.

NOTES

1. *Illustrated London News*, 12 June 1897, p. 807.
2. Frederick William Perry, *The Commonwealth Armies: Manpower and Organisation in Two World Wars* (Manchester: Manchester University Press, 1988), p. 96; Geoffrey Hodges, *Kariakor: The Carrier Corps: The Story of the Military Labour Forces in the Conquest of German East Africa, 1914 to 1918* (Nairobi: Nairobi University Press, 1999), pp. 34–5; 'British Island Colonies and the War', *The Times History of the War* vol. XVI (1918), pp. 73–108.
3. *Sunday Mirror*, 14 July 2002, p. 39; *Observer*, 21 July 2002, p. 6.
4. 'UK Army Has 10% Foreign Personnel', BBC News Online, 13 September 2006, <news.bbc.co.uk/1/hi/uk/5342624.stm>; 'More Foreign Recruits Sign up for British Army', BBC News Online, 24 May 2010, <news.bbc.co.uk/1/hi/uk/8702135.stm>.
5. An example of the strategy can be found at the Imperial War Museum, where between October 2004 and 2009, there was a collaboration with the African-Caribbean youth mentoring organisation '100 Black Men' to run a series of screenings under the title 'Black History through Film', in which archive films and television documentaries, mainly about non-white colonial troops in the two World Wars, were shown to young black Londoners and their mentors, parents or guardians.
6. James Campbell, 'Combat Gnosticism: The Ideology of First World War Poetry Criticism', *New Literary History* vol. 30 (1999), pp. 203–15.
7. IWM 84, IWM 128, IWM 195, IWM 370, IWM 413, IWM 483-4, NTB 272-2, NTB 312-1, NTB 313-1.
8. IWM 10, IWM 116, IWM 130-5+6, IWM 548. The IWM holds the Spanish-language version of *Feeding a Nation*.
9. IWM 663a, IWM 675b.
10. IWM 413 and IWM 3. See also NTB 319-02 for scenes of the Egyptian Labour Corps on the harbour in France and IWM 77 for scenes of members of the Egyptian Labour Corps unloading supplies in Baghdad.
11. IWM 410, IWM 226, IWM 231, IWM 168, IWM 184, IWM 176, IWM 230, IWM 699d and IWM 342/2.
12. NPU 11, IWM 196, IWM 319, IWM 269.

13. *50,000 Miles with the Prince of Wales* (1920), IWM 843.
14. IWM 26, IWM 32, IWM 37, IWM 41, IWM 42, IWM 45, NTB 328-1, IWM 508-36.
15. See IWM 65 for scenes of refugee women sewing at the British Army base depot in Baghdad. See also Arab men unloading stores from boats at Gaza and camels at Jaffa for the British Army, IWM 28.
16. IWM 501-8, IWM 501-13, IWM 502, IWM 508-67, IWM 564, IWM 1078, NTB 242-1.
17. *Messter Woche* vol. 46 (1915), IWM 483-4.
18. Though see Nicholas Hiley, 'Making War: The British News Media and Government Control 1914–1916' (Open University, unpublished PhD thesis, 1985). On Hilton de Witt Girdwood and filming Indian troops in 1915, p. 386 and pp. 392–4. Also: Nicholas Reeves, *Official British Film Propaganda during the First World War* (London: Croom Helm, 1986), p. 150 and pp. 170–1; Nicholas Hiley, 'Hilton de Witt Girdwood and the Origins of British Official Filming', *Historical Journal of Film, Radio and Television* vol. 13 no. 2 (1993); Andrew D. Roberts, 'Africa on Film to 1940', *History in Africa* vol. 14 (1987), pp. 189–227; Philip Woods, 'Film Propaganda in India, 1914–23', *Historical Journal of Film, Radio and Television* vol. 15 no. 4 (1995), pp. 543–53; Pierre Sorlin, 'The French Newsreels of the First World War', *Historical Journal of Film, Radio and Television* vol. 25 no. 4 (2004), p. 509. Production files are internal records held in the Imperial War Museum's Film Archive documenting requests by programme-makers for archive footage to be used in television productions and, occasionally, commercial feature films. A typical file will contain correspondence, technical records and contracts covering the research, viewing, copying and licensing of archival footage.
19. The 1990 loan scheme catalogue included a section called 'Commonwealth Contribution'. Three of the five titles covered non-white forces of World War II. An expanded Commonwealth Contribution in the 2000 edition includes *With the Indian Troops at the Front* (1916). The museum also published two multimedia resource packs for teachers, devoted to the history of non-white forces in the World Wars: *Together* (1994), covering World War II and *The Empire Needs Men!* (1998), on World War I.
20. *IWM Equality Strategy*, 2007–10.
21. IWM 667.
22. *With the Indian Troops at the Front* (British Topical Committee for War Films), IWM 202-01/02.
23. The arrival of the Indian Corps appears in *Our Empire's Fight for Freedom*, IWM 440-02; *Topical Budget 178-1*, NTB 178-01; *Pathe Animated Gazette* (1915), NPU 1006.
24. Paul Fussell, *The Great War and Modern Memory* (Oxford: Oxford University Press, 1977), pp. 82–90.
25. IWM 1080a and MGH 3725.
26. Luke McKernan '"The Modern Elixir of Life": Kinemacolor, Royalty and the Delhi Durbar', *Film History* vol. 21 (2009), pp. 122–36.
27. Joyce Collins, *Doctor Brighton's Indian Patients* (Brighton: Brighton Books, 1997). In April 2010, the Royal Pavilion, Brighton opened a permanent exhibition on the Indian war hospital.
28. David Omissi, *Indian Voices of the Great War* (London: Macmillan, 1999).
29. Rev. A. E. Horner, *From the Islands of the Sea: Glimpses of a West Indian Battalion in France* (Nassau: Guardian, 1919), p. 3.
30. *The Times*, 25 October 1915, p. 7.

31. For the connection between South Asian and Scottish military identities, see Heather Streets, *Martial Races and Masculinity in the British Army, 1857–1914* (Manchester: Manchester University Press, 2004).

32. David Killingray, 'All the King's Men? Blacks in the British Army in the First World War, 1914–1918', in Rainer Lotz and Ian Pegg (eds), *Under the Imperial Carpet: Essays in Black History 1780–1950* (Crawley: Rabbit Press, 1986). Despite the desire to project racial homogeneity within the metropolitan army, Ireland and Scotland provided substantial numbers of recruits, a situation that continued up to and during World War I. Martial race theories held that the Celtic races made natural soldiers, although the Irish came to be viewed with some ambivalence; at once childlike, unruly and emotional: Keith Jeffrey, 'The Irish Military Tradition and the British Empire', in Keith Jeffrey (ed.), *An Irish Empire?: Aspects of Ireland and the British Empire* (Manchester: Manchester University Press, 1996), pp. 94–122; H. J. Hanham, 'Religion and Nationality in the Mid-Victorian Army', in M. R. D. Foot (ed.), *War and Society* (London: Elek, 1973), pp. 159–81.

33. Lionel Caplan, *Warrior Gentlemen: 'Gurkhas' in the Western Imagination* (Oxford: Berghahn Books, 1995), pp. 88–90, 93, 103; David Omissi, *The Sepoy and the Raj: The Indian Army, 1860–1940* (London: Macmillan, 1998), pp. 28–9, 32–4.

34. Timothy H. Parsons, *The African Rank-and-File: Social Implications of Colonial Military Service in the King's African Rifles, 1902–1964* (Oxford: James Currey, 1999), p. 54.

35. *Manual of Military Law* (London: HMSO, 1914), p. 471

36. Omissi, *The Sepoy and the Raj*, pp. 159–62.

37. Kathryn Castle, *Britannia's Children: Reading Colonialism through Children's Books and Magazines* (Manchester: Manchester University Press, 1996).

38. Richard Smith, *Jamaican Volunteers in the First World War: Race, Masculinity and the Development of National Consciousness* (Manchester: Manchester University Press, 2004), pp. 47–8.

39. *The Battle of the Ancre and the Advance of the Tanks* (British Topical Committee for War Films, 1917), IWM 116; British Topical Committee for War Films, 1916.

40. Major A. B. Ellis, *The History of the First West India Regiment* (London: Chapman & Hall, 1885), pp. 13–15.

41. The literature on this subject is now extensive, but influential early studies include E. J. Leed, *No Man's Land: Combat and Identity in World War I* (New York: Cambridge University Press, 1979); E. Showalter, *The Female Malady: Women, Madness and English Culture, 1830–1980* (London: Virago, 1987).

42. R. A. Soloway, *Degeneracy and Degeneration: Eugenics and the Declining Birthrate in Twentieth Century Britain* (Chapel Hill: University of North Carolina Press, 1990); D. Feldman, 'The Importance of Being English: Jewish Immigration and the Decay of Liberal England', in D. Feldman and G. Stedman Jones (eds), *Metropolis London: Histories and Representations since 1800* (London: Routledge, 1989).

43. Smith, *Jamaican Volunteers in the First World War*.

44. *South African Native Labour Contingent: Somewhere in France* (Topical Film Company, November 1917), IWM 413.

45. National Archives WO32/5094 WO Minute AAG to AG, 23 January 1917.

46. Omissi, *Indian Voices of the Great War*, p. xxi.

47. Daniel Tetteh Osabu-Kle, *Compatible Cultural Democracy: The Key to Development in Africa* (Peterborough, ON: Broadview Press, 2000), pp. 44–8.

48. Topical Film Company, 1917, IWM 130-05+6

49. Christopher Pugsley, *Te Hokowhitu a Tu: The Maori Pioneer Battalion in the First World War* (Auckland: Reed, 1995). James Cowan, *The Maoris in the Great War: A History of the New Zealand Native Contingent and Pioneer Battalion: Gallipoli, 1915, France and Flanders, 1916–1918* (Auckland: Whitcombe & Tombs, 1926).

50. Marilyn Lake, 'Mission Impossible: How Men Gave Birth to the Australian Nation – Nationalism, Gender and Other Seminal Acts', *Gender & History* vol. 43 (1992), pp. 305–22.

51. *Visit of the Hon. W. F. Massey and Sir J. Ward to the Western Front 30 June–2 July 1918*, IWM 269.

52. Robert H. MacDonald, *Sons of the Empire: The Frontier and the Boy Scout Movement, 1890–1918* (Toronto, ON: University of Toronto Press, 1993), pp. 8–13.

53. Hodges, *Kariakor*.

54. Edward Paice, *Tip and Run: The Untold Tragedy of the Great War in Africa* (London: Weidenfeld and Nicolson, 2007).

55. IWM 84.

56. Malcolm Page, *KAR: A History of the King's African Rifles* (London: Leo Cooper, 1998); Parsons, *The African Rank-and-file*.

57. Cherry Kearton, *Adventures with Animals and Men* (London: Longmans, Green & Co., 1935), pp. 230–8.

58. Ibid., p. 245.

59. Ibid., pp. 250–1.

60. *Deir El Belah* (Topical Film Company, 1918), IWM 10.

61. Institute of Commonwealth Studies WIC/3/BWIR War Diary, 1st Battalion of the British West Indies Regiment, 1915–1919, pp. 75–8.

62. A. A. Cipriani, *Twenty-five Years After: The British West Indies Regiment in the Great War 1914–1918* (Port of Spain: Trinidad Publishing Co., 1940), p. 20.

4

American Philanthropy and Colonial Film-making: The Rockefeller Foundation, the Carnegie Corporation and the Birth of Colonial Cinema

James Burns

Between 1920 and 1940 agents of the British government produced dozens of films intended for colonial audiences. Some were made to teach agricultural and medical techniques, while others were designed to raise awareness about broader issues of hygiene and public health. By the beginning of World War II government-sponsored cinema shows had become a staple of imperial governance in British territories in Asia, Africa and the Caribbean. These films played an important role in the life of the colonised. They introduced hundreds of thousands of people to moving images. They reminded audiences of their place in a vast and diverse empire. They also served as instruments of propaganda that would be adopted by postcolonial governments. Scholars have long recognised the importance of state-sponsored films in the British Empire.[1] Yet despite its significance, the origins of the colonial film movement have hitherto remained obscure. Most scholars assumed that these programmes had emerged spontaneously in several regions, as British officials in diverse colonies worked at their own initiative during the late 1920s and early 1930s. Their primitive efforts enjoyed the moral, if not material support of influential individuals in London, who realised the potential contribution that cinema could make to imperial education. Left to their own devices, it was assumed, these local officials produced movies tailored to their specific audiences.

However the movement to 'uplift' the colonised with film was in fact heavily influenced by American philanthropic agencies, which were extending their influence into the British Empire during the interwar period. In the 1920s the Rockefeller Foundation produced two short films, *Unhooking the Hookworm* (1920), and *Malaria* (1925), which enjoyed wide distribution throughout the empire. Together these films impressed upon British administrators the value of the new medium to public-health education. But the Rockefeller films also persuaded many colonial officials that American movie-making was inappropriate for imperial audiences. This inspired administrators all over the empire to either shelve the Rockefeller films, edit them to suit local conditions or, in some cases, make their own productions on the same topics. Thus *Unhooking the Hookworm*, and *Malaria*, unwittingly encouraged the manufacture of locally produced colonial films during the early 1920s. By 1930 the films of the Rockefeller Foundation had helped persuade officials at all levels of the imperial bureaucracy of film's potential. Thus when the foundation decided to stop financing the production of colonial films in 1930, British officials approached a second American philanthropic agency, the Carnegie Corporation, for support. The corporation proved enthusiastic about the idea, and between 1935 and 1939 funded the making of films for colonial peoples in East Africa and the British West Indies.

Educational films emerged early in the cinema age. The first use of film in colonial education dates back to 1910, when the administration in the Philippines began showing American movies about tuberculosis to audiences in Manila.[2] During World War I the British government distributed propaganda films throughout the empire. But, with the exception of a few unusual cases, these were shown to white minorities in movie theatres.[3]

Unhooking the Hookworm was the first educational film to be produced with a colonial audience in mind. It was made to support the foundation's ambitious effort to eradicate hookworm infection throughout the world. The campaign against the parasite had begun in 1909, when John D. Rockefeller donated a significant part of his personal fortune to establish the International Health Board. Board officials asserted that the agency was an expression of Rockefeller's concern for the people of the American South, who suffered remarkable incidence of the affliction.[4] Yet many scholars have argued that the philanthropic enterprise was in part inspired by his desire to make the Southern workforce more economically productive.[5]

Regardless of Rockefeller's personal motives, the leadership of the International Health Board quickly recognised that its work in tropical regions could only be accomplished with the active co-operation of foreign governments. The British Empire contained an enormous number of hookworm sufferers, and thus cultivating British support for the campaign was crucial to its success. To this end, the International Health Board's head Wickliffe Rose travelled to London in 1913 to meet with British officials.[6] At a dinner held at Marlborough House, Rose presented a series of still photographs showing the campaign against hookworm currently underway in America. It was at this meeting that the idea for making a film about hookworm appears to have been hatched. According to Rose, the Secretary of State for the Colonies Lewis Harcourt was inspired to declare,

> I should not wonder if in future we come to look back upon this evening and the gathering around this table as the beginning of a new day in the administration of our colonial affairs and of better civilization for all countries in the tropics.[7]

Rose's appearance in London was a godsend to the Colonial Office. British officials had long been aware of the damage wrought by hookworm throughout the empire. But it was axiomatic that the colonies should be financially self-sufficient, and British politicians were loath to spend public funds on the health of colonial peoples. The International Health Board promised to invest significant resources in a dire colonial problem, while at the same time assuring British officials of their desire to work under the direction of local administrators and health professionals. Thus at their meeting the Colonial Secretary 'effectively handed Rose the keys to the British empire'.[8]

While the Rockefeller officials and British leaders articulated their goals for hookworm eradication in a discourse of altruism, they viewed the programme as crucial to the stabilisation of labour populations throughout the empire. According to historian Donald Fisher, the Rockefeller Foundation and the British establishment saw diseases such as hookworm as a drag on the fiscal health of the empire. In his words, while the Foundation and the British Government viewed the development of scientific medicine in Britain as a benefit to humanity, they also regarded these actions as utilitarian ... . Just as the Foundation had seen their 'Hookworm' campaign in the southern part of the United States both as humane and as a practical measure in economic terms, so they approached the world community with the same attitude.[9]

Soon after Wickliffe Rose's visit to London the first Rockefeller teams were dispatched to the British Caribbean territories. But the advent of the war in 1914 delayed the production of the proposed hookworm film. Over the next several years administrators in America reviewed possible scripts, and drafted a final version without any input from the Colonial Office. But they did integrate suggestions from Rockefeller agents working on the hookworm campaign in the Southern states, and in the Caribbean. Some of their suggestions emphasised the international dimensions of the hookworm problem. For example, an agent in the field submitted the following suggestion for opening the film,

> The camera might show a white man in the South at his construction work, a colored man in the South, a West Indian, a singalese [sic] of Ceylon, a Chinese Coolie in China, an African in the wilds of Africa, etc. the impression being conveyed that the idea of the importance of home sanitation is gripping all the races of the world.[10]

Another stationed in Trinidad encouraged the film-makers to develop a story that would feature Indian plantation workers on that island.[11]

As World War I wound down, plans for the production of the film gathered momentum. By 1918 the Rockefeller Foundation was receiving requests for moving pictures from local health officials in the United States.[12] At the same time, the war conditions had led to pioneering developments in mobile projectors, which could now be relatively easily transported on trucks. This was important, as many of the rural areas targeted by the campaign had no electricity.[13] Finally, six years after its initial conceptualisation, *Unhooking the Hookworm* was released in 1920.[14]

Despite the suggestions of the agents working in the Caribbean, the finished film was largely focused on hookworm's influence in the US. It imparted its message through the story of a white Southern family afflicted with the parasite. The film begins by showing a young boy lying on the porch of a farmhouse. When a friend asks him to go for a swim he begs off, saying he is 'too tired'. A title explains that the boy is lethargic because he suffers from hookworm. The boy's father takes him to a doctor, who gives him a pill that cures his infection. The film ends with a scene of the boy swimming with friends.[15]

While the story is about Americans, the film briefly addresses the international dimension of the problem by showing an illustrated world map with the areas of high hookworm infestation shaded in. It also contains one brief and somewhat incongruous scene of village life in India. Otherwise it remains focused on the experience of white Southern children. It also employs several 'sophisticated' (for 1920) film techniques. During the scene in which the doctor diagnoses and treats the young boy, the camera projects microscopic images of hookworm and their larvae. And there is a brief cartoon segment to demonstrate the growth of the worms inside the intestines. The film also utilises long titles in English. While these were translated into several other European languages for distribution, most colonial peoples would have been unable to understand the text without a translator.

Unhooking the Hookworm was initially screened throughout the American South, where it proved popular with local health officials. A state health officer in Kentucky hailed it as 'far and away the best public health film I have ever seen'[16] and claimed that it had encouraged many audience members to seek treatment. A health commissioner in Dublin, Georgia similarly wrote 'I have had wonderful results from the hookworm picture'.[17] The files of the Rockefeller Center Archive also include an effusive report from a community health officer in South Carolina, who attributed the dramatic increase in local interest in his work to the new movies.[18]

The goal of the film-makers had been, in the words of one of its field agents,

> to develop [sic] a hookworm film which is of <u>universal application</u>; one that can be shown in almost every part of the <u>world</u> where hookworms are found and which will tell the whole story of hookworm disease and its prevention in a simple manner.

It needed to be appropriate for an 'ignorant, superstitious, impressionable audience, many of whom cannot read'.[19] But soon after the film's release some Rockefeller officials began to question whether it would prove useful abroad. An agent working in Trinidad warned, 'Races other than the white race are easily distracted when a partially exposed white person is pictured. It invariably brings down a roar of laughter and continually distracts the audience from the point that is being made.'[20] Another correspondent explained that 'To the native of a tropical country there are no points of contact or association in the present film.' To a member of such an audience, 'Everything is foreign to him, from the homes, people, dress, and customs down to the great snakes they see depicted writhing in the human bowel.'[21] These concerns inspired Rockefeller officials to consider revising, or possibly remaking, the hookworm film.

Though nothing came of these plans, these comments reflect the concern that the white faces in the film would undermine the empathy of colonial people. One doctor working with the foundation suggested that a new film be shot in British Guiana, where 'one could find Hindus, Malays, Negroes, and Europeans, together with all types of unsanitary tropical conditions, as well as, tropical architecture and tropical local color'.[22] This suggestion implies that, while colonial audiences would not relate easily to white American actors, they would all recognise themselves in the stories of 'tropical' peoples such as 'Hindus, Malays, Negroes'. A suggestion made by a Dr Barnes was to include a cartoon character that he believed would appeal to all non-white audiences: 'Whiskers, dirt, and sunburn could make the color and nationality of the comic hero uncertain and therefore more cosmopolitan.' Such a film, he suggested, would include scenarios filmed in Siam, Alabama, Fiji and Brazil.[23]

This same correspondent also took issue with the fact that the tone of the hookworm film was out of step with the emphasis of the campaign in the Caribbean. Public-health officials there saw hookworm as mainly a problem affecting worker productivity. Thus a campaign to encourage people to try to control the disease should demonstrate the economic costs of untreated cases. However the Rockefeller film emphasised the cultural and social dimensions of the hookworm problem. The audience was meant to sympathise with the child because he was unable to enjoy a 'normal' childhood. As the doctor complained to Rockefeller officials, 'More emphasis should be laid on the fact that treatment for hookworm enables an erstwhile victim to do hard work with a welcome feeling of health.'[24]

These concerns that 'tropical peoples' would have difficulty relating to the experiences of whites in the movies would later become an article of faith among British film-makers in the colonies. However, at least initially, the Rockefeller officials assumed that their audiences would have no difficulty understanding the medium itself. The Rockefeller Foundation reports from agents in the field indicate that the majority of the people seeing the film had never seen movies before, even many of the white Southern audiences. Yet the correspondence lacks any discussion of the notion that racial differences might prove a barrier to eventual comprehension. Subsequent colonial film-makers would insist that 'primitive' audiences were slow to grasp the conventions of the medium, and therefore, could only understand technologically simple films.[25]

Despite these reservations, the film was being shown in the British West Indies shortly after its completion. There it rapidly became a fixture of health-education demonstrations including lectures and cartoons, which travelled throughout the islands. Reports filed by Rockefeller agents indicate that the film proved popular with rural audiences, and frequently drew hundreds of spectators to the travelling health shows. Even in rural districts with a reputation for intransigence to colonial initiatives, public-health officers could count on the movies to attract hundreds of people to watch their presentations.[26]

An interesting comment on the film was published in the Jamaican paper the *Daily Gleaner* shortly after it was screened for audiences in Kingston in 1922. The reporter waxed enthusiastic about the profound influence the film had on educating local people about the disease. It quoted a letter written by a woman who had resisted treatment until she saw the film: 'Sir, I beg you forgit [sic] past foolishness and send me more medicine. I attend show last night and see what happens inside me and beg for more of the very good govt. pill.'[27] The story observed that the film had been particularly influential upon 'people [who] had never seen motion pictures'.[28]

However, some local officials expressed doubts about the film's efficacy. A memo written not long after the screening of the first shows questioned whether such films could teach anything meaningful to Jamaicans. 'A hookworm film taken in the Southern States of America', one opined, 'could have conveyed very little to the audience' in the colony. If Jamaicans were to receive instruction from motion pictures, he argued, 'Locally made films are imperative if anything is to be got from them.' Much of this prejudice appears to stem from his low opinion of Jamaican audiences, though the final line of his letter suggests additional reasons for discouraging the future showing of more Rockefeller films: the 'culture ... distributed on the screen would be American (if this is not a contradiction in terms) and we want no culture from the U.S.A'.[29] These remarks reflect a widely held anxiety among colonial elites about the influence of American films, which grew throughout the decade as Hollywood began to conquer colonial markets.

The war had alerted some in the British establishment to the potential value of the cinema in the colonies. But it had also impressed many of them with the dangers of showing educational films intended for Western audiences to colonial peoples. This point was brought home to the Colonial Office when a scheduled showing of the American venereal disease film *Damaged Goods* (1919) caused a disturbance in Trinidad in 1920. According to the island's education officer, the screening drew a throng of 'rowdy disappointed applicants who had mobbed the attendances and broken down the door'. Those patrons who were able to secure tickets 'were taking the performance entirely in the wrong spirit. Any doubtful incident was greeted with shrieks of joy and the audience exchanged indecent jokes on the subject of the play.'[30] Incidents like this inspired the National Council for Combating Venereal Disease to ask the Colonial Office and the Rockefeller Foundation to co-operate in the production of a film about venereal disease to be shown in the empire. The council's president, Mrs Neville Rolfe, had travelled to Malaya in 1921 and had been impressed with the need for mass education to combat the spread of venereal disease among labourers there. She had also seen *Unhooking the Hookworm*, an experience which persuaded her that the foundation could produce a VD film that would be appropriate for colonial audiences.

Mrs Rolfe met with the Colonial Secretary Leo Amery in January 1925 to discuss 'the question of obtaining public health educational films with native backgrounds especially in relation to venereal disease'. She also met with George Vincent, president of the Rockefeller Foundation, who encouraged Mrs Rolfe to press the Colonial Office to formally support her proposal. According to Mrs Rolfe, Vincent assured her that the Rockefeller was willing to make more films for the colonies if they were officially requested. As she wrote in a letter to the Colonial Office,

> [T]hey are at the moment considering the production of a malaria film for use among native races, and if the Colonial Office could express the view that such films were needed it would probably go far towards deciding the Rockefeller Foundation to provide them.[31]

Rolfe's formal request to the Rockefeller Foundation contained strong praise for the hookworm film: 'Your own experiment in the anti-ancylostomiasis [sic] campaign has provided evidence that this method of propaganda is equally effective among native races.' She asked the foundation to produce 'a simple film exposition of the problem taken with native back-grounds, suitable for use in Africa, in Asia, and in the West Indies'. She concluded by suggesting that the foundation produce three separate films 'with an African background, with an Asiatic background, with an Indian background'.[32]

Mrs Rolfe also assured Vincent that the foundation would find willing buyers for the film, and that 'The British Government, we are aware, would avail themselves most gladly of such an opportunity.' Her confidence was based on her close relationship with colonial officials, which had led her to believe that they would support her request. However, the discussion within the Colonial Office about the making of a VD film reveals that by 1925 the relationship between the British government and the Rockefeller Foundation had grown complicated. As one official put it 'We gladly accept the Institution's help, but it is not politically desirable that we should ask for it officially.'[33] The foundation and the British government continued to work quite closely on colonial affairs, and during the negotiations about the VD film, they were in the process of establishing the London School of Hygiene and Tropical Medicine. But growing public concerns about American influence in the empire – particularly as it was projected by Hollywood – required colonial officials to demonstrate some discretion when it came to encouraging movie-making in the empire. The subject of Mrs Rolfe's film made her request particularly problematic. While colonial administrators had not objected to the subject of *Unhooking the Hookworm*, a film on venereal disease was quite likely to be banned in some colonies. As one administrator put it,

> An interesting situation would arise if a film produced with the Secretary of State's blessing were forbidden, and alternatively a very difficult situation if the Secretary of State were to insist on the showing of a film which the local authorities, with their special knowledge, considered undesirable from the race and colour point of view.[34]

These concerns ultimately quashed the idea that the Rockefeller should produce a VD film for the peoples of the empire.

But if the Colonial Office would not support the production of the VD film, it appears that it encouraged Rockefeller officials to carry on with a second film for 'native' audiences on malaria, which was completed later in 1925. However, despite the popularity of the hookworm film in the Caribbean, and the compliments it received from Mrs Rolfe, when it came time to make a second film, Rockefeller officials had determined that *Unhooking the Hookworm* had been inappropriate for any audiences other than white Southerners. Based on the views of their men in the field, the producers of the second film, *Malaria*, took into account the perceived limitations of its target audience. The chief concern raised about the film was that it presented colonial peoples with unfamiliar technologies. As an official of the foundation opined, 'in less "progressive" countries few people know what a microscope does'. In a similar vein, another official warned that 'the native or ignorant mind' would be confused by the sophisticated scientific apparatus involved in malaria's diagnosis and treatment. The most expansive comments were provided by Mark Boyd, an official of the Rockefeller Health Board, who warned of the danger of making films which were 'for the most part considerably above the intellectual capacity of the average rural audience either in the United States or abroad' and were particularly 'inappropriate for rural negro audiences'. He went on to explain 'No one realizes better than the southern negro the vast gulf that exists between whites and the negroes' and thus negroes could not be expected to learn from a film 'dealing with whites'. His comments influenced the production of the film *Malaria*, which was subsequently reshot to include scenes of African American actors to make it more intelligible to black audiences. According to reports, 'This modified film was enthusiastically received by Negro audiences wherever it was shown and I am sure made the rural negroes appreciate malaria as a negro problem.'[35]

Malaria was released in 1925. By this time the International Health Board had turned the campaign against hookworm over to local authorities in the American South, and in much of the Caribbean. But the hookworm and malaria films remained fixtures of public-health programmes in these regions throughout the decade.[36] They also began to find their way into British territories beyond the Western hemisphere. Everywhere the films were shown they appear to have drawn enthusiastic crowds.[37]

In 1927 the Colonial Office held discussions regarding the future of cinema in the empire. As part of the Colonial Office's preparations for the conference, a questionnaire was sent to each imperial administration. The returned surveys revealed that the Rockefeller films had made their way into diverse corners of the empire. While most colonies replied that they possessed few films, many had *Unhooking the Hookworm* and *Malaria*. In some territories, such as Zanzibar, these were the only two films in the government's possession.[38]

However, the replies to the survey indicated that local administrators were not impressed with the value of educational films made outside their territory. The Director of Medical and Sanitary Services in the Gold Coast commented: 'The strange atmosphere surrounding a film taken elsewhere would so detract from the main subject it was desired to teach as to entirely negative [sic] the value of the film'.[39] The governor of Tanganyika similarly asserted that

> any film of an educational nature or one aiming at promoting better health or hygiene amongst Natives of East Africa ... must not contain ideas of which there can be little conception among a primitive people but must be built up, as emphasized below, around a setting entirely concerned with familiar conditions.

The governor went on to describe the territory's experience with the Rockefeller films: 'The native audiences enjoyed the pictures but it is doubtful whether the lessons they were intended to convey were assimilated owing to the fact that the setting entirely concerned conditions in America.'[40] But the films had encouraged the local medical department to make its own hookworm film. According to the governor, 'The results indicate that a cinematograph film if prepared locally, is of value for propaganda purposes and the experiment is being continued at present by the production of two further small films.' One of the two films produced by the Tanganyikan government was about malaria.

In neighbouring Kenya, the British administration likewise took a dim view of the influence of foreign-made films on its African subjects. In 1927 the governor of the colony voiced the opinion that he desired to keep all films out of the colony.[41] When a colonial administrator did begin making films in Kenya a few years later, one was about hookworm.[42] And in 1935 when the Bantu Educational Kinema Experiment (BEKE) began making films to educate Africans in British East Africa, one of their first productions was *Tropical Hookworm* (1936).

By the time the Rockefeller agents left the Caribbean in 1924 the value of educational films appears to have been established.[43] In Trinidad, government officials began to integrate local footage into the Rockefeller films, and eventually abandoned them in favour of making their own.[44] By 1931 the government of Trinidad had produced a series of locally shot educational films, including one about malaria control that covered essentially the same ground as the Rockefeller film.[45] In Jamaica by 1929 government agents reported that the films were also beginning to include locally shot footage, insisting, 'Such local pictures should prove of higher value than imported ones, excellent though they be.'[46]

The Rockefeller films had a similar history in British South East Asia. Initially they appear to have generated a good deal of enthusiasm among audiences. *Unhooking the*

Hookworm was being shown as a feature in theatres in Singapore by 1923. When *Malaria* was released, both films became part of the colony's mobile education programme.[47] But in 1930 the *Straits Times* urged that local films be produced to replace those coming from America. Such films

> must be made really interesting in themselves if they are to appeal to local audiences, and that is where so many of those which we have seen, both at home and out here, are sadly at fault. The good will and the desire to instruct is there all right, but the power to interest and retain the attention is too often lacking.[48]

The following year the administration of the Federated Malay States began making its own films. Recognising that 'The possibilities of the cinema as a means of propaganda in Malaya have already been shown', two films were produced for $9,000, one for Malay audiences, and the other for Chinese. The Malay film was intended to teach rural peoples how to protect themselves from malarial mosquitoes.

As the Rockefeller films were making their way from territory to territory, in London there was growing controversy regarding the future of films in the empire. Throughout the 1920s British papers reported on the dangerous influence that American movies were exerting over audiences in India and throughout Asia. The corrosive effect of Hollywood on 'white prestige' in the empire was of particular concern to the king, and inspired British Prime Minister Stanley Baldwin to make a speech against the unfettered spread of the medium.[49] Anxieties about the cinema in the empire contributed to the convocation of a colonial conference entirely devoted to film in 1930. At this meeting there was an extensive discussion of the medium's potential value in the empire. But in a widely discussed minority opinion, committee member and veteran colonial administrator Sir Hesketh Bell warned of the dangers of showing movies to Africans that had been prepared for American audiences. He was clearly referring to the Rockefeller films when he wrote:

> Illustrations of the life history of the mosquito or of the devastating effects of the hookworm, which might be understood by more or less civilised coloured people, who have some notions about microbes and microscopes, would be quite bewildering to unsophisticated natives who have not the faintest idea of modern science and have only a rudimentary sense of proportion.[50]

Hesketh Bell's critique reflected a widely held view that colonial peoples were acutely susceptible to negative images absorbed through film. But a corollary to this assumption was that properly produced films would have an equally powerful beneficent influence on the colonised. This view came to be widely shared in the British government after 1930, though the exigencies of the Depression prevented the allocation of state resources in support of this idea. But by 1930 the idea of making educational films for the colonised had caught on and, during the early part of the decade, the Colonial Office received several unsolicited proposals from companies and individuals interested in the prospect. All of these emphasised the fact that indigenous audiences would have only a limited understanding of films made for Western audiences, along with the ethnic chauvinism of colonial peoples, which left them confused by foreign cultures and situations. Thus the idea of making a film of universal application, which had informed the making of *Unhooking the Hookworm*, was being eclipsed by an approach which emphasised the distinctive needs and capabilities of each colonial community.

As enthusiasm for colonial films was gathering momentum in London, the Rockefeller films were being revised or supplanted by locally produced films all over the empire. Ironically, they were being replaced by films made by people with no technical training. When their amateurish efforts proved confusing or risible to audiences, this was interpreted as further evidence of the limited capabilities of imperial audiences. Yet an editorial in 1930 that ran in the *Straits Times* offers an interesting evaluation of the Rockefeller films, and a prescient analysis of the future of colonial film-making. It began with a warning that a proposed educational film programme in the empire could 'as easily prove a colossal failure as a gigantic success'.[51] The choice depended on the expertise of the film-makers and the financial support of the Colonial Office. If the films were produced by medical or agricultural officers with no technical training, then the result would be a 'disaster'. In making this argument, the author went on to recommend that the Colonial Office consult with the International Health Board of the Rockefeller Foundation, 'whose medical propaganda films are far in advance of anything of the kind so far produced in Britain'. The author had seen showings of *Malaria* and *Unhooking the Hookworm* in Ceylon three years earlier, and declared 'Those films were masterpieces of the cinematographic art.'[52]

Malaria was the last film produced by the Rockefeller Foundation with a colonial audience in mind. In 1931 the Colonial Office asked the foundation to fund a study of the influence of educational films on the peoples of the colonies. In its application it suggested Malaya as a location for the experiment as, according to the anthropologist C. J. Seligman, 'the Malay has a good visual mind'. They also indicated that they would want to produce new films for the experiment. As they explained in their application, 'advantage ought really to be taken of the opportunity afforded for the production of new films in the territory selected' though they were quick to acknowledge that the existing health and hygiene films 'have been shown with valuable results to native races at various states of development'.[53] But Rockefeller Foundation officials begged off, saying that their focus had moved away from film-making and towards the funding of medical research.

With the Rockefeller Foundation out of the film-making business, colonial officials turned to the Carnegie Corporation for financial support. Indeed, in 1931 when the Malay film experiment was first proposed, it had been suggested that the corporation might be asked to fund it if the Rockefeller turned it down.[54] The most significant film programme supported by the corporation was the Bantu Educational Kinema Experiment. There is a rich literature about the origins and influence of the BEKE, which produced and distributed films in East and Central Africa between 1935 and 1937.[55] The BEKE's activities were covered in British and colonial newspapers, and the book written by the authors about the experience was widely reviewed. But while the BEKE received a great deal of positive press, it was denounced by local administrators throughout East Africa. Indeed, once the Carnegie money ran out, Northern Rhodesia was the only territory to express any enthusiasm or offer any financial support for continuing the experiment. Indeed, some officials blamed the BEKE for subsequently undermining the Colonial Office's enthusiasm for teaching Africans through film.[56]

Shortly after the BEKE wound down, the governor of Jamaica, E. B. Denham, inquired about the possibility of setting up a similar programme on the island.[57] In response, L. A. Notcutt, one of the BEKE's principals, sent an application to the Jamaican government offering to establish a similar film unit in the Caribbean. Local officials ultimately rejected Notcutt's application because of the poor reputation the BEKE had earned among the administrators in East Africa.[58] Instead, the director of education for Jamaica received a modest grant from the Carnegie Corporation to show films to rural peoples.[59] When this proved extremely popular, the government submitted a much more ambitious application to the Carnegie Corporation that was to include the production of health and agricultural shorts made especially for rural Jamaicans. In July 1939 the Colonial Secretary Malcolm MacDonald wrote to the island's new governor, Sir Arthur Richards, to endorse the plan, stating

> there is very great need for more locally produced films of an educational character for use in the West Indies and I am entirely in favour of an application being made to the Carnegie Corporation for a grant for this purpose.[60]

When the war broke out the following month it brought about a dramatic change in the trajectory of the 'films for the colonies' proposals. In 1939 the government created the Colonial Film Unit, with a mandate to make films for colonial peoples. This was of course something that the Colonial Office had been trying to do since 1913, but heretofore could only accomplish with the support of American philanthropy.

The idea of making films to educate colonial peoples was well established in the British Empire by the time the Colonial Film Unit was launched in 1939. Much of the initiative for film-making during the interwar period had come from British officials, in London, and in the colonies, who embraced cinema as a modern instrument of mass education. But the Rockefeller Foundation and Carnegie endowment played an important role in establishing the foundation that future film-makers would build upon. By producing films, and by funding the film-making efforts of others, these philanthropic organisations helped to create the colonial film project.

The support of the Rockefeller Foundation and the Carnegie Corporation for colonial film-making reveals the growing American involvement in the empire during the interwar period. However, until 1939, British administrators effectively harnessed this influence to their own aims. In London they did this by dictating the subject and style of the films produced. Abroad in the empire they accomplished this by editing films to suit local needs, or making their own, in some cases using American money. Ironically, American support allowed British administrators to produce and screen films whose approach to health education was antithetical to the original Rockefeller mission. The International Health Board had begun in 1909 with a model of public-health education that it regarded as universal, and this approach to film-making influenced the foundation's first film, *Unhooking the Hookworm*. But thereafter colonial film-making was informed by the assumption that the differences among colonial audiences made such a model impractical.

NOTES

1. See for example Rosaleen Smyth, 'The Development of British Colonial Film Policy, 1927–1939, with Special Reference to East and Central Africa', *Journal of African History* vol. 20 no. 3 (1979), pp. 437–50; Glenn Reynolds, 'The Bantu Educational Kinema Experiment and the Struggle for Hegemony in British East and Central Africa, 1935–1937', *Historical Journal of Film, Radio and Television* vol. 29 no. 1 (2009), pp. 57–78; and my own work *Flickering Shadows: Cinema and Identity in Colonial Zimbabwe* (Columbus: Ohio University Press, 2002).

2. 'Sanitary Education by Moving Pictures and Lantern Demonstration', *Report of the Philippine Commission to the Secretary of War 1910* (Washington: Government Printing Office, 1911), p. 92.

3. For example, in North Borneo war films were shown to local chiefs 'in order to give the natives some sense of the catastrophe' (*Straits Times*, 13 February 1918, p. 8).

4. *Science*, 5 November, 1909, pp. 635–6.

5. See E. R. Brown, 'Public Health in Imperialism: Early Rockefeller Programs at Home and Abroad', *American Journal of Public Health* vol. 66 no. 9 (September 1976), pp. 897–903 (p. 899).

6. J. Ettling, 'The Role of the Rockefeller Foundation in Hookworm Research and Control', in G. A. Schad and K. S. Warren (eds), *Hookworm Disease: Current Status and New Directions* (London: Taylor & Francis, 1990), p. 3.

7. Rockefeller Archive Center (RAC) RF RG 12.1, Wickliffe Rose Diaries, reference to meeting at Colonial Office in 'Notes on Journey to England and the West Indies 1913', p. 3.

8. Steven Palmer, *Launching Global Health: The Caribbean Odyssey of the Rockefeller Foundation* (Ann Arbor: University of Michigan Press, 2010), p. 57.

9. Donald Fisher, 'The Rockefeller Foundation Philanthropy and the British Empire: The Creation of the London School of Hygiene and Tropical Medicine', *History of Education* vol. 7 (1978), pp. 129–43 (p. 130).

10. RAC RG 1, Series 100, Box 5, Folder 42, 'Films-Reports 1917–1927, part 3', 'Preliminary Draft of Plan for Production of a Film on Hookworm Disease', 12 September 1917, unsigned précis for film.

11. RAC 100, 'Films-Reports 1917–1927, Part 1', 'Dersheimer to Howard' [IHB], from Port of Spain, Trinidad, 24 September 1919.

12. The Rockefeller files contain several such requests, including one from Columbia, South Carolina, RAC RF RG 5.1.2, Series 938 (1918) Box 72, F1030; '938 Films 1918', Letter from Universal Film Manufacturing Co. 23 April 1918 by Harry Levey, Manager, Industrial Deptartment, to Dr Meyers, of IHB.

13. RAC RF RG 5.1.2, Series 938 (1920), Box 103, F. 1431, 1432, 1433, '938 Films A–I 1920'. Letter to IHB from J. Sterling Moran, Community Motion Picture Bureau.

14. George Vincent, 'Fight upon Malaria', *New York Times*, 1 August 1921.

15. *Unhooking the Hookworm* is available to view online at <www.rockarch.org>.

16. RAC RF, RG 5.2, Series 200, SS-200, Box 1, Folder 3, 100, 'Films–Reports 1917–1927, Part 1' 5-26-21, 'Memorandum Concerning Comments on the Film "Unhooking the Hookworm", Dr A.T. McCormack, State Health Officer, Louisville, Ky'.

17. O. H. Cheek, commissioner of health, Dublin, Georgia quoted in RAC RG 1, Series 100, Box 5, Folder 39, 100 'Films-Reports 1917–1927', 5-26-21, 'Memorandum Concerning Comments on the Film "Unhooking the Hookworm"'.

18. RAC RG 5, Series 3, 246 J South Carolina County Health Work Reports, 1920, 246 J South Carolina County Health Work Annual Report, 1925, Folder 980. 'Narrative Report Fairfield County Health Unit S. C. Third Quarter 1920'.

19. RAC RG 1, Series 100, Box 5, Folder 41, 100 'Films-Reports 1917–1927', 17 December 1923, W. G. Smillie to John Ferrell, IHB.

20. RAC RG 1, Series 100, Box 5, Folder 39, 100 'Films 1922–1938'. Comment of W. C. Hausheer, quoted in 'Memorandum Concerning Comments on the Film "Unhooking the Hookworm"', 26 May 1921.

21. RAC RG 1, Series 100, Box 5, Folder 39, 100 'Films 1922–1938', 100 'Films–Reports 1917–1927'. Letter from W. G. Smillie to John Ferrell, IHB, in regard to proposed change in hookworm film, 17 December 1923.

22. RAC RG 1, Series 100, Box 5, Folder 39, 100 'Films 1922–1938', 100 'Films–Reports 1917–1927', Dr S. T. Darling to F. F. Russell, Leesburg, Georgia, 15 May 1924.

23. RAC RG 1, Series 100, Box 5, Folder 41, 100 'Films–Reports 1917–1927', Letter from Barnes to Dr Russell, nd.

24. These comments appear in an undated memo held in RAC RG 1, Series 100, Box 5, Folder 41, 100 'Films–Reports 1917–1927'. Dr Barnes is probably W. S. Barnes, who worked for the IHB on hookworm education in British Guiana.

25. For a discussion of British theories of film literacy, see my article 'Watching Africans Watch Movies', *Historical Journal of Film, Radio, and Television* (Summer 2000).

26. For example, a cinema operator in the Scott's Hall area of Jamaica where 'The cooperation in this area is the worst that has been met with for years' still attracted an average of almost 250 people to a series of free screenings. See RAC RG 5, Series 3, Reports, Routine, 437 H, 'Jamaica-Hookworm Reports', 1921–1922, 'Jamaica-Hookworm Reports', 1929, Folder 2250, Report of Unit, #1, July 1927.

27. 'Report of Hookworm Campaign', *Daily Gleaner*, 13 January 1922.

28. Ibid.

29. Jamaican National Archives, 1B/5/77/44, Memorandum on films dated 30 July 1930, though the report is not dated, and appears to have been drafted much earlier.

30. National Archives, Kew, CO/323/848, 'Reaction of Trinidad Audiences to VD film 1920', report from Letitia D. Fairfield, educational commissioner, Trinidad.

31. CO 323/943/2, 'Use of Films in Campaign against Venereal Disease: Proposed Appeal for Assistance to the Rockefeller Foundation', February 1925.

32. Ibid. Letter to Vincent from Mrs Rolfe, 5 February 1925.

33. Ibid. GG, 17 February 1925.

34. Ibid. Letter dated 11 March 1925 signed by 'GS'.

35. Quoted in Marianne P. Fedunkiw, 'The Rockefeller Foundation's Malaria Film, 1925', web published at <www.rockarch.org/publications/conferences/fedunkiw.pdf>.

36. See *Daily Gleaner*, 20 June 1925 for a discussion of the showing of both the hookworm and malaria films.

37. See Liew Kai Khiun, 'Wats & Worms: The Activities of the Rockefeller Federation's International Health Board in Southeast Asia (1913–1940)', pp. 15–16, web published at <www.ihp.sinica.edu.tw/~medicine/ashm/taniguchi%20KaiKhiunLiew.pdf> the Asian Society for the History of Medicine.

38. CO 323/000/26096, 'Reply from Zanzibar Says Government', 19 March 1927.

39. CO 323/000/26096, Government of Accra, 25 April 1928, Reply to 1 October 1927 confidential circular regarding interest in films for exhibition.

40. CO 323/000/26096, Letter from Grigg in Tanganyika, 7 October 1929. Grigg's pessimistic assessment of the Rockefeller films stands in contrast to remarks published in the *Annual Medical and Sanitary Report* of the Tanganyika Medical Department: 'at the end of 1925 the Zanzibar government kindly lent two cinematographic films "malaria" and "unhooking the hookworm" … . Explanations of the films were given in Kiswahili and the Natives appeared to take an intelligent interest.'

41. CO 323/990/1, *Report, Select Committee on Film Censorship* (Kenya), 29 July 1927.

42. J. Russell Orr, 'The Use of the Kinema in the Guidance of Backward Races', *Journal of the Royal African Society* vol. 30 no. 120 (July 1931), pp. 238–44.

43. Rockefeller Foundation Annual Report 1924, p. 143.

44. RAC RG 5, Series 3, Reports, Routine, 437 H, Jamaica-Hookworm Reports, 1929, Folder 2252, Report of #1 Unit, January 1929.

45. Orr, 'The Use of the Kinema in the Guidance of Backward Races', p. 242.

46. RAC RG 5, Series 3, Reports, Routine, 437 H Jamaica-Hookworm Reports, 1921–1922, Jamaica-Hookworm Reports, 1929, Folder 2252, Report of #1 Unit, January 1929.

47. 'Malaysia', *Straits Times*, 8 August 1928, p. 10.

48. 'Films for the Colonies', *Straits Times*, 12 September 1930, p. 12.

49. Stanley Baldwin, quoted in 'Films and the Empire', *The Times*, 24 May 1926. Ramsay MacDonald also spoke out about the dangers posed by commercial films in the empire in parliamentary debates, 16 March 1927, quoted in William Marston Seabury, *Motion Picture Problems: The Cinema and the League of Nations* (New York: Avondale Press, 1929), pp. 22–3.

50. *Report of the Colonial Films Committee* (London: HMSO, 1930), p. 22.

51. 'Educational Films', *Straits Times*, 20 August 1930, p. 10.

52. Ibid.

53. CO 323/1122/16, Films: proposed experimental scheme in Malaya, 'The Proposed Inquiry into the Effect of Films on Backward Races in a Selected British Dependence: Notes of a Meeting Held at No. 2 Richmond Gardens, Friday 30 January, 1931'.

54. Carnegie apparently turned the request down as well. See Smyth, 'The Development of British Colonial Film Policy', p. 442.

55. See Smyth, 'The Development of British Colonial Film Policy'; Reynolds, 'The Bantu Educational Kinema Experiment'; and Burns, *Flickering Shadows*.

56. CO 323/1744/13, 'Ministry of Information: Films for Mobile Film Units in Africa: Visit of Mr. Sellers to East–West Africa', Letter from Vincent Harlow of the Ministry of Information to Noel Sabine of the Colonial Office, 12 January 1940: 'as you are well aware, there is a strong and mistaken prejudice against the use of films in East Africa, which is largely due to the failure of the Bantu Cinema (sic) Experiment'. The Colonial Office had originally been opposed to the BEKE, but acceded when the funds were forthcoming from the Carnegie Corporation. See Smyth, 'The Development of British Colonial Film Policy', p. 442.

Empire and Film

57. CO 1377/838/3, 'Carnegie Corporation Grants', Letter from L. A. Notcutt to the Colonial Secretary of Jamaica, 14 April 1938.
58. Ibid. Malcolm MacDonald to Sir Arthur Richards, July 1939.
59. CO 137/838/3, 'Carnegie Corporation Grants'.
60. Ibid.

THE STATE AND
THE ORIGINS OF
DOCUMENTARY

5

The Cinema and the (Common) Wealth of Nations

Lee Grieveson

In the mid-1920s, the British state began to make use of film to support a political economy increasingly predicated on colonial territory, imperial trade and the utility of a newly configured Commonwealth bloc. It did so in part in collaboration with British industry and emergent monopoly and multinational capital. New institutions of film production housed within political parties and state offices created a series of films illustrating the import of empire trade, and in the process innovated the film form and practice that came later to be called 'documentary'. At the same time, the state worked to establish new global networks of distribution; novel practices of exhibition in various non-theatrical spaces like mobile cinema vans, schools and factories; and legislation to regulate the transnational movement and purported effects of non-'empire' films on metropolitan and colonial subjects and on economic and political order. This state-directed formation of cinema sought to make visible and material a political economy of early twentieth-century imperialism that was driven by what David Harvey has recently described as a 'dialectical relation between territorial and capitalist logics of power'.[1] All of which is to say this: cinema was utilised to respond to and reorientate economic and political problems in the metropolitan centre and, though at this moment less centrally, the (so-called) colonial periphery; to support the expansionary goals of monopoly and multinational capital, and the infrastructures of circulation so central to capitalist modernity; to build and strengthen ties in particular among the Commonwealth bloc countries; to respond to global shifts in trade and power; and to shore up a hegemony rendered increasingly shaky by the growing economic and political strength of, most notably, the United States of America. The cinema became, for a time, an important element in fostering the wealth of the nation and the elaboration of a capitalist and imperialist governmentality.[2]

What follows maps out this complex process. It does so as a contribution to a broader investigation of the ways cinema was used and developed for the purposes of shaping and managing the attitudes and conduct of mass populations by (and mostly within) newly interventionist liberal democracies facing the far-reaching economic and political upheavals of the early twentieth century. Liberal state rationality codifies knowledge to generate 'legitimate' agendas for state intervention or restraint in relation to its populations.[3] Economic crisis, and colonialism more broadly, mark limit points of liberalism as theory and practice, generating new agendas of intervention that also penetrate the cultural sphere.[4] Forms of state-directed non-theatrical cinema, and new practices of cultural policy and regulation, emerged, then, within the wider logics of capital accumulation and state 'security' that subtended the liberal political economy of capitalist imperialism in the interwar period.[5]

The broad outline of that political economy is this: the British state's response to the growing economic power of other industrialised nations, and devastating economic depressions that opened and closed the 1920s, was to develop a partial shift away from the classical free-trade liberalism that had been the guiding principle of economic strategies since the mid-nineteenth century, towards a policy of protectionism and 'imperial preference' that would place a tariff on goods imported from outside the territories of the empire. At the same time, the British government constructed new economic and political structures for the establishment of a Commonwealth bloc. The political and capitalist logics underlying this radical shift in macro-economic policy were varied. It would protect finance capital, which was dependent on the empire; it would, it was hoped, support a faltering British industry by delineating a protected empire market for the exchange of raw materials and manufactured goods while reinforcing the 'underdevelopment' of peripheral economies. The resulting stronger exports would thus ideally lower the levels of unemployment in the metropole and so counteract the political radicalism that accompanied worker disaffection with new Fordist manufacturing practices and that proposed socialist alternatives to liberal capitalist political economy. Finally, the economic and political ties with, in particular, the settler Dominions would fence off an economic bloc that could, it was hoped, sustain geopolitical hegemony.

The emergence of film production, distribution and exhibition within the confines of, first, the dominant Conservative Party, and then in the machinery of state, was a consequence of these precise economic and (geo)political contexts. The investment in culture and development of cultural policy is, indeed, one aspect of the newly interventionist liberal state in the interwar period, marking the ways in which culture was reconfigured as a crucial aspect of governance. Again, the broad contours of this film history can be quickly delineated: the Conservative Party established a film unit in 1925 to exhibit and produce films principally extolling its policies of protectionism to working-class British audiences; the Conservative government established and supported a film unit within the newly created Empire Marketing Board (EMB) in 1926 to support the board's wider goal of establishing networks of economic ties within the imperial and Commonwealth bloc; and, after lobbying in particular from the Federation of British Industries, the Conservative government enacted a form of tariff legislation for the film industry in 1927 that sought to counteract the perceived economic and political effects of the global movement and success of American films. Amid these developments, a series of films illustrating economic relations, the global flow of raw materials and manufactured goods, and the 'common' wealth of nations within the empire bloc, was produced, and widely circulated through new networks of global distribution. 'Documentary' cinema emerged, and was established in the space shared by state and corporate entities; the capital-intensive investment in film was made with the goal of publicising new economic and political forms.

The complex enmeshing of cinema and liberal political rationality and liberal imperial economics is at the centre of the history delineated here. It is a history that remains largely unwritten, reduced in the extant literature mainly to accounts of the formation and the functioning of the EMB film unit (and there largely without substantive engagement with the centrality of the economies of imperialism).[6] It is, though, imperative that we rethink the history of the state use of cinema in this period, situating 'documentary' in the broader contexts of sponsored and non-theatrical cinema as one part of a wider governmental recourse to media for the purposes of shaping the attitudes and conduct of populations within the complex political economy of the interwar years. The account of this will not only deepen our understanding of cinema history, but also our understanding of the enmeshing of political, economic and cultural apparatuses of hegemony, and, specifically, the way cinema as a form of mass media has been enlisted by states and corporations to articulate perspectives that support imperialist, or 'globalising', practices. I am probably not alone in believing that such a history might have particular resonance today.

'IMPERIAL PREFERENCE'

The liberal political economy of the eighteenth and early nineteenth centuries that ushered in new conceptions of property rights, market power and, indeed, imperialism was predicated on a constitutive tension, split between the urge to govern the polity in an economical manner with minimal intervention into the delicate balance of social and economic processes – the 'invisible hand' of Adam Smith's formative articulation of liberal economics – and the imperative to intervene to keep capitalist economies growing and to secure the correlative productivity and welfare of populations.[7] It was a dialectic that would be marked particularly acutely in the interwar period of the twentieth century. After global conflict between rival imperialist states, the principles of *laissez-faire* free-trade economics were widely challenged and ultimately swept away (if only temporarily) with the global Depression of the early 1930s, which prompted a retreat into national and/or economic blocs and the establishment of governmental 'welfare' interventions designed to shore up social and political order.[8] That these practices and governmental regimes were not always 'liberal' in the more general and now commonsensical sense of the word is well known.[9] In 1920s Britain, the dominant Conservative Party proposed a newly interventionist protectionist regime of tariffs on imported materials alongside a system of 'imperial preference' that would lower or withdraw those protectionist measures for countries within the empire.[10] Its policies marked a shift from what has been called the 'imperialism of free trade' that had from the mid-nineteenth century positioned Britain at the hub of global circuits of commercial and financial capital, as the first large transnational economy, towards a revised political economy that would necessitate the partial withdrawal from the global economy and the establishment of an imperial economic bloc with Britain at its political and financial centre.[11] These revisions would support, in particular, finance capital and large-scale industry, both increasingly dependent upon the empire. The policies were electorally unpopular (largely because of their potential impact on the price of everyday goods) and were opposed by the Liberal and Labour Parties.[12] In the absence, initially, of a clear mandate, the Conservative government used a series of imperial economic conferences throughout the 1920s to foster intra-imperial economic connections (at which, the importance of film to that project was discussed);

set in process the formal establishment of a Commonwealth bloc; and supported the creation of a number of other policy and cultural initiatives to foster the establishment of this newly configured emphasis on political economy. Later, in the aftermath of the cataclysmic global economic collapse of 1929, the Conservative-dominated national government withdrew Britain from the gold standard, the very symbol of liberal internationalism;[13] formalised the statutory identity of the Commonwealth in 1931; passed the Import Duties Act of 1932 that introduced a general tariff of 10 per cent; and in that same year introduced a system of imperial preference that supported quotas and other bilateral arrangements at an important imperial economic conference held in Ottawa.[14]

The governmental logics underlying this critical shift of emphasis in economic policy, in the elaboration of an imperial political economy, were varied and expansive. It was closely aligned with the support of finance capital, a crucial part of the Conservative Party's support base in London and the southeast of England.[15] The economic effects of tariffs would protect an ailing British industrial sector from the growing strength of other industrialised nations, particularly with respect to the chemical and electrical products generated from the second stage of the period of capitalist industrialisation.[16] It would consequently foster the growth of large-scale and export-dependent monopoly capitalism.[17] The support of a faltering economy, and correlative formation of the conditions subtending corporate capitalism, was critical to the governing agenda of the Conservative Party to advance propertied interests.[18] It would also, it was hoped, go some way towards resolving the vexatious and seemingly related problems of unemployment and working-class radicalism, put firmly on the political agenda because the Representation of the People Act of 1918 had extended the franchise to most working-class adult males.[19] The signs of that radicalism were increasingly visible in the interwar years, in the shadow of the Russian Revolution: trade-union membership increased in the early 1920s; the Labour Party became a viable political alternative; and labour militancy produced a series of industrial disputes (including most notably the General Strike of 1926 that threatened to disrupt the infrastructure upon which the country depended).[20] It was hoped that the introduction of tariffs would reduce unemployment and thus, in the words of one of its chief architects, Secretary of State for the Colonies Leopold Amery, detach 'the working people in this country from the anti-imperialist leaders of Socialism'.[21] The government also offered financial assistance to those emigrating, in particular to the Dominions, to counteract unemployment and to develop the economic utility of the empire.[22] In this way, the newly interventionist imperial political economy of tariff reform, and to a lesser extent empire settlement, fostered a corporate role for the state that was connected to nascent welfare interventions emerging in the 1920s and that was designed to reinvigorate the ostensibly beleaguered liberal capitalism.[23]

The correlative system of imperial preferences would buttress the metropolitan economy by sustaining the lucrative flow of the raw materials for industry and energy from the 'periphery' and their transformation into the more expensive manufactured goods created, sold and exported from the 'core'. It is now well known that the 'development of underdevelopment' of colonial economies, and their construction as 'complementary' to that of the advanced industrial core, was central to imperial political economy.[24] Its principles guided the creation of the system of 'development' economics, and imperial preferences; and the resultant imperial economic and political bloc. The former, as evidenced, for example, in the 1929 Colonial Development Act, would help finance economic and physical infrastructures in colonial spaces that would specifically facilitate the expansion and circulation of British products and finance capital.[25] The latter strategy subtended the 'Balfour Declaration' issued after the 1926 imperial conference, which declared Dominions 'autonomous communities'; the Statute of Westminster legally enshrined this conception of the Commonwealth in 1931.[26] The common wealth of nations would be fostered, though, of course, some were more autonomous and equal than others.

Economic ties developed with, in particular, the semi-industrialised Dominions of the Commonwealth across the 1920s, and most clearly at the Ottawa conference, were regarded as central to the establishment of an imperial economic and territorial bloc.[27] Alongside the benefits this would bring to the core economy, and to the project of cathecting the new working-class electorate with regard to a new consumer economy and to the Conservative Party, it was thought these ties could both conciliate the rising nationalist and anti-imperialist sentiments in colonised countries, and resist the growing economic and political dominance of the dollar and the US.[28] Canada would become particularly important for Britain's attempted containment of the world's next great hegemon (and was consequently included in the imperial preference system, despite opting out of the sterling area).[29] Later, this importance would play itself out through the fostering of connections between cultural institutions, particularly in relation to film and the category of 'documentary cinema' – one example of the ways in which the economic and political logics of the interwar years, and British late imperialism, shaped film texts, forms, policies and institutions. It is towards an account of that shaping process – of the enmeshing of cinema and capitalist imperialism – that I now turn.

'THE CINEMATOGRAPH IN EDUCATION'

Amid these complex economic and political shifts, the work of communication and culture assumed new priorities for political parties, the state and for corporate organisations interested in sustaining a liberal imperial economic order. It did so in the light of the sustained use of culture in the global conflict of 1914–18, when the British government turned to film in particular to influence the way the population (and indeed the government of the US) regarded the conflict. Various 'liberal' states came to similar conclusions about the importance of culture for shaping what came to be called 'public opinion'. Indeed, the study of 'propaganda' and 'public opinion' – communication studies – emerged in this post-war period, as scholars and policy-makers argued that mass media, and cinema in particular, had created a newly mediatised public sphere and were particularly influential in shaping the attitudes and the conduct of populations.[30] Working on the basis of similar assumptions, 'public relations' experts working for large corporate organisations began to pronounce on ways to engage media to best manage public opinion. The logic of these conceptions of the power of media and the malleability of individuals and populations could cut two ways. It would lead to jeremiads and a host of social-science investigations into the psychic and social effects of media that contributed to the creation of new regulatory frameworks. Yet also, and frequently at the same time, it could generate efforts to utilise culture as part of expansive strategies of governance by political parties, state bodies and a variety of non-governmental institutions. These efforts to manage opinion were integral to the newly interventionist practices of the liberal state.

It is in this context that a number of cultural forms and institutions were innovated to foster intra-imperial connections. The Foreign Office, for example, took over some aspects of the supervision of publicity and propaganda in 1918 from what was called the Ministry of Information during the war, closely monitoring nationalist movements.[31] In 1924 the government met half the costs of a large imperial exhibition held in Wembley in London that was designed, in the words of the official guide, 'to foster inter-imperial trade and open fresh world markets for Dominion and home products'.[32] The British Broadcasting Company began broadcasting in 1922, and its coverage included King George V's opening address at the imperial exhibition of 1924. It was constituted as a public utility in 1927 (when it became the British Broadcasting Corporation [BBC]); and began an 'Empire Service' in 1932 to broadcast throughout the empire and so cultivate ideas of imperial unity.[33] In 1930 the 'British Empire Games' began, not coincidentally in Canada, generating and promoting a Common-wealth union then in the process of formation.[34] And the British Council was established in 1934 as the institutional embodiment of what Nicholas Pronay has called the 'cultural propaganda approach'.[35] Together, the efforts to foster new cultural forms and build new media systems sought to generate an economic and political unity, at the same time sustaining the imperial order and forestalling subaltern resistance.

Film became particularly important to the political economy of interwar capitalist imperialism, largely because it was widely seen as the most popular and powerful form of mass media that in particular reached the politically important working-class audience.[36] The idea that film was a pedagogic form that could assist in the broader governmental project of fostering and stabilising imperial economic and political union gathered pace in the early 1920s. In a 1923 imperial education conference in London, for example, a day was devoted to discussing 'The Cinematograph in Education', accompanied by a screening of appropriate films and an exhibition of projectors suitable for educational uses.[37] The conference set up a committee to study the question of the pedagogical value of film further, and published the *Report on the Use and Value of the Cinematograph in Education*, arguing for the integration of film into school education.[38] Later in that same year an imperial conference focused on the development of empire trade discussed the 'utilization of the cinematograph film as an instrument for disseminating knowledge both here and overseas', and also as a supplement to aid British emigration to 'new lands'.[39] Film was uniquely positioned, a report on the conference observed, to show 'the benefit of educating the young and of strengthening the ties of sentiment, which mainly rests upon our knowledge of each other'.[40] In early 1924 the Treasury appointed a 'cinematograph advisor' whose 'duty it is to assist Government Departments generally in questions relating to cinemato-graphy and to supervise the preservation and use of films in the possession of the Government'.[41] In the same year, a report initiated by the Board of Education concluded that film was a powerful form capable of shaping the attitudes of its audiences. Its author, James Marchant, wrote to *The Times*, drawing out one of the implications of this conception of the pedagogical power of cinema:

> One aspect of the educational possibilities of the cinema has been repeatedly impressed upon me during the past seven years of investigation ... . That is that the time has fully come when the British and Dominion Governments should combine to produce a library of Imperial films to circulate around the Empire.[42]

As Tom Rice has shown, the extensive use of film within the 1924 imperial exhibition was an important moment in this gathering sense of the import of film for imperial economics, and for fostering intra-imperial unity.[43]

It was the Conservative Party itself that would at this point pursue most fully this conception of the economic and political utility of film, wrapping it together specifically with the party's efforts to communicate with the new nearly mass electorate and to establish a revised imperial political economy. The party established a film department within its central office in 1925, the first political party to do so. It stands as an important, if largely unnoticed, moment in the political use of film.[44] The department initially distributed and showed films in Britain that were 'mainly pictures of British industries and of the Empire', probably including a number of those sponsored and produced for the imperial exhibition by the Colonial Office, Dominion governments and business organisations like the important Federation of British Industries (FBI).[45] The filmed 'views of Britain's imperial glory' were shown in mobile cinema vans, at political meetings and also often in schools.[46] In 1926 the party started producing its own films, before in 1930 its film department was replaced by the ostensibly independent, but party-financed, Conservative and Unionist Film Association (CFA). CFA films were also made with advice and help from the film producers Alexander Korda and Michael Balcon, whose own series of films on the adventures of empire in the 1930s represented significant articulations of the logics of colonial rule.[47]

The party's establishment of a film unit was driven by the belief that film had been valuable to the British war effort, and thus in what *The Times* called film's 'utility for political work' with respect to the new working-class electorate.[48] J. C. C. Davidson, party chairman, said in 1926, 'The first job on which I set my mind was to apply the lessons of the Great War to the organization of political warfare.'[49] Many associated with the film unit had indeed worked on war propaganda.[50] In turn, the party's chief publicity officer, Joseph Ball, later noted that the 'enormous increase in the popularity of cinemas particularly among the working classes, pointed the way ... to the cinema film as a method of placing our propaganda before the electorate'.[51] Certainly, the party's logic regarding the utility of cinema mirrored that articulated in the same period from radically different political perspectives, notably the Soviet investment in cinema and also a scattered union use of film. For the Conservative Party, it was the pressing need to address the new working-class electorate, and to articulate in particular the political economy of imperialism as distinct from that of socialism, which pushed the party to its considerable material and ideological investment in cinema.

Accordingly, films made by the party frequently offered images and accounts of the productivity of capital investment and selective state intervention, showing in particular how this facilitated the development of colonial economies for the advantage of the British worker and economy. *West Africa Calling*, for example, made in 1927, set out to show how 'workers at home benefit by the policy of developing the Empire'.[52] The economic development led by Britain, the film proposes, made West Africa productive in various ways, and this in turn generated economic benefits in Britain. 'Years ago', the opening intertitles claim, 'West Africa was a country of forest ... swamps ... and desert', where 'national conditions made communications almost impossible'. The introduction of 'British enterprise has changed all this', creating a 'thriving trade' that both improves conditions for the 'native population' – the film shows schools and hospitals – and that generates employment for British workers and profit for British industry and capital. Lumber is 'turned to account with the help of British machinery', and huge mechanical diggers aid the 'British engineers ... developing the tin mines'. The shift from unproductive natural spaces (forest, swamp, desert) to exemplary spaces of liberal civility (hospital, school) is facilitated by capital, engineering and machinery, and state intervention. If this closely follows a late colonial logic, whereby political domination is legitimated by the promise of progress and technology is exchanged for subjection, the emphasis here focuses in on the proposed benefits that imperial economic development brings to working-class populations in Britain. In this way the film follows the political logics that presented imperialism as a solution to the travails of capitalist modernity, and forecloses, of course, the possibility of connections between subaltern populations.

West Africa Calling's account of this imperial political economy comes thereafter to focus on the creation of new infrastructures that facilitate mobility and the circulation of goods and capital. It is in these images, and the connections made between them through editing, that the film effects a visual corollary to the pathways that connect imperial economics, to the hidden movements of capital that escape imagining but underpin so much of the colonial archive. We are shown the new harbour at Takoradi in Ghana, as boats move past the huge cranes that load them with raw materials bound for England. We see the building of railroads, predicated on 'British steel sleepers and lines ... and rolling stock'. It is 'British cement', the film asserts, that is used in bridge building, and the newly constructed '[r]oads create a demand for British motor cars to run along them'. One brief scene shows British cars moving across the frame, with the margins at the front and the side of the frame occupied by an African woman carrying a basket on her head and by a slow-moving cart. The familiar dichotomy between technological modernity and tradition, so central to imperial rhetoric and iconography, is meshed here with an emphasis on the way British state, finance capital and technology transforms the space of West Africa to facilitate the circulation of, as the film puts it, 'food stuffs and raw materials' to Britain and 'increased employment in British workshops' to sustain imperial development. The sequence after the cars travelling across African roads shows cars being constructed in British factories, by workers employing modern (if not quite yet Fordist) technology (and, of course, the use of materials produced in colonial spaces, like the Malayan rubber that was so central to tyre production). Likewise, earlier a sequence featuring African workers laying railway sleepers switches to three shots of those sleepers being produced in a British factory. The emphasis on the infrastructure of roads, bridges and waterways as the material form that allows exchange over space is carried through and emphasised

West Africa Calling (1927)

in the editing of shots together towards the end of the film that switch between colonial spaces and the factories that the film proposes are mutually constituted and sustained. The images of material connections, emphasised through the connective tissues of editing, are central to the representation of the Conservative political economy that positions empire development and markets as central to the sustenance of the wealth of the nation.

The fascinated gaze of the camera machine at the various industrial machines that litter the film offers exemplary instances of what Brian Larkin has called 'the colonial sublime', the 'effort to use technology as part of political rule'.[53] West Africa Calling lingers over machines in motion. The film makes a distinction, though, between the way workers interact with machines, for in the sequences in colonial Africa the machines – like cranes – dwarf workers, who are always supervised in their relatively menial work of fetching and carrying by British officials, whereas in the short sequences in British factories the workers are unsupervised and demonstrate a mastery of complex technology. The gulf of technological superiority legitimises colonial rule; racialised labour supports the British working class. If this representation belies the history of how new technologies of mass production and Fordist work practices deskilled working-class populations, it does so in the goal of a political logic that seeks to cathect the working class to technological modernity and, perhaps even more substantively, to associate the power of machinery with that of capital and state. For the film, for Conservative political economy, the machinery of state powers industrial machinery, witnessed here (and so facilitated) by the actual and figurative machinery of film.

West Africa Calling's narrative of progress and modernity – from swamps to newly productive waterways, railways and roads – was an early example of a set of Conservative-financed and -produced films that presented lessons in political economy, and that similarly idealised the creation of infrastructures for the mobility of capital and goods. A number of these were produced in the early 1930s, in the context of the global economic Depression and as an explanation of the shifting contours of economic policy that saw the introduction of tariffs and imperial preference by the Conservative-dominated national government in 1931. Many of them purport to document the necessity of a revised political economy for the sustenance of British capital and industry. In the animated *The Right Spirit* (1931), John Bull's damaged car can only be fixed at Conservative leader Stanley Baldwin's 'Prosperity Garage', when it is filled from pumps labelled 'Safeguarding' (a term for the introduction of protectionist tariffs), 'Empire Unity', and 'Reduced Taxes'. The facilitation of the movement of the car by the Conservative garage is metonymic for the regeneration of the mobility central to economic well-being. *The Price of Free Trade* (1932) is a stilted, short, fictionalised encounter involving a Belgian trying to get work in Britain – he points out what he sees as the absurdity in preventing him from working while the steel he has made in Belgium can enter Britain freely – that concludes with an animated drawing showing the economic effects of the British production of steel. When steel is imported, there is a line simply between port and factory, yet when it is produced at home we see a multiplying series of lines drawn that connect quarries, mines, steelworks and factories. The emerging lines stand as images of the connections between productive sites and spaces, of the circulation of materials that facilitates employment and profit. *Two Lancashire Cotton Workers Discuss Safeguarding* (1935) is a short, scripted conversation between an older and younger worker, taking their lunch break. 'We shall have to look more to the empire', the older worker tells the younger one, 'and them more to us.' The tutelary role of the experienced worker explaining the complexities to the younger one, standing in for those newly admitted to the electorate, was a common characteristic of Conservative propaganda, and stood here as metonymic for the role of Conservative film more generally.[54]

The economic and political utility of the empire is shown in *Empire Trade* (1934). Unlike *West Africa Calling*, the film focuses on the Dominions (as well as India), those economies that were particularly important to Britain.[55] Its remarkable opening cuts – from the launch of a ship to several shots of a fast-moving train – recalling to mind the opening of the modernist *Berlin – Symphony of a Great City* (1927) – stand as visual markers for the speed of the circulation of goods and capital. The film's account of the economic interconnection between the core and periphery is supplemented by a message about the territorial import of the empire. The naval base of Singapore, we are told, 'keeps watch over the Malay states', while Aden is 'guarding the Suez canal, our trade route to the East'. Together, naval bases and the Suez Canal were critical to the circulation of British goods and to the country's geopolitical status. In *The Great Recovery* (1934) the problem of free trade is rendered in language that implies violation – 'for too long', we are told, 'London Bridge has been open to foreign ships' – before we see images of the Ottawa conference that established the details of imperial preference and thus in part the sanctity of Britain's economic borders.

The Conservative films represent an early example of the way media operated as part of a wider, networked infrastructure working to facilitate and mediate the goods that travelled along the same pathways.[56] Indeed, the party innovated a 'special machinery' of distribution and exhibition to show its films – a fleet of mobile cinema vans that toured Britain.[57] In order to bypass extant cinemas, the party invested in the design and construction of a number of these vans, with projectors that backprojected film onto a hooded screen at the back, thus enabling daylight projection. The elaboration of new machinery to foster the actual mobility of the virtual mobility of film was testament to the party's belief in the critical value of film to its elaboration of

Conservative Party's
mobile cinema van

economic policies in the interregnum before the establishment of those policies as legislation. And this was emphasised when the party fitted the cinema vans in 1927 with an early and expensive sound system.[58] That it was able to invest considerably in the capital-intensive business of film production and exhibition was, of course, a consequence of the party's financial backing by the city and big business. Or, put another way: the 'flash of capital' visible in the filmed accounts of the import of capitalist and imperialist economy, relayed by a ruling political party, was buttressed by the support of capital and industry.[59]

Vans were first used in August 1925, and were thereafter sent out in particular to rural areas and through small towns that had limited access to the cinema. Other vans carried film-projection equipment that could be set up in village and town halls, and other public spaces. Often films were shown prior to a political meeting, which would expound on the themes of the films.[60] At times, the vans also carried with them 'a number of showcases containing samples of Empire products in order that Empire food demonstrations may be combined with the film programme'.[61] Vans functioned in this way as mobile display and exhibition spaces, combining visual and material culture to encourage intra-imperial trade. And they did so as mobile spaces that extended the reach of government, making government mobile and capable of circulating among the new electorate. The conception of film as a way to enlarge the public sphere was elaborated in part in recognition of the way cinema had been constructed as an apolitical space of entertainment.[62] Later, the use of mobile cinemas was exported to the empire, frequently with the intention of engaging film to 'educate' colonial populations, to create modern colonial subjects and to bind populations into an imperial collectivity.[63]

The virtual and actual mobility of film was well suited to the elaboration of the imperial political economy so central to the Conservative Party's political agenda to mobilise new economic and political relations. The establishment of new visual forms, and new machines of distribution and exhibition, attests to the importance accorded media infrastructures. Yet the mobility of film, particularly of commercial American film, could also trouble economic and ideological forms. And film's importance for the political economy of capitalist imperialism was played also then through the elaboration and innovation of new structures of film policy and regulation. It is towards an account of the political economy of this new regulatory space that I now turn.

'TRADE FOLLOWS THE FILM'

The facilitation, and also regulation, of the movement of film, as a form of both material and cultural capital, become an issue for government debate and legislation starting in 1925, the same year that the Conservative Party initiated its own film unit and also in the midst of the ongoing debates about protectionism that followed the party's election victory in 1924. The calls to regulate the movement of, in particular, American films into Britain and across its empire – to establish a protectionist economy specifically for film – were twinned with efforts to foster a better-capitalised British film industry and the movement of those films across the Commonwealth and the empire, principally as markers for and generators of the intra-imperial movement of capital and manufactured goods. At stake in a series of debates and policy decisions on cinema and its mobility in the mid-1920s, then, was the innovation and establishment of a political space to foster the economic utility of cinema and to counter the nascent American economic imperial hegemony. For a time, the formulation of film policy became symptomatic of the broader struggles to foster British economic imperialism in the face of the rising economic power of the US.

It was an influential business organisation, the Federation of British Industries, which did most to initiate the debate and to push for state legislation. In a memo written in 1925 to Philip Cunliffe-Lister, president of the Board of Trade in the Conservative government, the organisation called for protection for the British film industry, and an increase in capital for British film production through the creation of a finance company or a 'Film Bank', which could, the memo observed, be called 'Imperial Cinematograph Corporation Ltd' and a British film studio.[64] Films produced by the Imperial Cinematograph Corporation, the memo continued, 'would use to the full the marvellous and varied resources of the Empire [and] could include subjects relating to British history and industry'.[65] The FBI's engagement with cinema extended beyond the goal to protect the British film industry for its own sake, and was driven also by the conception of the importance of film as a form of advertisement and propaganda that had, as we have seen, gathered pace in the post-war period.[66] For the FBI this meant that cinema had wider economic significance, and that the seemingly global dominance of American films thus threatened to damage British commercial interests both at home and in the empire markets that were so important to a British industry facing intense competition from other industrialised nations.

FBI members set up a series of meetings in 1925 to discuss the problems facing the British film industry, and the impact of this on industry more broadly. 'The influence of American fashions', the organisation noted in its first meeting, 'was beginning to affect the markets for goods even in this country and in the Dominions the tendency was even stronger than here.'[67] In a later letter to *The Times*, the president of the FBI offered a sharp economic analysis of some of the factors that supported the global circulation of American films, and its 'stranglehold over the film business throughout the Empire'.[68] If Britain were 'to stand up against the ever-growing flow of foreign rubbish and to check the gradual Americanization of our Empire', it would need to draw on the resources of the state to establish a protectionist tariff and to facilitate a heavily capitalised industry, like the one that had developed in the early 1920s in the US when Eastern finance capital supported the establishment of an oligopolistic studio system.[69] For the FBI, and British industry, the potential economic force of film necessitated state intervention, and the kind of protectionist legislation that was still some years away from full enactment.

The logic of the FBI's sense of the economic value of film was widely shared in the period. Variants on the phrase 'trade follows the film' were frequently repeated, positioning film as a form of advertisement that supplemented the circulation of goods and capital.[70] The American film industry itself articulated perhaps the most elaborate account of this conception of the economic utility of cinema at this moment, through the concentrated efforts of its public-relations arm, the Motion Picture Producers and Distributors of America (MPPDA), to foster the global distribution of its films. Will Hays, the head of the MPPDA, told the students at the Harvard Business School in 1927, 'I could spend all of my allotted time telling you how the motion picture is selling goods abroad for every manufacturer ... . "Trade follows the film."'[71] Likewise, in a theoretically savvy memo, Edward Lowry, the MPPDA's European representative, reasoned that motion pictures 'are such indirect and undesigned [sic] propaganda for the purveying of national ideals, mode of life, methods of thought, and standard of living', and as such 'are demonstrably the greatest single factor in the Americanization of the world and ... fairly may be called the most important and significant of America's exported products'.[72] The MPPDA made these arguments as part of its efforts to circumvent government intervention into its oligopolistic economic practices.[73] To these ends, the organisation also fostered close ties with the US State Department and the Department of Commerce, who supported the globalising efforts of the film industry as one element of the US government's own expansionist economic policies that saw, for example, the influx of US capital in particular into Latin America and Europe in the 1920s.[74]

Responding to the global reach of Hollywood and the expansionist economic goals of the US state, the London *Morning Post* astutely observed, 'The film is to America what the flag once was to Britain.'[75] Or, in other words, the global circulation of the filmic representation of American 'modes of life' and 'standards of living' symbolised, and participated in, the transition from a British imperialism based on the territorial power represented by the flag to the coming American-dominated world of economic and political power that was largely dislocated from geographical possession.

Cunliffe-Lister responded to the FBI's analysis of the economic force of cinema (which after all mirrored the logic partially subtending his own party's investment in film) by calling meetings with representatives of the production, distribution and exhibition sectors of the film industry and with the FBI to formulate a policy to counteract the dominance of American film and its impact on business and empire markets. In a memorandum to the cabinet in early 1926 he mapped out the problem film posed to economic order and the reasons underpinning American dominance. 'In Great Britain and throughout the Empire', he wrote, 'nearly every film shown represents American ideas, set out in an American atmosphere ... . The accessories are American houses, American motor cars, American manufactures and so forth.'[76] Undoubtedly, the movement of capital from Britain to the US was deeply problematic for the state, given the country's indebtedness to the US after World War I and the apparent shift in economic power visible in the post-war period. Audiences were easily influenced by American films, Cunliffe-Lister reasoned, because they were 'composed largely of young and "low-brow" people' (again, it was this conception of the malleable, working-class audience that had prompted the Conservative Party to invest in film itself, to better address the low-brow, recently enfranchised voters).[77] In a letter to *The Times* also in early 1926 he described film as 'the greatest advertising power in the world', a conception of the function of cinema that drove the FBI's anxieties and that brought it within his purview as president of the Board of Trade.[78] That action must be taken was not in doubt, but, trammelled by the lingering dictates of *laissez-faire* liberalism, and no doubt distracted by the General Strike, Cunliffe-Lister proposed that this was initially best driven by the film industry itself on a voluntary basis.[79]

The Conservative government's concern about the economic effects of American films was also supplemented by anxiety about the ideological effects film had on those easily influenced, low-brow audiences at home and across the empire. In a debate in parliament, significantly about the problem of unemployment, Conservative Prime Minister Stanley Baldwin stated:

> I think the time has come when the position of that industry in this country should be examined with a view to seeing whether it be not possible, as it is desirable, on national grounds, to see that the larger proportion of the films exhibited in this country are British, having regard ... to the enormous power which the film is developing for propaganda purposes, and the danger to which we in this country and our Empire subject ourselves if we allow that method of propaganda to be entirely in the hands of foreign countries. [80]

Widespread anxieties about the effects of film on working-class and colonial populations centred on their proposed capacity to displace British national culture, to foment political resistance and so to potentially disaggregate populations. In a meeting held by the FBI to consider the problem of film, Professor A. P. Newton of the Royal Colonial Institute bemoaned how American films that circulated widely in the Dominions 'hold everything British up to ridicule'. This had, Newton continued, 'a very bad influence on the comparatively plastic minds of the young'.[81] In an editorial in early 1927 *The Times* asserted that it was a 'public danger' that the 'false values of film' promoted the importance of 'wealth, luxury and notoriety' to audiences made up of 'the many newly enfranchised [with] slightly educated minds'.[82] Likewise, in March 1927 the film columnist G. A. Atkinson for the *Daily Express*, in a now oft-quoted statement, wrote:

> The plain truth about the British film situation is that the bulk of our picturegoers are Americanized ... . They talk America, think America, and dream America. We have several

million people, mostly women, who, to all intent and purpose, are temporary American citizens.[83]

Atkinson's choice of the word 'citizen' was surely not coincidental, for the promise of liberal citizenship held out by American film would be, or could be, seductive and disruptive for those varied populations in Britain and its empire who were not citizens but *subjects*. The presumption to liberal democracy so central to the textual economies of American film would be deeply problematic for a colonial power, even if those presumptions were frequently shot through with their own colonial rhetoric – the Western, after all, frequently narrated the history of American domestic colonialism – and indeed worked to buttress new forms of global economic hegemony.

Anxieties about the economic and political effects of cinema gathered pace throughout 1926 and were addressed in detail late in the year at the imperial conference in London. The conference would largely address economic issues, and would be the site where the preliminary organisation of a Commonwealth economic union was elaborated. Ongoing lobbying efforts by the FBI urged Cunliffe-Lister to add film to the agenda of the conference. 'The Committee view with great alarm', the FBI wrote,

> the practical monopoly which has been obtained by foreign film production concerns of the kinema programmes of the British Empire. They consider this must have a most detrimental effect on British prestige and must be seriously prejudicial to the best interests of the Empire, especially in those parts of the overseas Dominions which contain large coloured populations.[84]

To counteract this, the FBI submitted a memorandum to the conference recommending an immediate quota for the exhibition of 12.5 per cent British films in the British market.[85]

At the conference, a subcommittee was established to investigate film and its place within the empire. '[I]t is a matter of the most serious concern', the committee reported,

> that the films shown in the various parts of the Empire should be to such an overwhelming extent the product of foreign countries ... it is an undoubted fact that the constant showing of foreign scenes or settings, and the absence of any corresponding showing of Empire scenes or settings, powerfully advertises (the more effectively because indirectly) foreign countries and their products.

The report concluded by calling for 'suitable Government action' to encourage 'private enterprise in its efforts to place the Empire film industry on a sound footing'.[86] Unsurprisingly, the tenor of the report closely followed the logic of the FBI and Cunliffe-Lister's efforts to establish state aid to the British film industry in a way that was consistent both with the broader logics of the liberal governmental investment in cultural forms to generate economic and social and political stability and the specific efforts to establish a Commonwealth market to counter American dominance. The FBI accordingly issued a manifesto on how to market films in the crucial markets of the

Dominions, proposing the formation of a central distribution company to facilitate the dispersal of British and Commonwealth films, and an empire-wide quota scheme to regulate the spread of American films.[87] Film production and policy was innovated to establish and support an imperial political economy.

The tipping point for state intervention had been reached. Cunliffe-Lister responded to the conference report, and to the failure of the film industry to voluntarily reduce American film imports, by introducing a bill into parliament in March 1927 that would compel renters to acquire, and exhibitors to show, a prescribed number of 'British' films.[88] It defined a British film, significantly, in terms principally of employment (and thus of its economic utility as a site of work). The

> film must have been made by a British subject or a British-controlled company; the studio scenes must be photographed in a studio in the British Empire; the author of the scenario or of the original work must be a British subject; and not less than 75 per cent. of the salaries, wages and payments for labour and services.[89]

At the same time, the bill sought to address the question of block- and blind-booking, those trade practices established by dominant American studios to force distributors and exhibitors to book a raft of films at the same time, frequently sight unseen, in order to establish a trade monopoly. The British government hoped that the respective governments of the Dominions in particular would establish reciprocal agreements, thus supporting a film economy along the lines of the mooted imperial preference system. The bill closely followed the position staked out by the FBI, showing not only the close relation between the organisation and the Conservative Party but more broadly a political economy that was predicated on state support for industry.

Quota legislation did effectively support the production section of the film industry, over that of distribution and exhibition, in a way analogous to how tariff legislation worked more generally in supporting industry and finance capital. It was partly for this reason that the Labour Party refused to support the bill, and that some commented that it was driven entirely by the demands of the FBI, and by the interests of business and finance capital.[90] The Act certainly did, as *The Times* predicted, attract 'new capital ... to the British industry'.[91] The vertically integrated combines Gaumont-British and British International Pictures were established in 1927, with a capital investment predicated on the stable markets created for British films by the quota legislation.[92] It was in this way, if not in other ways, that the quota legislation was effective, for the efforts to foster capital investment in the film industry had been a core concern throughout the process (it was, for example, important to the FBI and formed a large part of Cunliffe-Lister's memo to the cabinet in early 1926).

Economic ties and common markets were complexly enmeshed with the imperative also to forge political and affective 'bonds'. After reading the already cited resolution of the imperial conference into the record of the debate, Cunliffe-Lister asserted:

> Everybody will admit that the strongest bonds of Empire – outside, of course, the strongest of all, the Crown – are just those, intangible bonds – a common outlook, the same ideas, and the same ideals which we all share and which are expressed in a common language and a common literature. Should we be content for a moment if we depended, upon foreign literature or

upon a foreign Press in this country? From the trade point of view, the influence of the cinema is no less important. It is the greatest advertising power in the world. Just let the House imagine the effect upon trade of millions of people in every country, day after day, seeing the fashions, the styles, and the products of a particular country. It inevitably influences them in their trade purchases.[93]

The economic 'influence' was, yet again, supplemented by concern about ideological influence, by the potential power of film to destroy the hierarchies of difference and the bonds of deference essential to colonial governance. 'I do not suppose that there is anything which has done so much harm to the prestige and position of Western people and the white race', said the Conservative former president of the Board of Trade and chancellor, Sir Robert Horne, 'as the exhibition of films which have tended to degrade us in the eyes of peoples who have been accustomed to look upon us with admiration and respect'.[94] Likewise, the Conservative MP Herbert Williams remarked that the

evil of showing to coloured races and to, shall we say, less educated people than the average inhabitant of this country, representations of the lives of white people which are completely contrary to the life the bulk of us live ... [has] done great harm.[95]

Always implicit in these concerns about misrepresentation was the idea that there was a form of representation that would best sustain Britain's 'prestige' and the right to govern. 'The success of our government of subject races depends almost entirely on the degree of respect which we can inspire', a report attached to a Colonial Films Committee established by the government in 1929 stated. 'Incalculable is the damage that has already been done to the prestige of Europeans in India and the Far East through the widespread exhibition of ultra-sensational and disreputable pictures.'[96]

At the base of these concerns about the damage done by representation were ideas about the effects of films on supposedly malleable populations, and thus the capacity of film to undercut the structures of authority central to liberal and colonial governmentality. Regulatory discourses frequently argued that mimetic responses to films were more evident in subaltern populations. 'The backward races within the Empire', a government-sponsored report asserted in 1933, 'can gain and suffer more from the film than the sophisticated European, because to them the power of the visual medium is intensified.'[97] At play also in the margins of these debates were nascent concerns about not only the representation of misbehaving white characters, but also about the structures of empathy that were so central to the textual economies of, in particular, American fiction film and that enabled positions of alignment and allegiance between populations that undercut the premises of colonial logic and practices. The problem of film was, in Babli Sinha's suggestive phrasing, its 'threatening deterritorializing potential', its capacity to mix spaces and populations, to undercut boundaries and to foster utopian possibilities that ran counter to economic and political structures of imperial hegemony.[98]

The state accordingly invested great importance to the establishment of systems of film regulation in this period, making manifest the close ties between ideas about film as a form of cultural imperialism evident in debates about quota legislation and the establishment and sustenance of institutions to curtail the visibility and mobility of films that were regarded as potentially threatening to economic order and governance. The importance accorded to this task was considerable. For example, the president of the British Board of Film Censors (BBFC) was Edward Shortt, who had previously been home secretary, tasked with dealing with industrial unrest and the threat of a General Strike. Shortt was noted, Nicholas Pronay has shown, for his mastery of 'internal security, counter-subversion and counter-insurgency', and his engagement with the regulation of cinema was tied to these governmental aims.[99] The regulation of Soviet film and its articulation of a radically different political economy were also important in this context.[100] The imperial dimensions of film regulation were intensified in the 1920s (there was some overlap, for it was feared that Russia was utilising propaganda to foment colonial nationalism in South Asia, and a Colonial Office memorandum in 1927 remarked that 'film exhibitions in Malaya and elsewhere in the East [were] a factor in the spread of communist doctrines').[101] The BBFC banned, in 1923, any films showing British officials in 'equivocal situations' involving colonial women, and a new series of injunctions was elaborated between 1926 and 1930, which banned: 'The showing of white men in a state of degradation amidst Eastern or Native surroundings'; 'Liaisons between coloured men and white women'; and 'Equivocal situations between white men and coloured people'.[102] The Colonial Office wrote to all colonies and protectorates asking them to outline the censorship measures in place;[103] and remarked that colonial governments needed to begin to supply films as counter-attractions: 'It is, I am afraid, clear that private enterprise does not provide Colonial Dependencies with the best class of film, and consequently it may become necessary for Colonial Governments themselves to provide films.'[104] Again, government intervention was needed to supplement the free market. The Colonial Office recommended the adoption of mobile-cinema projection, like that pioneered by the Conservative Party.[105] Later, the Colonial Films Committee worked to set up a machinery of distribution within the colonies, specifically with the help of the FBI.[106]

The logics of censorship thus intersected with those that underpinned film production by groups like the Conservative Party and the elaboration of film policy that was predicated on conceptions of the affective power of film and the malleability of subaltern populations and audiences. Or, put another way: the regulation *and* production of culture were connected as two sides of a coin, linked by the imperatives to facilitate capital flow, protect industry, govern working-class and colonial populations and so to sustain the project of liberal and colonial governmentality.

'THE SWEEP OF COMMERCE'

The conceptions of the economic and political import of film emerging in the 1920s in the context of the economic and political logics of imperialism led also to the establishment of a state-run film unit in early 1927, while the debates about the economic and ideological effects of film rumbled on in parliament. The film unit was housed within the Empire Marketing Board, a department established by the Conservative Party – with significant support from the Board of Trade and Cunliffe-Lister – to promote inter-imperial trade in lieu of the formal establishment of a protectionist economy that would be postponed until the onset of the Depression.

At a state level, film production was thus directly connected to the sustenance of an imperial political economy, to the visual illustration and elaboration of imperial economic relations. The establishment of the EMB film unit was consistent with the Conservative Party's own use of film, and with the widespread belief in the economic and political utility of cinema for the maintenance of liberal economic and political order. Its subsequent history is relatively well known, for the film unit is often seen as the starting point for the history of British documentary cinema. All I have said here thus far offers a somewhat different sense of the place of the EMB and of documentary within the wider economic and political history of the conceptions and practices of the utility of cinema proliferating in the interwar period. The formation of the aesthetics and institutions of documentary can be seen in this way as one strand in the broader history of the forces that brought cinema and the political economy of liberalism – and here specifically of late liberal imperialism – into close association.

The history of the EMB was itself tied up with the Conservative Party's strategy to elaborate a new imperial economy in the interwar period. The party's election defeat in 1923 was attributed in large part to the tariff question. When it returned to power in late 1924, on the back of a renunciation of the direct imposition of tariffs, the party sought other ways to encourage a protectionist economy and closer economic ties within the empire. One of these was the establishment of an Imperial Economic Committee (IEC) with a budget of £1 million per annum to be spent on finding 'entirely new and untried ways of developing trade with the Empire, trade which will bring in Empire stuff in lieu of foreign stuff'. The IEC recommended in 1925 that the money be spent by an 'executive commission' that would produce 'continuous publicity on a national scale with a view to spreading and fostering [the idea] that Empire purchasing creates an increased demand for the manufactured products of the United Kingdom and therefore stimulates employment at home'.[107] Cunliffe-Lister at the Board of Trade supported this version of what has been called 'non-tariff preference', arguing that the improved marketing of empire foodstuffs in Britain would reduce a reliance on foreign imports – and thus the dollar gap with the United States – as well as stimulate colonial economies to enable them to purchase British manufactured goods.[108] Leopold Amery at the Colonial Office also supported this, and the executive commission to carry out this economic task was established as the Empire Marketing Board in May 1926, with Amery as its first chairman. The board, the IEC recommended, 'should be charged with the duty of conducting the movement for trade in Empire produce'.[109] Alongside publicising empire goods in the UK and, in the words of Amery, selling 'the idea of Empire produce and purchase', the EMB also furnished economic analysis and intelligence that included notes on various commodities, trade pamphlets for various exporters, the provision of statistics on market prospects and consumer behaviour, and world commodities surveys.[110] And it supported scientific research into problems of agricultural production.

At its first meeting in June 1926, the members of the EMB observed that they would be implementing a new government policy of publicity that was unprecedented in peacetime.[111] In this respect the EMB marked a significant moment in the connection of state economic goals with cultural work that was clearly informed by the new ideas about government, 'public relations' and the sustenance of liberal democracies that had proliferated in particular in the immediate post-war period. The membership of the board reflected this, for it included a number whom were drawn from the BBC – the institutional embodiment of ideas about culture as a public utility – and from the advertising profession, that other crucial industry that mushroomed in the 1920s, predicated on ideas about the effects of media and its economic utility.[112] The publicity goals of the board were marshalled by its secretary, Stephen Tallents, who had played a significant role in the management of the General Strike, as secretary to the cabinet committee dealing with the strike that had supported in particular government use of the BBC radio network to elaborate its response and its political critique of union action.[113]

Tallents elaborated on the logic that animated his and the EMB's sense of the governmental import of culture in a pamphlet entitled *The Projection of England* published in 1932. 'When England by her sea power won her place in the sun', Tallents wrote, 'her shadow was the longest of them all. To-day that morning of the world is past ... . The shadows of the peoples are more equal and the long shadows have grown less.'[114] England needed to elaborate 'the art of national projection' to 'create a belief in her ability to serve the world under the new order as she has served it under the old'.[115] That is, maintain 'supremacy' in the revised geopolitical configuration marked by transformations in imperial rule – the lessening of England's shadow – and by the emergence of a 'new order' dominated by the US and to some extent Soviet Russia.[116] Along the way, Tallents bemoaned how American dominance had 'turned every cinema in the world into the equivalent of an American consulate', and also discussed the innovations of Soviet cinema.[117] The projection of geopolitical supremacy needed to be supplemented by the communication of economic 'qualities' and primacy. 'If we are to win their custom, we must first win their minds', Tallents wrote. '[A]nd to win their minds we must set ourselves to project by all means of modern international communication a picture of England's industrial qualities.'[118]

Visual culture was important to the EMB, and its goal of 'winning' minds, as Tallents's use of 'projection' suggested. The board commissioned modernist artists to produce posters, which were widely displayed.[119] It quickly discussed the possibility of deploying film to support establishing a system of non-tariff preference and to 'sell the idea of Empire'. Tallents had in fact discussed this with the author Rudyard Kipling in August 1926, immediately after the formation of the EMB and shortly after the end of the General Strike and around the time the Conservative Party was beginning its own film programme.[120] Kipling suggested that the EMB should undertake the production of a major feature film 'in which intrinsic entertainment value would be paramount, and which would be suitable for distribution on its merits in the ordinary commercial way to the trade'.[121] Kipling also proposed that the board hire Walter Creighton to carry this out. Creighton had produced the Wembley tattoo at the 1924 imperial exhibition, with help from Kipling, and was thus well versed in the production of imperial spectacle. After a film committee was established at the EMB in February 1927, Creighton was appointed in March, with the support of Colonial Secretary Amery. Creighton had no actual knowledge of film production, and was employed because of his connection with Kipling, whose fame and association with imperial storytelling would, it was thought, help guarantee the film's success.[122] Kipling was also very closely associated with the Conservative Party, which was led by his cousin Stanley Baldwin. The board proposed that Creighton travel to Canada and the US to gather knowledge of film production, from both commercial studios and from the Canadian Government Motion Picture Bureau, and to scout locations for the imperial epic he and Kipling imagined.

While Creighton was away, John Grierson was employed by Tallents initially on an *ad hoc* basis to develop the EMB's film activities.[123] Grierson's intellectual history is now relatively well known: a Glasgow philosophy graduate, he had recently returned from the US, where he had been a Rockefeller-funded scholar based originally at the famed sociology department at the University of Chicago.[124] Grierson had become interested in the social psychology of popular media, like others within the social sciences at Chicago, had met Walter Lippmann, whose work on public opinion and democracy was widely influential, and had gravitated thereafter increasingly towards examining the social and political function of film. Tallents commissioned him initially to write a report for the EMB on 'popular appeal in cinema' and its potential use by the government. The lengthy 'Notes for English Producers', written between February and April 1927, was influenced by the social-science work Grierson had studied in the US; it would be an influential document for the establishment of a theory and practice of what later came to be called documentary cinema.

'[C]inema is recognised', Grierson began, 'as having a peculiar influence on the ideological centres to which advertisement endeavours to make its appeal ... because it is an ideal medium for all manner of suggestion.'[125] The conception of 'suggestion' here came directly from work in sociology, psychology and the emergent discipline of social psychology that argued that individuals and social groups were 'suggestible' and so were formed through mimetic contact with others. Theories of suggestibility, sympathy and mimesis were directed at that central liberal problematic – the question of how individuals were bound into social order – in the context in particular of the migratory movement and the establishment of urban democracies characteristic of the early twentieth century.[126] It is this intellectual context that spawned the proliferation of social-science investigations on the mimetic effects of cinema in the 1920s, and the popularisation of those in regulatory discourses and practices (like those articulated by the Board of Trade in Britain, for example, and others engaged in the project of managing colonial populations and so creating and maintaining liberal imperial order). If the immediate aim of Grierson and Tallents was to assess how film could foster imperial economic co-operation, in line with the remit of the EMB itself, the broader agenda established as central right at the start of the documentary film movement concerned the way that the suggestive and ideological power of cinema could be harnessed to liberal governmental rationality.

Grierson dismissed the utility of the pre-existing models of film form exemplified by commercial American cinema, government-financed Soviet cinema and, to a lesser extent, actuality cinema. 'American producers', Grierson wrote, 'are so bound up with what they call "human interest", and so insensitive to the dramatic importance of scene and setting, that they invariably allow the more private preoccupations of their characters to destroy the sweep of events.'[127] Yet, he continued, the 'Russians, to take "Potemkin" as a guide, have gone to the other extreme. Communist interests have made them somewhat blind to personal themes', and this finds its 'cinematic expression in an emphasis on crowds, ships, streets and factories, to the almost complete exclusion of individual life'.[128] Grierson's political theory of film sought to articulate a space for state-sponsored British cinema and for its enactment of the liberal problematic to form the interdependence of individual and social formation. The appropriate register for this was a realism that meshed 'scene and setting', and 'the sweep of events', with a proper focus on aspects of individual life. Arguing for the establishment of a practice of cinema that was positioned between the poles of economic individualism and collectivism, Grierson's government-sponsored memorandum on film was clearly driven by the same logics that shaped the British state's efforts in the interwar period to establish a political role for the country in what Tallents had described as the 'new order' dominated by the coming hegemons, the US and Soviet Russia. The problem of cinema was, once again, a microcosm of the economic and geopolitical problems facing the British state.

The examples of this new state-mandated political formation of cinema that emerged from Grierson's paper, and indeed later practice, were, not surprisingly, closely tied to the imperative to elaborate a new imperial political economy, for it was that task that was central to the Conservative Party and government and to the institution it formed to further those aims, the EMB. 'Where no story existed', he proposed, imagining a film that might be produced by the board,

> there would be no great difficulty in creating original scenarios round the adventures of the great explorers, around the different phases of Colonial life, and round the great commercial and industrial enterprises of the time. We might, for instance, have a picture of the search for the Northwest passage, a picture of the exploits of the Hudson's Bay Company, a picture of the crossing of Canada before the railways came ... a picture of South African diamond mines or of Western Australian gold fields, of the building of a canal, a bridge, a dam, a railway (the Trans-African Railway for example).[129]

Likewise, the intertwined stories of 'discovery and colonisation' and the establishment of infrastructures should, Grierson asserted, be central to the films the board produced. Its films could thus take advantage of 'the visually dramatic material in which the Empire is so rich' to show and develop accounts of

> the sweep of commerce ... the ships, the docks, the factories, the furnaces, the streets, the canals, the plans, the plantations, the caravans, the parades, the dams, the bridges, all over the earth ball that carry the flag of English energy.[130]

Grierson's paper on the proposed utility of cinema was circulated widely, at the same time that the debates on the economic and political effects of cinema were taking place in parliament and in the pages of the press. Cunliffe-Lister praised the report, which he described 'as really very interesting indeed', as he worked on framing the quota legislation that was predicated on similar ideas about the suggestive power of cinema.[131] Grierson was subsequently employed by Tallents to help design the EMB's use of cinema, a job that entailed both a theoretical and practical elaboration of the way cinema could be effectively employed by the state to further its economic and political goals. He quickly set to work. Late in 1927, he arranged a series of screenings at the Imperial Institute, inviting various members of the government to attend and to participate in a discussion about the films and 'the various possibilities of the film in educational, scientific, marketing and propagandist work'.[132] Likewise, in October 1927 Grierson organised a screening of films on a train carrying members of the Imperial Agricultural Committee from Edinburgh to London. Among the films was one 'showing the saving of labour and greater efficiency which comes with the electrification of the land'.[133] Watching the pictures of the modernisation of farming on a speeding train was no doubt uniquely appropriate for the government and the EMB's goals to establish infrastructural networks to facilitate imperial economies and to rationalise imperial production. The close ties between cinema and the railway, often commented upon by contemporary and subsequent observers, were forged here on the rails of imperial economics, the sustenance of the imperial 'complementary' economy by which colonial economies were tied to agriculture and raw materials.[134]

The innovation of new non-theatrical exhibition spaces, like the Imperial Institute and the train, was quickly established as a critical task for the EMB's elaboration of the filmic corollary to the projected imperial economy. Grierson wrote another position paper, 'Further Notes on Cinema Production', to assess the situation. 'All those interests which do not (and cannot) find their ends satisfied by the commercial organisation', he wrote, 'are beginning to look elsewhere; and this they must do.'[135] Along the way he commented approvingly on the FBI's efforts to utilise cinema by drawing 'up a list of films for the encouragement of private and institutional exhibitions'.[136] The crossover between the goals of the FBI and the EMB in fostering imperial trade was, after all, considerable. In mid-1928, the EMB innovated the use of 'automatic projectors' in public spaces to show short 'poster' films that advertised some element of imperial produce, like for example South African fruit or Canadian apples. The first of these was positioned in Victoria Station in London, an appropriate space of transit. 'The model' of the poster film, Grierson wrote, 'is the American "trailer", – the short film advertisement which heralds the 'coming soon' of another Hollywood masterpiece.'[137] Hollywood's advertisement for itself was a successful model to be copied for the advertisement of imperial goods. Later in 1928 the EMB sponsored a mobile cinema van in Leicestershire – once again linking cinema with mobility in ways that refracted the idealisation of economic mobility visible in the films of imperial produce it was showing.[138] Grierson referenced the Conservative Party's successful pioneering use of mobile cinema vans.[139] The elaboration of mobile cinema networks, and non-theatrical exhibition spaces, was a critical formative moment in the establishment of a media infrastructure to facilitate the flow of goods and thus an imperial economic bloc.

The long-term goals of the EMB in respect to non-theatrical distribution and exhibition centred on the use of its films by teachers, either bringing schoolchildren to the cinema established by the EMB at the Imperial Institute or by circulating films to schools to illustrate classes on geography, economics and the empire.[140] The integration of film, pedagogy and imperial economics was pursued consistently by the EMB in the early 1930s, operating on the assumption that film was most appealing to children – who were, it was widely argued, particularly suggestible subjects – and that it could thus function as a pedagogical technology. Its ideas and assumptions in this respect would support the British government's later development of film production for colonial populations, who were likewise regarded as particularly susceptible to the suggestive and persuasive powers of cinema.

EMB films would work both as advertisements for specific products and for 'the idea of empire' more broadly. The strategy initially innovated by Grierson and Tallents was to utilise pre-existing film, principally from the Dominions, that showed examples of agricultural produce or raw materials. The early poster-film experiments *Canadian Apples*, *Lumber* and *South African Fruit*, for example, functioned as short advertisements for these products, in line with the EMB's rhetoric on the importance of buying empire goods to better sustain the British and imperial economy. *Conquest* (1929) was a more expansive project, a compilation film on 'the pioneering development' of Canada that reused scenes from Hollywood Westerns and from footage shot by the motion picture bureau in Canada to tell a story about the settlement and 'conquest' of Canada.[141] The film drew, if unwittingly, links between the Western genre and the 'drama' of 'discovery and colonization' that Grierson had written about in the government memorandum on the economic and political utility of cinema. Grierson and the young film-makers he employed produced a number of compilation films in the early months of the EMB's film production, reusing existing footage drawn mainly from the Commonwealth and innovating new practices of editing that were partly influenced by Soviet cinema. The compilation film pioneered by the EMB marked in its very form the imperative to elaborate the imperial political economy that the board sought to visualise and foster, for in the mingling of footage from across the nascent Commonwealth the films made concrete the idealisation of the circulation of goods and capital at the base of the efforts to create the British-led imperial economic bloc. Grierson discovered, in his theory and practice, that montage could be divorced from its radical function in Soviet film, and repositioned in the service of the closely linked imperatives of the consumer and imperial economy. Advertising executives would learn well from this innovation.

Illustrating the 'complementary' imperial economy, and its utility for Britain, was established as a central goal of the EMB's film production right from the outset. The first film the board commissioned was the one imagined by Kipling, Creighton and Tallents, though it was not finally completed and released until 1930. *One Family*, as the film came to be called, presents an elaborate fantasy of Commonwealth economic integration.[142] It tells the story of a young boy who imagines visiting various Commonwealth countries to collect the ingredients that go to make up the king's Christmas pudding. The film begins with the young boy getting ready to go to school, as his mother chivvies him along and his father reads the newspaper. Along the way to school, he sees a shop window advertising the empire produce that goes into making a Christmas pudding. The film is here directly connected to a broader EMB campaign that took the Christmas pudding as a central symbol of the importance of empire produce. The pudding functioned in this respect as a concrete symbol of the way empire goods could serve to produce an object that marked in its nature the commingling of produce central to the nascent Commonwealth-bloc imagination and that also marked something specific to British traditions. In the film this is further marked by the fact that the pudding was being made for the head of the Commonwealth, the British king.

At school, the boy asks about the empire, but is bored by the teacher's dull recounting of territories and falls asleep. The film sets out to teach a better, more engaging, lesson about the empire, enacting the pedagogical value of film proposed by government supporters of the use of cinema. We see the boy's dream of entering the grand space of Buckingham Palace to meet the king (who remains unseen) and setting off on an adventure to gather the products that make up the Christmas pudding. The boy is guided by a set of women dressed in robes, who symbolise different Commonwealth spaces (India is included, but it's the one space we do not visit, indicative both of the moves to reposition the country as a Dominion in the 1920s but the uncertainty and hesitation about that – the film's representation is in this way clearly linked to broader geopolitical imperatives). A typical sequence has the boy looking outwards from the palace, to magically see into South Africa – where he then enters the frame, to be shown and told about some aspect of the farming and harvesting of foods (in this example, of South African grapes from a white-owned farm, but picked by black labourers). Other sequences show the produce being transported to England. A small cask of brandy is lowered from a huge steamer ship, docked in England; in another sequence of shots we see ships dock at large grain factories in Canada to gather flour for the pudding, before setting off for England. Upon arrival, the products are fed into huge machines that produce the pudding, a symbol of the advanced industrial technology of the metropole.

This industrial-process narrative is enfolded within a sort of domestic one, for the film begins with the young boy getting ready for school with his mother and father and ends with his realisation that the Dominions are 'a family too'. The domestic narrative so central to narrative fiction is translated to a geopolitical narrative of proposed Commonwealth unity, imagining a family of nations gathered together under the benevolent patriarch of the king and Britain. If its principal goal was to advertise the importance of imperial produce and economy, the film also worked to visualise and generate the 'common allegiance' within the Commonwealth bloc that the 1926 Balfour Declaration on the formal establishment of Commonwealth ties had affirmed as critical, as indeed had those who sought to elaborate the quota and regulatory framework for Commonwealth films. The film presents a visual record of the ties that were being delineated at state level, and its shifting between fantasy and reality is eloquent testimony in itself to the way that the film was positioned and imagined as a text and form that could translate fantasy – or political will – into the real world.

At the core of many of the EMB films were images showing the harvesting of products in colonial spaces and their transport and arrival in the metropole. This is a dominant trope across the board's work, indeed across the colonial archive in the interwar period more generally, for it offers the clearest visual record or account of the efforts to establish the so-called complementary imperial economy. *One Family* is consistent with many other EMB films in this respect (though it has been subsequently largely ignored in the critical literature on the unit, one consequence, as Martin Stollery has astutely observed, of the broader ignorance of the imperial contexts for the emergence of British documentary cinema).[143] The better-known *Cargo from Jamaica* (1933), for example, directed by Basil Wright, shows the harvesting of bananas and their transport, on the heads of colonial subjects, to be manually loaded onto a large ship. Arriving in London, the cargo is efficiently transported by conveyor belts from the ships to warehouses.[144] The contrast between the use of bodies and technology – not only the conveyor belt, but also the undoubtedly British-built and -owned ship – of course acutely marks the standard contrast between an

Cargo from Jamaica (1933)

advanced technological modernity and its double, the 'primitive' economy of colonised labour and agricultural produce. The ubiquity of the large transport ship in EMB films and a great number of British colonial films is in this way instructive, for the ships mark not only the idealisation of technology and transport, but also stand as concrete symbols of the literal mobility of the British finance capitalism that sustained the shipping industry and thus British economic control of the global circulation of materials and goods.

The elaboration and sustenance of the economic and political ties of the Commonwealth, played out on the film screen, were further underpinned by networks of exchange in film institutions established in particular between Canada and Britain. Canada's position was uniquely significant to the establishment of a Commonwealth bloc, for it offered a bulwark against the expansionist US. The director of the Canadian Government Motion Picture Bureau, Captain Frank Badgely, had visited the EMB in May 1928. At the meeting, Badgely shared with Tallents, Grierson and others on the film committee the experience the unit he led had gained as a state-financed film production unit and distribution and exhibition network that sought to utilise film to, in part, articulate a national perspective to counter the economic and media dominance of the US.[145] Creighton had visited Canada immediately upon his appointment by the EMB. Grierson likewise visited Canada, and the US, in 1931, approvingly surveying film-production methods in the Canadian unit.[146] The EMB unit authorised him to purchase 'film material suitable for the Board's purposes'.[147]

In 1932 Grierson and the EMB set about organising a film screening at the crucial imperial economic conference in Ottawa, in discussion also with the Federation of British Industries and the Canadian Government Motion Picture Bureau.[148] A 'further plan was to supplement' these screenings with 'shows throughout Canada from the rear of Canadian Pacific Railway trains'.[149] In many ways these plans marked the culmination of the EMB's efforts as regards cinema, for they directly connected film to the political project of establishing an imperial economic bloc, itself concluded at this conference when the 'imperial preference' system was instigated.

Watching films of economic projection, of the circulation of goods and creation of an imperial political economy, in the conference halls and from the back of a train travelling across the economically and politically crucial space of Canada marks in this sense a significant moment in the conception and practice of the economic and geopolitical utility of British colonial cinema.

The EMB's finest hour was one of its last. It was disbanded shortly after the imperial preference economic system was set up, because its function in establishing non-tariff forms of preference was rendered redundant.[150] Key personnel – Tallents, Grierson – moved to the auspices of the Post Office, setting up the GPO film unit, which would itself make the idealisation of forms of circulation a central task. Often it did so in conjunction with corporate organisations, as David Trotter and Scott Anthony show in this volume. The dream of the economic and geopolitical value of cinema lived on. In 1938 Grierson was commissioned by the Imperial Relations Trust to travel to Canada, New Zealand and Australia to survey the possibilities of setting up a film centre in each of these countries with a view in particular of 'strengthening the link between Britain and the dominions if war came'.[151] The Imperial Relations Trust was administered by Tallents, and was seemingly connected to Britain's secret service as part of the propaganda efforts to cement Commonwealth and colonial unity for the war hovering on the horizon. Grierson's assignment was, Gary Evans has shown, specifically 'to set up a Northern American propaganda base to urge Canada and (more important) the United States into an active partnership with Britain at war, if war should come'.[152] Grierson was also invited by the Canadian government, and the report he wrote for them about film in mid-1938 was enthusiastically received. He returned in late 1938 to draft the legislative bill that created a National Film Board, and was a year later invited by the Canadian government to take up the position as first director of the board.[153] Grierson's further elaboration of documentary cinema, supported by the state, was directly connected to the geopolitical goals that had partly subtended the establishment of the Commonwealth.

Yet the economic and political realities of this dream of 'Commonwealth' unity and British primacy floundered amid growing resistance to colonial oppression and also because the US directly countered the British economic project. Hollywood films offered seductive visions of a liberal capitalism somewhat at odds with its colonial formations. Other colonial or Dominion states resisted Britain's entreaties to forge imperial connections to counteract American and Hollywood dominance.[154] Later, the US would make the dissolution of the system of imperial preferences, and the opening up of the world to US economic penetration, a condition of its economic support to Britain in the post-World War II settlement. In so doing, it initiated a new configuration of economic liberalism, with the US at its hub, to be managed by a set of ostensibly international institutions like the World Bank and the International Monetary Fund – but that is a different story of imperial economics.[155]

If film offered, for a time, a way of sustaining British economic and geopolitical primacy, it couldn't resist the sweeping changes that altered the economic and political landscape in the interwar years. The films of the 1920s and early 30s analysed here come to look ever more fictional, divorced as they were from the realities of Britain's economic and geopolitical position. 'Documentary' cinema indeed tries to 'mummify' change, to borrow the words from a significant theorist of the indexical nature of cinema.[156] The complex indexicality of the cinematic image, and of documentary, would be ever more bent towards the fantastical maintenance of a dying dream of economic and geopolitical dominance. Archives institutionalised this position on cinema's potential to mummify change, and it is no coincidence that the EMB's film library was bequeathed to the Empire Film Institute, which later turned this material over to the British Film Institute (itself created after a commission had been established in 1929 to survey the ways in which cinema could be deployed to further British national interests).[157] The archive formed in part to help halt the forces that repositioned Britain's hegemony now houses the films that register, if frequently only through their purposeful absence, those same forces – and that provide the material basis for the project of which this essay is a part.

NOTES

This essay was written with help from the support of the Leverhulme Foundation, and the Arts and Humanities Research Council. It has benefited from help in particular from Tom Rice; from Lora Brill, Kay Dickinson, Peter Krämer and Colin MacCabe; and from the librarians and archivists at the British Film Institute, the British Library, the Public Records Office, the Modern Records Centre at the University of Warwick and the Department of Special Collections at the Bodleian Library in Oxford. This is for Colin.

1. David Harvey, *The New Imperialism* (Oxford: Oxford University Press, 2003), p. 180.
2. I use the conception of 'governmentality' as 'the conduct of conduct' in this essay in the sense in which it is used in Michel Foucault's later philosophy, as a way of conceptualising and detailing the establishment of various epistemological and institutional practices focused on the management of bodies and populations so as to shape, guide, correct and modify the ways in which individuals and groups conduct themselves. On this see, in particular, Michel Foucault, 'Governmentality', in Graham Burchell, Colin Gordon and Peter Miller (eds), *The Foucault Effect: Studies in Governmentality* (London: Harvester Wheatsheaf, 1991), pp. 87–104. The imperial centre co-opted its colonies as laboratories for experiments with economic, administrative and educational systems. On this see, for example, Gyan Prakash, *Another Reason: Science and the Imagination of Modern India* (Princeton, NJ: Princeton University Press, 1999); David Scott, *Refashioning Futures* (Princeton, NJ: Princeton University Press, 1999); and Ann Laura Stoler, *Race and the Education of Desire: Foucault's History of Sexuality and the Colonial Order of Things* (Durham, NC: Duke University Press, 1995).
3. Foucault, 'Governmentality'; Michel Foucault, 'Security, Territory, and Population', in Paul Rabinow (ed.), *Michel Foucault: Essential Works of Foucault, 1954–1984: Volume 1, Ethics* (London: Penguin, 2000); and see also Patrick Joyce, *The Rule of Freedom: Liberalism and the Modern City* (New York: Verso, 2003), and the essays collected in Andrew Barry, Thomas Osborne and Nikolas Rose (eds), *Foucault and Political Reason: Liberalism, Neo-liberalism, and Rationalities of Government* (London: UCL Press, 1996).
4. The constitutive connections between liberalism and imperialism are explored in Bernard Semmel, *The Liberal Ideal and the Demons of Empire: Theories of Imperialism from Adam Smith to Lenin* (Baltimore, MD: Johns Hopkins University Press, 1993); and Uday Singh Metha,

Liberalism and Empire: A Study in Nineteenth-century British Liberal Thought (Chicago, IL: University of Chicago Press, 1999).

5. I use the phrase 'capitalist imperialism' here in ways that draw directly on an extensive Marxist tradition of analysis of the capitalist dynamics underpinning imperialist expansion and exploitation. Lenin's classic analysis located the origins of imperialism in the competitive logic of capitalism: '[C]apitalism's transition to the stage of monopoly capitalism, to finance capital', he wrote, 'is connected with the intensification of the struggle for the partitioning of the world.' See V. I. Lenin, *Collected Works*, vol. XXII (Moscow: Progress Publishers, 1965), p. 255. The accumulation of capital surplus by industrialised nations, Lenin and others argued, caused the turn to overseas investments and markets. Lenin's insights about the interrelation of the economic and the geopolitical are pursued by David Harvey's work on the historical and contemporary logics of capitalist imperialism. In *The New Imperialism*, and elsewhere, Harvey shows how 'imperialism of the capitalist sort' focuses on the flow of 'economic power ... across and through continuous space ... through the daily practices of ... trade, commerce, capital flows, ... labour migration, technology transfer ... flows of information, cultural impulses and the like' ((Harvey, *The New Imperialism*, p. 26). What Harvey describes as 'accumulation by dispossession' is predicated on a plundering of resources to enable the profitable expansion of capital, and a concurrent destruction of non-market social forms. See David Harvey, *Spaces of Global Capitalism: Towards a Theory of Uneven Capitalist Development* (London: Verso, 2006), in particular pp. 69–116. The Marxist tradition of political economy, and its analysis of the forms and forces of imperialism, is also continued and deepened in important work by Giovanni Arrighi, *The Long Twentieth Century: Money, Power, and the Origins of Our Times* (London: Verso, 1994); and Alex Callinicos, *Imperialism and Global Political Economy* (London: Polity, 2009).

6. Though see the instructive accounts in Martin Stollery, *Alternative Empires: European Modernist Cinemas and the Cultures of Imperialism* (Exeter: University of Exeter Press, 2000), pp. 140–202; and Priya Jaikumar, *Cinema at the End of Empire: A Politics of Transition in Britain and India* (Durham, NC: Duke University Press, 2006), pp. 13–64.

7. Adam Smith, *The Wealth of Nations*, 1776 (London: Methuen, 1961, two volumes). The threads of connections linking Smith, political economy and liberal governmentality are traced out by Mary Poovey in *A History of the Modern Fact: Problems of Knowledge in the Sciences of Wealth and Society* (Chicago, IL: University of Chicago Press, 1998), pp. 214–18 and pp. 236–48.

8. Eric Hobsbawm, *Industry and Empire: An Economic History of Britain since 1750* (London: Weidenfeld and Nicolson, 1969), pp. 174–211; Eric Hobsbawm, *The Age of Extremes: A History of the World, 1914–1991* (New York: Pantheon Books, 1994), in particular pp. 93–7.

9. Wolfgang Schivelbusch, *Three New Deals: Reflections on Roosevelt's America, Mussolini's Italy, and Hitler's Germany, 1933–1939* (New York: Picador, 2006), in particular pp. 1–48.

10. The economic policies of the Conservative Party in the 1920s are outlined in Philip Williamson, *National Crisis and National Government: British Politics, the Economy and Empire, 1926–1932* (Cambridge: Cambridge University Press, 1992), pp. 43–54. On the broader economics of British imperialism in the interwar period, see B. R. Tomlinson, 'Imperialism and After: The Economy of the Empire on the Periphery', in Judith Brown and William Roger Louis (eds), *The Oxford History of the British Empire: Volume IV, The*

Twentieth Century (Oxford: Oxford University Press, 1999); Michael W. Doyle, *Empires* (Ithaca, NY: Cornell University Press, 1986); Barry Eichengreen, 'The British Economy between the Wars',' in Roderick Floud and Paul Johnson (eds), *The Cambridge Economic History of Modern Britain, Volume II: Economic Maturity, 1860–1939* (Cambridge: Cambridge University Press, 2004). The Conservative Party had previously unsuccessfully proposed a tariff system, in the early years of the twentieth century, in response to the increasingly protectionist economic policies of other major industrialised nations. On this, see E. H. Green, *The Crisis of Conservatism: The Politics, Economics and Ideology of the British Conservative Party, 1880–1914* (London: Routledge, 1995).

11. John Gallagher and Ronald Robinson, 'The Imperialism of Free Trade', *Economic History Review* vol. VI no. 1 (1953). The liberal policies of free trade subtended the expansion of informal economic control in the nineteenth century, when the British state devised policies to support the investment of the surplus capital generated from the world's first industrialised economy and to keep the world open to the circulation of capital that would be routed through Britain.

12. The Conservative Party campaigned in the 1923 general election on the tariff question, but was defeated by the Labour Party. It was widely thought that the tariff question damaged its campaign, for it was seen to necessitate an increase in the cost of daily foodstuffs. Tariff protection was more popular with businesses than consumers; the Conservative Party's policies would be directed more to sustaining the industrial and financial economy. See Ian M. Drummond, *Imperial Economic Policy 1917–1939: Studies in Expansion and Protection* (London: George Allen and Unwin, 1974), pp. 28–9.

13. The general adoption of a gold standard by the currencies of the chief European nations between 1863 and 1874, a fixed and rigid relationship between the unit of the currency and a fixed quantity of gold, simplified the operations of a single free and multilateral system of world trading that tended to rely and pivot on London. The gold standard was suspended in 1914, but Britain rejoined the standard in 1925, before leaving again in 1931.

14. The Dominions were given temporary, and the colonies permanent, exemption from the import tax of 10 per cent established by the 1932 Act. On these policies, and the economic and political thinking behind them, see Tim Rooth, *British Protectionism and the International Economy: Overseas Commercial Policy in the 1930s* (Cambridge: Cambridge University Press, 1992), pp. 71–100; P. J. Cain and A. G. Hopkins, *British Imperialism, 1688–2000*, 2nd edn (New York: Longman, 2002), pp. 464–71; Hobsbawm, *The Age of Extremes*, pp. 106–7.

15. In their influential book *British Imperialism, 1688–2000*, Cain and Hopkins emphasise the importance of finance capital, and the drive to create an international trading system centred on London and mediated by sterling, to British imperialism. World trade, they show, was to be provided through loans to foreign governments, and subsequently through direct investment and was to be controlled by the City and the Treasury. This would all be tied together by a regime of free trade and the resulting expansion of global commerce was to be handled, transported and insured by British firms. Likewise, Lance E. Davis and Robert A. Huttenback estimate that the capital invested in Europe in 1910–14 ranged between 9–12 per cent and over the same period in the empire the figure was between 39–40 per cent. See Davis and Huttenback, *Mammon and the Pursuit of Empire: The Political Economy of British Imperialism, 1860–1912* (New York: Cambridge University Press, 1986),

pp. 40–1 and p. 46. For debates about Cain and Hopkins's thesis, some of which reasserts the importance of industrial pressure groups, see Raymond E. Durnett (ed.), *Gentlemanly Capitalism: The New Debate on Empire* (New York: Longman, 1999).

16. The introduction of a partial tariff during the war in 1915, the McKenna Duties, was specifically targeted at new industrial products – at gramophones, clocks, watches, automobiles and celluloid, those new technologies enabling, in differing ways, the compression of space and time so central to modernity. Later, the 1921 Safeguarding of Industries Act protected those 'key industries' that Germany had become dominant in, including most notably chemicals and electrical products. For details see Rooth, *British Protectionism and the International Economy*, p. 37.

17. Hobsbawm, *Industry and Empire*, pp. 180–4; Cain and Hopkins, *British Imperialism, 1688–2000*, p. 415.

18. On the political logics of early twentieth-century Conservatism, see, for example, Green, *The Crisis of Conservatism*, in particular pp. 59–119 and pp. 223–41.

19. On Conservative conceptions of class in the 1920s, see Ross McKibbin, 'Class and Conventional Wisdom: The Conservative Party and the "Public" in Inter-war Britain', in his *The Ideologies of Class* (Oxford: Oxford University Press, 1991), pp. 259–93; and David Jarvis, 'British Conservatism and Class Politics in the 1920s', *English Historical Review* vol. 111 no. 440 (February 1996), pp. 59–84.

20. 'For the first time in history', Hobsbawm writes, 'a proletarian party became and remained the major alternative government party' (Hobsbawm, *Industry and Empire*, p. 176). Trade-union membership increased from 4 million in 1913 to 8 million in 1919. See Eichengreen, 'The British Economy between the Wars'. On the General Strike see, for example, Gordon Ashton Philips, *The General Strike: The Politics of Industrial Conflict* (London: Weidenfeld and Nicolson, 1976).

21. Leopold Amery, *My Political Life*, vol. 1 (London: Hutchinson, 1953), p. 253, cited in Stephen Constantine, '"Bringing the Empire Alive": The Empire Marketing Board and Imperial Propaganda, 1926–1933', in John M. MacKenzie (ed.), *Imperialism and Popular Culture* (Manchester: Manchester University Press, 1986), p. 196. Amery was Secretary of State for the Colonies between 1924–9 and for Dominion Affairs between 1925–9.

22. The 1922 Settlement Act, offering financial support to those emigrating in particular to the Dominions, was also devised specifically to counteract unemployment and to develop the economic utility of the empire. See Drummond, *Imperial Economic Policy 1917–1939*, pp. 32–5 and pp. 43–85.

23. The British state's development of structures and institutions to prevent crisis and conflict in this period is described in Keith Middlemas, *Politics in Industrial Society: The Experience of the British System since 1911* (London: André Deutsch, 1979), in particular pp. 174–214.

24. The classic accounts of this are Andre Gunder Frank, *Capitalism and Underdevelopment in Latin America* (New York: Monthly Review Press, 1969); and Immanuel Wallerstein, *The Capitalist World-Economy* (Cambridge: Cambridge University Press, 1979). On the conception of the relations between core and peripheral economies in the liberal theory emerging in the eighteenth century, see Semmel, *The Liberal Ideal and the Demons of Empire*, pp. 17–38; on the impact of these strategies on colonial economies see, for example, W. Rodney, 'The Colonial Economy', in A. Adu Boahen, *General History of Africa: VII Africa under Colonial Domination 1880–1935* (Paris: UNESCO, 1990), pp. 153–61.

25. The Colonial Development Act of 1929 created a fund of £1 million a year, to which colonial governments could apply for development assistance. Assistance could be given only to schemes with a demonstrable economic benefit to Britain. Rooth, *British Protectionism and the International Economy*, pp. 30–1; Stephen Constantine, *The Making of British Colonial Development Policy, 1914–1940* (London: Frank Cass, 1984).

26. L. J. Butler, *Britain and Empire: Adjusting to a Post-imperial World* (London: I. B. Tauris, 2002), pp. 5–6. Arthur Balfour served in the Conservative government of 1924–9 as Lord President of the Council.

27. The settlement empire of Canada, Australia, New Zealand and South Africa had become increasingly economically important to Britain, largely because their economies could sustain the purchase of imports and because they were dependent on British finance capitalism for infrastructural development. These countries provided 50 per cent of empire imports between 1909–13 and received 54.6 per cent of exports to the empire. By 1934 empire trade provided 35.3 per cent of British imports and received 43.9 per cent of exports. The Dominions accounted for 61.09 per cent and 53.01 per cent respectively. See A. R. Dilley, 'The Economics of Empire', in Sarah Stockwell (ed.), *The British Empire: Themes and Perspectives* (London: Blackwell, 2008), p. 103.

28. 'By accepting the constitutional equality and autonomy of the Dominions', Philip Williamson writes, 'the Conservative government had intended to outflank secessionist movements and under the new guise of "Commonwealth" enable the white Empire to be maintained through ties of sentiment, defense needs, and economic interest' (Williamson, *National Crisis and National Government*, p. 80). On the effects of the economic Depression in the early 1930s on anti-imperialist activity, see Hobsbawm, *The Age of Extremes*, pp. 106–7.

29. When Britain left the gold standard in 1931, it established a 'sterling area' and 'encouraged' the white settler Dominions to peg their currencies to sterling (the formal empire had no choice), and this aimed specifically to reduce the dollar gap caused by trade and post-war debt to the US. The British had lost about a quarter of their global investments during the war, mainly those in the US, which they had to sell to buy war supplies. The US ended the war as the main international lender, supplanting Britain. See Ian M. Drummond, *The Floating Pound and the Sterling Area, 1931–1939* (Cambridge: Cambridge University Press, 1981); Hobsbawm, *The Age of Extremes*, p. 97; Cain and Hopkins, *British Imperialism, 1688–2000*, pp. 449–53.

30. See for example J. Michael Sproule, *Propaganda and Democracy: The American Experience of Media and Mass Persuasion* (Cambridge: Cambridge University Press, 1997).

31. Philip M. Taylor, 'British Official Attitudes towards Propaganda Abroad, 1918–39', in Nicholas Pronay and D.W. Spring (eds), *Propaganda, Politics and Film, 1918–1945* (London: Macmillan, 1982), p. 28.

32. Marjorie Grant Cook in collaboration with Frank Fox, *The British Empire Exhibition 1924: Official Guide* (London: Fleetway Press, 1924), cited in Tom Rice, 'Exhibiting Africa: British Instructional Films and the Empire Series (1925–1928)', in this volume. See also John MacKenzie, 'The Imperial Exhibitions', in *Propaganda and Empire: The Manipulation of British Public Opinion, 1880–1960* (Manchester: Manchester University Press, 1984), pp. 96–120.

33. Paddy Scannell and David Cardiff, *A Social History of British Broadcasting. Volume One 1922–1939, Serving the Nation* (London: Basil Blackwell, 1991), pp. 3–22; D. L. LeMahieu,

A Culture for Democracy: Mass Communication and the Cultivated Mind in Britain between the Wars (Oxford: Clarendon Press, 1988), pp. 141–50. John Reith's manifesto for constructing the BBC as a public utility cited George V's opening address at the empire exhibition as a crucial example of the way media could form collective identities.

34. The first 'British Empire Games' was held in 1930 in Canada. Its name was changed to the British Empire and Commonwealth Games in 1954 and to the British Commonwealth Games in 1970. The British in its title was lost in 1978.

35. Nicholas Pronay, 'The Political Censorship of Films in Britain between the Wars', in Pronay and Spring, *Propaganda, Politics and Film*, p. 113. On the British Council, see also Philip M. Taylor, *British Propaganda in the 20th Century: Selling Democracy* (Edinburgh: Edinburgh University Press, 1999), pp. 76–8; and on the development of cultural institutions between the wars, see Janet Minihan, *The Nationalization of Culture: The Development of State Subsidies to the Arts in Great Britain* (New York: New York University Press, 1977), pp. 172–215.

36. Lee Grieveson, 'Visualizing Industrial Citizenship', in Devon Orgeron, Marsha Orgeron and Dan Streible (eds), *Learning with the Lights Off* (Oxford: Oxford University Press, 2011).

37. *The Times*, 4 June 1923, p. 7.

38. Rachael Low, *The History of the British Film, 1918–1929* (London: George Allen and Unwin, 1971), p. 53.

39. *The Times*, 4 June 1923, p. 7.

40. *The Times*, 10 October 1923, p. 11.

41. *Hansard*, 8 December 1925, vol. 189, cc238–9.

42. *The Times*, 11 June 1924, p. 8.

43. Rice, 'Exhibiting Africa'.

44. Timothy Hollins offers the only substantive engagement with this development: 'The Presentation of Politics: The Place of Party Publicity, Broadcasting and Film in British Politics, 1918–1939', University of Leeds, 1981; and Hollins, 'The Conservative Party and Film Propaganda between the Wars', *English Historical Review* (1981), pp. 359–69.

45. *The Times*, 8 April 1926, p. 9.

46. Hollins, 'The Conservative Party and Film Propaganda between the Wars', p. 363.

47. Jeffrey Richards, 'Patriotism with Profit: British Imperial Cinema in the 1930s', in James Curran and Vincent Porter (eds), *British Cinema History* (Totowa, NJ: Barnes & Noble Books, 1983), pp. 25–41. Korda's productions included *Sanders of the River* (1935), *The Drum* (1938) and *The Four Feathers* (1939); Balcon's *Rhodes of Africa* (1936) and *King Solomon's Mines* (1937). The CFA was run by Sir Albert Clavering, who was well connected in the British film industry.

48. *The Times*, 13 April 1926, p. 12.

49. J. C. C. Davidson, *Memoirs of a Conservative. J. C. C. Davidson's Memoirs and Papers 1910–1937*, ed. R. Rhodes James (London, 1969), p. 337, cited in Richard Cockett, 'The Party, Publicity, and the Media', in Anthony Seldon and Stuart Ball (eds), *Conservative Century: The Conservative Party since 1900* (Oxford: Oxford University Press, 1994), p. 548.

50. Cockett, 'The Party, Publicity, and the Media', p. 548.

51. Joseph Ball, cited in Stephen G. Jones, *The British Labour Movement and Film, 1918–1939* (London: Routledge and Kegan Paul, 1987), p. 19. Joseph Ball was appointed director of publicity, a newly created post, in 1927.

52. The film was produced for the Conservative Party by British Instructional Films. See Tom Rice, *'West Africa Calling'*, <www.colonialfilm.org.uk/node/1329>.

53. Brian Larkin, *Signal and Noise: Media, Infrastructure, and Urban Culture in Nigeria* (Durham, NC: Duke University Press, 2008), p. 39.

54. There is a similar structure in a serial feature in Conservative newspapers, whereby the fictional character Mrs Maggs talks to her younger colleague, Betty the Maid, about the issues of the day. See David Jarvis, 'Mrs Maggs and Betty: The Conservative Appeal to Women Voters in the 1920s', *Twentieth Century British History* vol. 5 no. 2 (1994), pp. 129–52.

55. The commentator explains how colonies purchase manufactured goods from Britain and thus maintain employment in Britain. India, we learn, 'takes more of our manufactured goods than any other part of the Empire and gives employment to as many as 130,000 British workers'. Likewise, 'by purchasing our goods', the Malay States 'create regular employment in this country'; Australia keeps '77,000 British workers regularly employed through buying British goods' (and its iconic Sydney Harbour Bridge was 'built by a British firm with British materials'); and Canada 'gives employment to 67,000 Britons'. On this film, see Tom Rice, *'Empire Trade'*, <www.colonialfilm.org.uk/node/1312>.

56. Larkin's account in *Signal and Noise* of the development of media infrastructures in Nigeria is an important model here for the way we might conceptualise the relations between new circuits of media distribution and exhibition and the political economy of colonialism.

57. *The Times*, 13 April 1926, p. 12. In the 1931 election season, the cinema vans visited seventy-nine towns; during the 1935 election, an estimated 1.5 million people watched films from the vans. Siân Nicholas, 'The Construction of a National Identity: Stanley Baldwin, "Englishness" and the Mass Media in Inter-War Britain', in Martin Francis and Ina Zweiniger-Bargielowska (eds), *The Conservatives and British Society, 1880–1990* (Cardiff: University of Wales Press, 1996), p. 134.

58. The financial organisation of the film unit is visible in part in the records held in the Conservative Party Archives at the Bodleian Library in Oxford. See in particular CC04/1/34, and F/N 47–48. There were twelve van operators in 1929, earning from £5–8 a week each, with a subsistence allowance; in 1935 the weekly cost of running eleven vans was £263. The expenses for film production, and film and van maintenance, were considerable. The CFA's budget in 1934 was triple that of the whole budget for the Conservative publicity department. See Cockett, 'The Party, Publicity, and the Media', p. 560.

59. I take this phrase from Eric M. Cazdyn, *The Flash of Capital: Film and Geopolitics in Japan* (Durham, NC: Duke University Press, 2002).

60. J. A. Ramsden, 'Baldwin and Film', in Pronay and Spring, *Propaganda, Politics and Film*, p. 133.

61. *The Times*, 8 April 1926, p. 9.

62. 'The problem of exhibiting political propaganda film', wrote the chief of publicity Joseph Ball in 1926,

> is one of such difficulty that at the present time it is only by the production and use of our own cinema vans that they can be placed before the public, the managers of cinematograph theatres being unanimous in their opposition to the exhibition of any film of a political character. (Joseph Ball, cited in Hollins, 'The Conservative Party and Film Propaganda', p. 361)

63. On this see practice see Larkin, *Signal and Noise*, pp. 73–122; and Zoë Druick, 'Mobile Cinema in Canada in Relation to British Mobile Film Practices', in Wolfram R. Keller and Gene Walz (eds), *Screening Canadians* (Marburg: Universitätsbibliothek Marburg, 2008), pp. 13–34.

64. FBI memo, reproduced in *Kinematograph Weekly*, 6 August 1925, pp. 30–1.

65. Ibid., p. 31.

66. The FBI had previously sponsored a number of short films in 1924, some of which were shown at the British Empire Exhibition at Wembley.

67. Minutes of a conference on the subject of British film production, held at the offices of the Federation of British Industries, on Wednesday 6 May 1925, MSS200/F/1/1/159, p. 2, Modern Records Centre, University of Warwick. It is noticeable that the FBI refers specifically to Dominion markets, for it was those that were particularly important to British industry.

68. Max Muspratt, president, Federation of British Industries, *The Times*, 21 January 1927, p. 10.

69. Ibid.

70. Joseph P. Kennedy in 1927, for example, proposed that 'films were serving as silent salesmen for other products of American industry'. In 1931 the commerce secretary, and later president of the US, Herbert Hoover praised the industry 'as a powerful influence on behalf of American goods'. Both these are cited in Toby Miller, Nitin Govil, John McMurria, Richard Maxwell and Ting Wang, *Global Hollywood 2* (London: BFI, 2005), p. 65.

71. Will Hays, 'Supervision from Within',' in Joseph P. Kennedy (ed.), *The Story of the Films as Told by Leaders of the Industry to the Students of the Graduate School of Business Administration George F. Baker Foundation Harvard University* (Chicago, IL: A. W. Shaw and Company, 1927), cited in Miller *et al.*, *Global Hollywood 2*, p. 65.

72. Edward G. Lowry, 'Certain Factors and Considerations Affecting the European Market', Internal MPPDA memorandum, 25 October 1928, reproduced in Andrew Higson and Richard Maltby (eds), *'Film Europe' and 'Film America': Cinema, Commerce and Cultural Exchange 1920–1939* (Exeter: University of Exeter Press, 1999), p. 353. Lowry astutely observed that the FBI was the most important organisation in lobbying for legislation to restrict the importation of American film into Britain and its empire (p. 364).

73. Richard Maltby, 'Introduction: "The Americanization of the World"', in Richard Maltby and Melvyn Stokes (eds), *Hollywood Abroad: Audiences and Cultural Exchange* (London: BFI, 2004).

74. Richard Maltby and Ruth Vasey, '"Temporary American Citizens": Cultural Anxieties and Industrial Strategies in the Americanisation of European Cinema', in Higson and Maltby, *'Film Europe' and 'Film America'*, p. 39.

75. *Morning Post*, cited in Andrew Higson and Richard Maltby, '"Film Europe" and "Film America": An Introduction', in Higson and Maltby, *'Film Europe' and 'Film America'*, p. 9.

76. Philip Cunliffe-Lister, president of the Board of Trade, memorandum, 'The British Film Industry', 6 February 1926.

77. Ibid. Cunliffe-Lister had previously worked on the publicity subcommittee of the supply and transport committee, an organisation whose tasks included strike-breaking. Cunliffe-Lister was, with Leopold Amery, a fierce advocate for tariff legislation throughout the 1920s. After serving as president of the Board of Trade, Cunliffe-Lister served also as Secretary of State for the Colonies (1931–5), a fact that itself, Priya Jaikumar notes, demonstrated 'the enduring weld between colonial affairs and national industry' (Jaikumar, *Cinema at the End of Empire*, p. 44).

78. *The Times*, 6 April 1927, p. 15.

79. When the talks between the different sectors of the industry broke down, the leading trade journal *Kinematograph Weekly* noted dryly, 'The General Strike intervened' (*Kinematograph Weekly*, 5 August 1926, p. 31).

80. Baldwin, cited in Margaret Dickinson and Sarah Street, *Cinema and State: The Film Industry and Government, 1927–84* (London: BFI, 1985), p. 19. In late 1926, the Conservative Party conference called for encouragement of the production and display of British films, particularly 'the encouragement of the production of sound British films propagating British ideals'. See *The Times*, 22 September 1926, p. 7

81. Minutes of a conference on the subject of British film production, p. 3.

82. *The Times*, 22 March 1927, p. 15.

83. *Daily Express*, 18 March 1927, p. 6, cited in Mark Glancy, 'Temporary American Citizens? Audiences, Hollywood Films and the Threat of Americanization in the 1920s', *Historical Journal of Film, Radio, and Television* vol. 26 no. 4 (October 2006), p. 461.

84. FBI, report of its overseas committee, *Kinematograph Weekly*, 22 April 1926, p. 42.

85. Low, *The History of the British Film*, p. 96.

86. 1926 imperial economic conference report, cited in Lowry memo, in Higson and Maltby, *'Film Europe' and 'Film America'*, pp. 354–5.

87. See Dickinson and Street, *Cinema and State*, p. 27. In a later letter to the government, the FBI made this question of imperial preference central:

> In considering the various ways in which to counteract the great advantage held by the American producing companies through their possession of so large and wealthy a market, attention has been given to the possibilities of improving the position of British pictures in British overseas markets.

This memorandum was attached to an FBI letter to the government entitled 'Cooperative Marketing of British Empire Films. FBI Offer to Government', 10 November 1926, cited in Priya Jaikumar, 'An Act of Transition: Empire and the Making of a National British Film Industry, 1927', *Screen* vol. 43 no. 2 (Summer 2002), p. 127.

88. 'I think the importance of securing greater production and wider distribution of British films is generally recognized throughout the country', Cunliffe-Lister said, in introducing the bill.

> The necessity was enforced in the strongest language by the Imperial Conference last Autumn, in a Resolution which I will read to the House. The Resolution was as follows: The Imperial Conference, recognising that it is of the greatest importance that a larger and increasing proportion of the films exhibited throughout the Empire should be of Empire production, commends the matter and the remedial measures proposed to the consideration of the Governments of the various parts of the Empire with a view to such early and effective action to deal with the serious situation now existing as they may severally find possible. (*HC Deb*, 16 March 1927, vol. 203, cc2039–112)

89. Ibid. The bill emerged from committee in July 1927 and passed its third reading in parliament in November. It was debated in the Lords in December and became law. The Cinematograph Films Act provided that in the first year the distributors' quota should be

7.5 per cent, and the exhibitors 5 per cent. Both quotas were to increase by stages to 20 per cent in 1936, and remain at that level until 1938 when the Act expired.

90. In a debate in parliament, Colonel Day argued that the bill had been driven by the demands of the FBI:

> There can be no doubt that the only people in the trade who want this Bill and who are the driving force in connection with it are the producing group of the F.B.I. They have been the people in the fore all the way through. When there has been any announcement to be made in the Press of a modification of the quota, etc., they have been the first people to rush into print with it. As the right hon. Gentleman knows quite well, when an alteration was made in certain Clauses of this Bill, although we were sitting in Committee at the time, the first intimation that we had in that Committee of that alteration was by reading in the 'Times' a letter from representatives of the F.B.I., saying what the modifications were going to be. (*HC Deb*, 14 November 1927, vol. 210, cc691)

The Labour Party opposed the 1927 Act, believing that it targeted working-class cinemagoers and was consistent with Cunliffe-Lister's support for a protectionist economy. Philip Snowden, former Labour chancellor, accused Cunliffe-Lister of 'being simply a tool in the hands of the Federation of British Industries' (*The Times*, March 1927, p. 8, cited in Jaikumar, *Cinema at the End of Empire*, p. 41).

91. *The Times*, 14 March 1927, p. 15.

92. Andrew Higson remarks, 'economic protectionism boosted the confidence of the production sector of the industry and attracted unprecedented levels of external investment'. See Andrew Higson, 'Polyglot Films for an International Market: E. A. Dupont, the British Film Industry, and the Idea of a European Cinema, 1926–1930', in Higson and Maltby, *'Film Europe' and 'Film America'*, p. 275.

93. In a fascinating justification for action, Cunliffe-Lister referred to the dominance of American films and the effects on trade with Latin America:

> I wonder if hon. Members have seen the evidence which was given by the Department of Commerce of the United States before a Committee of the Congress, I think, in January, 1926. The Department was justifying to the Committee an appropriation for the cinema section, and Dr. Julius Klein, in charge of the Department, said this: I do not think it is any exaggeration to say that the motion picture is perhaps the most potent single contributor to a better understanding of the United States in Latin America … . It is invaluable in all markets where there is a high percentage of illiteracy among the people, for from the pictures they see they get their impressions of how we live, the clothes we wear, and so forth. In fact, there has been a complete change in the demand for commodities in dozens of countries. I can cite you instances of the expansion of trade in the Far East, traceable directly to the effects of the motion picture. Then he went on to speak of how in South America, before the War, if you went into the stores, you found that the bulk of the commodities were of British origin. He said that in 1919 or 1920 he was shipwrecked on the coast of Peru and went ashore to be re-outfitted; he found that in all the shops there were no longer British articles, but that American articles had taken their place. On making inquiries

he found that a great deal of that change was due to the fact that the people were constantly seeing American films and American styles. That is completely borne out by our own representatives in these countries. (*HC Deb*, 16 March 1927, vol. 203, cc2039–112)

Again, cinema was a problem of political economy.

94. Ibid.
95. Ibid.
96. Sir Hesketh Bell, Minority Report in the Colonial Films Committee Report, 1930, cited in *The Film in National Life* (London: George Allen and Unwin, 1933), p. 133.
97. Bell, *The Film in National Life*, p. 126.
98. Babli Sinha, '"Lowering our Prestige": American Cinema, Mass Consumerism, and Racial Anxiety in Colonial India', *Comparative Studies of South Asia, Africa and the Middle East* vol. 29 no. 2 (2009), p. 305.
99. Pronay, 'The Political Censorship of Films in Britain between the Wars', p. 112.
100. Jones, *The British Labour Movement and Film*, p. 105; *The Times*, 16 June 1930, p. 11.
101. 'Memorandum Prepared in the Colonial Office, Colonial Film Conference, 1927: Cinematograph Films', CO 323/990/1, p. 1. On these concerns more generally, see Kevin Narizny, 'The Political Economy of Alignment: Great Britain's Commitments to Europe, 1905–1939', *International Security* vol. 27 no. 4 (Spring 2003), pp. 184–219.
102. Pronay, 'The Political Censorship of Films in Britain between the Wars', p. 104.
103. W. Ormsby Gore, for the Secretary of State for the Colonies, Letter to all colonies and protectorates (except Malta), Palestine and Tanganyika, 1 October 1927, CO 323/990/1.
104. 'Memorandum Prepared in the Colonial Office, Colonial Film Conference, 1927', p. 12.
105. 'Travelling Cinemas', enclosure no. 4 in circular despatch dated 1 October 1927, CO 323/990/1.
106. Report of the Colonial Films Committee, CO 323/109/10.
107. Imperial Economic Committee, cited in David Meredith, 'Imperial Images: The Empire Marketing Board, 1926–1932', *History Today* vol. 37 no. 1 (January 1987), p. 31.
108. Robert Self, 'Treasury Control and the Empire Marketing Board: The Rise and Fall of Non-tariff Preference in Britain, 1924–1933', *Twentieth Century British History* vol. 5 no. 2 (1994), p. 160.
109. Report of the Imperial Economic Committee, cited in 'The Work of the Empire Marketing Board, Report No. 1', July 1926, 1, CO 323/962/7, p. 1.
110. Amery, *My Political Life*, p. 352. The remit of the EMB was expanded in 1930 to enable British goods to be advertised within the empire. The board had previously worked on the logic that advertising empire goods in Britain facilitated empire purchasing of British manufactured goods.
111. 'The Work of the Empire Marketing Board, Report No. 1', p. 2.
112. See the details in Constantine, '"Bringing the Empire Alive"', pp. 203–4. The advertising executive William Crawford was appointed as vice-chairman of the board. Crawford's thinking on the power of advertising, and its connections to education, were influential on the board. '[T]he real power of advertising', Crawford had written, 'is not to sell goods, but to form habits of thinking' (Crawford, cited in LeMahieu, *A Culture for Democracy*, pp. 163–4). This logic connected to Amery's conception of the board as a way of 'selling the idea of Empire'.

113. See Amery, *My Political Life*, p. 347; Philip Williamson, *Stanley Baldwin: Conservative Leadership and National Values* (Cambridge: Cambridge University Press, 1999), pp. 83–7; and J. A. Ramsden, 'Baldwin and Film', in Pronay, *Politics, Propaganda and Film*, p. 133.

114. Stephen Tallents, *The Projection of England* (London: Olen Press, 1955), p. 11. Pamphlet first published in 1932.

115. Tallents, *The Projection of England*, cited in F. A. Hoare, 'Educational Cinematography', *Films and Education* (London: Commission on Educational and Cultural Films, 1932), p. 9.

116. Tallents, *The Projection of England*, p. 12.

117. Ibid., p. 24 and pp. 29–30.

118. Ibid., p. 19.

119. Stephen Constantine, *Buy and Build: The Advertising Posters of the Empire Marketing Board* (London: HMSO, 1986).

120. 'Note on a Proposal for the Preparation of a Film under the Auspices of the Empire Marketing Board', CO 760/37 EMB/C/1, 28 January 1927, pp. 1–3.

121. 'Minutes of the First Meeting of the EMB Film Committee Conference Held at the Board's Offices', CO 760/37, 1 February 1927, p. 1.

122. 'The collaboration of Mister Kipling', the EMB's memorandum recorded, 'would, it was felt, prove of the greatest value to the film as a commercial asset', Minutes of the First Meeting of the EMB Film Committee Conference Held at the Board's Offices.

123. Stephen Tallents, 'The Birth of British Documentary', *Journal of the University Film Association* vol. 20 no. 1 (1968), p. 17.

124. The most complete account of Grierson's intellectual and aesthetic formation is Ian Aitken, *Film and Reform: John Grierson and the Documentary Film Movement* (London: Routledge, 1990), pp. 16–89. The Rockefeller Foundation was an early pioneer of industrial public relations.

125. John Grierson, 'Notes for English Producers', BT 64/86 6880, April 1927, p. 1.

126. Lee Grieveson, 'Cinema Studies and the Conduct of Conduct', in Lee Grieveson and Haidee Wasson (eds), *Inventing Film Studies* (Durham, NC: Duke University Press, 2008).

127. Grierson, 'Notes for English Producers', p. 17.

128. Ibid., p. 18. On Grierson's extensive writings about Soviet cinema, see, for example, Stollery, *Alternative Empires*, pp. 147–9.

129. Ibid., p. 20.

130. Ibid., p. 17.

131. Cunliffe-Lister, letter to Leopold Amery, 10 May 1927, BT64/86 I.M.5511, cited in Swann, *The British Documentary Film Movement, 1926–1946*, p. 13.

132. 'Exhibition of Films at the Imperial Institute Theatre, Film Conference, Empire Marketing Board', 12 September 1927, 1. The EMB gave a grant of £6,000 to the Imperial Institute to convert a room into a cinema hall, and £1,000 for running of the cinema (*The Times*, 31 October 1927, p. 8).

133. *The Times*, 24 October 1927, p. 18.

134. Wolfgang Schivelbusch, *The Railway Journey: The Industrialization of Time and Space in the 19th Century* (Berkeley: University of California Press, 1986); Lynne Kirby, *Parallel Tracks: The Railroad and Silent Cinema* (Durham, NC: Duke University Press, 1997).

135. Grierson, 'Further Notes on Cinema Production', CO 760/37 EMB/C/4, 28 July 1927, p. 8.

136. Ibid., p. 9.

137. Grierson, 'Film Propaganda', CO 323/1102/2, p. 7.

138. Empire Marketing Board, Film Committee, 'Minutes of the Seventh Meeting', 13 November 1928, p. 2.

139. Grierson, 'Government Cinema Activities in the United States', EMB/c/15, 12 September 1928, p. 2.

140. Grierson proposed establishing a film library at the Imperial Institute in a memorandum in March 1928. See 'The Empire Marketing Board and the Cinema', CO 760/37 EMB/C/9.

141. Forsyth Hardy, *John Grierson: A Documentary Biography* (London: Faber and Faber, 1979), p. 58.

142. The film is available on the colonial film website, alongside an article by Tom Rice. See <www.colonialfilm.org.uk/node/40>.

143. Stollery, *Alternative Empires*, p. 157.

144. Wright later complained that Grierson himself added this sequence, and that in doing so he depoliticised the critique of colonial labour practices buried in his film. See Elizabeth Sussex, *The Rise and Fall of British Documentary: The Story of the Film Movement Founded by John Grierson* (Berkeley: University of California Press, 1975), p. 33.

145. Empire Marketing Board, Film Committee, 'Minutes of the Sixth Meeting of the Film Committee', 7 May 1928, pp. 1–2.

146. Grierson wrote that the Canadian Government Motion Picture Bureau

> made our Unit seem a very poor relation indeed ... . In cinema qualities we have not so much to learn on this side, but on the equipment side and in the creation and management of circulation we have almost everything [to learn]. (Grierson, cited in Hardy, *John Grierson*, p. 63)

147. Empire Marketing Board, Film Committee, 'Minutes of the Sixteenth Meeting', 8 January 1931, p. 47.

148. Empire Marketing Board, Film Committee, 'Minutes of the Twenty-first (Special) Meeting 6 May 1931, p. 62.

149. Ibid.

150. On the dissolution of the EMB, see Constantine, '"Bringing the Empire Alive"', pp. 218–20.

151. Gary Evans, *John Grierson and the National Film Board: The Politics of Wartime Propaganda* (Toronto, ON: Toronto University Press, 1984), p. 49, cited in Joyce Nelson, *The Colonized Eye: Rethinking the Grierson Legend* (Toronto, ON: Between the Lines, 1988), p. 43.

152. Evans, cited in Nelson, *The Colonized Eye*, p. 43.

153. See the account in Nelson, *The Colonized Eye*, pp. 43–60; and Zoë Druick, *Projecting Canada: Government Policy and Documentary Film at the National Board of Canada* (Montreal, QC and Kingston, ON: McGill-Queen's University Press, 2007).

154. See Jaikumar, *Cinema at the End of Empire*, in particular pp. 41–64.

155. It is one taken up brilliantly by Neil Smith in *The Endgame of Globalization* (London: Routledge, 2005), in particular pp. 53–121; by Harvey in *The New Imperialism*; and by Giovanni Arrighi, 'Hegemony Unravelling – 1', *New Left Review* vol. 32 (March–April 2005), pp. 23–80, and Arrighi, 'Hegemony Unravelling – 2', *New Left Review* vol. 33 (May–June 2005), pp. 83–116. Cordell Hull, US Secretary of State, described the Ottawa Agreement as 'the greatest injury in a commercial way that has been inflicted on this country since I have been in public life' (Hull, cited in Callinicos, *Imperialism and Global Political Economy*, p. 168).

156. André Bazin, *What Is Cinema?*, trans. Hugh Gray, vol. 1 (Berkeley: University of California Press, 1967), p. 15.

157. The Commission on Education and Cultural Films set up in 1929 published its report as *The Film in National Life* in 1932. The political and economic analysis of film with respect to the empire, circulating widely in the immediate aftermath of the quota debates, was restated:

> The British [film] industry needs a larger market within which to extend it scope. The British Empire is an obvious field, but it is untilled. Distribution is largely controlled by American capital. The British industry has a legitimate and encouraging opportunity to enlarge its field: but it is an opportunity which must be courageously seized, and without delay. (*The Film in National Life*, p. 48)

It was this report that subtended the establishment of the British Film Institute, and shortly thereafter the National Film Archive.

6

Exhibiting Africa: British Instructional Films and the Empire Series (1925–8)[1]

Tom Rice

In co-operation with the British Colonial Office, colonial governments and corporate sponsors, the film company British Instructional Films released three series of pictures between 1925 and 1928, which promised to show the 'peoples, homes and habits' of the British Empire.[2] These short, one-reel films covered the breadth of the British Empire, and included titles on Hong Kong, Iraq, Malta, India, the West Indies and, most prominently, Britain's African colonies. Easily dismissed as commercial failures and almost completely overlooked within critical studies of British cinema, the series represents a way through which both governments and commercial producers worked out the *how* and *where* in colonial film-making. *How* would governments and commercial producers utilise and address colonial topics and *where* would these films be exhibited?

This essay is in many respects a history of colonial cinema in the 1920s. The series was developed out of the Wembley exhibition of 1924–5. The films, principally financed by colonial governments, were re-edited and titled by British Instructional Films after negotiations with the Colonial Office. They were then briefly shown in cinemas, before playing within an emerging non-theatrical market. By the end of the 1920s some of these films were also playing back within the colonies. What is at stake here is literally the *place* of film within colonial policy.

How, then, did colonial governments look to utilise film? How did they represent the colonies to British audiences? How, in turn, did the Colonial Office organise this material as a means of visually recording, navigating and mapping the Empire for British viewers? In closely analysing a number of films from the Empire Series that primarily relate to Africa, the essay attempts to answer these questions, while also examining the ways in which commercial producers recontextualised this material for a paying audience. Certainly the problems encountered by producers, distributors and exhibitors when working with the Empire Series indicate some of the broader challenges facing British cinema. For example, the promotion and reception of this series within the British press responds closely to discourses surrounding American cultural imperialism, the paucity of British films within the colonies and state concerns regarding the representation of the empire on screen. The series thus connects to popular concerns surrounding British cinema in the 1920s.

Taken together, my analysis positions the Empire Series as a valuable means of understanding the establishment and legitimisation of a formalised production, distribution and exhibition network for colonial films. The Wembley exhibition is integral to this development. While much has been written on this important exhibition, which attracted 27 million visitors over its two seasons, little mention has been made of the ways in which film was incorporated there. The exhibition connected a broader culture of imperial display to particular economic policies of the early 1920s. This context would, I argue, shape the dominant exhibition modes for colonial documentary, which would be largely pedagogical and non-theatrical. It also prefigured the dominant rhetoric of colonial documentary, in its promotion and endorsement of a newly configured imperial economy. These films foreshadow the work of the Empire Marketing Board in defining individual colonies by products and industries, and in propagating a post-war imperial identity predicated on trade and economics. They also play though on a popular fascination with the 'primitive' and project, in particular through their intertitles, an image of the empire back to British audiences that largely endorses the dominant government attitudes in, for example, highlighting British primacy, the social and industrial development of the colonies and the critical importance of imperial loyalty.

The empire exhibition illustrated a growing recognition, on the part of the Colonial Office and colonial governments, of the possibilities of film and of its value as a pedagogical tool. The imperial conference of 1926 and the Cinematograph Films Act of 1927 consolidated and formalised some of these ideas, while the establishment of the Empire Marketing Board in 1926 and the opening of the Imperial Institute's cinema a year later further helped to generate a distribution network and educational outlet for colonial film. The story of the Empire Series fits within these more established developments and reveals a moment at which producers, governments, distributors and exhibitors were still trying to negotiate and establish a viable colonial film policy.

FROM AFRICA TO WEMBLEY: COMMERCIAL PRODUCERS AND COLONIAL GOVERNMENTS

Covering 216 acres of parkland and attracting over 27 million visitors during its two seasons, the British Empire Exhibition of 1924–5 was the largest of all imperial exhibitions.[3] It served, in part, as a public celebration of the strength and unity of the post-war empire. Historian Deborah L. Hughes has argued that this promotion of imperial unity was motivated by a 'commercial agenda that sought to link imperial markets and close ranks against competition from Europe and America'.[4] The official guide to the exhibition presented the event as a 'stock-taking of the whole resources of the Empire', intended 'to foster inter-imperial trade and open fresh world markets for Dominion and home products'.[5] The exhibition also purported to reimagine Britain's imperial identity, as its rhetoric shifted from one of conquest to one of duty and development. This development was represented not only through industrial progress, but also through an increasing promotion of 'liberal' civilisation values.

Historical accounts of the exhibition have hitherto failed to address the prominent role afforded to film at the event. Among the 100,000 feet of film exhibited were two films produced by the Department of Overseas Trade, *Highways of Empire* and *Resources of Empire*, which played at the HM Government Pavilion in 1925 and further films produced for, among others, the General Post Office, the War Office, the Ministry of Health and Royal Mint.[6] While these productions emphasised broader developments and connections throughout the empire, many free films also played in cinema halls within the specially constructed pavilions that represented and housed each colony and Dominion. For example, the cinema within the New Zealand pavilion showed 'every aspect of New Zealand life, industry and scenery', while from 11.30 am to 9 pm, the Australian pavilion cinema showed 'all phases of Australian life'. The South Africa pavilion had two cinemas, showing daily 'one [film] of South Africa's industries, the other of the history, scenery and travel facilities of the country'.[7] The Walled City of West Africa, which represented Nigeria, the Gold Coast and Sierra Leone, also contained a free cinema hall managed by the Kinematograph Co. of 197 Wardour Street. As well as showing Nigerian and Gold Coast pictures for two and a half hours every afternoon and evening, it was also hired out by colonial commissioners during the vacant late-afternoon slot, showing film from, among other places, Cyprus, Fiji, Palestine and the West Indies.[8]

These pavilions also featured films from commercial sponsors, alongside those commissioned by colonial governments. This is evident in the example of the West African pictures, which were filmed in the spring of 1923 by the London-based Greville Brothers. The Greville Brothers (V. H. and N. A. Greville) were commissioned by the governments of Nigeria and the Gold Coast to make films specifically for the exhibition, but during their trip secured further commissions from commercial enterprises. They produced films for Elder Dempster and Co., J. S. Fry and Sons (*The Wealth of West Africa*, 1927) and the Keffi Consolidated Tin Mining Co. (*Tin Mining in Northern Nigeria*, 1924), with these films intended 'for showing at the Exhibition and elsewhere to all those people who are displaying, in striking contrast to the apathy of recent years, a real interest in the industrial development of the British Crown Colonies'.[9] The commercially sponsored productions were shown alongside the government material and screening reports emphasised a conformity of style, content and titling across the productions. Private investment was essential in financing the planned 'development' of West Africa and so both industry and state sought to promote trade and investment within West Africa, primarily through the representation of local products and industries.[10]

The Greville Brothers secured 40,000 feet of film during their expedition, and presented these rushes in a series of screenings before prominent colonial officials, including Sir Gordon Guggisberg and Sir Hugh Clifford, the governors of the Gold Coast and Nigeria respectively.[11] Describing two of the completed productions in April 1924, the London-based weekly *West Africa* recognised the influence of these films, claiming that 'it is beyond doubt that they will give to 99 people out of every 100 at Wembley who know nothing of West Africa their master impression of the country'. Mr Broadbridge, the chairman of the Keffi Consolidated Tin Mining Company, explained that its film responded to a widely held belief that the 'Nigerian share market suffered because of a deficiency in publicity'. He added that the films ensured that 'the properties of the company had been brought to this country instead of the people of this country having to go to the properties in Nigeria'.[12] Both industrial

A poster advertising 'The Walled City of West Africa'. The free cinema hall showed two and a half hours of pictures from Nigeria and the Gold Coast every afternoon and evening. Image courtesy of Mary Evans Picture Library/Onslow Auctions Ltd

companies and colonial governments to varying degrees saw these films as a means to increase trade, to promote economic development and, through a romanticised image of traditional Africa propagated at the exhibition, attract potential settlers.[13] They recognised the influence film could exercise in shaping popular impressions of the empire and, even before the Wembley gates opened, plans were already afoot to utilise and exploit these films beyond the exhibition's closure.

BRITISH INSTRUCTIONAL FILMS AND THE CREATION OF THE EMPIRE SERIES

In October 1923, Sir Edward Davson, a prominent figure on numerous imperial trade committees, had suggested using these films in the 'development of Empire trade and the encouragement of emigration to the Dominions'. In a letter to *The Times*, he explained that these films 'will represent the greatest collection of geographical films that has ever been made, and it would be regrettable if, in a year's time, they were scattered or destroyed'. He continued:

Empire and Film

I suggest that an organisation should be formed, possibly under the auspices of the Imperial Institute, to take them over at the close of the exhibition and to send them in charge of competent lecturers in continuous exhibition throughout the Kingdom.

Davson suggested that the films would serve to 'educate our people ... in an appreciation and knowledge of our Dominions and Colonies, of their scenery and the life of their people, of their industries and products'. He further argued that, as the scheme developed, the films could be sent overseas, to build up imperial interdependency among the varied lands of the empire.[14]

These ideas were taken forward by Graham Ball, a film expert attached to the Department of Overseas Trade. On 27 May 1924, Ball called together those representatives of the colonial governments who were participating in the exhibition, in order to discuss a proposal for a series of short films drawn principally from those currently playing at Wembley. Ball now proposed that about 26,000 feet of film should be divided into fifty-two short films, with each section 'confined to a particular colony'. He suggested that this series could be called 'Scenes in the British Empire'.

Ball acknowledged that the main purpose of these films was 'propaganda' and recognised that, as the 'long travel or topographical film is not popular', demand would be small unless the series was pushed by a firm of renters with 'skilled sellers'. His plans, though, remained ambitious. He hoped to book in 400 theatres and make a total booking of £250 on each film, while further representatives suggested that theatres could show one film a week throughout the year, before showing them in schools or overseas in other parts of the empire.[15]

The plans for the series thus reveal a desire to use film to educate and teach British audiences about the colonies, to promote imperial trade and emigration, to position 'educational' shorts within a cinematic programme and to exploit commercially the widely viewed films of the empire exhibition.[16] Although intended for British audiences, these initial discussions also suggested that these same titles could play overseas and project an image of the empire back to the colonies.

After negotiating with several firms – including Gaumont, which offered to 'edit, re-title and re-assemble' the films and release one a week – an agreement was signed in October 1924 with British Instructional Films (BIF), which gave the firm the sole rights to produce this series of shorts.[17] Founded in 1919 by H. Bruce Woolfe, BIF sought to produce films that were both broadly educational and entertaining to non-specialist audiences. It had accrued a reputation, in particular, for its coverage of overseas imperial tours and in 1923 had agreed to film the Empire Cruise of the Special Squadron 'after a last minute appeal from the admiralty'. The tour covered 38,000 miles over ten months during 1923 and 1924, and the completed six-reel film, *Britain's Birthright*, was released to cinemas on Empire Day 1925. When it played before the Duke and Duchess of York at Shepherd's Bush Pavilion in July, it was shown alongside the latest edition of BIF's fourteen-part series of the Prince of Wales's tour of Africa.[18]

The Empire Series, which was released theatrically in three sets (each of between six and twelve films) in November 1925, February 1927 and June 1928, comprised predominantly films shown at the empire exhibition, material shot during the Empire Cruise and footage filmed during the Prince of Wales's tour of Africa. The series, compiled by BIF under contract to the Colonial Office and using films produced for colonial governments and also for the Admiralty, incorporated material from three different sources, produced by a variety of companies and with different ideological aims. For example, much of the African footage, such as *An African Derby* (1927) and *Basutoland and Its People* (1925), came from existing BIF material filmed for the Admiralty during the Prince of Wales's tour, and promoted British primacy and imperial loyalty through the centrality of the royal family and colonial authority. Other films, such as the Jamaican title, came directly from those showing at Wembley, and thus responded to the aims of the specific pavilion. The Jamaican film, which was shot in January 1924 by Raymond S. Peck, director of the Canadian Government Motion Picture Bureau, and overseen by the Tourist Trade Development Board in Jamaica, was intended primarily, as the West Indian pavilion itself was, as a means of attracting tourists and potential settlers to the island.[19]

While the colonial governments were primarily motivated by individual concerns, the Colonial Office sought to unite these disparate parts within a centralised imperial ideal. In extending the work of the empire exhibition, it sought to make connections between the colonies, principally to map the spaces and materials of the empire for British audiences. BIF helped to achieve this as, most notably through the inter-titles, it homogenised these images of the empire and related them back to Britain. It created a representation, in particular of the African colonies, that was largely consistent across its output, and which responded both to a popular interest in the 'primitive' and to the government's increasing emphasis on trade and development.

'PEOPLES, HOMES AND HABITS': REPRESENTING THE COLONIES[20]

The format of the Empire Series followed the organisation of the empire exhibition itself in being arranged geographically by colony, and so reiterated this notion of individual, and vastly different, colonies and Dominions united within the 'imperial family'.[21] With titles like *Tin Mining in Nigeria* (1925), *Zanzibar and the Clove Industry* (1925), *Black Cotton* (1927) and *Gold Mining in the Gold Coast* (1928), a number of the films defined the colonies by products and industries, emphasising a post-war imperial identity centred around trade and economics. Yet also, as advertisements noted, the films focused, in particular, on the 'peoples, homes and habits' of the colonies, displaying the Africans as subjects of study in a manner that often closely mirrored the work of the exhibition. The exhibition contained an anthropological exhibit displaying 'the immense variety of races in different stages of development within the British Empire', while the Walled City had housed about sixty Hausa, Yoruba, Mendi, Ashanti and Fanti visitors within a 'native village' and workshop. The ethnographic shots within the films, displaying the Africans in close-up, in profile and emphasising distinguishing physical characteristics, similarly presented the Africans as exhibits for British audiences.[22] The exhibition context certainly helps to shape the iconography, structure and themes of these films, and more broadly of subsequent colonial non-fiction cinema. Understanding the ideological aims and strategies of the empire exhibition is thus integral to our understanding of the Empire Series.

The display of African life, both within the exhibition and on film, was ostensibly intended to challenge traditional perceptions of Africa. The exhibition commissioner for Nigeria stated, upon its closure, that

> by our films, by our exhibits, by our pictures and dramas, by our craftsmen and by our own enthusiastic devotion to our adopted country, we have dispelled, in a large measure, the wild ideas current as to the state of Nigeria, the horror of its climate, the backwardness of its people.[23]

The exhibition, and the films therein, was widely presented in progressive terms and credited with redefining Africa in the popular imagination. An early review for the Greville Brothers' West African films praised them for avoiding 'the sort of paralysing "muck" about plurality of wives and so forth, over which the cheaper sort of London daily "rags" have been spreading themselves'.[24] The official guide to the exhibition further stated that *The Gold Coast of To-Day* (1924) 'illustrates in detail the astonishing development of the country, and the habits, industries and tribal customs of its progressive people', presenting the film as 'evidence that Africa is marching on the path of civilisation with other parts of the Empire'.[25]

In illustrating this 'development', historian David Simonelli has argued that the empire exhibition ultimately served 'to present colonial peoples and their nations not as potential industrial partners, but as quaint objects of anthropological study'.[26] Certainly, the films and exhibition responded to a popular fascination in 'the primitive' and to traditional imperial notions of exploration and discovery. In a company catalogue, the Greville Brothers claimed that they were 'responsible for the unique conception of producing films of the little-known and still savage places of the world, [and] are both travellers of wide experience and profound knowledge of the dark and uncivilised regions'. Earlier productions for the company included *The White Man's Grave* (1921) and their films, and more broadly those of the Empire Series, endorsed well-established visual signifiers of traditional Africa: for example, the image of Africans climbing trees features repeatedly throughout these films.[27]

The exhibition, and the subsequent films, exemplifies then the paradoxical nature of Britain's engagement with its African colonies, celebrating both a modern imperialism that promotes economic development, and traditional notions of 'primitivism'. In his examination of the West African pavilion at Wembley, Daniel Mark Stephen recently argued that 'the popularity of the West African exhibits coincided with the emergence of "blackness" and "the primitive" as powerful British cultural commodities'. '[L]arge numbers of visitors rejected colonial claims in favour of their own seemingly more potent culture', Stephen writes, adding that 'in spite of strenuous efforts on the part of colonial officials, a decidedly illiberal imperial message, both modern and Victorian at the same time, was successfully communicated by public audiences at Wembley, undermining official claims to a reformed imperialism'.[28] Such contradictions between an official 'liberal' message and a continued popular fascination in 'the primitive' were similarly foregrounded in the Empire Series. The series was caught between an emphasis on economics and the accompanying 'liberal' ideals and a longer history of primitivism, still popular in fiction and African expedition films. The notion of British development within the

'Also its students of form eager to back their fancy …'. Bringing the empire to British audiences in *An African Derby* (1927). Courtesy of BFI National Archive

colonies was dependent on representing the pre-existing 'primitive' nature of the lands and people, and the mode of titling adopted by BIF across its films acknowledges and responds to British audiences' fascination with traditional notions of undeveloped Africa. The intertitles directly address and privilege the British viewer, endorsing a hierarchical imperial relationship predicated on British primacy and social difference.

A closer consideration of these titles helps to unravel the ways in which the series represented and defined both the African colonies and this imperial relationship to British audiences.[29] First, *An African Derby* presents the people and events of Basutoland within a distinctly British context, as the titles position the action of a Basuto race meeting in relation to the Epsom Derby. A title remarks that 'excitement runs high as the field rounds "Tattenham Corner"', referring to a famous section at Epsom, and the winning jockey is described as a 'dusky Donoghue', a reference to six-time Derby winner Steve Donoghue. This is common in other BIF pictures. For example, in *Britain's Birthright* Singapore Harbour is described as 'the Clapham Junction of the East', while in *Palaver: A Romance of Northern Nigeria* (1926), a title explains that the Africans are far removed from 'civilisation' as they are 'stranded 5030 miles from Piccadilly Circus'.

The titles within *An African Derby* 'Westernise' this event within Basutoland, and this works both to emphasise British primacy, and to incorporate this image of Africa within the hierarchy of the British Empire. The disparity between the intertitles and the images, between the British and African customs, is also used here to generate comedy. References to the 'leaders of fashion' and the 'extremely "chic"' models are followed by ethnographic shots of Africans on display, wearing modest local costume. This comedic device is not uncommon. Indeed, the 1924 spoof exploration film *Crossing the Great Sagrada* derives its comedy from this disparity between the image and title. However, while *Crossing the Great Sagrada* exposes the artificiality of these colonial narratives, producing comedy from cultural stereotypes and ultimately questioning the authenticity and authority of these ethnographic documentaries, the Empire Series does not question the validity of its representation, and indeed employs historical titles to authenticate its evidently staged image of Africa.

Empire and Film

On the one hand then, the series, like *Britain's Birthright* before it, highlights the differences between the Africans on screen and the British viewer. For example, in *Basutoland and Its People*, a shot showing the local method of cutting hair is followed by an intertitle stating 'They polish them with sand and water!' The inclusion of the exclamation mark highlights how alien this custom is intended to appear to the viewer, finding humour in the 'unsophisticated' customs of the Africans. This is further illustrated in *Kinematograph Weekly*'s review of *An African Derby*, which described the race meeting as 'quaint'.[30] In *Oil Palm of Nigeria* (1928) the commentator notes the 'superstitions' – as opposed to religion – of the locals, endorsing the popular Western notion that the Africans put their faith in superstition. The 'peculiar figure' of the Juju is compared to 'our old time marionette'. The use of the word 'our' here further differentiates the British viewer from the African on screen.

On the other hand, positioning the African sequences within a British context also incorporates this image of Africa within the empire. BIF's 1928 catalogue noted that 'some of the similarities between African and European peoples manifest themselves' in *An African Derby*, while the opening title in *Zanzibar and the Clove Industry* states that 'the island of Zanzibar is about the size of a small English county', as it positions the island within the empire, albeit as a junior partner.[31] The empire exhibition, and indeed the imperial conference of 1926, sought to present the empire as a manageable space and, in redefining the term 'Commonwealth', portray the colonies not as conquered lands but as economic and cultural allies. The Empire Series is indicative of the ways in which the Colonial Office organised the individual parts within the empire, but also of the ways in which BIF represented the relationship between Britain and its colonies across a number of series.

This familial relationship between Britain and the colonies and between the viewer and those depicted on screen is also evident in BIF's coverage of the Prince of Wales's tour. In one sequence, in which the prince attends a race meeting in Accra, a title notes that 'the native "bookie" is just as eloquent as his brother of Epsom'. The tour still notes the 'ever-changing panorama of barbaric splendours', depicts medicine men and local customs, yet it shows this disparate empire united, in this case, through its support for the royal family. Both the prince's tour and the naval tour were intended to illustrate to the colonies British support for the empire, yet the films, now bringing these images back to British audiences, serve to highlight the colonies' reciprocated support and loyalty. This popular support is indicated in the prince's tour by repeated (staged) shots of the cheering, watching crowds, pushing at the camera, while in *Britain's Birthright*, the crowds rush to see 'the world's greatest battle cruisers', a powerful representation of Britain's primacy, strength and technological advancement.

This emphasis on imperial loyalty also serves a political purpose in generating support within Britain for colonial development programmes. The need for development is promoted across the series in a number of ways. First, as discussed, through the mode of address, as by relating the colonies to Britain it both incorporates Africa within the empire and emphasises its still-undeveloped nature. This is reiterated both through the ethnographic shots and in titles, which note, for example, that 'Palm-oil is prepared in a crude and primitive way', and that locals in Zanzibar use 'the primitive loom of Ancient Arabia'. Second, the series illustrates the commercial value of the colonies to Britain. In *Britain's Birthright* a ship from Hobart transports 'fruit and wool for the mother country', while *Tin Mining in Nigeria* shows a shipment loaded for Britain, demonstrating, according to BIF, 'to what extent, at the present time, the prosperity of one country waits upon that of another'. *Oil Palm of Nigeria* also shows the product loaded onto a ship bound for Liverpool as these industrial pictures often conclude by showing the product on its way to England, creating a visual record of the circulation of materials and products throughout the empire.[32] Finally, the films outline the perceived developments already introduced. These developments are often moral and social ones, as the series repeatedly presents the British as liberators who brought peace to Africa. For example, a title within *Basutoland and Its People* reports that 'Incessant tribal warfare was the rule until 1884, when the Imperial Government took control. Since then peace has reigned.' They also though take the form of commercial and industrial developments. 'When Singapore was purchased for Great Britain in 1819, it was an utterly deserted island', an intertitle states in *Britain's Birthright*. 'To-day it is a great modern city, boasting fine public buildings.'

This rhetoric of development is especially notable in those films relating to the Gold Coast, a colony which features particularly prominently within the BIF catalogue. The films from the Gold Coast again reveal this dichotomy between 'progress' and 'primitivism'. *Blazing the Trail* (1927) documents the developments in transport, contrasting shots of modern British machinery and scientific research with those of African workers transporting material on their heads. *Northern Territories Gold Coast* (1928) explores the social developments under British supervision and, in highlighting these, again plays on popular perceptions of Africa. A staged sequence shows 'warriors in full dress' charging at the camera, before an intertitle explains that, thanks to the British, the locals are now 'quite peaceful' and 'do not find use for their bows and poisonous arrows'.

The Gold Coast also serves to exemplify a changing economic relationship between Britain and Africa, and this is prioritised both within the Empire Series and within other sponsored shorts, such as *West Africa Calling* (1927), which BIF produced for the Conservative Party.[33] The Gold Coast was integral to BIF's representation of the empire, enabling the company to promote a discourse of discovery, expansion and development across a variety of titles produced for trade and governments at home and overseas. Indeed, BIF was also commissioned by the Gold Coast government to record the official opening of Takoradi Harbour in 1928. The building of the harbour, which featured regularly within BIF films, is especially important within this promotion of a modern imperial economy. Through its films from the Gold Coast, BIF was able to show both the intensive production of natural resources within a modern colony and, particularly through the images of Takoradi, the resultant circulation of these products throughout the empire.

'SUPPORT THESE SPLENDID BRITISH SUBJECTS': PROMOTION AND EXHIBITION

When the second set of the Empire Series was released to cinemas in February 1927, *Kinematograph Weekly* wrote:

We refuse to believe that this technically excellent and absorbingly interesting series will not receive great appreciation from audiences all over the Kingdom. It is a reproach to the showmen, we fear, to learn that this type of film does not book satisfactorily.

The review concluded by stating that 'we again urge all showmen to support these splendid British subjects, which are great stuff and should supplant much of the utter drivel now seen in "Shorts"'.[34]

This review indicates both the apparent commercial failings of the series, and the terms in which the series was championed as 'British' in opposition to the dominant American industry. In 1925 when letters in *The Times* had questioned why the 'admirable cinematograph displays' at Wembley were not commercially available, the writers had presented their omission within this context, asking 'What is wrong with the British Film industry that when these poor children cry out for bread we give them stones?', while another added 'One wonders really how sincere the British film producers and those engaged in the industry are in their claims for sympathy against American encroachments.'[35] These fears surrounding the hegemony of the American film industry on the British market were closely aligned to those concerning the representation of the empire on screen. During 1925, Prime Minister Stanley Baldwin had called for action after noting the 'danger to which we in this country and our Empire subject ourselves if we allow that method of propaganda [film] to be entirely in the hands of foreign countries'.[36] When BIF released *Britain's Birthright* a couple of months earlier, *Kinematograph Weekly* had complained that 'the American flag gets more than its fair share of publicity', and promoted *Britain's Birthright* as a 'picture that every schoolboy and girl should see, since the flag needs "showing" nearly as much in England as it does in the Colonies'.[37]

The publicity and discussions concerning the Empire Series engaged with and fuelled these popular discourses regarding American cultural imperialism, and also responded to the paucity of British films within the colonies and Dominions. A *Times* report in 1926 complained that 'among what might be termed "national" film subjects the record of distribution in our own Dominions is lamentable in the extreme', noting that *Britain's Birthright* was 'refused by all the Dominions' and only shown by private enterprise.[38] These concerns were widely discussed at the imperial conference of October 1926 and culminated in the Cinematograph Films Act of 1927. The Act, while intended to reinvigorate the British film industry by enforcing a 'quota' of British films to be exhibited and distributed within Britain, was also, as Priya Jaikumar has shown, 'equally shaped by imperial aspirations' in extending these initiatives throughout the empire.[39]

The Empire Series was thus released into cinemas at a moment when film discourse was promoting 'British' film subjects and challenging producers and exhibitors, at home and overseas, to present the empire on screen and to regain control of its representation. However, despite these demands the best role and position for these imperial shorts was still unclear. BIF initially sought to promote the commercial exhibition of the series in November 1925, only a few weeks after much of the material had been shown for free at Wembley. Furthermore, sponsored films from the exhibition continued to screen non-theatrically across the country with additional lectures and exhibits contextualising the films. In the month following the closure of

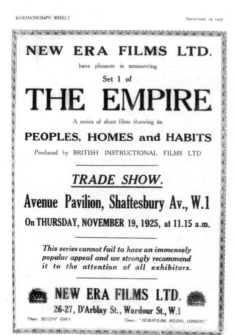

NEW ERA FILMS LTD.

have pleasure in announcing

Set 1 of

THE EMPIRE

A series of short films showing its

PEOPLES, HOMES and HABITS

Produced by BRITISH INSTRUCTIONAL FILMS LTD

TRADE SHOW.

Avenue Pavilion, Shaftesbury Av., W.1

On THURSDAY, NOVEMBER 19, 1925, at 11.15 a.m.

This series cannot fail to have an immensely popular appeal and we strongly recommend it to the attention of all exhibitors.

NEW ERA FILMS LTD.

26-27, D'Arblay St., Wardour St., W.1

'Phone : REGENT 5318-9.   'Grams : " NURAFILM, WESDO, LONDON."

A trade advertisement in *Kinematograph Weekly* in November 1925 for the first of three sets released as part of the Empire Series. The poster's claims that the series could not fail to have an 'immensely popular appeal' were soon disproved

the exhibition, for example, the Elder Dempster film was screened to the 'boys of Ampleforth College, York', at the YMCA hall in Bournemouth, to members of the African Progress Union in London and, along with other West African pictures from Wembley, at an exhibition of empire products held by the Guildford Women's Conservative Association.[40] For BIF the series thus marked a moment in which it was still determining how best to present these imperial subjects. How should commercial companies and governments use film to educate audiences about the empire? Could these films play within commercial spaces as entertainment? Were these films inherently connected to exhibitions and reliant on a contextualisation and scientific validity not provided by widespread theatrical distribution? In short, what was the future for short imperial films?

By 1927 BIF explained, with reference to the Empire Series, that it was 'now concentrating on making the films available for educational purposes'. The majority of the films, including *Britain's Birthright* and the *Official Record of the Tour of H.R.H. the Prince of Wales* (1925), were now advertised for non-theatrical hire through BIF's education department, while BIF discussed with the Imperial Institute 'the need for a central bureau for distributing Empire films'.[41] Amid the aforementioned imperial film discourses, BIF had traditionally emphasised the pedagogical function of its imperial films, and reviews responded to this. The journal *West Africa*, in discussing the third set of the Empire Series, noted 'how valuable they would be if used in schools throughout the Empire', while *Kinematograph Weekly* had promoted *Britain's Birthright* as a film of 'the greatest educational value', which would provide schoolchildren with 'a wide vision and a better idea of the extent and possibilities of the Empire than any number of books'.[42] *Britain's Birthright* had been 'arranged' by Professor Arthur Percival Newton, Rhodes Professor of Imperial History at King's College, London, and he was also asked by Bruce Woolfe to check the historical accuracy of pictures within the Empire Series. The Imperial Institute praised BIF for taking 'the trouble to seek the advice of eminent authorities such as Professor Newton, from an educational point of view'.[43]

The perceived educational value of the films did not help them find a commercial audience. Instead, the films would be repositioned at the forefront of an emerging non-theatrical imperial film market. The films of the Empire Series reappeared from 1927 within an educational context in what was, in many respects, the natural successor to the cinemas at the empire exhibition. The Imperial Institute cinema, which opened in July 1927, showed imperial films four times a day to children, and from the outset regularly screened films from the Empire Series, such as *A Day in the Life of a District Officer* (1925).[44] The institute, described by its director as a 'permanent Wembley', displayed the 'products of each and every part' of the empire and the cinema, funded by the Empire Marketing Board, continued this focus on trade and imperial productivity. The ideals of Wembley were now established permanently within this institution, with film (and primarily BIF films) once more forming a part of this imperial pedagogy. Reports noted the 'educational effects of these films' and stated that 'the value of this propaganda is fully appreciated by the government of most of the dominions and colonies and has renewed their interest in the galleries'.[45] A memorandum from the Imperial Institute in 1927 acknowledged its preference for these BIF films. The 'productions of British Instructional Films are in every way superior to those obtained from other sources', it stated, adding that the company had 'succeeded most happily in introducing little scenes of native life, recreations, native types and customs into nearly all of their films'.[46]

While the Empire Series, displayed free of charge for schoolchildren and adults as part of a broader exhibition, had effectively returned to its roots, its failure at the cinema prompted the Crown agents to speculate in 1927 on the best generic framework for these imperial subjects. 'Experience with the Empire Series would appear to indicate that purely propaganda or educational films are not the type to succeed commercially', they noted.[47] The commercial failure of these films thus pushed the creation of new distribution networks and spaces of exhibition for colonial films.

CONCLUSION: MOVING IMAGES AROUND THE WORLD

In 1927 BIF revealed fresh plans to work with colonial governments in producing films 'of an educational character demonstrating local resources and development'. These films, defined as 'educational' and promoting trade and development, were now intended specifically for exhibition within the colonies. As a member of the Film Producers' Group, BIF actively promoted the trade of British films overseas, with this proposed 'interchange' of educational and imperial films again intended to spread 'imperial knowledge' and 'counteract the influence of the foreign photoplay'. BIF signed a deal in 1928 to screen their existing productions in Australia and New Zealand and were again at the forefront of plans announced in 1930 to 'promote the better distribution of British films in the colonies' and to supply films of an 'educational value to the native races'. Reports outlining the formation of this Colonial Films Committee noted that BIF already 'send instructional and interest films to places so far distant as the West Indies, Nigeria and the Gold Coast, the Malay States, India and New Zealand for exhibition in places other than those of entertainment'. The story of the Empire Series had now come full circle, as many of these films, shot in the colonies and then exhibited in Britain at Wembley, in cinemas and non-theatrically, returned to the colonies and Dominions.[48]

BIF continued to work with colonial governments and local industries and had now positioned itself at the forefront of an emerging educational film market.[49] It was not the only commercial company working within this field though, and in 1927 the Colonial Office rejected BIF's request for exclusive production and distribution rights with colonial governments and within colonial territories. The Crown agents explained that another company had recently been commissioned to produce 10,000 feet of film for the Federated Malay States. These films would again highlight the 'scenic, life, habits, customs, industries' of the area, and were divided into seventeen sections 'for education and trade use', some of which would feature at the Imperial Institute cinema. The company commissioned to produce these films was the Greville Brothers.[50]

By 1927 the Crown agents acknowledged that the Empire Series had 'not been a success as regards the cinema theatres and the amount so far received on behalf of the participating colonies is negligible'.[51] The commercial failure of the series helped to shape the ways in which colonial films were distributed and exhibited throughout the empire. From this point on there is clearly a greater realisation on the part of governments and the film industry that colonial documentary would be principally pedagogical, and would operate outside commercial circuits. This realisation is an important stepping stone for both the Empire Marketing Board and the more widely known history of British documentary. It also further highlights the significant and previously overlooked role of the empire exhibition within film history. This framework for colonial non-fiction cinema extends and formalises the Wembley model, while the organisation and subject matter for colonial shorts, in foregrounding trade and economics and defining individual colonies by products and industries, again follows practices adopted at Wembley.

After 1927, BIF's imperial subjects were more often either shown in non-theatrical spaces (for example, *West Africa Calling* played on the Conservative Party mobile cinema vans) or presented within a fictional framework, such as *Stampede* (1929).[52] During the 1930s, as head of Gaumont British Instructional, Bruce Woolfe initiated further series of empire shorts, produced with support from colonial governments and commercial sponsors.[53] In predominantly showing local industries and 'day-to-day' life' within the colonies, the films again sought to map these disparate regions and to illustrate the industrial productivity and economic value of the empire. These films were now though promoted primarily as educational pictures for schools, supple-mented by teaching notes and intended for classroom use. Viewed alongside the opening of the new Empire Film Library at the Imperial Institute in 1935, the films ultimately reveal the codification of a distribution and exhibition network for imperial shorts that was first negotiated through the Empire Series.

NOTES

I would like to thank Lee Grieveson for his extremely helpful comments on earlier drafts of this article.

1. For further historical information and analysis on the films mentioned within this article, visit 'Colonial Film: Moving Images of the British Empire' at <www.colonialfilm.org.uk>. In addition, films from the series can be viewed here.
2. 'Memorandum by Graham Ball on the Suggested Scheme for a Series of Empire Films', accessed at the National Archives, CO 323/919/11; *Kinematograph Weekly*, 19 November 1925.
3. The exhibition ran from 23 April–1 November 1924 and then reopened on 9 May until 31 October 1925. The attendance of 17.5 million in 1924 dropped to 9.75 million in 1925. See John MacKenzie, 'The Imperial Exhibitions', *Propaganda and Empire: The Manipulation of British Public Opinion, 1880–1960* (Manchester: Manchester University Press, 1984), pp. 96–120. See also David Simonelli, '"[L]aughing Nations of Happy Children Who Have Never Grown Up": Race, the Concept of Commonwealth and the 1924–25 British Empire Exhibition', *Journal of Colonialism and Colonial History* vol. 10 no. 1 (Spring 2009); Jonathan Woodham, 'Images of Africa and Design at the British Empire Exhibitions between the Wars', *Journal of Design History* vol. 2 no. 1 (1989), pp. 15–33; Daniel Mark Stephen, '"The White Man's Grave": British West Africa and the British Empire Exhibition of 1924–1925', *Journal of British Studies* vol. 48 no. 1 (January 2009), pp. 102–28.
4. Deborah L. Hughes, 'Kenya, India and the British Empire Exhibition of 1924', *Race and Class* vol. 47 no. 4 (April–June 2006), pp. 66–85.
5. Marjorie Grant Cook, in collaboration with Frank Fox, *The British Empire Exhibition 1924: Official Guide* (London: Fleetway Press, 1924). See also MacKenzie, *Propaganda and Empire*, pp. 96–120.
6. 'Particulars of Cinematograph Films Owned by the Department of Overseas Trade and Other Departments Participating in the British Empire Exhibition', accessed at the National Archives, BT 61/26/9.
7. *The British Empire Exhibition 1925: Official Catalogue* (London: Fleetway Press, 1925). The South African pictures were produced by African Film Productions. For more information see Thelma Gutsche, *The History and Social Significance of Motion Pictures in South Africa, 1895–1940* (Cape Town: Howard Timmins, 1972), p. 322.
8. Cook and Fox, *The British Empire Exhibition 1924*, pp. 69–70; 'West Africa and the Empire Exhibition', *West Africa*, 29 March 1924.
9. *West Africa* offers detailed reports on the filming and initial screenings of the unedited footage. See for example: 'Gold Coast Industries: Private View of First Films for British Empire Exhibition', *West Africa*, 28 April 1923, p. 422; *West Africa*, 5 May 1923, p. 451; 'The Gold Coast Film', *West Africa*, 19 May 1923, p. 533; 'The Nigeria Film', *West Africa*, 16 June 1923, p. 657; 'Nigeria Filmed for the British Empire Exhibition', *West Africa*, 23 June 1923, pp. 670–3; *West Africa*, 30 June 1923, pp. 726–7.

10. In discussing the New Zealand film, *New Zealand Truth* suggested a potential conflict between the sponsors' interests and requirements and those of the exhibition. The paper argued that the industrial sequences would benefit from further editing as, at present, they are 'more suggestive of advertisement for the firms concerned than of real attraction to the people who are likely to visit the big exhibition'. It did state though that 'there is no doubt that one of the most effective means of advertising New Zealand at the forthcoming British Empire Exhibition will be by the film depicting the Dominion's commercial and scenic resources' ('N.Z.'s Official Film', *New Zealand Truth*, 19 January 1924, p. 1).

11. Regarding the Nigerian material in July 1923, *West Africa* wrote that

> the complete film would take about six hours to show. This is, of course, impractical. It will, when edited, captioned, titled and put into sequence, be finally made into five or six separate reels for showing as required to vary the interest of the public. ('The Nigeria Film', p. 757).

12. 'Two Films That Matter', *West Africa*, 26 April 1924, p. 393; 'Tin Mining in Nigeria', *West Africa*, 5 April 1924, p. 305.

13. Woodham, 'Images of Africa and Design at the British Empire Exhibitions between the Wars', p. 21.

14. Edward Davson, 'Empire Films', *The Times*, 10 October 1923, p. 11.

15. 'Memorandum by Graham Ball on the Suggested Scheme for a Series of Empire Films'.

16. *Kinematograph Weekly*, in reviewing the first set of films in November 1925, suggested that 'this series of one-reelers promises to be of value not only as an extension of the Wembley idea, but also as entertainment' (*Kinematograph Weekly*, 19 November 1925).

17. The films would be distributed by New Era Films.

18. For more information, see Tom Rice, 'Britain's Birthright', Moving Images of the British Empire, 2010, <www.colonialfilm.org.uk/node/6219> and Tom Rice, 'Official Record of the Tour of H.R.H. the Prince of Wales, Part 3', <www.colonialfilm.org.uk/node/1705>. See also Christopher M. Bell, *The Royal Navy, Seapower and Strategy between the Wars* (London: Macmillan, 2000), pp. 168–9; Ralph Harrington, '"The Mighty Hood": Navy, Empire, War at Sea and the British National Imagination, 1920–60', *Journal of Contemporary History* vol. 38 no. 2 (April 2003), pp. 171–85. BIF secured the exclusive rights to the Prince of Wales's tour from the Admiralty in April 1925. See *The Times*, 28 April 1925, p. 12; *The Times*, 14 July 1925, p. 12.

19. 'The Jamaica Film', *Daily Gleaner*, 26 June 1925, p. 8. The *Daily Gleaner* noted that the Jamaican film, which was playing twice a day in the West India cinema, was 'now in the hands of British Instructional Films Limited, who are preparing it for inclusion in their series for display all over the country'. Peck had come to Jamaica in January 1924 to film 'the beauties of Jamaica and her social and industrial pursuits'. See 'Here to Take Pictures of Island's Life', *Daily Gleaner*, 17 January 1924, p. 13. See also 'Film to Advertise Jamaica', *Daily Gleaner*, 2 February 1924, p. 12.

20. *Kinematograph Weekly*, 19 November 1925.

21. This structure assumes particular significance after the imperial conference of 1926. The conference, and the resultant Balfour Declaration, acknowledged the growing political independence of the Dominions, and defined them as 'autonomous communities within the British Empire ... united by a common allegiance to the Crown'. This message of imperial

unity is prevalent in EMB productions, such as *One Family* (1930), which was made with British Instructional Films.

22. Simonelli, '"[L]aughing Nations of Happy Children Who Have Never Grown Up"'. *Crossing the Great Sahara*, which records the 3,500 mile journey from morthern Nigeria of Captain Angus Buchanan, played at the Palace Theatre in London for three weeks and then ran for a further six weeks at the Philharmonic Hall in the early part of 1924. The film was supported by displays of approximately 500 birds and animals that Buchanan had brought back from his travels and, within this context, the film presented the Africans as subjects of scientific study.

23. 'British West Africa and the British Empire Exhibition', *West Africa*, 7 November 1925, p. 1483. The chairman of the West Africa exhibition committee similarly praised the exhibition for dispelling 'some of the abysmal ignorance that has existed for so many years about West Africa affairs and conditions generally', and complained in particular of the ignorance 'which plays such as "White Cargo" tend to keep alive by conveying entirely erroneous impressions to the public'.

24. 'Two Films That Matter', p. 393.

25. Cook and Fox, *The British Empire Exhibition 1924*, p. 67.

26. Simonelli, '"[L]aughing Nations of Happy Children Who Have Never Grown Up"'.

27. 'Greville Brothers Company Catalogue', c. 1927, accessed at BFI Special Collections.

28. Stephen, '"The White Man's Grave"'.

29. *West Africa* had praised the titles in the Greville Brothers' Wembley pictures, noting that 'instead of loutish jocosity, we get such titles as "We are privileged to witness"'. They were more critical of those adopted in the Empire Series, reserving particular criticism for the 'unusually facetious' titles within *An African Derby*. See 'The Nigeria Film', p. 657; 'Two Films That Matter', p. 393. 'Films of West African Life', *West Africa*, 19 February 1927, p. 175. The mode of titling is not exclusive to the African films within the Empire Series. See Tom Rice, 'Baghdad', <www.colonialfilm.org.uk/node/47>.

30. *Kinematograph Weekly*, 24 February 1927, p. 76.

31. British Instructional Films, *Catalogue of Films for Non-theatrical Exhibition* (1928).

32. Ibid. For an excellent, detailed analysis of the ways in which these films imagine an 'idealised political economy', see Lee Grieveson's essay within this collection, 'The Cinema and the Common (Wealth) of Nations'.

33. See Grieveson, 'The Cinema and the Common (Wealth) of Nations'; Tom Rice, 'West Africa Calling', <www.colonialfilm.org.uk/node/1329>.

34. *Kinematograph Weekly*, 24 February 1927, p. 76.

35. 'Films at Wembley', *The Times*, 15 October 1925, p. 15; 'Films at Wembley', *The Times*, 17 October 1925, p. 8.

36. Colonel Sir Arthur R. Holbrook, 'British Films', *Royal Society of Arts Journal*, 3 June 1927, pp. 684–709.

37. Trade Shows Surveyed', *Kinematograph Weekly*, 12 March 1925, p. 58.

38. 'Film and the Empire', *The Times*, 24 May 1926, p. xiv. When *Livingstone* (1925), a film defined somewhat ambitiously as 'the most remarkable film ever made as a result of British industry', failed to secure distribution in America or Africa, its producer and the British press presented this as a slight on British industry and argued that British films could only challenge their foreign counterparts 'if the African and other dominion markets were really thrown open to British films'. 'See British Films in South Africa', *Bioscope*, 19 August 1926, p. 22; 'The Cinema In Africa', *The Times*, 5 October 1926, p. 10.

39. Priya Jaikumar, *Cinema at the End of Empire: A Politics of Transition in Britain and India* (Durham, NC: Duke University Press, 2006), p. 5.

40. 'The Elder Dempster Film', *West Africa*, 31 October 1925, p. 1439; 'An Excellent Effort', *West Africa*, 14 November 1925, p. 1516.

41. 'Letter from Crown Agents to the Under Secretary of State, Colonial Office', 11 July 1927, accessed at the National Archives, CO 323/985/23. BIF established an education department in November 1925.

42. 'Four Good Films of West Africa', *West Africa*, 16 June 1928, p. 764; 'Trade Shows Surveyed', p. 58.

43. 'Encouragement in Production of British Films', 1927, accessed at the National Archives, CO 323/985/23.

44. 'Gold Coast Films in London', *West Africa*, 9 July 1927, p. 895. At its opening, films including *Zanzibar and the Clove Industry* and *Baghdad* were also shown, while *Rough Diamonds*, taken in South Africa and included in the first set of the series, played to audiences during 1928. See *Daily Mirror*, 7 April 1928, p. 9.

45. 'Free Cinema', *Daily Mirror*, 20 August 1927, p. 9; *Daily Mirror*, 15 October 1927, p. 9; 'The Cinema in Education: Popularizing the Imperial Institute', *The Times*, 31 October 1927, p. 8. The cinema proved an enormous draw for the institute, as its visitor numbers increased from 2,400 to 8,000 per week during its first month.

46. 'Encouragement in Production of British Films', 1927, accessed at the National Archives, CO 323/985/23.

47. The Crown agents further suggested that *Palaver*, a BIF feature shot in Nigeria, which 'combined fiction with a background of local customs ... would appear to be the type of film which is most likely to appeal to cinema audiences in this country'. *Palaver* shared much in common with the Empire Series, in terms of personnel, its close links with colonial governments, and in promoting itself as an authentic study of African life, yet it reflected a growing tendency to re-contextualise these imperial studies within a fictional framework. For more information on *Palaver*, see Tom Rice, 'Palaver', <www.colonialfilm.org.uk/node/1342>.

48. 'State Film Shows', *Straits Times*, 6 August 1927, p. 3; 'British Films: Agreement for Oversea Distribution', *The Times*, 26 January 1928, p. 10; 'The Film World: British Pictures for South Africa', *The Times*, 23 January 1929, p. 14; *The Times*, 9 April 1930, p. 14. Furthermore, a film from the Empire Series was exhibited in Kenya and Uganda in 1929 as part of one of the earliest experiments into African film audiences. *Black Cotton* – now labelled *Cotton Growing in Nigeria* – was one of three films supplied by the Empire Marketing Board and taken out to East Africa by Dr Julian Huxley as part of what film historian Rachael Low described as a 'small but influential experiment'. There is no evidence that BIF adapted their films specifically for these overseas audiences. See Rachael Low, *The History of the British Film, 1929–1939: Documentary and Educational Films of the 1930s* (New York and London: Bowker, 1979), p. 43.

49. BIF advertised in *The Times* in 1928 to 'Principals of Industrial Undertakings', outlining the ways in which the cinematograph could be used as a 'direct aid to industry and commerce'. See *The Times*, 25 January 1928, p. 13.

50. Much of this footage was primarily intended to encourage British immigration to Malaya and to 'remedy' the 'disquieting shortage' of British civil servants within Malaya. For more information on this expedition, see Tom Rice, 'Malaya. No 12: Its Relation to the Empire', <www.colonialfilm.org.uk/node/1656>.

51. 'Letter from Crown Agents to the Under Secretary of State, Colonial Office'.
52. In 1928 Bruce Woolfe travelled to India to oversee the production of *Shiraz*, a BIF co-production with UFA, which was followed a year later by *A Throw of Dice*. In 1929 he also contacted the high commissioner in Southern Rhodesia, explaining that he was working on a script with John Buchan on the life of Cecil Rhodes, although this was never produced.
53. In 1936, Woolfe initiated a six-month filming expedition to the West Indies 'with the blessing of the West India committee' which was intended as the first part of a complete film series 'showing the whole Empire as it is for the benefit of school children in various parts of the British possessions'. This was followed a year later by four 'Indian geography shorts'. While there is little evidence to suggest that any of these films were widely seen, particularly given the paucity of school projectors in circulation, these films illustrate the continued legacy of the original Empire Series. See 'Filming the Caribbean for the Classroom', *Daily Gleaner*, 15 August 1936, p. 23; 'Entertainment into Instructional: G.B.I.'s Indian Geography Shorts', *Today's Cinema*, 27 May 1937, p. 7; 'New Instructional Films: Empire Series Planned by Gaumont-British', *The Times*, 15 July 1939, p. 10. See also Tom Rice, 'Gaumont-British Instructional', <www.colonialfilm.org.uk/production-company/gaumont-british-instructional>; Priya Jaikumar, 'An "accurate imagination": Place, Map and Archive as Spatial Objects of Film History' in this volume.

7

Imperialism and Internationalism: The British Documentary Movement and the Legacy of the Empire Marketing Board

Scott Anthony

For the past twenty years, at least, film historians have struggled with the apparent paradox that, while the British documentary movement publicly tethered itself to a social democratic mission, its funding came from a conservative state focused on the maintenance of imperial power and less impressed by the claims of labour and modernity. This essay addresses this paradox by re-examining the ways in which the aesthetic conventions, political ethos and social networks created by the Empire Marketing Board (EMB) would continue to influence British documentarists' representations of the empire throughout the interwar period and beyond.

The British documentary movement owed its existence to the Empire Marketing Board (1926–33). Created in the wake of the imperial economic conference of 1924, the EMB's emergence was an important part of a governmental drive to meet the challenges of new global technologies including aviation and telephony.[1] A brainchild of the imperialist Conservative politician Leo Amery, the EMB was to cement 'imperial-mindedness' by promoting the inter-empire exchange of scientists, educationalists and engineers. Amery hoped that the board would prepare the ground for a pan-imperial market walled off by tariffs, and the ostensible role of the EMB film unit was to publicise the opportunities the empire offered. The EMB's stark imperialist mission has encouraged film historians (especially those subsequently influenced by 'new left' thinking) to see a telling schism between what John Grierson and the British documentarists said they were doing and what they actually did. Or, as Brian Winston's pithy put-down had it, 'Right wing money, left-wing kudos and films of dubious social value in the middle'.[2]

Most important for historians of the British documentary movement is the fact that while the board fell victim to the slump, its ethos retained a considerable hold over its film-makers. Stephen Tallents, the architect of the EMB film unit, became an advisor to the Imperial Relations Trust. John Grierson, the movement's figurehead, would play a pivotal role in the shaping of the National Film Board of Canada, as well as advising the governments of Australia, New Zealand and South Africa. Former EMB film-makers would continually return to the subject of the empire and imperial relations throughout the course of their careers – from Paul Rotha's documentaries for Imperial Airways to Harry Watt's Commonwealth Westerns like *The Overlanders* (1946) and *Where No Vultures Fly* (1951).[3]

Winston's interpretation of this paradox is simply to see Grierson and his acolytes as either dishonest or deluded. Another interpretation has been to draw a distinction between the 'progressive' aspects of the British documentary movement's work, those that contribute towards what Ross McKibbin described as the 'cultural redistribution of esteem', and the 'propagandist' elements.[4] This distinction could be supported by contrasting the movement's marquee films with the cruder touring educational films, contrasting *The Song of Ceylon* (of which more later) with its offcuts *Dance of the Harvest*, *Monsoon Island*, *Negombo Coast* and *Villages of Lanka* (all 1934).[5] It would mean making a distinction between the films made for prestige, on which the movement risked its institutional chips, and those made for more utilitarian reasons, on which the movement would compromise. The attraction of this argument for defenders of the documentary movement is that it protects Grierson's reputation as a 'progressive' and transforms the documentary movement's dealings with the worlds of business and government into necessary means to a subversive end.[6] The reality is probably messier than such a neat formulation allows.

The task ahead is to move beyond assessing exactly how reactionary (or otherwise) the EMB was and instead re-situate the kind of imperialism the board and its film-makers espoused into a broader interpretative context. As a beginning it's worth emphasising that the British establishment in the 1920s can be forgiven for thinking that the British Empire had had a 'good war'. Unlike the Austro-Hungarian, German, Ottoman or Russian empires, the British Empire had not only staved off collapse but grown in size and governmental complexity (for example, with the creation of mandated territories).[7] As the interwar period progressed, the empire could even be understood as a transnational bulwark against aggressive ethno-nationalist authoritarian states. Thus the view that the British Empire had a role as a quasi-internationalist prototype of 'the world economic unit of the future' was less fanciful to the civil servants, technocrats and scientists working at the EMB than more polemical contemporary judgment generally allows.[8] The board may have been Amery's brainchild, but in sum it is probably best understood as an example of what Arthur Marwick described as a forum of 'middle opinion', which helped generate piecemeal reformist (rather than revolutionary) 'agreement'.[9]

Marwick was describing the political landscape of interwar Britain, but there is also a relevant strand of imperial history that stresses the importance of 'middle grounds'. The exercise of imperial rule depended on long lines of bureaucratic, social, political and cultural command. Constant work, bargaining and negotiation at these varied 'middle grounds' was a fact of empire.[10] As well as operating as a forum for inter-imperial relations, the EMB also represented the interests of a rising technocratic class, a lower stratum of inter-imperial bureaucracy with distinct professional and class interests as well as scientific expertise. Thus while the EMB film unit did play on conventional establishment fears – in particular the threat of 'Americanisation' – the EMB's enthusiastic propagation of agro-science, road building and hydro-electricity gave it a quite different tenor to rival imperial ventures. The mode of the Empire Marketing Board, for example, is distinct from that of the British Empire Film Institute, which more obviously drew on populist, bellicose late nineteenth-century iterations of imperial propaganda.[11] One of the many interesting idiosyncrasies about the EMB film unit was not just that it was committed to documenting life across the empire (rather than simply asserting its greatness) but that its cinematic work was produced in creative dialogue with the examples of 'development' offered by the Soviet

Union. As Tallents reflected on the opportunities that existed for building a cinematic portrait of the empire:

> We have ready to our hand all the material to outmatch *Storm Over Asia* by a film that should be entitled *Dawn Over Africa*. The history of our imperial development is rich in themes not less great than that of the Turkestan–Siberian Railway. The story of the Hudson Bay Company alone would provide a theme, which, incidentally, would not be dependent, as is that of *Turk–Sib*, upon an illusionary representation of successful achievement. In the countryside and country life, which have inspired so noble a body of English poetry and painting, we have themes not less beautiful than *Earth*, and we are under no necessity, as was Dovjenko, to disguise them under the appearance of political propaganda.[12]

Indeed, Russia's relationship to the outlying socialist republics offered a model of centripetal (as well as centrifugal) imperial development that chimed with the approach of the liberal technocrats who staffed the board. Hence in an EMB film show, episodes of *Drifters* (1929), *Conquest* (1930) and *A Southern April* (1928) might be intercut with *Earth* (1930), *Turk–Sib* (1929) and Lydia Stepanov's *Giant Harvest* (1930).[13] This is not to say that the board sat at the vanguard of revolutionary Communism, but to recognise a Wellsian interest (which exploded into wider public conscious after the Wells–Stalin talk of 1934) in state-sponsored modernisation that eventually came to make a broad equivalence between the EMB's ambitions, Stalin's five-year plans and Roosevelt's New Deal.[14] Technocratic ambition unified the EMB's project rather than political rhetoric and the (possibly deliberate) fuzziness with which the board's ultimate goals were expressed enabled it to build a broad coalition of interests. The impulse that drove its work was less the desire to be 'right' (or 'left') but the determination to push things forward. If 'inertia' was the dominant mode of high politics in interwar Britain, the EMB and its documentarists were on the side of 'engagement'.

Understood this way, the board's dissolution in 1933 not only reflected its lack of constituency in high political circles, but the economic weakness of technocratic networks that the EMB had been plugged into. Former EMB film-makers remained dependent on commissions from colonial governments, agro-scientists, petroleum companies, telecommunications businesses and aviation interests. Documentary films, like aviation and media communications, were transnational operations whose staff believed that the future belonged to them but whose immediate future depended on their ability to lobby for subsidies and survive an ever more hostile, nationalist environment.[15]

Kevin Grant, Philippa Levine and Frank Trentmann have argued that 'from the late eighteenth century to the early twentieth centuries, the British Empire was the principal conveyor-belt for both transnational social movements and for inscribing the idea of civil society into colonial relations', and overall this seems a reasonable description of the role the British documentary movement attempted to play.[16] Of course, there were many different strands of internationalist thought during the interwar period and internationalism did not necessarily lead to a more egalitarian and progressive stance on imperial (or global) relations, but we should acknowledge that the EMB's scientific staff and film-makers believed that they were engaged in a democratising project and that the vast majority of their contemporaries (whether friends or foes) accepted this too. As John Taylor later recalled,

> today you look back on it and say oh the Empire Marketing Board and imperialism and so on but Tallents, Sir Stephen Tallents, who ran it was a Liberal and would be much more in tune with Commonwealth than Empire.[17]

●

The rise of corporatism was perhaps the defining intellectual development of the British business world in the 1930s.[18] Legislative intervention, long-term fiscal planning, investment in high technology and greater focus on improving the skills of workers were the pillars of a string of high-profile government interventions into the commercial sphere that included the Central Electricity Board, Imperial Chemical Industries and Imperial Airways. Granted a ten-year subsidy in 1924, Imperial Airways underwrote Britain's aviation industry, pioneered routes to India, South Africa and Australia and by 1938 was experimenting with both conventional and composite aircraft to achieve a non-stop North Atlantic service.[19] The prolonged economic pressures of the slump era, however, made its existence precarious. Symbolically, political proponents of financial orthodoxy were able to draw rhetorical mileage in the comparison between the state's nannying of aviation with Britain's historically buccaneering approach to sea trade. Imperial Airways' dilemma was neatly summarised by the *Daily Telegraph* aviation correspondent, Major C. C. Turner:

> Sir Alan Cobham once pertinently quoted the case of a railway in Malaya, which never paid its way and was never likely to pay its way, yet the whole prosperity of the Colony depended on that railway. To close down the railway would have meant universal ruin. The same is true, or at least will soon be true, of airways throughout the British Empire.[20]

In 1936 Paul Rotha's Strand Films was commissioned to produce a cycle of documentary films (including *Air Outpost*, 1937, *African Skyways*, 1940 and *The Future's in the Air*, 1937) to help secure Imperial's reputation.[21] This cycle of films Paul Rotha produced for Imperial Airways at Strand provides an example of how a kind of technocratic liberalism was able to weather the social, political and economic turbulence of the interwar period, as well as a demonstration of how closely nascent internationalism could be intertwined with imperialism.[22] Because no viable consumer market for aviation existed, the films were to sell the idea of aviation by creating a new type of national mythology, which wove the development of civil aviation into a story about Britain's relationship with the wider world. The underwriting of civil aviation was to be defended as an investment in the future of global civilisation. Made at a moment when technologies were becoming global, but politics seemingly ever more national, the cycle of films made by Strand Films for Imperial Airways can be used to exemplify the unpredictable ways in which imperial and internationalist concerns would converge as the prospect of war loomed closer.

The films were the brainchild of C. F. Snowden Gamble, who had been appointed advertising manager in 1931 in an effort to protect the firm from slump-era cuts and to stem a tide of negative publicity. As well as broadening out the idea of advertising

Imperial's film-makers. A six-month period flying the empire routes provided the basis for Strand's films

from the simple buying of newspaper adverts to the more sophisticated practice of public diplomacy, Gamble was to use the mass media as a vehicle for his techno-evangelism. To the frustration of his managers, Gamble unyieldingly propounded the belief (often expressed in the words of H. G. Wells) that aviation would enable the human race to go 'from strength to strength in an ever splendid widening "circle of adventure and achievement"'.[23] Donald Taylor recalled that Gamble's ambition was to utilise art, education and technology to enable a citizen to become 'a true democrat'.[24] Gamble spoke of developing a language appropriate to an emerging international mentality.[25]

Strand's lead film was to be *The Future's in the Air*, a big-budget four-reeler directed by Taylor with a script by Graham Greene and a score by William Alwyn that followed the progress of an Imperial plane flying from Southampton to Brisbane. Ostensibly made to mark the Post Office's launch of the 'all Empire mail by air mail' scheme, the film was intended to more broadly enthuse empire loyalists, workers in new hi-tech industries and schoolchildren, as well as to be screened to sceptical politicians and commercial audiences.

One of the most striking aspects of *The Future's in the Air* is its attempt to articulate how rapid technological progress had the potential to reshape global civilisation. By appropriating elements of modernist art and borrowing from contemporary imaginative writing – such as J. W. Dunne and Nevil Shute – Strand's film attempts to interpret the social, political and economic significance of aviation.[26] Naval strength had underpinned Britain's rise to global prominence, aviation promised to reconfigure Britain's place in the 'coming world economic unit of the future'. As an economic commentator perceptively put it at the time:

If air communications with passengers and mails develop as they seem likely to develop ... they will not permit any community to live and develop on its own, cut off from the rest of the world, no matter how inaccessible to land and sea transport it may be. Many will regard the prospect of this levelling process with disfavour ... . Certainly when the larger influences of the East are brought to bear more immediately upon Western civilisations, there will be interesting developments. It cannot be denied that the introduction of large-scale world-air transport systems must, in the end, tend to produce world homogeneity.[27]

Such insights run through the formal make-up of Imperial Airways films. For example, shortly after the opening titles of *The Future's in the Air* finish, we are introduced to 'one of the men who will fly this machine through space and time' as we observe the final stages of an Imperial Airways pilot's training. Dramatic landscapes are aurally juxtaposed with technical information as the narration is increasingly fragmented by sequences where the Imperial Airways plane is posited as a sort of teleporter: the plane is filmed dramatically flying out of cloud cover and over desert, jungle or mountainous territory before disappearing again. Reusing footage of Sharjah airfield from *Air Outpost*, *The Future's in the Air* draws our attention to how 'shoes from Bond Street tread the desert sand, shiny suitcases from Piccadilly reflect the glare of an Arabian sun'.

At a more metaphorical, imaginative level, the broad sweep of the Imperial Airways films invites comparison with the classic tropes of nineteenth-century colonial fiction. While the Conradian explorer journeyed inexorably deeper into humanity's evolutionary past as he trekked ever further into Africa, the interwar imperial narrative hopped by aeroplane between dimensions of the past, present and future in a manner befitting an intellectual age defined by Einstein. The understanding of world history owes as much to the interwar vogue for disjunctured historical narratives as the Whiggish tradition that supposedly underpinned the 'trusteeship' model of British imperialism.[28]

More prosaically, *The Future's in the Air* expresses a commonplace insight of the age – flying radically jumbles perceptions of space and time. Perhaps the most striking sequence in *The Future's in the Air* sees a succession of static shots of the tail fins, wings, nose and landing gears of an Imperial Airways plane intercut with details from the pyramids and hieroglyphics. 'Thou comest forth each day over heaven and earth, thou passest through the heights of heaven', the narration quotes from *The Book of the Dead*, 'thy heart hath decreed a day of happiness in the name of travel'. The sequence echoes a perception frequently expressed in aviation travelogues on the BBC:

Cairo seems to have everything. It's a miniature Paris, it's the gateway to the Orient, it's the capital city of one of the oldest civilisations in the world, its European, oriental, Arab, English and everything else rolled into one. Nowhere else except in Cairo would you see an expensive English car being towed home to its garage by a donkey with a policeman on a bicycle hanging on to the back.[29]

What makes the Imperial Airways films so interesting is that the documentarists not only recorded the impact of this travel on their concertinaed perceptions of space and time, but they were forced to try to build a new explanatory framework in which to express these insights. The film-makers found it impossible to simply drop simple and simplistic ideas of progress into the narrative of their films – a new epistemological framework was required.

Air Outpost (1937): imaginative visual equivalences between ancient civilisations and new technology are a staple of Strand's films

Internationalist modernist art and documentary cinema would prove crucial to thinking through the impact of aviation on empire. On the advice of Marcus Brumwell at Stuart's advertising agency, Gamble had turned Imperial into a major patron of modernist design. Thus, for example, Theyre Lee-Elliott developed a modernist corporate logo ('Speedbird'), which was then sculpted into concrete by Barbara Hepworth and used as the basis for a short psychedelic film by Len Lye.[30] The choice of modernist design reflected both its supposed 'internationalist' qualities, Brumwell's belief that advertising could work as an enlightened social mediator and the hope that aviation would play an important role in creating a harmonious human global civilisation.[31] Post-war, Brumwell controlled the advertising account of the International Civil Aviation Organisation (ICAO) and the similarities between the ICAO's later 'development' publicity and Imperial Airways' pioneering efforts are striking. He also became a prime mover in the 'Gaitskell Group' that recast the Labour Party (under Harold Wilson) in a more technocratic mould.[32]

Undeniably the development of European aviation was animated by both national and imperial competition, but aviation proved an intrinsically internationalist technology requiring pan-national legal, technical and organisational standards. During the interwar period, Imperial subsidised the establishment of Indian Trans-Continental Airlines and Quantas and an influential strand of liberal thought at the time further pressed for the creation of an international air police force. Imperial Airways' immediate legacy was pre-eminence in fields such as meteorology and radar, which helped enable Britain to fend off German air attacks during World War II (the offensive capabilities laboriously developed by the RAF, in contrast, proved ineffective until the very closing stages of the conflict).[33]

Civil aviation was a technology of diplomats and specialists rather than explorers and speculators. Imperial's films were laden with representations of social and technological interconnectedness, distributed through a range of associational organisations in a manner thought to encourage a moral and emotional sense of togetherness, and screened against an 'internationalist' backdrop that continually emphasised how aviation was reshaping global geography and that this physical reconfiguration had political consequences. The films do not celebrate Imperial Airways passengers (who are frequently mocked) but the humanitarian potential of aviation.[34]

•

Strand's film-makers spent six months on the empire routes shooting their films. With typical entrepreneurialism, Rotha attempted to sell the footage his film-makers collected as many times as possible. Thus alongside the films made for Imperial Airways, Strand produced *Five Faces of Malaya* (1938) (for the Malayan government) and *Dawn over Iran* (1938) (for Anglo-Iranian Oil). These films are shot through with a peculiar vision of liberal imperialism. The focus of these films is not on empire as a motor of progress, but the ways in which modern administrative, commercial and technological apparatus can co-exist with an array of local customs and cultural and political structures. If the Imperial Airways films provide a 'big picture' understanding of the impact of contemporary social, economic and technological change, these spin-off films afford a close-up picture of how new technologies were changing the everyday experience of empire.

Five Faces of Malaya filters the *Weltanschauung* of the Imperial Airways films in a particularly interesting way. Alexander Shaw's film argues that Malaya is five nations in one – a nation of Malays, Sakai, Indians, Chinese and Europeans. Each of these 'nations' is furthermore associated with a different way of life. For example, Tamils are associated with the development of Malaya's rubber industry, the Chinese with the expansion of tin mining and the British with playing golf. Many historians of Malaya would understand *Five Faces* as an exemplar of the 'ethnic division of labour': discrete ethnic identities in counterpoise with each other, each with their own specialisation of labour. Writing from his interwar experience of Malaya, J. S. Furnivall criticised this development as a byproduct of Britain's cynical approach to colonial administration:

> Everywhere a native social order, with the plural features characteristic of a society based on personal relations, has been converted into a definitely plural society, with three or more component sections, living side by side but separately, and with no common social life.[35]

Building on these insights, it has been argued that, to put it crudely, such racial 'divide and rule' was a consistent and intentional consequence of colonial government.[36] This is an argument that has since been challenged – for example, it has been argued that the hardening and politicisation of this racial plurality actually occurred in Malaya's transition to independence – but in any case these discussions are too polarised to shed much light on a reading of a film as subtle as *Five Faces of Malaya*.[37]

More to the point, the film's explicit propagandist purpose was to encourage the unification, rather than entrenchment, of Malay society. Demand for Malaya's rubber and tin had been reduced by the Great Depression, and Malaya's ethnic mix was further disturbed by the rise of Chinese and Indian nationalism. After a militaristic Japan attacked China, uniting Malays with Hindus, Muslims, Buddhists and Confucians became an ever more urgent matter of territorial security. *Five Faces of Malaya* was thus part of the Colonial Office's project of 'Malayisation', an attempt to build a coherent national identity flexible enough to fit the variegated politics of the federated states.

The *Future's in the Air* (1937): the imagery of the Imperial Airways films borrows from Empire travelogues and Soviet cinema

The propagandist brief meshed with Shaw's own experience.[38] His film may have been shaped by the concerns of colonial administrators, but Shaw did not believe that the film's political function undermined its authenticity or its sincerity. 'Five races, five creeds – and oddly enough they all get on fairly well', he wrote to Paul Rotha,

> after all the nonsense one has heard about the British Empire at least one can say that if there are going to be Empires, Malaya would serve as a pretty good model for how they should be run – although of course I have collected a few really good "damn the wog" incidents.[39]

There is also some evidence that Shaw befriended the anthropologist H. D. Noone during his visit.[40] The contrast between the interest taken by Shaw and the 'expertise' of a London-based anthropologist who wrote a feature on *Five Faces* for the film magazine *World Film News* is telling. 'Beautiful people these and worth a whole film to themselves', writes the unnamed doctor, 'Let the other chap worry about new roads, new railways, telephones and sewers – amused and tolerant and non-cooperating. The Malay's only clock is the sun and he is generally late on that.'[41]

Thus alongside a certain amount of archness (Tamils are associated with the rubber industry, the British with *golf*), it is important to recognise that *Five Faces* was intended to express genuine idealism. A key characteristic of the film is the speculative connections it makes between different historical periods, peoples and professions. These connections offer a way of inserting unexpected disjunctures into the film's standard voice-of-God commentary and serve to pique the viewers' curiosity.

As the film progresses, the surprising correlations between Malaya's five apparently separate 'faces' congeal into a filmic worldview. One of the reverently filmed sultans turns out to be an Oxford-educated lawyer. Traditional dress is eventually shown to coexist with modern fashion. Electrical pylons are interspersed with distinctive native trees. A traditional Malayan wedding meal is shown to blend together a collection of spices and food items that tell the story of Malaya's development.

The important point is that *Five Faces of Malaya* offers viewers an anthropological imagining of empire. Thus, even when *Five Faces*' argument is tinged with a residue of racial hierarchy, as when the narration describes the Sakai as 'indolent and optimistic', it is the British that the film *shows* idly sitting around. Ultimately, the Malayan story of multiple races, customs and professions is presented as a series of equivalences and the colonial classes' extravagant tea-drinking becomes as valid (or ridiculous) as the people who dwell in mangrove swamps. *Five Faces of Malaya* deals in relativism rather than universalism. Here the film both reflected the relatively high status government then accorded anthropology and a wider intellectual trend that saw anthropological apparatus that had previously been focused on 'simple', 'primitive' cultures being brought to bear on the 'complex', 'developed' societies of the West.[42] Crucial to understanding Shaw's film, and much of the British documentary movement's work, is recognising its exploratory nature. Grierson had trained as a social scientist and the films of his movement often work as enacted theses – they operate like the best guesses of a participant observer rather than the premeditated effort of the cinematic propagandist.

Artistically, of course, the mode of representation evident in *Five Faces of Malaya* fits into a broader modernistic context. When the film was made, dealers and critics such as Roger Fry, Oscar Raphael and Sydney Burney were collecting, selling and exhibiting tribal art from China, Malaya and Indonesia (as well as Africa and South America) while artists such as Jacob Epstein were self-consciously drawing on 'primitive' non-Western art. *Five Faces'* principal cinematic source, however, is the Empire Marketing Board's *The Song of Ceylon*. An aggregative modernist bricolage of ancient rituals and modern communications, *The Song of Ceylon* ambitiously attempted to do for the cultural and commercial relations of the British Commonwealth what Walter Ruttman had done for Berlin and Dziga Vertov had done for Moscow. *Ceylon*, like *Five Faces*, was both respectful of the indigenous culture it filmed and alive to the satirical opportunities offered by sharp cutting between 'primitive' rituals and the obsequious workings of British commerce.[43]

The relationship between the films produced by Rotha for Imperial Airways and the cinematic idiom established at the Empire Marketing Board seems clear. In the same way that films such as *Industrial Britain* (1933) sought to bind together the classes, regions and industries of interwar Britain, the Imperial Airways films attempted to imaginatively encompass the empire. In the same ways that the documentary films of the 1930s can be seen to prepare the way for home-front solidarity during the war, the colonial films anticipate the 'the people's Empire' sentiment of World War II propaganda as delineated by Wendy Webster.[44]

Indeed, the Imperial Airways documentaries, with their images of African mechanics and Arab meteorologists, favour the cosmopolitan global citizen over the desires of the privileged passengers. We can see Imperial's pictoral idealism influencing post-war bodies such as the ICAO ('An Indonesian pilot is flying a British aircraft into a Ceylonese airfield', as one ICAO pamphlet put it, 'on a French landing aid manned by a Greek'[45]) as well as the Shell Film Unit. Stuart Legg's *Song of the Clouds* (1956), for example, which promoted the work of the International Air Transport Association, was distributed by bodies such as the World Health Organisation. By moving beyond picturesque cinematic travelogues of empire, the British documentary movement's films illustrate how old ideas of imperialism were stretched towards new conceptions of internationalism. Beyond this it might even be possible to see Grierson's appointment as Director of Mass Communications and Public Information at UNESCO as marking the philosophical end point of the Empire Marketing Board film unit's aims. 'Its principal effect (was) to change the connotations of the word "Empire"', Grierson later reflected of his work at the board, 'our original command of peoples was becoming slowly a co-operative effort in the tilling of soil, the reaping of harvest, and the organisation of a world economy'.[46] We do not need to accept such self-aggrandisement in full to recognise the continuity of thought and the direct aesthetic, social and political lineage.

NOTES

This article could not have been written without the assistance of Paul Jarvis and Jim Davies at the British Airways Archive, Mark Duguid at the BFI, Sue Breakell at the Tate and Simon Elliott at the University of California, Los Angeles. Many thanks also to Tim Boon, Marc Matera, Martin Stollery and Lee Grieveson for their advice and suggestions.

1. Ashish Rajadhyaksha, 'Colonial Film Policy in India after the 1925 Imperial Conference', presentation to Colonial Film: Moving Images of the British Empire conference, Birkbeck College, London, 7 July 2010.
2. Brian Winston, *Claiming the Real: The Documentary Film Revisited* (London: BFI, 1995), p. 60.
3. Basil Wright would acclaim Harry Watt's Australian Western, *The Overlanders*, as the true heir of EMB idealism. The 'sweep, range and essential humanity' of Watt's tale of ranchers in the Outback proved, 'that there are more Commonwealth nations stories able to fire people's imagination than Hollywood ever imagined'. See Basil Wright, 'The Cinema', *Spectator* vol. 177 no. 6172 (11 October 1946), p. 364.
4. See Ross McKibbin, *Classes and Cultures: England 1918–1951* (Oxford: OUP, 1998; 2000).
5. A definitive exploration of the filming of Wright's Ceylonese films can be found in J. Hoare, '"Go the Way the Material Calls You": Basil Wright and *The Song of Ceylon*', in Scott Anthony and James Mansell (eds), *The Projection of Britain: A Complete History of the GPO Film Unit* (London: BFI, 2011).
6. This seems to stem from an unspoken assumption that art must serve morally improving ends and that film art, as a new democratic form of art, is predisposed to be progressive. This is an argument that has been forcibly refuted in John Carey, *What Good Are the Arts?* (London: Faber, 2005).
7. See Susan Pedersen's recent work on the mandate system such as 'Metaphors of the Schoolroom: Women Working the Mandates System of the League of Nations', *History Workshop Journal* vol. 66 no. 1 (2008), pp. 188–207.
8. An argument made in Bernard Porter, *The Absent-minded Imperialists: Empire, Society and Culture in Britain* (Oxford: OUP, 2004).
9. See Arthur Marwick, 'Middle Opinion in the Thirties: Planning, Progress and Political "Agreement"', *English Historical Review* vol. LXXIX no. CCCXI (1964), pp. 285–98.
10. See L. Lees, 'Colonial Towns as Middle Grounds: British Malaya, 1874–1920' (unpublished paper, University of Pennsylvania, 2005); and Robert Young, *Colonial Desires: Hybridity in Theory, Culture and Race* (London: Routledge, 1995); Richard Price, '"One Big Thing":

Britain, Its Empire and Their Imperial Culture', *Journal of British Studies* vol. 35 no. 3 (July 2006), pp. 602–27.

11. For examinations of the use made of empire in domestic British politics, see Dane Kennedy, *Britain and Empire, 1880–1945* (London: Longman, 2002) and Andrew Thompson, *Imperial Britain: The Empire in British Politics, 1880–1932* (London: Longman, 2000).

12. Stephen Tallents, *The Projection of England* (London: Faber, 1932), p. 31–2.

13. National Archives, CO 758/89/3, 'A Private Demonstration of Economic Propaganda Films', 24 October 1930.

14. See J. M. Powell, 'The Empire Mmeets the New Deal', *Geographical Research: Journal of the Institute of Australian Geographers* vol. 43 no. 4 (December 2005), pp. 337–60. The EMB's work would also inform the drafting of the Colonial Development Act of 1929; see Stephen Constantine, *The Making of British Colonial Development Policy, 1914–1940* (London: Routledge, 1984) and William Louis, *In the Name of God Go!: Leo Amery and the British Empire in the Age of Churchill* (London: W. W. Norton, 1992).

15. A point borne out by the fact that Amery's enthusiasm for funding ambitious imperial development schemes in the midst of the slump earned him the nickname the 'Mad Mullah'. See Corelli Barnett, *The Collapse of British Power* (London: Pan, 1972), p. 129.

16. See 'Introduction', in Kevin Grant, Philippa Levine and Frank Trentmann (eds), *Beyond Sovereignty: Britain, Empire and Transnationalism, c.1880–1950* (New York: Palgrave, 2007).

17. John Taylor: BECTU Interview Part 2, <www.screenonline.org.uk/audio/id/945640/>. For more on Tallents, see Scott Anthony, *Public Relations and the Making of Modern Britain: Stephen Tallents and the Birth of a Progressive Media Profession* (Manchester: MUP, 2011) and Stephen Constantine, 'Tallents, Sir Stephen George (1884–1958)', *Oxford Dictionary of National Biography*, Oxford: Oxford University Press, September 2004; online edn, October 2008 <www.oxforddnb.com/view/article/36412>.

18. See Keith Middlemass, *Politics in Industrial Society: The Experience of the British System since 1911* (London: André Deutsch, 1979).

19. The Mayo composite aircraft that began crossing the Atlantic in 1938 saw a large plane take off carrying a smaller one 'piggy back'. The experiment was prompted by the commercial need to better balance space allocated to fuel, mail and passengers. See Charles Gibbs-Smith, *Aviation: An Historical Survey from Its Origins to the End of World War II* (London: Stationery Office, 1970) and A. S. Jackson, *Imperial Airways and the First British Airlines 1919–1940* (Lavenham: Terence Dalton, 1995).

20. National Archives, INF17/51, 'The Supply of Films to the Empire Film Library by Messrs Imperial Airways', *Imperial Airways Gazette*, C. C. Turner, 'As Others See Us', p. 7.

21. These films built on Rotha's earlier work for Imperial such as *Contact* (1933). See Tim Boon, *Films of Fact: A History of Science in Documentary Films and Television* (London: Wallflower Press, 2008) and Martin Stollery, *Alternative Empires: European Modernist Cinemas and the Culture of Imperialism* (Exeter: University of Exeter Press, 2000).

22. Many of the EMB's collaborators would become involved in the post-war establishment of internationalist organisations. See Mark Mazower, *No Enchanted Palace: The End of Empire and the Ideological Origins of the United Nations* (Princeton, NJ: Princeton University Press, 2009) and Frank Trentmann, 'After the Nation State: Citizenship, Empire and Global Coordination in the New Internationalism, 1914–1930', in Grant *et al.*, *Beyond Sovereignty*, pp. 34–53.

23. BA Archive, 'Premier of New Films about Imperial Airways', *Imperial Airways Gazette* vol. 9 no. 12 (1937).

24. Donald Taylor, 'Official Publicity', *The Times*, 18 April 1944, p. 5.

25. BA Archive, 'The Man Who Had Designs on an Airline,' *BOAC News*, 24 November 1972.

26. Dunne was a visionary writer who argued (in books such as *An Experiment with Time*) that time was not linear, a discovery which led him to question accepted models of epistemology and posit an esoteric understanding of causality. His ideas were widely disseminated, most famously in the 'time-travelling' plays of the popular playwright J. B. Priestley. See John Baxendale, *Priestley's England: J. B. Priestley and English Culture* (Manchester: MUP, 2007).

27. Oliver Stewart, 'Air Communications and the Far East', *Pacific Affairs* vol. 8 no. 3 (September 1935), p. 351.

28. See Richard Overy, *The Morbid Age: Britain and the Crisis of Civilisation, 1919–1939* (London: Penguin, 2009).

29. BBC Broadcast, John Day Wentworth, 'Flight over Egypt', *BBC Radio*, 10 August 1938.

30. The Len Lye film can be viewed online. See <www.youtube.com/watch?v=MzcwxFxsXUM>.

31. See J. Brumwell, *Bright Ties Bold Ideas. Marcus Brumwell Pioneer of 20th Century Advertising, Champions of the Artists* (Truro: Tie Press, 2010) and Tate Archive, Brumwell papers, J. R. M. Brumwell, 'The Decline of Art in Advertising?,' *Penrose Annual* vol. 47 (1953), p. 40.

32. See Guy Ortolano, *The Two Cultures Controversy: Science, Literature and Cultural Politics in Postwar Britain* (Cambridge: CUP, 2009).

33. Richard Overy, 'Air Power in the Second World War: A War Winner?', Lecture delivered at the University of Cambridge, 3 November 2010.

34. 'Sometimes a passenger may show what seems to be childlike ignorance about flying (but) we must never look, or even feel, surprised or superior', pleaded one of Brumwell's staff pamphlets, 'It is unkind and anyway he may be the greatest living authority on some subject of which we are all very ignorant.' See Tate Archive, Brumwell papers, Box 17, *The Public and Ourselves* (1938), p. 5.

35. John S. Furnivall, *Progress and Welfare in Southeast Asia: A Comparison of Colonial Policy and Practice* (New York: Institute of Pacific Relations, 1941), p. 61.

36. See Maurice Freedman, 'The Growth of Plural Society in Malaya', *Pacific Affairs* vol. 33 no. 2 (1960), pp. 158–68; Lim Teck Ghee, 'British Colonial Administration and the "Ethnic Division of Labour" in Malaya', *Kajian Malaysia* vol. 1 no. 2 (1984), pp. 28–36.

37. For example, it is now thought unlikely that the colonial state actually had the power to enforce this rigid 'ethnic division of labour'. Increasingly, interest has focused on the importance of economic choice and the ways in which the administrative assumptions of the British colonial administration were challenged. See Tim Harper, *The End of Empire and the Making of Malaya* (New York: Cambridge University Press, 1998) and Mahathir bin Mohamad, *The Malay Dilemma* (Singapore: Donald Moore for the Asia Pacific Press, 1970).

38. Shaw's understanding of the workings of interwar Malaya are of a kind increasingly now coming into intellectual fashion. The impact of the slump in Malaya, it is now asserted, encouraged both economic diversification and intercommunal consciousness. Although the slump impinged on the personal aspirations and material wealth of Europeans and colonial administrators, the cultural and educational gap between Asians and Europeans closed, and this in turn laid the foundations for political, social and economic change. See Christopher Baker, 'Economic Reorganisation and the Slump in South and Southeast Asia', *CSSH* vol. 18 no. 3 (1981), pp. 325–49; Lok Kok Wah, 'From Tin Mines Coolies to Agricultural Squatters:

Socio-economic Change in the Kinta District during the Inter-war Years', in Peter Rimmer and Lisa Allen (eds), *The Underside of Malaysian History: Pullers, Prostitutes and Plantation Workers* (Singapore: Coronet, 1990), pp. 72–96; J. N. Brownfoot, 'Sisters under the Skin: Imperialism and the Emancipation of Women in Malaya, c.1891–1941', in J. A. Mangen (ed.), *Making Imperial Mentalities: Socialization and British Imperialism* (Manchester: MUP, 1990), pp. 46–73. On the slump-era struggles of European settlers in Malaya, see Virginia Thompson, *Postmortem on Malaya* (New York: Macmillan, 1943).

39. UCLA, Paul Rotha papers, 'Shaw to Rotha', 18 February 1937.

40. Noone was a maverick anthropologist who disappeared into the jungle. He later worked for the British intelligence services. See Dennis Holman, *Noone of the Ulu* (Oxford: OUP, 1958), Richard Noone, *Rape of the Dream People* (London: Hutchinson, 1972) and Christopher Bayley and Tim Harper, *Forgotten Armies: The Fall of British Asia, 1941–45* (London: Allen Lane, 2004).

41. 'Five Faces', *World Film News* vol. 3 no. 2 (May/June 1938), p. 55.

42. This is a formulation borrowed from Peter Mandler. See Peter Mandler, 'The Idea of Intercultural Relations from the 1920s to the 1950s', presentation to 'We the Peoples: Democratising International Relations in Britain and Beyond, 1870–1950' workshop, St John's College, Cambridge, 9 January 2010.

43. On its release, Graham Greene had praised Basil Wright's film for its intellectual sweep and cultural sensitivity. See Graham Greene, *Mornings in the Dark* (London: Penguin, 1995), p. 93.

44. Wendy Webster, *Englishness and Empire, 1939–1965* (Oxford: OUP, 2005), pp. 68–91.

45. Tate Archive, Brumwell papers, *10 Years of Postwar International Civil Aviation* (1955).

46. John Grierson, 'The EMB Film Unit', in Forsyth Hardy (ed.), *Grierson on Documentary* (London: Collins, 1946), pp. 48–9.

COLONIALISM AND THE REPRESENTATION OF SPACE

•

8

Representing Connection: A Multimedia Approach to Colonial Film, 1918–39

David Trotter

The aim of this paper is to build on the premises established by Lee Grieveson in his illuminating account of the mutual reinforcement and mutual reconfiguration of the British film industry and the British imperial project between 1926 and 1933.[1] These premises are that: a) during the 1920s a new paradigm of empire took shape in Britain, with the emphasis on the gradual formation of a global economic bloc of self-governing nation-states, an emphasis enshrined as the British Commonwealth by the Statute of Westminster in 1931; b) this new paradigm posed, for British capitalism, and for the (mostly Conservative or Conservative-led) British governments of the period, a problem of representation, or, if you prefer, propaganda; and c) from 1926, British cinema had an important part to play in solving this problem, under the auspices of the Empire Marketing Board (EMB) and other organisations, and underwent in the process a fundamental alteration, both formally, as a result of the emergence of documentary as a hallmark or signature genre, and institutionally, by means of the development of a range of non-theatrical distribution networks. My aim is at once to narrow the focus of the argument, by concentrating on images of Ceylon, a Crown colony until 1948; and to broaden it, by approaching cinema as one of several media, some visual, some not, each to a significant degree given over, during the period between the World Wars, to promotion of the imperial project.

Grieveson describes British documentary cinema as an instrument of capitalist imperialism: that 'contradictory fusion', as David Harvey has put it, of two logics of power, one concerned primarily with command over and use of capital, the other primarily with command over and use of the human and natural resources specific to a territory or territories.[2] The purpose of the EMB's extensive investment in film was to enable both domestic and colonial audiences to bear witness to the circulation of raw materials and manufactured goods that constituted the Commonwealth's common wealth. Grieveson takes as his main example *West Africa Calling* (1927), which demonstrates the capacity of British capital and technology to convert African swamp and desert into factory, hospital and school. 'It is in these images', he argues, 'and the connections made between them through editing, that the film effects a visual corollary to the pathways that connect imperial economics, to the hidden movements of capital that escape imagining but underpin so much of the colonial archive.' In EMB films, images of 'material connection, emphasised through the connective tissue of editing, are central to the vision of the Conservative political economy that positions empire developments and markets as central to the sustenance of the wealth of the nation'.[3] Representing material connection was a task enthusiastically undertaken by the two films I will discuss here: Basil Wright's *The Song of Ceylon*, and a British Pathé newsreel, *The Ceylon Tea Industry* (both 1934).

The connective pathways presented on screen in films like *West Africa Calling* and *The Ceylon Tea Industry* were the product of the 'round after round of time-space compression', which have by Harvey's account remorselessly driven the 'evolution of the geographical landscape of capitalist activity'.[4] The concept of time-space compression, originating in Marxism, indeed in Marx himself, but currently put to a variety of uses, can be taken to encompass the ways in which human societies have sought to convert distance into durations of shorter and shorter span with a view to the efficient and profitable exchange of goods and information. According to Barney Warf, time-space compression constitutes a 'mechanism' for the production of 'places' as 'nodes within increasingly wider networks of mobility and power'.[5] By 1930, there was a general understanding that the most recent round of time-space compression involved technological advances in aviation and in wireless telegraphy and telephony. Films about the global movement of raw materials by train, truck and ship have to be seen in the context of the pre-eminence then attributed in fact and fantasy to air routes and telecommunications networks. Telecommunication had already become, and still remains, capitalism's essential lubricant.[6] To put it another way, the media that substantially remade empire in their own image during the period between the World Wars were the new media of wireless telegraphy and telephony, not the old medium of film. But radio signals do not 'have' an image. So efficient are they in making connections, by the compression of distance into instantaneity, that there is nothing left to represent, nothing that requires representation. We could not see the message moving even if we wished to. However, such almost absolute time-space compression did not render cinema redundant. The job of the representational media, including cinema, was to render palpable once again a connectivity that had become at once more necessary than ever before and more abstract.

REPRESENTING CONNECTION: NEWSPRINT AND OTHER MEDIA

Connection had long been understood as the key to that enhancement of the mere occupation of territory thought most likely to consolidate Great Britain's commercial and military power in an increasingly competitive world. The British government invested heavily in an 'all-red' global submarine cable network connecting the centre of empire to its most far-flung peripheries. By 1902, British capitalism controlled most of the world's major commercial cables, while the government had at its disposal a secure means of communication with all strategically significant colonial territories and naval bases.[7] That network played no small part in the defeat of Germany in World War I. What really put the cat among the cable-laying pigeons, however, was the invention of radio.

Guglielmo Marconi's first experiments in the new medium, in the 1890s, had shown that radio waves curve around obstacles, including the earth's surface, and that the distance they travel is proportional to their length and to the strength of the transmitter. During the period up to and beyond World War I, the great powers and even greater corporations sought continually to outdo each other in the field of long-wave radio transmission. Before the war, the world's most powerful transmitter was located at Nauen, near Berlin; after it, at Sainte-Assise, near Paris. In the 1920s, the Post Office built a super-station at Rugby capable of reaching Australia or the entire Royal Navy at once, submarines included. It had twelve towers, each 250 metres high, supporting an antenna which covered ten square kilometres. Although radio was by now essential to shipping, it remained an adjunct to cable-borne telegraphy in long-distance communication. Cables, though more costly, were more reliable, and more secure. But the demand for communications grew so fast after the end of the war that both cable and wireless companies had as much business as they could handle.[8] The connections to be represented were those made possible by a new medium (wireless telegraphy) in competition with an old one (cable telegraphy); and by a surge of investment in a new mode of transport, the aeroplane, which could itself be conceived, as we shall see, as in some sense a medium.

On 3 February 1920, *The Times* reported that Major-General Sir F. H. Sykes, Controller General of Civil Aviation, had given a lecture on the topic of imperial air routes at the Royal Geographical Society to an audience including the Prince of Wales and a generous selection of dignitaries. Sykes's theme was that the British Empire would henceforth be sustained by air rather than sea power, and by the development of telecommunication technologies. The empire, he said, possessed a unique capacity to establish 'air depôts, refuelling bases, and meteorological and wireless stations in every part of the world'. This network of depots and stations had already taken shape in his mind. 'Egypt', he went on, 'for some time to come must be the "hub" or, as I have long called it, the Clapham Junction of the India, Australia, and Cape routes, and the heart of the whole system of their expansion.' Winston Churchill responded on behalf of the Air Ministry, arguing that the impulse given to aviation by war should be maintained during peace.[9] Sykes's lecture provided a template for the representation of empire as connectivity. But how was such a system to be established?

The Times took up the cause of time-space compression. Distance, a leading article announced,

is the chief barrier between the scattered British peoples. But geographical distance should be measured not by the absolute standard of mileage on sea or land, but by mileage divided by the time taken to traverse it. Theoretically the time-mile is now a fraction of a second for aeroplanes, approximately a minute for airships and railway trains, under ninety seconds for light road-transport, and from two to ten minutes for various forms of sea transport.

The smooth and secure functioning of empire required 'the quickest transport and the most nearly instantaneous wireless and cable communication'.[10] *The Times* had for some time been doing rather more than merely report government initiatives to reinforce or recreate empire through connection. Its proprietor, Alfred Harmsworth, Lord Northcliffe, was at once a staunch imperialist and the chief exponent of the serialised photographic encyclopedia. The ambition of the Northcliffe press was, as Michael North has put it, 'to construct an empire of information at least as extensive as the British Empire itself'.[11] On 4 February 1920, the day after it had reported Sykes's speech about imperial air routes, *The Times* published the map of the route to be taken by an air expedition it had itself funded to blaze a trail the length of Africa from Cairo to the Cape: landing grounds, emergency landing grounds, wireless stations.[12] The flight was undertaken by Alan Cobham, a World War I fighter-ace hitherto reduced to providing joy-rides at airshows. *The Times* charted his progress from Cairo to the Cape assiduously. In 1921, Cobham joined the De Haviland Aircraft Company. He made the trail-blazing spectacular his business. Indeed, he made time-space compression his business. Speaking at a luncheon given in his honour by the British Empire League in May 1925, he argued for more and better imperial air routes. 'By aviation could be effected the quick passage of letters and individuals and acceleration of business. Life could only be judged in measures of time.'[13]

The maps accompanying and promoting the flights undertaken by Cobham and others represent empire as connection. By the 1920s, Michael Heffernan observes, news media were no longer content merely to describe or picture remote colonial territories. They also became engaged in 'actively constructing' the idea and reality of empire as 'an integrated space of flows, an abstract concept made real by the telegraph, radio, and aviation networks through which news items circulated between the imperial periphery and the metropolitan core'.[14] The newspaper map represents connection as contiguity: as a chain of depots, bases and stations. The best way to conceive empire's 'integrated space of flows' – that 'abstract concept' – was to pin it to the earth's surface. Addressing the imperial conference in October 1926, Sir Samuel Hoare, Secretary of State for Air, announced that he and his wife were soon to attempt the new Cairo-to-Karachi route. The next step, he thought, should be an extension to Bombay and Calcutta. And how about Rangoon? 'If, in the not remote future, links can be inserted in some such way as I have suggested, a long chain of great tensile power will have been forged across the Empire's framework.'[15] Hoare's remarks indicate not just that political and economic connection could be imagined concretely, but that concreteness itself had taken on an important political and economic function. Empire's integrated space of flows would only ever be fully known as a paradigm of global integration if and when it became fully contiguous throughout that space, fully tensile: one link clasping, flexed against, the next.

Contiguity proved a tall order, but not an impossible one. Imperial Airways, established by multiple merger in 1924 with a working capital of £1 million, two government-appointed directors on a board of ten, and the promise of £1 million of subsidies over the next ten years, took on the task of developing the major empire routes. Regular passenger services from Croydon Airport reached Delhi in 1929, Cape Town in 1932, Brisbane in 1934 and Hong Kong in 1936.[16] 'A single operating company, partly financed by the British government, has the job,' as the American magazine *Popular Mechanics* put it, 'of linking together an empire that compasses the globe and includes more than 350,000 people.' There was even the possibility of a 'globe-circling airway, 20,000 miles long', operated in conjunction with Pan-American's Pacific line: English the only language spoken throughout.[17] Imperial Airways posters of the 1930s show an inverted Y with its base in London and its stem forking at Cairo: in one direction, the route stretches down through Entebbe, Nairobi and Salisbury (Harare) to Johannesburg and Cape Town; in the other, across to Baghdad, Basra, Karachi and Delhi, and then down to Rangoon, Bangkok, Singapore

Air Post (1934)

and beyond. Cairo, Sykes's Clapham Junction, was regarded as the key link in the chain. Rather, the idea of Egypt, or of 'the Egyptian', overwhelmingly familiar in Britain since Howard Carter had reopened King Tutankhamen's tomb on 29 November 1922, anchored a whole way of thinking about connection – about empire as an integrated space of flows. In one of the most evocative of all the Imperial Airways posters, an airliner approaches a pair of sharply etched pyramids from the general direction of Karachi (snow-capped peaks) by way of Baghdad (minarets). These destinations had to be held within a single glance if the territories they occupied were to be understood as newly contiguous. Martin Stollery notes that the promotional films made by Strand for Imperial Airways in the late 1930s often include planes over pyramids: the ancient engineering feat now viewed afresh in all its grandeur courtesy of a modern one.[18]

   Passengers alone were not enough to establish contiguity. There were simply not enough of them. From the outset, civil aviation had required subsidy. Postal services soon became instrumental in its growth, offering lucrative contracts to private carriers between selected cities. In Nevil Shute's *So Disdained* (1928), a veteran pilot recalls the early days of the London–Paris flights.

> We carried the much advertised Air Mails. That meant the machines had to fly whether there were passengers to be carried or not. It was left to the discretion of the pilot whether or not the flight should be cancelled in bad weather; the pilots were dead keen on flying in the most impossible conditions. Sanderson got killed this way at Douainville. And all he had in the machine was a couple of picture postcards from trippers in Paris, sent to their families as a curiosity. That was the Air Mail. No passengers or anything – just the mail.[19]

The Air Mail became at once agent and emblem of connectivity. On the one hand, it greatly reduced the amount of time monetary orders spent in the mails, thus accelerating capital's invisible flow;[20] on the other, it was easy to visualise as a series of linked physical actions (publicity material often features the transfer of a bulging mailbag from van or launch to plane). A British Pathé newsreel of 1932 reports that the thirty-eight-seat liner inaugurating the weekly London-to-Cape Town service would accommodate no more than three passengers on this occasion in order to leave room for an 'enormous quantity of mail'.

Air Mail was a chain of events anyone could initiate simply by placing a letter in a letterbox. During the 1930s, Imperial Airways rebranded itself in spectacular fashion by securing a contract to carry *all* the British Empire's mail at a flat rate of a penny halfpenny per half ounce. The Empire Mail Scheme, launched on 29 June 1937, made use of a fleet of twenty-eight gleaming modernist flying-boats which became the company's best advertisement. To be sure, they carried more passengers in even greater luxury. But their *raison d'être* was to deliver packets of information rapidly and reliably. The Empire Mail Scheme didn't just represent connection. It converted a particular mode of transport into a telecommunications medium. That said, we shouldn't necessarily assume that air travel created a 'discontinuous geography of collected rather than connected points'.[21] There was nothing at all impalpable about the links forming the empire mail chain. The British Pathé newsreel announcing the scheme's first return flight from Australia shows the boat's captain not in the cockpit, but in a launch headed out into the harbour, mailbag in hand.

Palpability was a quality not easy to associate with the new media of wireless telegraphy and telephony, which set about compressing time-space during the 1920s, as a supplement to, or in competition with, cable. In 1921, *The Times* could still envisage a 'chain' or girdle of stations 'connecting the communities of the empire by geographical steps of about 2,000 miles each'.[22] The long-wave station built at Rugby had physical presence enough and to spare. However, Marconi and his research engineers had been working with bandwidths under 200 metres. They knew that radio waves could be intensified by reflection; and that, because the reflector had to be proportional in size to the square of the wavelength, the method would only work for short-wave radio. Using a parabolic reflector made of wire, they were able to direct much of the transmitter's energy towards a receiver equipped with a parabolic antenna. In May 1924, Marconi announced that messages transmitted from Cornwall using his 'beam' system had been received by engineers in Australia, India, South Africa and North and South America. Short-wave radio was a great deal cheaper than long-wave, and it transmitted at up to 200 words per minute, faster than long-wave, faster even than cable. The British government signed a contract with Marconi to build short-wave stations in Canada, Australia, South Africa and India. These stations were owned and operated by the Post Office. The BBC's Empire Service began broadcasting on short wave on 19 December 1932.[23] 'The most striking development of all the electrical arts during the last quarter of a century', declared Edward Appleton, Wheatstone Professor of Physics at London University,

> has undoubtedly been the advance in radio-communication. Such development has been much more than the registration of purely technical improvements, for wireless, by way of broadcasting, has introduced a new medium of cultural and political enlightenment in our social life and, by way of the overseas wireless telephone, has brought the parts of the Empire into closer and more intimate touch than ever before.

Progress in the development of high-definition television, Appleton continued, meant that the BBC would before too long be in a position to inaugurate a London service operating on ultra-short waves.[24]

For a variety of reasons, commercial, political and technical, short-wave radio did not simply displace long wave, any more than wireless transmission displaced transmission by submarine cable.[25] In fact, an Imperial Wireless and Cable Conference held in January 1927 recommended the merger of all British communications interests. The plan was approved by parliament in August 1928. In April 1929, the new conglomerate, Imperial and International Communications, assumed control over 253 cable and radio stations, and more than half the world's cables. Each point on the network was now linked to all the others by at least two separate channels of communication. Cable and Wireless, as it was from 1934, had become as monumental a 'pillar' of empire as Imperial Airways.[26]

Short waves do not curve around the earth's surface. Instead, they bounce off the upper layers of the atmosphere, reappearing far from their origin by means of a 'skip' effect. They make it hard to imagine contiguity as a principle of connection. This is one data flow which cannot be mapped without interruption from point to point across a network. Short-wave radio exemplified the dilemma confronting representational media from the mid-1920s onwards. Representing connectivity had just got a lot harder. Maps of the period that display the imperial cable and wireless network tend to show radio beams curving delicately around the earth's surface to their remote destinations as though the transmitters were all long wave. There could be continuity in fantasy – in representation – where there was now none in fact. It may be significant that Appleton's *Times* article on developments in short-wave radio, which has nothing at all to say about transport, should none the less include a large photograph of different kinds of aircraft on the tarmac at Croydon. A range of visual images was still necessary.

What of Ceylon, in all this? Ceylon became something of a representational crux for capitalist imperialism, because while the island was an important and venerable Crown colony, and indeed one sometimes still held up as a model of annexation, it remained for much of the period on the periphery of the new imperial networks.[27] Speaking at Norwich in October 1925, Sir Samuel Hoare argued that for political, strategic and commercial purposes, 'flying lines' should be driven as rapidly and as extensively as possible across the empire. All around the world there were British territories or spheres of influence 'which at almost regular intervals could be used as landing grounds or links in the great Empire air chain'. There was no technical reason, Hoare concluded,

> why Bombay should not be brought within four days of London instead of 14, why Calcutta and Colombo should not be reached in six or seven days instead of 16 or 17, why Singapore should not be reached in eight days rather than 24, and Melbourne in 13 instead of 32.[28]

It was to be some time, however, before Colombo could claim a status equal to those other cities. On 15 December 1927, *The Times* reported the imminent departure of two RAF officers who planned to undertake a 'propaganda flight and reconnaissance of air transport prospects' in India, Burma and the Federated Malay States. They planned to fly on to Ceylon, though that would require the conversion of their machines into seaplanes at Calcutta.[29] The map of 'World Markets and Empire Trade' supplied with the *Graphic*'s British Industries Supplement on 19 November 1927 shows Ceylon as a crucial link in the network of shipping routes; as does that which features in Elsie K. Cook's 1931 *A Geography of Ceylon*. 'The air-route to Australia', Cook explains, 'does not touch Colombo, but goes via Karachi and Rangoon.'[30] By 1937, there were reports of 'the creation, stage by stage, of an organization which is throwing a chain of marine alighting, mooring, and re-fuelling points across India, equipped with all the latest devices available, and reinforced by an amplified service of wireless and meteorology'. Ceylon was at last to be 'brought regularly within the great Empire network of air-mail routes'.[31]

The story was the same with regard to telecommunications. Ceylon had long since been connected to the rest of the world by cable. An Eastern and Associated Telegraph Companies map of 1922 shows links in three directions: to Aden, Malayasia and the African coast. But it was not until October 1935 that a reliable telecommunications route was finally established between London and Colombo: by radiotelephone to India and then onwards by landline and cable.[32] In 1937, ten years after the inauguration of the world's first long-distance radiotelephone circuit, between Britain and the United States, Ralph Bown, a Bell Telephone Laboratories engineer, was able to report that connection had been established between 93 per cent of the world's telephones. An accompanying map shows Ceylon connected firmly by indirect links to Britain in one direction and Australia in the other. London was at this point the only hub enjoying direct communication with every major world city.[33]

Ceylon, in short, became a representational crux during – and on account of – its belated integration into the empire transport and telecommunications chain in the early 1930s: shipping, but not yet aviation; cable, but not yet telephony. My hypothesis is that, as a result of this belatedness, films made about Ceylon in the early 1930s hesitate between the idea of empire as the occupation of territory and the idea of empire as connectivity.

CEYLON ON FILM

During the 1880s, tea cultivation, originally regarded as a last resort or makeshift, became Ceylon's 'staple industry'.[34] In 1883, 1,000,000 lbs of Ceylon tea had been imported into Britain; by 1888 the figure was 18,533,000 lbs.[35] Thereafter, despite some attempt at diversification, Ceylon *was* tea, with one or two other natural resources on the side; at least until the Japanese invasion of Malaya in December 1941 cut British industry off from its primary source of rubber. The identification of a particular colonial territory as the source of a particular commodity marketed the commodity in Britain; the commodity's marketing in turn further identified the territory as a British colony. The mechanism of that mutual reinforcement of status, as metropolis and periphery, was the relentless elaboration of some familiar distinctions: nature/culture, labour/capital, cultivation/technology, feminine/ masculine. In James Joyce's *Ulysses* (1922), Leopold Bloom, halted before the window of the Belfast and Oriental Tea Company in Westland Row, regards the legend on the packets: 'choice blend, made of the finest Ceylon brands'. The name conjures the Far East. 'Lovely spot it must be', Bloom muses: 'the garden of the world, big lazy leaves to float about on, cactuses, flowery meads, snaky lianas they call them. Wonder is it like that.'[36]

If anyone could claim responsibility for the contents of Bloom's daydreaming, it was probably Sir Thomas Lipton. Lipton began to advertise in the *Graphic* and other illustrated magazines in January 1892, two years after his company had acquired its first tea estates in Ceylon. These advertisements depict the tea estate as an oriental garden brought into being and thereafter ordered by European capital, scientific expertise, management skills and access to transport. It was an idea stabilised throughout by the gendering of the relation between nature and culture, labour and capital. As Anandi Ramamurthy has shown, 'the otherness of South Asia could best be represented for Lipton's through the image of a Tamil woman tea picker'.[37] In the 1920s, at a time of intensifying class conflict in Britain, such arrangements were sometimes taken to exemplify the benefits and benevolence of capitalist imperialism in general. In April 1926, Alfred Wigglesworth put forward as a model of mutually advantageous co-operation between capital and labour

> the expansion of the tea industry in Ceylon and Assam, rubber in Malaya, gold mining in South Africa, cocoa by natives in West Africa, jute in Bengal, wool in Australia and food stuffs in Canada, New Zealand and other sections of the Empire.

It was time, Wigglesworth concluded, 'to emulate such progress at home'.[38]

As Grieveson has demonstrated, the harvesting of products in colonial spaces and their subsequent transfer to and arrival at the metropolis became a 'dominant trope' in EMB films. For example, the portrayal of bodies and machines in *Cargo from Jamaica* (1933), directed by Basil Wright, 'marks acutely the standard contrast between an advanced technological modernity and its double, the "primitive" economy of colonized labour and agricultural produce'. The ubiquity of the large cargo ship in these films testifies at once to the idealisation of transport and technology as instruments of control, and to the 'literal mobility', as Grieveson puts it, of British finance capitalism, its grip on global circulation.[39] Two representational regimes have been fused. The cargo ship stands in metaphorically for civilisation as opposed to the primitive. Metonymically, it connects to machines, in the metropolis, and to bodies performing the work of machines, in the colonial space. The harvesting-and-transport trope amply informs *Gardens of the Orient*, a film about the cultivation of tea in India and Ceylon made by the GPO unit in 1936, and distributed by the very grandly named Empire Tea Market Expansion Bureau. In other Ceylon films, however, the representational regimes don't fuse quite so seamlessly.

The Ceylon Tea Industry, like *Cargo from Jamaica*, is a harvesting-and-transport film. It tells the story of the colonial production of tea, from cultivation through processing and quality control to export by cargo ship. Apart from a brief episode concerning recreation and religious ceremony, the narrative is straightforwardly sequential. Each scene connects metonymically to the next as one part of a coherent representation to another. Metonymy gains an additional edge once the tea has been packed into crates. We see the crates being transported by cart and railway from the estate to a central warehouse, and then by cart and elephant from the warehouse to the docks. Each crate is marked with a clearly visible LIPTON. The whole of which each image forms an interconnected part is not so much a territory as a corporation. This is capitalist imperialism in action.

The Ceylon Tea Industry, like Cargo from Jamaica, can also be read metaphorically. Like the Lipton's advertisements in the Graphic and other magazines, it further reinforces the opposition between labour and capital in the shape of technical expertise by gendering labour not just as female, but as exotically feminine. Indeed, when it came to exoticism, cinema's own technical expertise proved more than a match for mere magazine illustration. The camera pans across a hillside thronged with women picking tea. Cut to a medium shot of an individual picker: beautiful, bare-shouldered, wearing elaborate nose- and ear-rings. She breaks off the top of the plant and holds the leaves up to the camera, with level gaze. Cut to a close-up of her fingers holding the leaves. The sequence concludes with a medium shot of a group of women picking in unison. What these changes in shot scale have accomplished is both to connect the leaves the woman has picked metonymically to all the other leaves that will make up a consignment, and to isolate her metaphorically as an embodiment of otherness. The metaphoric micro-system becomes complete when, later in the film, we encounter white-coated European male tea-tasters at work in a laboratory, presumably on the same consignment. Thus far, the film's vertical axis (metaphor) could be said to predominate over its horizontal axis (metonymy).

But that's not the whole story. After the consignment of tea has been tested for quality, it makes its way by cart – and, rather less plausibly, by elephant – to the docks, where labourers load it into a lighter, and then, the Lipton trademark still very much in evidence, into the waiting cargo ship. The ship departs. That, we might suppose, is the end of it. Gardens of the Orient was to conclude in just such a fashion with the loading of crates of tea onto a liner, which departs ceremonially to a majestic final flourish of commentary. 'Thus the fragrant leaf begins its long journey over thousands of miles of land and sea to fill the world's tea-cups with the essence of perfection.' Alternatively, we might expect to follow our chosen consignment across the high seas to a British port equipped with British cranes and conveyor-belts. In fact, neither conclusion applies. What greets us instead is a shot of camels laden with Lipton tea passing a battered sphinx, in the direction of a distant pyramid. And then, aligning the company with empire itself: 'Lipton's – the organization on which the sun never sets.' There is no reason to believe that the company regarded Egypt as a particularly important market. The only explanation for the presence of sphinx and pyramid in the Pathé film is the prominence Egypt had achieved since the mid-1920s, both in fact and in fantasy, as the Clapham Junction of imperial air networks. The film has in effect grafted a new piece of circuitry (aviation), for which there was as yet no material basis in Ceylon, onto an old one (shipping). Of course, the camels could be taken, along with the elephant and all the other beasts of burden, both animal and human, to symbolise the primitive condition of the colonial in general. But this is a film that wants to make its point by metonymy as well as by metaphor. Lipton's, after all, depended for its profitability on those long chains of 'great tensile power' enveloping the 'Empire's framework'. The more tensile the chain could be made to appear, by association with technological advance, the better.

The Song of Ceylon, a four-part documentary commissioned from the GPO film unit by the Ceylon Tea Propaganda Bureau in 1933, was from the outset, and still remains, the focus of intense debate on account of its 'strange mixture of anthropological observation, travelogue, poetic rhapsody, and sound-image experimentation'.[40] Much recent commentary has been concerned with the film's 'authoring of otherness': its construction of yet another garden of the orient replete with unalienated labour and, in a departure from previous savourings of oriental femininity, a gentle homoeroticism. Stollery points out that in Song, as in the Imperial Airways films, modernity takes the form of speed, but here 'speaks with the hurried and intrusive "Voices of Commerce"': the montage of voice, sound and electronic interference laid over images of labour in its third and most vividly experimental section.[41] Opinions still vary as to how successful Wright and his co-director Walter Leigh were in reconciling tradition with modernity through a poetics of cinema. What is not in doubt is that Song represents Ceylon metaphorically, as an edenic 'virgin island' ripe for exploitation. I want to conclude by suggesting that the sound montage of the 'voices of commerce' section, recorded in the GPO's Blackheath studio, also constitutes a metonymic representation of connectivity per se.

Walter Leigh firmly believed that the contrapuntal use of sound would produce a 'new and far more expressive form of film art'. Audiences, he wrote, had to learn to listen to sounds 'bound up with, and yet separate from, the picture': sounds whose primary value was allusive. 'The sense of the sounds is related to the sense of the picture, and a specific emotion results.' So far, so Soviet. Yet the allusion, in Song, was to the achievements of imperialist capitalism. 'Morse and radio announcers reciting market prices are heard over shots of tea-pickers', Leigh explained, 'sounds of shipping over the gathering of coker-nuts.'[42] The opportunity, and perhaps the danger, lay in the divergence of the sense of the sounds from the sense of the picture. Charles Davy, reviewing Song for Cinema Quarterly, argued that the third section was its weakest part, 'for the voices are ghostly, and the influence of England on Ceylon is not at all ghostly; it is a forcibly transforming influence, leading to fever and conflict'.[43] It seems to me that these voices are indeed ghostly, but that their ghostliness has a purpose.

The theme of the the the 'voices of commerce' is the harvesting of crops for export. 'New clearings', the narrator intones, 'new roads, new buildings, new communications, new developments of natural resources.' To put it more precisely, the sequence pays particular attention to the ways in which modern transport systems and communications technologies have already enhanced, and might yet further enhance, the incorporation of a hitherto relatively isolated local economy into the world market. The natural resources at issue are tea and copra. As in The Ceylon Tea Industry and Gardens of the Orient, we witness (again, with the help of women in close-up) the harvesting of the crop, its passage through the factory and transfer to a cargo ship. As Leigh himself noted, 'sounds of shipping' accompany the collection of nuts: 'for Australia', a voice announces, 'calling Toulon, Naples, Port Said, Suez, Aden, Colombo'. Ceylon, we are to understand, has long been firmly embedded in the imperial network of sea routes. But will that prove enough to keep the island economy competitive as time-space compression accelerates? Other voices dictate letters and recite market prices. Morse Code jabs and flickers along the sequence of images. Such methods of communication constitute further links in the empire chain: they facilitate and speed

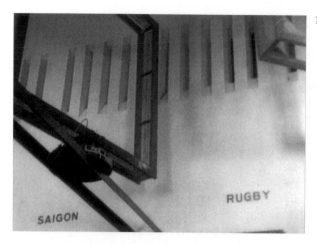

up commerce. Soundtrack and image-track have been edited contrapuntally, so that the source of one is never the source of the other. But the mutual reinforcement of the rhythm of one by the rhythm of the other does strongly imply that the 'voices of commerce' have been folded into the garden of the orient, and animate it throughout.

Doubts remain, however. One brief sequence appears to concern the reception of messages about the movements of steamers by wireless telegraphy and their onward transmission by broadcast radio (the voice and the pulses of code are heard simultaneously). But the broadcaster speaks French, and a kind of intertitle informs us that this particular wireless traffic, though it may well involve Colombo, has in fact passed between Saigon and Rugby.

These thoroughly up-to-date communications technologies, replete with antennae and arrays of knobs and valves, seem to bear an oblique relation only to what we have been shown of Ceylon; though almost immediately telegraph poles shadow the spindly trees in a scene set somewhere in the interior. The most up-to-date technology of all, wireless telephony, cannot be represented *in situ*, since in 1933 there was no direct communication by telephone between Britain and Ceylon. The sound montage does, however, include a telephone conversation during which two British men, speaking in clipped professional tones, discuss the blueprints for a new factory. This exchange, which has no visual correlative, achieves a sonic clarity almost entirely unknown to telephone systems, then or now. 'New buildings', the film's narrator had announced. But the eerily soundproofed debate about blueprints takes place not so much between discrete physical locations in Britain, Ceylon or indeed anywhere else, as in the abstract space of capital flows. The ghostliness of the 'voices of commerce', like that of the conclusion of *The Ceylon Tea Industry*, arises out of the attempt to graft a new piece of circuitry (wireless telephony), for which there was as yet no material basis, onto an old one (correspondence by letter or telegram).

Wright and Leigh evidently, and for good reason, found instantaneous connection of the kind made possible by wireless telegraphy and telephony hard to represent visually. They didn't try to conceal the fact. The Rugby–Saigon exchange, for example, requires a palpably laborious articulation of shots: a tilt up the transmitter's aerial, then a tilt down from the receiving antenna into the radio hut; and then, as though that wasn't schematic enough, the intertitle identifying the signal's source and destination. Metonymy, the figure best able to represent the transport and tele-communications chains that had reconfigured empire into Commonwealth, simply couldn't cope with short-wave radio's discontiguous skip effects. It isn't just metonymy that has fallen short rhetorically, or 'the visual' in general. After all, the telephone conversation about blueprints remains a purely aural event: an event altogether too pure in its aurality to contribute to the 'sense' of a film about Ceylon, or indeed anywhere in particular beyond the studio in which it was staged. Representation fails, as a form of knowledge and power, when confronted by a connectivity that no longer has any need for it. The ghost heard wailing among the 'voices of commerce' might be the ghost of cinema itself.

NOTES

1. Lee Grieveson, 'The Cinema and the (Common) Wealth of Nations', in this volume.
2. David Harvey, *The New Imperialism* (Oxford: Oxford University Press, 2003), p. 26.
3. Grieveson, 'The Cinema and the (Common) Wealth of Nations', pp. 80–1.
4. Harvey, *The New Imperialism*, p. 98. See also Harvey, *The Limits to Capital* (Oxford: Blackwell, 1982); and Harvey, *The Condition of Postmodernity* (Oxford: Blackwell, 1989), Part III.
5. Barney Warf, *Time-space Compression: Historical Geographies* (London: Routledge, 2008), p. 9. Warf provides a lucid overview and critique of competing theories of time-space compression. I have tried to follow his example, if not exactly his method, in attending to the historical 'particularities' of the phenomenon in all of their 'messy complexity' (p. 39).
6. Gwen Urey, 'Telecommunications and Global Capitalism', in Bella Mody, Johannes M. Bauer and Joseph D. Straubhaar (eds), *Telecommunications Politics: Ownership and Control of the Information Highway in Developing Countries* (Mahwah, NJ: Lawrence Erlbaum Associates, 1995), pp. 53–83. For a comprehensive account of the history of these developments, see Peter J. Hugill, *Global Communications since 1844: Geopolitics and Technology* (Baltimore, MD: Johns Hopkins University Press, 1999).
7. Daniel R. Headrick, *The Invisible Weapon: Telecommunications and International Politics 1851–1945* (Oxford: Oxford University Press, 1991), pp. 93–8.
8. This paragraph relies heavily on Daniel R. Headrick, 'Shortwave Radio and Its Impact on International Telecommunications between the Wars', *History and Technology* vol. 11 (1994), pp. 21–32.
9. 'Empire Air Routes', *The Times*, 3 February 1920, p. 6.
10. 'Imperial Communications', *The Times*, 7 July 1921, p. 11.
11. Michael North, *Reading 1922: A Return to the Scene of the Modern* (New York: Oxford University Press, 1999), p. 126. For Northcliffe's personal reflections on the state of the empire, see *My Journey Round the World (16 July 1921–26 February 1922)*, ed. Cecil and St John Harmsworth (Philadelphia, PA: J. B. Lippincott, 1923).
12. 'From London to the Cape by Air', *The Times*, 4 February 1920, p. 9.
13. 'Aviation and the Empire', *The Times*, 22 May 1925, p. 13.

14. Michael Heffernan, 'The Cartography of the Fourth Estate: Mapping the New Imperialism in British and French Newspapers, 1875–1925', in James R. Akerman (ed.), *The Imperial Map: Cartography and the Mastery of Empire* (Chicago, IL: University of Chicago Press, 2009), pp. 261–99, 293.

15. 'The Imperial Conference', *The Times*, 29 October 1926, p. 9.

16. Gordon Pirie, *Air Empire: British Imperial Civil Aviation, 1919–1939* (Manchester: Manchester University Press, 2009).

17. 'Wings over the British Empire', *Popular Mechanics* vol. 64 (1935), pp. 674–7, 674, 676–7.

18. Martin Stollery, *Alternative Empires: European Modernist Cinemas and Cultures of Imperialism* (Exeter: University of Exeter Press, 2000), pp. 167–8. Michael North describes Carter's exploits as 'the first truly modern media event' (North, *Reading 1922*, p. 19).

19. Nevil Shute, *So Disdained* (London: Cassell, 1928).

20. Warf, *Time-space Compression*, p. 148.

21. D. Simonsen, 'Accelerating Modernity: Time-space Compression in the Wake of the Aeroplane', *Journal of Transport History* vol. 26 (2005), pp. 98–117, 100. For widely differing but equally informative accounts of the consequences of such acceleration for national sovereignty and national identity, see Gillian Beer, 'The Island and the Aeroplane: The Case of Virginia Woolf', in Homi Bhabha (ed.), *Nation and Narration* (London: Routledge, 1990), pp. 265–90; and David L. Butler, 'Technogeopolitics and the Struggle for Control of World Air Routes, 1910–1928', *Political Geography* vol. 20 (2001), pp. 635–58.

22. 'Empire Wireless Chain', *The Times*, 7 April 1921, p. 9.

23. Headrick, 'Shortwave Radio and Its Impact on International Telecommunications between the Wars', pp. 24–5. See also Hugill, *Global Communications since 1844*, ch. 5; and Aitor Anduaga, *Wireless and Empire: Geopolitics, Radio Industry, and Ionosphere in the British Empire, 1918–1939* (Oxford: Oxford University Press, 2009), pp. 63–72.

24. 'World-Wide Radio', *The Times*, 3 May 1935, p. 54.

25. For a detailed account, see Dwayne R. Winseck and Robert M. Pike, *Communication and Empire: Media, Markets, and Globalization, 1860–1930* (Durham, NC: Duke University Press, 2007), pp. 306–29.

26. Headrick, 'Shortwave Radio and Its Impact on International Telecommunications between the Wars', p. 27. See also Hugill, *Global Communications since 1844*, pp. 118–19, 128–34.

27. Professor A. P. Newton, 'Forgotten Deeds of Empire', *Saturday Review*, 19 September 1936, p. 376.

28. 'Air Defence', *The Times*, 21 October 1925, p. 11.

29. 'Air Transport in the East', *The Times*, 15 December 1927, p. 13.

30. Elsie K. Cook, *A Geography of Ceylon* (Madras: Macmillan, 1931), p. 221.

31. 'Air Route Developments', *Saturday Review*, 21 July 1937, pp. 73–7, 73.

32. 'Growing Use of Telephones', *The Times*, 25 October 1935, p. 11.

33. 'Transoceanic Radiotelephone Development', *Proceedings of the Institute of Radio Engineers* vol. 25 (1937), pp. 1124–35.

34. 'The Tea Industry of India', *Gentleman's Magazine* vol. 270 (May 1891), pp. 457–63, 458.

35. Anandi Ramamurthy, 'Tea Advertising and Its Ideological Support for Vertical Control over Production', in his *Imperial Persuaders: Images of Africa and Asia in British Advertising* (Manchester: Manchester University Press, 2003), pp. 93–130, 96. See Denys Forrest, *A Hundred Years of Ceylon Tea, 1867–1967* (London: Chatto and Windus, 1967), pp. 170–1.

36. James Joyce, *Ulysses*, ed. Jeri Johnson (Oxford: Oxford University Press, 1993), p. 68.

37. Ramamurthy, 'Tea Advertising and Its Ideological Support for Vertical Control over Production', p. 119.

38. 'Britain's Purge', *Saturday Review* vol. 3677 (17 April 1926), p. 503.

39. Grieveson, 'The Cinema and the (Common) Wealth of Nations', pp. 97–8.

40. Jamie Sexton, 'The Audio-visual Rhythms of Modernity: *Song of Ceylon*, Sound, and Documentary Film-Making', <www.scope.nottingham.ac.uk/article.php?issue= may2004&id=249&section=article>. I'm grateful to Jonny Hoare for sharing with me a knowledge of the film far more detailed than my own.

41. Stollery, *Alternative Empires*, p. 196. See also William Guynn, 'The Art of National Projection: Basil Wright's *Song of Ceylon*', in Barry Keith Grant and Jeanette Sloniowski (eds), *Documenting the Documentary* (Detroit, MI: Wayne State University Press, 1998), pp. 83–98.

42. Walter Leigh, 'The Musician and the Film', *Cinema Quarterly* vol. 3 (1935), pp. 70–4, 73–4.

43. Charles Davy, 'The Song of Ceylon', *Cinema Quarterly* vol. 3 (1935), pp. 109–10, 110.

9

An 'accurate imagination': Place, Map and Archive as Spatial Objects of Film History

Priya Jaikumar

INTRODUCTION

A commonplace hermeneutic of postcolonial scholarship has been to expose affiliations between territorial power and modes of knowing, recording and ordering the world. How is such a politics of place relevant to film historiography? This query occasions my interrogation into a set of British geographical films about Indian towns, dating to 1937. In their specifics, the films display the uses of visual media in geography. As graphic evidence that helped to stabilise a field of disciplinary knowledge, they reveal how the status of imperial geography was tested and formalised through visuals about colonies. As projections of colonial India deployed in educating British pupils who are addressed as future citizens of a nation and an empire, they highlight intersections between the visual practices of geopolitics and of curricular geography. In the longer perspective, scrutiny of these visuals also necessitates reflections on modes of film historiography that frame contemporary acts of interpretive contextualism.

Historiography faces particular challenges in discussing and codifying a colonial visual archive, many of which stem from a crisis of categorisation endemic to the colonial process, where the acquisition of sovereignty over bodies and resources across diverse political formations accompanied the constitution of liberal European nations. If unable to confront this link and the legacies of Europe's contradictory political affiliations, discourses on colonial film risk being trapped in modes of description that merely reinforce the problematic place of colonialism in European democracies. For any discipline to enlighten us on colonial cinema, it must comprehend and disrupt the logics of seeing, being and thinking that made such films possible in their own time, and assimilable within a longer history of world cinema, culture, politics and industrial practice. Such epistemic questions of category – of where, why, and how we situate/d colonial objects, people and places then and now – are fundamentally spatial ones. What follows is an argument for exploring space as a critical analytic in film historiography, provoked by colonial films whose exegesis involves breaking an old pact between territorial power and epistemic truth.

FOUR BRITISH GEOGRAPHICAL FILMS, 1937

British Instructional Films (BIF), formed by H. Bruce Woolfe in 1919, was known for its war, educational and science films and, according to film historian Rachael Low, this market niche may have contributed to the company's survival during the difficult post-war years of British film production, from the 1920s on.[1] Reformed later as Gaumont-British Instructional (GBI), the company's geographical films adopt a hybrid format of actuality and animation, where animation refers to cartographic drawings and moving symbols on maps. Under the 'Indian Town Studies' series, GBI's geographical shorts include *Thar Desert Town: Bikaner* (1937), *A Central Indian Town: Udaipur* (1937), *A Foot-hill Town: Darjeeling* (1937) and *A Himalayan Town: Katmandu* (1937).[2] These films re-edited footage shot during the making of *Wings over Everest* (1934), also utilised in GBI's geographical series entitled 'The Secrets of India' (1934), and possibly in some of its fiction films.[3]

Though the earlier 'Secrets' series shares footage with the 'Town Studies' series, and covers the same Indian towns, based on catalogue descriptions and surviving films, it appears that their tone was very different.[4] In the 'Secrets' series, *Bikaner* shows its viewers Indian nautch girls, and *Udaipur* begins with the king's palace, as a voiceover informs us that it is the dwelling of 'his Highness the Maharana of Udaipur, direct descendant of the sun god, and natural leader by birth and tradition of all the Indian leaders of the Hindu faith'.[5] Blatantly mythic and orientalising images (and music) have no place in the 'Indian Town Studies' of 1937, which are formally curricular and prefer factual description. They enjoyed limited 'Saturday morning educational' screenings in 35mm format at select Gaumont British theatres across twelve cities in the UK, indicating that they aimed for some popular viewership, but their primary purpose was to supplement school curricula as 16mm non-flam films for substandard projectors.[6]

Notwithstanding tonal differences, the geographical series of 1934 and 1937 were both influenced by BIF's more popular 'Secrets of Nature' series (1922–33). Key personnel involved in the 1934 'Secrets of India' series produced the critically acclaimed 'Secrets of Nature' series, carrying with them commonalities that extended beyond analogous titles holding a revelatory promise (as distinct from an analytic one, available in GBI's fascinating and entirely animated short *The Expansion of Germany*, 1937). BIF's nature films and the lesser-known geographical films overlap in perspective, as both connect a species typology with product range. *Skilled Insect Artisans* (1922), for instance, compares silk production from an Ailanthus moth against the silk of an Admiral moth, echoing the human geography of the India series that relates Indians to varied typologies of labour and leisure activity. Both sets of film are characterised by a presentist, nominal mode that preclassifies types of insects and people.[7] The nature films and geographicals also interweave hybrid compiled and shot footage, evocative of BIF's earlier war-reconstruction films like *Allenby's Campaign* (1919), *Ypres* (1925), *Mons* (1926) and *The Battle of Coronel and Falkland Islands* (1927). This raises the question of whether we can delimit colonial films to films primarily depicting colonies. It would appear that BIF's Indian geographical films are best explained when placed in the context of their production company, rather than exclusively in the context of colonialism. More broadly, foundational to the institutional parameters of this wide range of cinematic content was a perspective of visual objectivity and cosmopolitan affect, given the frequent combination of fiction with actuality footage, reference to real events and scientific typologies, and interest in other lands, creatures and peoples. As part of GBI's catalogue of productions, the 1937 geographicals are a glimpse into disciplinary and cinematic orders of knowledge that were in formation while being mutually influential in a wider education of British citizens in the natural and political world. Insisting on distinct visual practices between biology, ecology, human geography and anthropology when these fields were as yet formalising their distinctions within educational institutions would, in the first instance, be anachronistic. The recommendation of the 'Indian Town Studies' for geography classes aimed at students of ten or eleven years of age and over was an act of disciplinary disaggregation, and part of the process of institutionalisation of imperial geography.

To begin with the formalisation of film form in such films, the edits combining narrative and actuality in nature and geographical films were part of an evolving understanding of how the cinematograph could grasp the 'real', with its emergent rather than imposed sense of drama. Mary Field, director of BIF's 'Secrets of Nature' series and producer of the 'Secrets of India' series, opposed dramatic fiction to 'non-dramatic film, such as a travel picture or a "Secret of Nature"' film, thus aligning geography and nature films by saying that '[a]ll you can do is to have a general idea of what your film is to be about and then set to work to collect material that may prove useful in making it'.[8] BIF's non-dramatic films were edited to convey stories gleaned from the world with broad directives, but in the absence of a prior script. The geographicals in particular, born of incidental material shot on site combined with collated material, depended heavily on footage edited together with maps, animations, diagrams and repeated voiceover tropes to introduce regularities unifying diverse Indian towns through a network of overlapping symbols. As I discuss in the next section, in the case of the 1937 series, the logic of these symbols derived from imperial geography's evolving modern perspective that emphasised internationalism, empathy and comprehension of the British Empire's diversity as well as its interconnectedness. This perspective was linked to an ideology aimed at inculcating an appreciation for the natural beauty and political stature of the British Isles, when placed in scalar comparison to a world within which the imperium was cast as an internally cohesive and comprehensible unit.

In the films, diverse colonial Indian townships are made legible when their footage is presented through overlapping metrics and grids. Places in India with distinct roles in imperial administration – Afghanistan, an unmanageable frontier of nomadic tribes and invasions; Darjeeling, a frontier land that served as a British summer resort and tea plantation; Bikaner and Udaipur, Rajputana princely states under the sovereignty of the British monarch – are levelled by visual tropes. Repeatedly, viewers encounter vocational or ethnic types of inhabitants (the cobbler, metalworker, pan-wallah and cartridge makers of Afghanistan in *The North West Frontier*, 1928); North Indians, Tibetans, Nepalese and Europeans in *Darjeeling*), using an incongruous range of transportation (camels, motor cars, bicycles and horse carts in *Bikaner*; trains, oxcarts and coolies in *Darjeeling*) and quaint modes of entertainment (dancing dolls in *Darjeeling*; the royal procession in *Bikaner*), portraying the place's awkward relationship to modernity and temporal progression.

The films *Bikaner* and *Darjeeling*, available to view at the new digital archive on British Empire films (<www.colonialfilm.org.uk>), reveal several formal similarities.[9] Both start with identical maps of India marking the same places: they combine the physical markers of the Plain of the Indus (at west), Plain of the Ganges (east), Himalaya Mountains (north-east), and Deccan (south), with the political markers of Delhi, Bombay and Calcutta. These maps are animated by arrows, letters, moving dots and lines that show, in the case of Bikaner, gates and wells in the walled city and, in the case of Darjeeling, the route from Siliguri and the path of a two-foot gauge railway. Both films use voiceovers that act as laser pointers to an image: 'Take a good look at this map of India. The arrow points to the Deccan'; 'Take another look at Bikaner on the map'; 'If you look at the people in the market, you will see all kinds of north Indians.' 'Notice ... the different kinds of faces.' Creating a similar visual trajectory for the lands, a frictionless path of arrows and dots take the viewer on an ever-narrowing journey, from the map of India to a township. Our sequential introduction to different modes of transport and the marketplace, with its vocationally or ethnically varied consumers, leads to a few key built environments such as temples at the spiritual end, and observatories or irrigation systems at the technological end. This tour culminates with architectures of governance, ranging from the maharaja's palace in *Bikaner* to the government house in *Darjeeling*, residence to the governor of Bengal in the summer months. In this pattern, the films are similar to the silent BIF film about Afghanistan mentioned above, *The North West Frontier*, also available in the digital archive.

The visual building blocks of these geographicals are location shots, edited together with maps and diagrams.[10] Within a semiotic vocabulary, the cinematic image and the diagrammatic map are at odds with each other. Maps are symbolic designations of a place drawn from a cartographic system, rather than from the lexicon of technologically reproduced reality.[11] They are part of an iconography of enumeration, whereas cinematic shots of locations and crowds can register photographic detail in excess of framing discourses. In Christopher Pinney's words, 'No matter how precautionary or punctilious the photographer is in arranging everything that is placed before the camera, the inability of the lens to discriminate will ensure a substrate or margin of excess ...'.[12] But historical context also defines the role of maps and photographs as orders of representing reality, and British schools of the period encouraged mapwork based on photographs that represented an experientially tested realm of the familiar. The British *Handbook for Geography Teachers* (1955; 1932) recommends that photographs of one's neighbourhood or holiday visits serve as the basis for map drawings, in order to establish maps as 'representations of reality'.[13] Abstraction and fantasy are discouraged, as is the tendency to tell 'picturesque but inauthentic stories ... under the heading of Geography' in dealing with 'Life on Other Lands'.[14]

Consequently, of greater interest than a geographical film's use of maps as text or image is the idiom of scientific nominalism that these films share with the map-making process. Regional map-making was to be the training ground for colonial geography, through developing the student's facility for what was termed an *accurate imagination*, a phrase I pursue because it was crucial to the abstractions that accrued rational status with regard to colonies. For schoolchildren, colonial maps, photographs and films were sanctioned by truths outside the experiential variety, simply because unlike the frequently visited neighbourhoods that served as factual corollaries of early map-drawing efforts, colonies were inaccessible except through the imagination. Lacking reliable observational accreditation, the credibility of colonial geography came from the authority of educational institutions and the state, naturalised through the notion of an accurate imagination. Institutional adjudications over questions of visual veracity and emergent notions of a rational imagination gained significance in this context.

Two aspects of this observation are worth carrying forward. First, geography's rationalist claim to accuracy was made through the realm of imagination, specifically defined as a visual and aesthetic realm. This legitimated the entry of literature and film into geography, by framing fiction and filmic record as illustrative evidence, and reciprocally conceiving of geography as accessible to the imagination (in addition to being an object of factual study). Second, while formally and affectively distinct, cinema and cartography were linked to the visual truths of imperial geography, by which I mean geography's perspectival prescriptions of Britain's position in relation to the world. Geographical films that formally combined the artifice of cartographic symbolism with a photographic registration of detail reveal linkages sanctioned between Britain and its empire, and between empire and visuality, in the spatial education of modern British citizens. GBI's 'Indian Town Studies' suppressed the fantastic aspects of colonial films with which they shared footage, becoming of greater practical use to imperial geography through their more stable, sombre visual regimes. Distinctions that mark this series as curricular as opposed to theatrical productions become institutionally entrenched with the formalisation of geography, and of film in education. The British Film Institute (BFI), host to discussions on best practices related to geographical films in the 1930s, was important to such formalisations, as was the Imperial Institute before it. All this illustrates not just the diverse institutional histories that we must study to understand films about colonies, but cinema's relation to a range of productive rationalities that made certain truths about colonial space axiomatic.

Such perspectives are available to us now, not only because it is possible to situate the geographical films in their contexts, but also because we can see them in relation to alternative and actively anti-imperial ways of knowing, recording and ordering colonial space. This, for me, is in large part the attraction of the new digital film catalogue. Inspired by the greater availability of colonial films in digital archives, our sifting through the material offers us a rare opportunity to reorder the matrices of comprehension through which colonial space was grasped at a previous time of imperial filming, screening and archiving. With its new platform and accelerated access, the digitisation of colonial cinema revives concerns about the colony as a space produced through the organisation of knowledge in archival, scholarly and disciplinary practices. The digital reintroduces dreams of accuracy through its (illusory) promise of more complete preservation and access, as it stores infinitely more material in infinitesimal spaces while making that material available to the imaginations of a wider public. It gives the idea of an accurate imagination traction beyond its precise historical usage, reviving longstanding frictions between the desire for a total or accurate history, the questionable faith in the visual as evidentiary proof of accuracy and presence and the active need to reimagine historical visual material.

AN ACCURATE IMAGINATION

> One of the chief functions of geography in school is to help children *to imagine accurately* places, people, activities which lie beyond immediate experience … . Using always the experience of the child as the starting-point, the geographer has, in addition to many other aids … a wide range of visual aids to assist him.[15]

These words open the section on 'Visual Aids' in the *Handbook*, where the writer evaluates lantern slides, film strips, films, wall charts, diagrams, samples and three-dimensional models for geographical teaching. The idea of an accurate imagination, which relied on the development of rational method to extrapolate one's mode of looking at the world from known (seen and experienced) to unknown (unfamiliar or seen through facsimile) realms, was derived from the geographer James Fairgrieve's textbook *Geography in Schools* (1926). Fairgrieve, who would later supervise BIF's Afghanistan short *The North West Frontier*, states that the 'function of geography in school is to train future citizens to *imagine accurately* the conditions of the great world stage, and so help them to think sanely about political and social problems in the world around'.[16] The connection between visuality as a technique for developing an accurate imagination, and an accurate imagination as the path to building a sense of world citizenship plays an important part in the acceptance of films as tools for teaching international geography. The path to cinema's inclusion as a legitimate aid to geographical education is paved by claims about the centrality of a certain kind of visualisation to geography and to citizenship.

G. J. Cons, supervisor of the GBI's 'Indian Town Studies', general editor of the *Handbook for Geography Teachers* in 1955, and Senior Tutor and Lecturer in Geography at the University of London's Goldsmiths College, named geography an 'outlook subject', orienting an 'educated person' to the 'geographical perspective' of an age.[17] 'Outlook', 'educated', 'perspective' and 'age' are key words, pointing to a collaboration between the late Victorian formalisation of empire and popular education in Britain, alongside the institutionalisation of disciplinary geography and a visual (perspectival) imagination in the early twentieth century. Degree-granting geography departments didn't start until 1917, but discussions on how to instil in the growing citizenry a sense of place and point of view within their region, nation and world emerged with the consolidation of empire in the late nineteenth century, impacting incorporations of geography into school curricula.[18] Imagination was an important way to reach broader audiences who may have had less exposure to world affairs, particularly with the expansion of male suffrage and the mandate to educate the working classes. The paradigm of an accurate imagination in British geographical education appears in the context of expanding popular education and citizen building. Colonies served as limit-sites that proved or disproved the viability of a conceptual weld between imagination and accuracy, because their physical inaccessibility and the preponderance of fantastical visual representations challenged the ideal of a broad-based rational education in imperial affairs, while also making it more urgent.

In his definition of an accurate imagination as a means to train future citizens in rational thinking about world affairs, James Fairgrieve owed a debt to his professor, Halford Mackinder, the pioneer of modern geography in Britain. Member of the

British parliament and the Royal Geographical Society, champion of the Oxford University extension lectures, proponent of a 'new geography' and liberal imperialism and key architect of the concept of 'geopolitics', Mackinder was the first to systematically connect geography with what he called a 'special form of visualisation'.[19] Beyond establishing the significance of visual aids in classrooms, Mackinder influentially proposed that 'imagination or visualisation was the specifically geographical mode of thought'.[20] In a lecture delivered in 1911, titled 'The Teaching of Geography from an Imperial Point of View, and the Use Which Could and Should Be Made of Visual Instruction', Mackinder suggested that 'The power of visualization was meant for real things, rich in shape and colour … . Let our literary teaching appeal to the mind's EAR, and our geographical and historical teaching to the mind's EYE.'[21] While fiction was to be appreciated for its cadences, the scientific study of reality demanded pictorial comprehension.

Despite disciplinarily straddling the natural and social sciences, in the wake of explorers like Francis Youngblood and educators like Mackinder there was a push to reclaim an appreciation of natural beauty in modern geography, defined as a discipline encouraging rational analysis and comparative thinking to rouse the more affective faculties of appreciation and sympathy.[22] The 'visualising eye and the rationalising eye'[23] had to work in concordance to appreciate simultaneously the scientific *and* aesthetic significance of topographical forms. Politics entered at the most subliminal level, as an (unconscious) affectivity that accompanied (tutored) rationality: 'The real geographer *sees* the world drama as he reads his morning paper. He gesticulates unconsciously as he thinks … . In other words, he sees it in perspective of space.'[24] What geography had to produce was an instinctive sensory comprehension of spatial meaning, so that visualising topography offered a condensed enactment of Britain's and the world's historical destiny.

Central to this formulation was Mackinder's notion of Britain's topographical 'insularity and universality', which the *Handbook* proposes as cornerstone facts and values in the teaching of British geography.[25] A student's primary-school education began with an intimate knowledge of Britain as an island group or a 'Homeland', with its insular regional features. Britain was also privy to the 'great human contrasts' of nature and biology because the Isles were offshore to Europe and territorially pivotal to the world's 'universal history'.[26] So a secondary level of education oriented students to colonies and lands farther afield from England. Topography was understood to produce a geographical vision, and this vision could serve as evidence and valuation of the space. Britain's insularity and universality were measurable topographical features, values, and constituted the progressive stages in the geographical education of a pupil. The movement was outward because a perspectival encounter with one's humanity demanded the ability to visualise the entire world within a comparative framework, anchored in a superior locational position that was simultaneously territorial and evaluative. In a Heideggerian sense, the being was inserted into the world picture and the world *as* picture with a secure scientific understanding of his/her place within this visualisation.[27]

The pronouncedly visual transaction between being and the world is relevant to the present discussion in a couple of ways. First, as scholars of visual studies note, the Heideggerian notion of a picturised and consequently controllable world highlights the imperialising impulse of European modernity.[28] Second, Heidegger is making the argument that the formation of modern sciences rests upon the emergence of mathematical principles of research procedure. Scientific knowledge is institutionally formalised because of repeatable methodological techniques that require a transformation of the world and its experience into manipulable units of representations, which can serve as objects for disciplinary technologies. There is an expanded role for the aesthetic under modernity. For Heidegger, this reflects the alienating objectification of every aspect of life in modernity but, to invoke Walter Benjamin, it simultaneously describes the entry of the ordinary into the realm of aesthetics upon which the emergence of a modern sensibility (and, for Heidegger, the modern sciences) was predicated. Aesthetics, under modernity, no longer points to rarefied objects of art, but becomes the grid through which the world is transformed into measures of representation, open to manipulation by the state and disciplinary practices as much as by the masses.

Going a step further, the modern invention of the state itself depended on transforming subjects into composite rational, sensory and emotional units of representation that could be organised and addressed as a population and an electorate. Educing a modern citizen from the subject requires an education of the senses, as argued by David Lloyd and Paul Thomas, who note that for representative democracies like Britain – where the part stands for the whole, and the state for its populace – a prior ethical formation invested in the universalisation of particular experience is called upon. Aesthetic education is central to this ethical formation, because the 'aesthetic provides the theoretical ... articulation of the citizen-subject, whose education is not aimed so much at particular objects of knowledge as at forming an ethical disposition that is most clearly elaborated within the concept of culture'.[29] Rejecting the Foucaultian turn to governmentality on grounds of its inability to grasp the representative state as a utopian aspiration of the collective, Lloyd and Thomas emphasise the Romantic roots in Reformist England's definition of culture and the state. Nevertheless, what Michel Foucault made visible with his methodological removal of the constituent subject was the dispersal of a disposition towards the modern subject across a range of micro-domains, corresponding with (and facilitated by) the decline of transcendental sovereignty. This redefinition shows the secular liberal state as boundless, remade through the management and disposal of all things governing life. The state functions not only as an explicit authoritative agent, but more profoundly as something that is reformulated into a logic guiding everything from disciplinary practices to everyday encounters. While this does not imply incontrovertible state power, because the suasiveness of a liberal political regime can be manifest or repulsed across intimate spaces of subjective experience and public spaces of collective decision, it does highlight the pervasiveness of and permeability between culture, power and state rationalities.[30] Under such a dispensation, the contest of politics lies in how the world is visualised, framed and negotiated representationally.

To turn this discussion to the case at hand, an accurate understanding of the world in British geography during the 1930s was underwritten by the ironies of a historical collaboration between the liberal and imperial ideologies that constructed Britain's perspective of the world. Uday Mehta writes that 'the irony of the liberal defense of empire stands, because in some at least intuitively obvious sense, that defense vitiates what we take liberalism to represent and historically stand for', namely, the principles of representative democracy and equal rights under law.[31] A focus on colonies as the object of rational study allowed British education to maintain its distinction, through its deference to coeval modes of analysis and proposed linkages between neutral observation and empathetic appreciation, from the overtly political and propagandistic uses of visual instruction in Fascist or Communist nations. The larger goal of geography, as framed by Mackinder and embraced by subsequent British geographers, was to promote imperial *understanding*.[32] The geographical films of 1937 were suggested for school curricula because they utilised referential tools – maps, factual voiceover narration, ambient sound and location shots, occupational and architectural detail – to create a rationalist framework for understanding the similarities and differences between Indian towns and more familiar, domestic surroundings. A liberal faith in objective study as the means to improve one's understanding of self and the other proved, in a self-affirming way, 'the great truth that the land of Britain is one of the most humanised in the world'.[33]

Given this dedication to objective study, colonies presented tactical challenges to the accurate imagination of their topography. They were unavailable for field trips, physically further afield, less familiar and, within the calculus of British governance, more chaotic than the domestic. They were prone to becoming subjects of fantasy, and in need of stronger monitoring by texts of scientific observation, travel or administrative record. As a space and as a unit of representation, colonies presented some problems to the evolving discipline of modern geography and to the aesthetic education of British citizens, which placed faith in the rational cultivation of imaginative, visual and perceptual faculties. One of the first concerns raised about visual material for the teaching of imperial geography was the relative paucity of appropriate images or footage. Mackinder noted that colonial images had

> usually been collected either without system by passing visitors whose main object was other than educational, or by residents who, from the very fact of their familiarity with the scenes, are apt to omit pictures of the contrasts which for the stranger are the most salient. Such collections as are available have usually been made for special purposes, as for the promotion of religions missions, or of emigration.[34]

Arbiters of what counted as legitimate visual material on colonies for the educational market increased in significance with the emphasis on an accurate imagination. As Edward Said and Arjun Appadurai remind us, imperialism's impulses of exoticising and classifying the colonies have been intertwined in complicated ways. Appadurai distinguishes the 'heat of the novel, the light of the camera' from the 'cool idiom of number' when it came to describing colonial populations and territories.

> Illustrating literally the power of the textual 'supplement' … numerical tables, figures, and charts allowed the contingency, the sheer narrative clutter of prose descriptions of the colonial landscape, to be domesticated into the abstract, precise, complete and cool idiom of number.[35]

Geographical films, though part of the cinematic world of heat and light as described by Appadurai, aspired to nominalism.

The first committee commissioning appropriate educational images for circulation in the empire appears to be the Visual Instruction Committee of the Colonial Office, started in 1902 to gather lecture slides. Its project was to spread visual instruction in Britain 'on the same lines in all parts of the Empire', beginning with Ceylon, the Straits Settlement and Hong Kong, and expanding to include material on India and the Dominions.[36] Between this early period and the 1950s, institutions producing visual geographical material for education multiplied to include several public and private institutions, such as Aims of Industry Ltd, the British Film Institute, British Instructional Films, the Central Film Library, Educational Foundation for Visual Aids, Encyclopaedia Brittanica Ltd, the Gaumont British Film Division, the Imperial Institute, MGM Instructional Department, Scientific Film Association, Sound Services Ltd, Wallace Heaton Ltd.[37]

A few factors are worth noting. Institutes and companies from the public and private sphere participated in the production and circulation of imperial images for education, so easy distinctions between the state's mandate and market orientation towards geographical education are untenable.[38] In 1927, A. E. Bundy of British Instructional Films Ltd sought a commission from colonial governments on behalf of Bruce Woolfe and others, to 'make cinematograph pictures of an educational nature' and for 'preferential rights in the distribution of fictional subjects produced in the Empire'. The private firm did not earn contracts for preferential commercial film distribution (an undefined if frequently desired privilege during the 1920s), but it was making its request on the basis of a history of governmental co-operation on educational and non-fiction films.[39] Under these conditions, a coincidence in vision between private and state-sponsored educational films was strategic and felicitous. Moreover, as a collective that competed in the non-theatrical market, exchanges between production institutions and film reviews in educational publications created a domain of sanctioned opinions in the first half of the twentieth century. By the 1950s, these publications included *Film User*, *Journal of Education*, *Look and Listen*, *Monthly Film Review* (BFI), *School Government Chronicle*, *Visual Education* (which reviewed film strips).[40]

The GBI geographicals of 1937 met the standards of modern geographical education as defined within such discursive fields. They were anti-adventure colonial films that suppressed visual tropes of danger, excitement, the sublime and the picturesque, and assumed a spectator who was appreciative but evaluative. Other contemporary films did not make this cut, such as the 1936 short *Romantic India*, which is a grab-bag of stock footage on Indian tea, rice mills, temples, the Darjeeling train and elephants. It was deemed unsuitable 'in the teaching of geography' and listed for 'theatrical exhibition' by the *Monthly Film Bulletin*.[41] Various geographical shorts shared an imperial ideology, but only some received curricular approval because they submitted to disciplinary norms.[42]

READING FOR LIFE ITSELF

So far I have argued that the geographical films accepted in school curricula demonstrated the anatomy of a rational imagination, which was part of British imperial geography's disciplinary formation. I now depart from this kind of historiography to leverage through the cracks of the rationalist imagination, by considering that the concept of an accurate imagination was based on an assumption of geographical and national consensus over accuracy. While this makes aesthetics a matrix for imperial ideology, it also makes it unreliable in conveying the actual *shifts* in what counted as accurate. For the GBI geographicals, the map and the photograph were key visual formats that could extend a stable, referential status to the cinematic medium. This was only possible through the suppression of contemporaneous contestations over the function and use of colonial maps and photographs as accurate or referential tools for reality and its governance. Moreover, the notion of an accurate imagination was aided by the concept of accurate representation, which gave imagination the 'logic of visualization'.[43] Towns in India were visualised to make them intelligible and transparent, with vision transforming a place, its people and the fullness of their lives, into abstract space.[44]

When I watch these films today – films that make colonial bodies indistinguishable from topography – I am nevertheless startled by the location shots, crowd shots and close-ups of people in Bikaner, Udaipur or Afghanistan, in their own place, in their own time. I experience a sense of visual familiarity and intimacy with people, almost more vivid because they are hedged by the film's levelling narration. Without claiming to access or restore the lives and places flattened by visual representations of imperial geography, I aim to methodologically unseat the primacy of the film's disciplinary perspective in delivering them to us, by looking for alternative records of colonial place to understand the exclusions upon which such geographical visions were based. This necessitates re-reading the films from a postcolonial present, which opens up copious material in British and Indian archives organised not around film, but around various graphic modalities of imperial administration (such as mapping, documenting, memo-writing and photographing place) connected to the films of colonial terrains. With a more capacious archive, the objects and interpretive matrices familiar to film studies can be questioned for their arbitrary delineation of visuality to cinematic texts, which cannot tell us the whole story. Conversely, the present demands a more rigorous turn to film *qua* film, so that we can reclaim the affectual distinctions between geographical films as disciplinary objects of their period, against the cinematic event that is a repeatable and renewable (though always placed) encounter between spectators and texts. Even as ideological fictions, geographical films rely on a locational cinemato-graphy that carries the technical ability to preserve a fragment of time and place as a moving image, to reveal its details to other eras such as our own.

In ways that have been rehearsed several times since the 2001 US invasion of Afghanistan, the Northwest Frontier Province was proving ungovernable to the British. By 1937, the Government of India was receiving complaints about the entry of nomadic Afghans into British India with improper travel documents, like passports without photographs, or unauthenticated photographs. The Afghan Passport Rules provided for 'the issue of passports without photographs to nomads, carriers and labourers – presumably because of the difficulty in obtaining photographs in Afghanistan – and because nomads etc have been locally exempted in the N.W.F.P and Baluchistan from the Indian Passport Rules'.[45] This exemption was set to expire in 1938, which provoked discussions in preceding years between the Ministry of External

Affairs and the Home Department over the best course of action. The above quote is borrowed from one such exchange. Eventually, the administration accepted that while it was desirable for the Afghan government to 'encourage the art of photography in Afghanistan by sending some of their subjects to India for training', it wasn't possible to enforce photographs because the Afghan border was too large and porous, photo studios and visa acquisition points too far apart, and booksellers in India not in possession of Afghan almanacs.[46] R. B. Elwin, Undersecretary to the Government of India, Home Department, concluded caustically that 'any Afghan can cross the frontier when and where he likes without meeting anybody'.[47]

These nomadic Afghans who escape photography, or leave a frustrated trail of bureaucrats pursuing their accurate visual trace, are not part of the lexicon of images in BIF's *The North West Frontier*. The cobbler, metalworker and cartridge maker of the film are depicted within fixed environments, and filming them is an invisible, uncontroversial procedure that cannot address the unrecordability of certain subjects. Geographicals show a rootedness of locals in an environment, and a lack of ambiguity about the viewer's position in relation to it. 'This is a view of the walls from the outside', says the narrator about the walls of Bikaner. 'And now we are looking at the walls from the inside of the town.' This stability of our status in relation to the place contrasts with the more chaotic conditions surrounding photography as a mode of representation and control within the colony.

Moreover, mobility is a central part of the geographical films' theme and spectatorial perspective, but it is simultaneously a discriminatory index, in that the fluidity of the map and camera is contingent on the presumed stasis of the recorded subjects. The film *Bikaner* follows the journey of water into town, and ends with the maharaja's journey in royal procession through town. Busy street scenes show traffic moving dynamically and diagonally toward or away from the camera. But metaphorically, the restless people are static. The town is uncomfortably wedged in time and the people situated within a presentism of typologies, enabled by a nominalism of the imperial imaginary that, as Arjun Appadurai argues, treated Indian tribes and castes as 'abstractable from the regional and territorial contexts in which they function[ed]'.[48] Unlike the abstraction of the populace formative of Western liberal democracies, the modern imperial state represented India's population as a series of special groups, rather than as a collective of individuals. The civilisational snapshot of a place naturalises the colony, and the optic of scientific classification divests it of the conflict of history.

The same may be said of the cartographic symbols in the films, which convey none of the challenges of standardising maps of India during this period. Maps share with film screens the quality of flattening space. For accurate cartography this means projecting the uniform scale of a spherical globe onto alternative shapes like cylinders, cones and planes, which distort constancy unless certain standards of transcribing latitudinal and longitudinal distances onto a flat surface are accepted. Under the leadership of the British government in 1909, an international conference of interested (imperial) nations was convened to publish a series of sheets mapping the entire world following uniform standards.[49] This standard was referred to as the International million map of the world, the *Carte Internationale du Monde*, according to which a map of the world on a scale of one to a million was proposed.[50] The publication of such maps ushered a new era of cartography, promising a uniform idiom for comprehending the world:

> a map of the world on a uniform system, in which all sheets are arranged to fit together along the margins – uniform in their manner of reckoning longitudes from the meridian of Greenwich; uniform in their manner of reckoning heights in meters above the mean level of the sea. They will have the same method of indicating the relief of the land, the same conventional signs for towns and roads, the same styles of lettering to distinguish between physical and political features. In a word, the whole map will be written in the same language, without difference even of idiom.[51]

In 1937, Colonel Campbell, director of map publication in India, led discussions to replace the varieties of maps available on India with 'one popular standard' that would conform to the *Carte Internationale*.[52] Conforming Indian topography to international standards posed some problems. The *Carte Internationale* road classifications allowed for three kinds of roads, unlike the 'Survey of India' maps, which recorded roads of many varieties. In India, three classes of roads were reserved for 'wheeled traffic' alone. Then there were the 'generally motorable' 'transfrontier' roads (fourth category); 'transfrontier' roads for 'other wheeled traffic' (fifth category); 'pack animal' roads (sixth category); and 'footpath' (seventh category).[53] The heterogeneous transport pictured in the GBI geographicals, ranging from camels, horses and ox-carts to pedestrians, rickshaw-wallahs and automobiles was precisely the problem in fitting Indian topography within any recognised criteria of the International series. On 2 September 1937, a letter went out from the Surveyor General's Office in Calcutta to the Secretary at the Central Bureau of the Ordnance Survey Office in Southampton, England, requesting special exemption.

> Sir, I have the honour to state that we are contemplating a change in our 1/M map policy. A conference will be held in Delhi in early December at which the RAF, Civil Aviation Directorate, the Army, and others interested will be represented … we would like, if we can do so without seriously impairing the international value of the maps, to facilitate and expedite the change, by adopting a more convenient contour and layer interval than those laid down … . Should we be unable to satisfy the interests represented at the conference, by adherence to three classifications … we would like the liberty to adopt say one more classification, the necessary modifications being made in symbols used.[54]

Needless to say, this request was not granted by the Ordnance Survey Office on the grounds that 'Central Bureau has no power to authorise modifications of the style of the Carte Internationale du Monde au Millionième', since those standards were set by an international community of Western nations in London in 1909 and in Paris in 1913. 'Such supplementary editions to the 1/1M Map produced by various countries as do not practically conform to the decisions of the Conference shall not be regarded as forming part of the International Map of the World.'[55] Official-seeming cartographic symbols standardised across the 'Indian Town Studies' edited out the resistance of the land to productions of visual regularity, to allow an international comprehensibility otherwise impeded by non-cinematic graphic translations of the landscape, which were more accurate or at least more useful to motorists, army officials and aviators on site. The films fulfil the fantasy of a cosmopolitanism that was contingent on erasing the particularity of the land.

The equivalence between the writing out of a place and the writing upon it is described by Henri Lefebvre's notion of differential space, which emerges from the differences that must be eliminated to make lived space into abstract space.[56] Narrating a history of the confrontations foundational to the appearance of representational or abstracted space allows us to retrieve a sense of location through the analytic of space. Information about colonial location proliferates in imperial geography, but the same gesture abstracts the thing at the core of its discipline: location. Conceiving of space as a product rather than object of study reveals geographical knowledge as an artifice in itself, and allows locations a reality greater than their artefactual status within disciplinary knowledge. Geographical films play a curiously dual role in this dynamic between reducing a location to artefact against permitting place its liveness. Despite being defined by the disciplinary demands of geography, the films animate a place and its past by capturing the crowds, their environments, their faces and movements in the moment, making them live in an eternal present. Film is at once what condemns the represented place to abstraction and what redeems it. Cinema's potential to quicken perception, in Siegfried Kracauer's sense of its ability to move us to novel encounters with a world when its details are isolated and distilled by reality's technological reproducibility, is not countenanced by Lefebvre.[57] For Lefebvre, films are intrinsically abstracting entities that cannot yield anything beyond the illusion of time and space.

'Can images of this kind really be expected to expose errors concerning space?' asks Lefebvre. 'Hardly ... . On the contrary, images fragment; they are themselves fragments of space. Cutting things up and rearranging them, *découpage* and *montage* – these are the alpha and omega of the art of image-making.'[58] The redemption and manipulation of reality (through a photographic image) appear at two ends of a spectrum of possibilities for cinema that I want to keep alive as a debate with historical resonances, but circumvent as a choice, through my focus on colonial films that show us the importance of a different kind of question about cinema's relation to the temporal and spatial dimensions of the real.

As the preceding films show, time and place are not neutral entities but dense products of a political encounter. Anne McClintock identifies this as a feature of colonial discourse that places colonies in 'anachronistic space' (reminiscent of the metropole's past) and 'panoptic time' (condensing in a glance the relative advancement of the Western subject).[59] Once we understand time and place as products of colonial knowledge, they become untrustworthy units of film historiography in themselves. Simultaneously, cinema's technological ability to liberate material reality from the chronology and corrosion of time through its techniques of montage and facilities of recording push for a form of historiography sensitive to the medium's multiple and ongoing presents. So our question should not only be what or how colonial films add to a pool of knowledge about a period or a nation in film, history and politics, though these are crucial questions. We additionally need to ask how film spatialises reality, how this spatialisation of reality does or does not situate place within certain teleologies of narrative and history, and how historical narrative in turn spatialises

Empire and Film

knowledge in its treatment of colonialism. The first is a question about medium, the second about politics and the third about disciplinary paradigms that facilitate our interpretations of a medium and its politics. In the case of the 1937 GBI films, the final question draws attention not only to the disciplinary practices of geography but also to film studies, which is itself not placeless but defined largely with reference to the Euro-American academy, of which I am a part.

My point is that the act of writing a film historiography of imperial Britain or colonial India is not just about Britain or India or the 1930s, though it is most certainly also that. Undertaking such writing forces us to simultaneously confront categorical assumptions foundational to film theory and history, because those categories cannot be transplanted to the context of colonialism without qualification. This is a productive crisis that throws up wide-ranging questions: What makes a film colonial? What is colonialism's entanglement with early film history and modernity? How do we account for the blurred boundaries between actuality and fiction films in the colonial context, where fantasies betray the needs of *realpolitik*, and documented colonies appear phantasmagoric? Do colonial films need their own theoretical vocabulary, or must cinema itself be examined differently in light of what we learn with regard to these films? What if, as Brian Larkin argues, the emergence of cinema relates not just to 'that ur-form of industrial modernity, the commodity' but equally to the politics of state power?[60] What if a film's screen space is conceived not only in relation to the viewer's mobilised virtual gaze, as Giuliana Bruno and Anne Friedberg suggest, but through the lived, social spaces abstracted by that mobility?[61] These questions gain relevance as colonial films from India and Africa become more widely available for review, calling into question our categories for organising them in relation to currently acceptable grids for studying film and film history.

CONCLUSION

While space has emerged as an important category in tracing cinema's links to cities, urbanism, architectural design and modernity, foregrounding categories of analysis in the writing of film history calls for the treatment of space as a critical optic in historiographic writing.[62] Such a spatial turn is particularly suited to track the self-evidence that accrues around historically contingent categories, by interrogating how people and places acquire their boundaries, their emplacements and their relationalities to other people and places, studied in this essay within a series of films, and within their contexts of exhibition and comprehension.[63] I have focused on the spatial imaginary of films about Indian towns, which deploy the referential tools of maps and location shots in responding to a historical need to address (and create) informed British citizens through modern education.

Philip Rosen has proposed that the 'attempt to conceptualize historicity in theory or practice must implicitly or explicitly acknowledge the referential ambitions of any historiography'.[64] The referential dimension of history writing may have potentially obscured the relevance of spatial questions to the discipline. Rosen uses film theorist André Bazin's work to think through intriguing similarities between cinema and historicity, linking in particular film historiography's referential ambitions to Bazin's elaboration of a spectator's faith in the temporal simultaneity between reality and its mechanical reproducibility. Such a linkage permits Rosen to sidestep questions of space in favour of questions of temporality as central to both historiography and film theory. But connecting historiography's referential impulse to complex realist theories of temporal simultaneity denies the spatial dislocations upon which the reconstituted continuum of history is founded, of which Bazin is cognisant as he considers edits and camera movements able to maintain a sense of reality's ambivalent fullness.

This is not to suppress Rosen's point that space is 'also a basic Bazinian category'.[65] It is merely to note that Rosen's reading of filmic space primarily in terms of the spatial likeness or contiguity between world and image permits an ascendancy to issues of temporality, because that is what obsesses the Bazinian subject with regard to the credibility of an image.[66] Admittedly '[s]patial likeness and deviance are finally not the crux of Bazinian realism'.[67] But Rosen's lesson that the subject is key to any reading of Bazin teaches us that, in addition to the credibility of the photographic image – which derives from a faith in the temporal simultaneity of world and image at a moment in the past – its ability to humanise by endowing all things with a visual, spatial and potentially moral equivalence are significant to his phenomenology. Elements of filmic space (including, to follow Rosen, motion and perspectival composition) are relevant to the kinds of transactions a film permits between the world, the image and spectator under a Bazinian system, just as space is relevant to the historiographic process of preservation through the retrieval, storage and translation of a past spatial logic.

Cinema's spatial dimensions may additionally provide inspiration for a non-linear historiography. The Soviet film-maker Sergei Eisenstein saw cinematic montage as a 'means to "link" in one point – the screen – various elements (fragments) of a phenomenon filmed in diverse dimensions, from diverse points of view and sides'.[68] The spatial trope of an analytic montage to provoke a fullness of vision, or at least to instigate the realisation of vision's partialities, is well suited to colonial film historiography, because it can allow each film to be undercut by an analysis of its management of *other* potential relations between memory and history, society and subject. Postcolonial scholarship elaborates on the deconstructive – or in Eisensteinian terms, the cinematic – mode of historiography as necessary to dismantling the prerogative of certain geographical territories to theoretical, rather than merely empirical, knowledge. Fundamental categories that explain the world, such as history or philosophy, are indexed to events that occur in what Dipesh Chakrabarty calls a 'hyperreal Europe', while others have no existence outside their qualifying particularity.[69] Location defines one form of knowledge, and is defined by another.

A critical colonial film historiography offers an opportunity to break the conspiracy between epistemic formations and places of production, allowing us alternative routes to spatialise knowledge. Read in these ways, the GBI shorts bring links between epistemic, geographical and cinematic space to the foreground, forcing us to seek an ethical response and an appropriate historiography for people and places who are preserved in time, but wrenched from their spatial contexts through acts of imperial film production, circulation and preservation.

NOTES

Part of the research for this essay was conducted with the help of a grant from Advancing Scholarship in the Humanities and Social Sciences, offered by USC's Office of the Provost. Anjali Arondekar and Kara Keeling's early comments on this essay were very helpful, as were bibliographic suggestions from Stephen Legg. The article developed from a presentation given at the University of Pittsburgh, and I thank the audience for their generous and provocative suggestions.

1. Rachael Low, *The History of the British Film 1918–1929* (London: George Allen & Unwin, 1971). Noting that there was an 'unfounded optimism' in the post-war years as production companies such as Hepworth, Gaumont and Pearson, and even later companies such as Ideal and Stoll, expected to return to markets they had enjoyed prior to 1914, Low observes that many producers were forced to quit with the decline in business from 1920 to 1924. The British film business became less viable with its lack of capital and distribution capabilities and the influx of Hollywood films. British Instructional Films, in addition to Herbert Wilcox and Michael Balcon of Gainsborough, withstood these pressures by 'making films of a completely different character' (p. 107; also see p. 129).

2. See *Monthly Film Bulletin* vol. 4 no. 8 (31 December 1937), pp. 261–2 for descriptions of these films. All four films were produced by Mary Field, supervised by G. J. Cons, with diagrams by R. Jeffreys.

3. For the 1937 reuse of footage from 1934, look under 'Appraisal' of 'Foothill Town: Darjeeling' in *Monthly Film Bulletin* vol. 4 no. 8 (31 December 1937), p. 261. Also referred to in <www.colonialfilm.org.uk/node/1645>.

4. Compare *Fair City of Udaipur* (1934), available for view at <www.colonialfilm.org.uk/node/857> with my descriptions of the 1937 series.

5. For descriptions of the 'Secrets' series, see *Monthly Film Bulletin* vol. 1 no. 5 (June 1934), pp. 35–6. This older series follows the tradition of early reels from India, many of which are catalogued under exploitative titles like 'Nautch Girls Dancing' and 'A Hindoo Sacrifice', putting them in the realm of the shocking, titillating and outrageous. As I discuss further, such extremes were insufficiently accommodative of disciplinary geography's proposed balance between an 'artistic' and 'scientific intention' in organising topographic and ethnographic material for educational purposes. See *The Elge List 1902: Gaumont and Company, Reel 2* (London: BFI, World Microfilms Publications Ltd, 1982).

6. *To-day's Cinema* vol. 49 no. 3708 (9 September 1937), p. 1; *Monthly Film Bulletin* vol. 4 no. 8. (31 December 1937), pp. 261–2.

7. I wouldn't carry this analogy too far. The nature film's transition from creature to product highlights an omission in geographical films: the latter never names the conditions under which product is extracted from labouring entities. Referring to the silk moth, an intertitle tells us: 'To secure the silk it must be unwound before the moth spoils it by dissolving the end of the cocoon.' This is followed by a shot devoid of moths, with just a spindle winding thread from cocoons. 'When the silk, which sometimes is a double thread more than a mile long, is wound off, the dead body of the pupa comes to light.' A human hand enters the frame, giving scale to the visuals and holding a pupa from different angles. The cinematographic capture of the beauty of the insect, combined with an instrumental attitude to the extraction of its product that renders the creature redundant, is not

transportable to geographical films though it may be present in industrial films. The elided middle of the geographical shorts is imperialism, which has transformed India as dispersed territory into India as a source of labour, raw material and market. The naturalisation of this process suppresses imperial need as the central rationale behind generating a particular range of products. In speaking of the colony as a space, Achille Mmembe talks of it as 'a formation of terror that combines massacre and bureaucracy' (Mbembe, 'Necropolitics', *Public Culture* vol. 15 no. 1 (2003), p. 23). Geographical shorts replicate bureaucratic vision as reality, but show little of the rest.

8. Mary Field and Percy Smith, *Secrets of Nature* (London: Faber and Faber, 1934), p. 189.

9. The 'Indian Town Studies' were thematically less coherent than BIF's 'Empire Series', (1925–8) discussed by Tom Rice in his essay, 'Exhibiting Africa: British Instructional Films and the Empire Series (1925–8)' in this volume.

10. G. J. Cons, who supervised these films, held a lecture and screening on 27 May 1937 for a mixed audience of film, education and BBC representatives, explaining 'how the shorts came to be edited' from entertainment films. Unfortunately, no transcripts of this presentation survive. *To-day's Cinema* vol. 48 no. 3620 (27 May 1937), p. 7.

11. Following the semiotics of C. S. Peirce, who was also an expert on map projections.

12. Christopher Pinney, 'Introduction: How the Other Half ...', in Christopher Pinney and Nicholas Peterson (eds), *Photography's Other Histories* (Durham, NC: Duke University Press, 2003), p. 6.

13. G. J. Cons (ed.), *Handbook for Geography Teachers* (London: Methuen and Co., 1955), p. 23. In 1932, Miss D. M. Forsaith, a Lecturer in Geography at Goldsmiths College, edited the *Goldsmiths' College Handbook for Teachers of Geography*. The standing sub-committee in geography of the University of London undertook revisions of this version in 1955, under the editorship of G. J. Cons, also Lecturer at Goldsmiths College. I have not found the 1932 edition, and use the revised version as the basis for my discussion. The new edition incorporated changes such as an age-specific arrangement of information, and a section on 'Visual Aids'. With its emphasis on imperial understanding, the 1955 edition reveals the extent to which the political circumstances of Britain shifted over two decades, so using the later text to frame films from 1937 needs defence. I argue that a departure from strictly chronological thinking is essential when it comes to colonialism, in order to confront how the past shapes and lingers in the present. There is an arc of continuity that my citational practice allows me to emphasise. The 1955 *Handbook* uses writings from the 1920s to create its arguments, as we will see, and its emphasis on visual media in geography and on comprehension and imagination (rather than on rote knowledge) relates to a political shift in Britain favouring an emphasis on interdependence and bilateralism in imperial affairs, which dates to the interwar period, and connects the 1930s to the 1950s. (For a discussion of how concessions to bilateral rhetoric influenced commercial film policy starting in the 1920s, see my book *Cinema at the End of Empire: A Politics of Transition in Britain and India* [Durham, NC: Duke University Press, 2006], pp. 41–103). An initiative in 1950 toward internationalisation in geographical education, organised by UNESCO at Canada's McGill University with geographers from twenty-three countries, including the British Commonwealth, evokes this blurred sense of time, as it grafts an 'international' regime on the 'colonial' world with no reassessment of intellectual paradigms. See C. D. J. Back, 'The Teaching of Geography in Relation to the Development of International Understanding: UNESCO Seminar', *Australian Geographer* vol. 5 no. 9 (June 1951), pp. 250–3.

14. Cons, *Handbook for Geography Teachers*, pp. 12–13.
15. Ibid., p. 115.
16. Fairgrieve, quoted by Ashley Kent, 'Geography: Changes and Challenges', in Maggie Smith (ed.), *Teaching Geography in Secondary Schools: A Reader* (London: Routledge, 2002), p. 4.
17. Cons, *Handbook for Geography Teachers*, pp. 2, 1.
18. By 'growing citizenry', I am referring to an expansion of male suffrage (with the Representation of the People Act, 1884), and a broadening state mandate to educate the working classes, as compulsory education was instituted in 1880 and made free after 1892. For a discussion of the kinds of 'institutionalisation and professionalisation of geography' that accompanied this from 1830–1918, see Avril Maddrell, 'Discourses of Race and Gender and the Comparative Method in Geography School Texts 1830–1918', *Environment and Planning D: Society and Space* vol. 16 (1998), pp. 81–103.
19. Halford Mackinder, 'The Teaching of Geography from an Imperial Point of View, and the Use Which Could and Should Be Made of Visual Instruction'. *Geographical Teacher* vol. 6 (1911), p. 80. It is important to maintain a distinction between the centrality of the visual within an emerging geographical *dispositif*, shared across the first half of the twentieth century in Britain, and the more changeable attitude that prevailed in school classrooms towards technologies of visualisation, such as film strips versus silent or sound motion pictures. Mackinder used the lantern slide extensively in his public lectures, and condemned the cinematograph as 'too cumbrous and expensive' an apparatus, that would 'render thought unnecessary' (Mackinder, 'The Teaching of Geography,' p. 85). This view of the cinematograph in education was not held in the 1930s or 1950s, though Mackinder's ideas on the significance of accurate visualisation to modern geography prevailed. For more on Mackinder's use of visual media and his role in geographical education as well as geopolitical theory, see James Ryan, *Picturing Empire: Photography and the Visualization of the British Empire* (Chicago, IL: University of Chicago Press, 1998) and Gerry Kearns, *Geopolitics and Empire: The Legacy of Halford Mackinder* (Oxford: Oxford University Press, 2001).
20. Cons, *Handbook for Geography Teachers*, p. 10.
21. Mackinder, 'The Teaching of Geography', p. 80.
22. Ibid., p. 79:

> New conditions [regarding unity of policy] prevail to-day in every part of the King's Dominions ... to be obtained only by the free consent of the several peoples. This consent, if it is to be relied upon, must be based on a reasonable agreement in regard to aims, and sympathy in regard to difficulties.

23. Cons, *Handbook for Geography Teachers*, p. 10, quoting Mackinder. Also consider: '"When you understand all about the sun and all about the atmosphere and all about the rotation of the earth, you may still miss the radiance of the sunset." Geographical field work makes such a gap in experience less likely' (Cons, *Handbook for Geography Teachers*, p. 4).
24. Mackinder, 'The Teaching of Geography', p. 80.
25. Cons, *Handbook for Geography Teachers*, p. 2.
26. Mackinder, 'The Teaching of Geography', p. 82. He continues, 'In these days, when international affairs have become worldwide, it is necessary that the great human contrasts which are the outcome of universal history should be generally known ...'.

27. See Martin Heidegger's 1938 lecture 'The Age of the World Picture', in Julian Young and Kenneth Haynes (eds and trans.), *Martin Heidegger: Off the Beaten Track* (Cambridge: Cambridge University Press, 2002), pp. 57–73.

28. For an application of Heidegger's essay in discussions of photography, maps and early cinema, see Tom Gunning, 'The Whole World within Reach: Travel Images without Borders', in Jeffrey Ruoff (ed.), *Virtual Voyages: Cinema and Travel* (Durham, NC: Duke University Press, 2006), pp. 25–41, and Christopher Pinney, 'Future Travel: Anthropology and Cultural Distance in an Age of Virtual Reality: Or, a Past Seen from a Possible Future', in L. Taylor (ed.), *Visualising Theory* (London: Routledge, 1994), pp. 409–28.

29. David Lloyd and Paul Thomas, *Culture and the State* (New York: Routledge, 1998), p. 7.

30. Admittedly, the repulsion of power or its negotiation at an individual level are not Foucault's focus.

31. Uday Mehta, *Liberalism and Empire: A Study in Nineteenth Century British Liberal Thought* (Chicago, IL: University of Chicago Press, 1999), p. 4.

32. There is great durability to these principles of education, which were enshrined in 1950 in the UNESCO seminar mentioned previously, though the seminar was dedicated not to 'imperial' but 'international understanding'. 'International understanding is an attitude. An attitude that cannot be taught, but it can be fostered by intelligent thinking about facts.' Such thinking occurred when the teacher aroused in students 'an objective, but at the same time a sympathetic and lasting interest in other people and their problems' (Back, 'The Teaching of Geography in Relation to the Development of International Understanding', p. 252).

33. Cons, *Handbook for Geography Teachers*, pp. 8–9.

34. Mackinder, 'The Teaching of Geography', p. 84.

35. Arjun Appadurai, 'Number in the Colonial Imagination', in Carol A. Breckenridge and Peter van der Veer (eds), *Orientalism and the Postcolonial Predicament: Perspectives on South Asia* (Philadelphia: University of Pennsylvania Press, 1993), p. 323.

36. Mackinder, 'The Teaching of Geography', pp. 84–5.

37. Cons, *Handbook for Geography Teachers*, p. 118.

38. Scholars writing about the contradictory working of state and free-market logics particular to interwar Britain provide valuable insights into the novel institutional experiments characterising this period. In this anthology, see Lee Grieveson's essay 'The Cinema and the (Common) Wealth of Nations' on the contradictions of capitalist and territorial power operative in the British state's attitude towards cinema within the imperium in the early twentieth century. In *Cinema at the End of Empire*, my reading of the 1927 Quota Act as a policy aimed at mobilising the empire as a unit of trade rather than territory falls into this line of inquiry.

39. National Archives, CO 323/985/23. See letter dated 5 August 1927 from the Comptroller-General, Development and Intelligence, to the Undersecretary of State, Colonial Office, describing this request.

40. Cons, *Handbook for Geography Teachers*, p. 120.

41. *Monthly Film Bulletin* vol. 4 no. 8 (31 December 1937), p. 262. The original copy of this film was provided by the Government of India, and was re-edited by C. E. Hodges Production Ltd. An earlier review in the *Monthly Film Bulletin* is equally negative and lists the film for 'theatrical exhibition' rather than instruction:

Each of the sequences has its own interest but they have only the vaguest relation to each other and there is practically no indication of their locality. The "tea-time" music and the wordily uninformative commentary are of less assistance than bare titles would have been. (*Monthly Film Bulletin* vol.2 no. 23 [September 1935], p. 182)

42. Aside from an instrumental rationality expressed here, there was also incidental consensus over educational material when such a consensus was tactically efficacious. For instance, in 1937, the BFI printed some criticism of films held by the Empire Film Library at the Imperial Institute. When the latter reacted with the objection that, unlike the BFI, it was dependent on High Commissioners and empire governments for films, so that criticism from national organisations may lead its supply sources to dry up, the BFI 'tactically dropped their idea of criticising publicly the films in our Empire Film Library'. See Letter dated 20 May 1937 from H. A. F. Lindsay of the Imperial Institute to J. H. Jones of the Department of Overseas Trade, National Archive, T161/844.

43. Henri Lefebvre, *The Production of Space* (trans. Donald Nicholson-Smith) (Malden, MA: Blackwell, 1991), p. 96.

44. The last sentence is an echo of Lefebvre's comment in *The Production of Space*: 'People *look*, and take sight, take seeing, for life itself' (p. 75).

45. C. S. A. G. Savidge, Undersecretary to the Government of India, external affairs (EA), memorandum dated 13 December 1937. The migrants came through Assam, Shillong and Burma. See National Archives of India, Home (Political) 'Afghan Travel Documents: Request to the Afghan Government That All Passports Issued to Afghan Subjects Should Contain a Specimen Signature or Thumb Impression of the Holders', F 17/437/38.

46. National Archives of India, Home (Political). Letter from Savidge dated 18 May 1938, F 17/437/38.

47. National Archives of India, Home (Political). Letter from Elwin dated 15 July 1938, F 17/437/38.

48. Appadurai, 'Number in the Colonial Imagination', p. 326. Appadurai's argument is about how this migrates into the national communal imaginary.

49. There were twenty-one attendees at the London conference, though I have not been able to find the entire list. The next conference held four years later in Paris repeated nine delegates from the London conference, and I am using these attendees as representative of the international community that defined 1/M standards. Nations in Paris included Britain, France, Germany, Belgium, Denmark, Holland, Italy, Russia, Sweden, New Zealand and India (represented by a British member of government). See 'Carte Internationale du Monde au Millionème', *Geographical Journal* vol. 43 no. 2 (February 1914), pp. 178–82.

50. Consult G. R. Crone, 'The Future of the International Million Map of the World', *Geographical Journal* vol. 128 no. 1 (March 1962), pp. 36–8, for details of the conference.

51. *The Edinburgh Review*'s report is reproduced in 'The International Map of the World', in Edward J. Wheeler (ed.), *Current Literature* vol. 53 (July–December 1912), p. 55, under the 'Science and Discovery' section.

52. National Archive of India, Home (Public). 'Herewith a sample volume of a proposed new series of map for India', 516/1928.

53. This was the system followed by the existing India and Adjacent Countries (I and AC) series, which was to be replaced by the 1/M series. See 'Survey of India–Map Policy Conference', in National Archive of India (Education. Forests, 32-14/37).

54. Ibid.
55. Ibid., Letter dated 25 October 1937.
56. Lefebvre, *The Production of Space*.
57. This is Miriam Bratu Hansen's instructive reappraisal of Kracauer in her 'Introduction' in Siegfried Kracauer, *Theory of Film: The Redemption of Physical Reality* (Princeton, NJ: Princeton University Press, 1997), pp. vii–xlv.
58. Lefebvre, *The Production of Space*, pp. 96–7.
59. Anne McClintock, *Imperial Leather: Race, Gender and Sexuality in the Colonial Context* (New York: Routledge, 1995), pp. 32–7, 40.
60. Brian Larkin, *Signal and Noise: Media, Infrastructure, and Urban Culture in Nigeria* (Durham, NC: Duke University Press, 2008), p. 12.
61. Giuliana Bruno, *Atlas of Emotion: Journeys in Art, Architecture and Film* (London: Verso, 2007); Anne Friedberg, 'The Mobilized and Virtual Gaze of Modernity: Flâneur/Flâneuse', in *Window Shopping: Cinema and the Postmodern* (Berkeley: University of California Press, 1993), pp. 15–32.
62. See, for example, Mark Shiel and Tony Fitzmaurice, *Cinema and the City: Film and Urban Societies in the Global Context* (Oxford: Wiley-Blackwell, 2009) and Edward Dimendberg, *Film Noir and the Spaces of Modernity* (Cambridge, MA: Harvard University Press, 2004).
63. The terms (boundaries, emplacements, relationalities) self-consciously mimic Michel Foucault's tracing of the Western history of space in his essay 'Of Other Spaces', *Diacritics* vol. 16 no. 1 (Spring 1986), pp. 22–7.
64. Philip Rosen, *Change Mummified: Cinema, Historicity, Theory* (Minneapolis: University of Minnesota Press, 2001), p. 7.
65. Ibid., p. 29.
66. Rosen asserts:

> For Bazin the photographic or cinematic image always provides the spectator with absolute brute knowledge that the objects visible in the frame *were at one time* in the spatial 'presence' of the camera, that they appear from an irrefutable past existence. Furthermore, this 'presence' of the camera to object lasted *for a certain amount of time*. (Rosen, *Change Mummified*, p. 29)

67. Ibid., p. 19.
68. Yve-Alain Bois, 'Introduction, Sergei Eisenstein: Montage and Architecture', *Assemblage* no. 10 (December 1989), p. 111.
69. Dipesh Chakrabarty, *Provincializing Europe: Postcolonial Thought and Historical Difference* (Princeton, NJ: Princeton University Press, 2007), p. 40.

188

Empire and Film

10

Domesticating Empire in the 1930s: Metropole, Colony, Family

Julie Codell

This paper will explore what I call the domestication of empire, the correlation of a narrative about family life with topics of imperial bureaucracy and ideology. This parallel, symbolised by editing cuts between metropole and colonies, is prominent in two films made during the 1930s era of prolific production of commercial empire films in both Britain and the United States: *The Four Feathers* (*FF*, 1939, Zoltan Korda) set in the Sudan in 1898 and *The Sun Never Sets* (*SNS*, 1939, Rowland Lee) set in West Africa's Gold Coast (modern Ghana) in the 1930s. My argument is that these films' constant editing back and forth between metropole and colony was an ideological strategy to domesticate empire by tying the domestic life of exemplary multi-generational families of civil servants to imperial ambitions, a special bond between family and empire which also permitted characters to critique and debate their imperial mission, resolved, in the end, by their decision to serve empire.

However, the collapse of imperial idealism with family life also generates a central conflict in these films in which centuries of family service to the empire is suddenly threatened. In both films a son initially refuses to enter civil service or join his regiment shipping out to the Sudan, arguing for individual agency and against social and familial pressures to carry out such duty in favour of their own personal wishes to do something else and remain in Britain. Refusing to submit to expectations conditioned by generations of family imperial service, these scions pit classical narrative's conventional focus on individualism against social norms. Both films resolve these tensions, however differently, to permit these sons to return home triumphant after severe tests of masculinity and loyalty but not always within prescribed imperial institutions.

Unlike most 1930s empire films in which characters reside in the colonies, coping with colonial insurgency and steadfast in their commitment to empire, these films' protagonists are contrained by the expectations of their families, who served in the military (*FF*) or civil service (*SNS*), a legacy that also legitimates their questioning the efficacy of empire, its purposes and sacrifices. In *SNS* the older son Clive's first name fittingly recalls Robert Clive (1925–74), famous as Clive of India, who defeated the French at the decisive Battle of Plassey (1757). In addition, the family's last name is Randolph, perhaps an allusion to imperial advocate Winston Churchill's Tory, pro-empire father.

A feature of the domestication of empire is that female desire, often antagonistic to empire either by being completely absent (e.g., *The Lives of a Bengal Lancer*, 1935,

Henry Hathaway) or thwarting imperial devotion (e.g., *Gunga Din*, 1939, George Stevens; *The Rains Came*, 1939, Clarence Brown) or criticising imperial missions (*Rhodes of Africa*, 1936, Berthold Viertel),[1] is harnessed in these films in an intense endorsement of males' imperial duties. Yet, like the men's view of family tradition as burdensome, the women condemn life in the colony (*SNS*) or never go there at all (*FF*).

In these two films decisions on colonial policy and practice are debated in London and at the protagonists' well-to-do homes, seeming to depoliticise empire by making it a family matter woven into the fabric of domestic life, as male and female family members both have investments in imperial service. These investments make the debates as much about family ties as about the national good, intertwining domestic life and nation into a single imperial force, perhaps to suture audiences to characters' domestic lives with which audiences might identify. But in this attempt the films ironically demote colonial life. In *SNS* Africans are subordinated to a battle for control of empire taking place between British civil servants and evil Russian scientist Zurof (Lionel Atwill), who is trying to take over Britain's African empire, an allusion to 1930s European politics and a defence of England as a benevolent, 'good' empire as opposed to the venal imperial ambitions of Germany and the Soviet Union.[2] Among 1930s empire films, these two are the most denigrating of indigenous populations – demonised Arabs in *FF* and infantilised Africans in *SNS*. Unlike *King Solomon's Mines* (1937, Robert Stevenson), *Rhodes of Africa* and *Drums* (1938, Zoltan Korda; US title, *The Drum*), which engage colonised populations' participation, usually in indirect rule, these films' protagonists serve without visibly affecting colonial subjects.

Using the promise of domestic stability to justify empire, these films none the less communicate an anxious empire from which characters wish to escape, perhaps reflecting empire's increasingly destabilised position amid rising anti-imperialism in India and Africa, and Americans' outspoken sympathy for Gandhi, isolationism at the outset of World War II and general hostility to British imperialism, despite their own imperial ambitions since 1898. The back-and-forth editing emphasises sharp differences between British and colonial landscapes: wealth vs poverty, spaciousness vs overcrowding, pruned foliage vs untamed jungle, mansion vs huts, rich greenery vs life-sapping desert. Within these insistent dichotomies, imperial problems remain unresolved despite, or even because of, the happy family resolutions in these films. The filmic space reimagines colonial space as distant and degraded, heightened by editing that emphasises differences between metropole and colony and tensions between public and private spheres, unhappily merged in Africa, but properly separated in England.

As 'Rule Britannia' plays, *The Sun Never Sets*' opening rolling text declares:

> [To] The countless millions bred in the British Isle who, through the past four centuries, have gone forth to the far corners of the earth to find new countries, to establish laws and the ethics of government, who have kept high the standard of civilization—this picture is respectfully dedicated.

Then the film cuts to a map of the Gold Coast accompanied by 'oriental' music and the text: 'heat – humidity – fever – known for years as "the white man's grave"'.

This is followed by an aerial shot of the African compound of huts, and a medium shot of an anxious Helen (Barbara O'Neil) waiting for her duty-bound husband Clive Randolph (Basil Rathbone), so that they can return to England. Asked if she would return to Africa, she replies, 'Never, I hope, never'. Clive speaks a native language as he and the chief face each other and Africans sing a Westernised song. In the car Helen and Clive, thrilled to be returning to England, laugh while Africans seen through a window behind them gradually disappear.[3]

Then the film cuts to the sea and sky as if from the boat that carries Helen and Clive home. In London, the 'Seat of Empire' intertitle appears over a shot of the Houses of Parliament. In the farewell ceremony before Clive left, a chair was brought out for the chief, so London as the 'seat' contrasts punningly with the chief's meagre chair, among the film's many contrasts between Africa and England. Then there is a low shot of Big Ben above Thomas Thornycroft's backlit sculpture of Boudicca and her daughters in a horse-drawn chariot. Boudicca, a symbol of British nationalism by the nineteenth century, led an uprising against the Romans; she slaughtered populations in towns she razed to the ground, resisting the Romans for two years until they defeated her. The statue is an ambiguous image of a native queen fighting colonisers, surely commenting on British resistance to Germany, not the British Empire.

Then the film cuts to Downing Street, followed by an intertitle 'Colonial Office' and Clive's discussion with his supervisor, who commends Clive's fifteen years of service and anticipates a promotion for him so he can remain in London. At this point, 'home' embraces the Colonial Office, and Clive's supervisor is a family friend. Then at the grand Randolph country house, Clive's younger brother John (Douglas Fairbanks, Jr) argues against entering the service. Clive and John in the middle distance on the left, along with their uncle, are in front of a piano beneath a portrait of an ancestor who looks like an eighteenth-century East India Company nabob. When John shouts that he will not go into the service, Mother (Mary Forbes) looks shocked in close-up. John argues that he has a right to have some say over his life and justifies this by citing family failures: Uncle Gerald after thirty years in India got only a 'petrified liver'. Clive would have cracked up without Helen. Grandfather (C. Aubrey Smith) spent forty years in the service but made one mistake and was sacked. John wants more than a pension and his fiancée Phyllis (Virginia Field) wants a home, not 'a succession of bungalows in far-flung parts of the empire'.

Empire and a proper home are opposed in John's argument and fittingly John and Clive face each other before the large hearth beneath a mantelpiece filled with family memorabilia. Uncle Simon (John Burton) plays 'Pop Goes the Weasel', identifying John's protest with childishness. Maturity is associated with service, childishness with a focus on oneself, identifying individualism as a problem for both family and state. John insists that the family has been sacrificed to imperial service and that it is time the sun set on the empire.

Phyllis adds her protests. As the women mobilise to change her mind, John goes upstairs and finds Grandfather, who at first endorses John's hostility to service. In a lush study filled with colonial memorabilia, Grandfather pins flags of all the Randolphs in service on a map, including American Randolphs, one of whom was an early governor of Virginia. Those who have died, one recently in Nigeria, have their flags put into a special box. Asked what he got from the service, Grandfather says only a sense of belonging, feeling a part of something bigger, unlike those who

> go around the world thinking only of themselves and their pockets, never taking part in any thing that matters. They find later they don't belong anywhere. I pity them very much. When I die, I shall leave you something, it isn't money, but the old maps and books and family history. Don't bat an eye, I shall be cursing the service, as you did, as we all do, but we belong.

John is chastened and meets Phyllis; both realise that John must enter the service.

Suddenly the film cuts back to Africa's dusty landscape, with the clichéd image of a map. Scientist and madman Zurof is questioned by British Commissioner Carpenter (Douglas Walton) about exploiting natives in his goldmine and bribing chiefs, practices 'contrary to British policy'. This 'meanwhile back in the colony' scene shows how badly things are going in Africa without Clive. When Carpenter leaves, Zurof and his accomplices discuss a plan to buy native land.

The film cuts back to Clive at the Colonial Office doubly disappointed at not getting his new post and being sent back to the Gold Coast to investigate Zurof. Clive's supervisor says, 'There are troublesome things taking place in different parts of the empire that we don't like and don't understand', a fictional reference to the film's plot, but also a reference to real rising Gold Coast protests against British rule. Clive comments that his family will consider the assignment a black eye.

Then the film cuts to the formally attired family at dinner over a well-loaded table, all denigrating the Gold Coast as the worst possible assignment. A servant's remark that they are keeping food hot for Clive prompts Grandfather to tell a lively story about *his* grandfather and Clive of India, in which the signal for danger was the phrase, 'the plum pudding is hot', a story his family cuts short, having heard it often. John will later use this phrase to signal his single-handed infiltration of Zurof's radio broadcasting compound. Clive arrives to face their expectations of his 'promotion', only to tell them that he's going with John to the Gold Coast. Helen, now pregnant, is visibly disappointed, but is determined to go with Clive. She eventually suffers a miscarriage in Africa, further identifying that continent as a place that thwarts domestic harmony and even threatens future generations, at curious conflict with the family's pride in its extensive imperial service, but foreshadowed by Grandfather's earlier mention of a cousin who died in Nigeria.

As they exit the front door en route to Africa, John reads the motto over the door: 'Ite et gloria fulgentes redite', which he translates. He jokes, 'it's a far, far better mess I'm going to make of these than have ever been made before', echoing Sidney Carton's self-sacrificing speech in *A Tale of Two Cities* and foreshadowing his later willingness to die to save both the empire and his brother's reputation. Mother, the moral force who frowns on John's resistance to serve and insists that women should support their husbands, gives everyone flowers (a reminder of tamed English gardens, perhaps) as they leave for Africa. Grandfather assures her that 'most of them' will return and then puts John's and Clive's flags on his map.

In Africa, John comments on the smell of Africa, described as old tyres by civil servant Cosey (Melville Cooper). A close-up shot of the ground underscores Africa's extremes – we see dust, then monsoon rains and floods – contrasting with England's cultivated botanical richness. Clive interrupts the sale of native land to Zurof's men and upbraids the chiefs as greedy, willing to sell their land and people for gold, and thus rendering British intervention necessary to save them from themselves. Africa is uninhabitable; Africans are childish.

In addition to the family manor, Britain is represented by the Colonial Office, which discourages any mixing of family and professional service. Clive's supervisor may be a family friend, but the top-level administrators reject Clive's report identifying Zurof as a threat and condemn him, not only for taking Helen to Africa but for neglecting his official duties to tend her during her miscarriage. For this dereliction, Clive is relieved of his post. Clive's failure is due to John's desultory performance: he mislays an important message; believes Zurof's lies about Officer Carpenter (who Clive tries to reach in torrential rain); reveals a secret message to Zurof; and sends a phony message precipitating Clive's return, causing Clive to fail to reach Carpenter, who dies. This destruction of his career and perceived failure to do his job sends Clive into a feverish rampage, distressed that he will be viewed as a laughing stock by service cohorts. John, who accused Clive of being driven by 'duty, duty, duty', must repair this damage by later risking his life to infiltrate Zurof's headquarters.

Clive and Helen are sent to the coast while John, worn out and drinking excessively, remains in their place. Suddenly Phyllis appears and she and John form a new imperial couple. She helps John recover and rededicate himself to work. John recites the family motto ('Go forth and return with honour'), but plans to quit the service and work for Zurof. He is afraid to go home, but Phyllis brings the family's love and the box of flags signifying the Grandfather's death. Grandfather had asked that John put his flag in the box, a request that transforms John, who recites the family motto again, now in Latin, as he places the flag in the box. He and Phyllis marry in Africa.

Then the film's pace quickens. Following scenes of terrorist action in Africa and the Colonial Office's discussion of Zurof creating havoc in order to boost prices of the molybdenum that he mines, John carrys new bride Phyllis across the threshold to find a message from London requesting that he find Zurof. Here John must sacrifice celebrating his wedding night to carry out his duty ('a job for Clive'), encouraged by Phyllis. They must get Cosey drunk to remember the important message that John lost, a rather silly moment of comic relief, which reveals the existence of the radio tower.

Alluding to contemporary events, the film montages Zurof's vision of taking over the world with scenes of marching soldiers, military mobilisation, anxious Office bureaucrats, all linked by a voiceover about war preparations and intertitles: 'mobilization', 'propaganda', 'uprisings', 'rebellion', 'revolt' and 'invasion'. These references collapse German aggression and colonial unrest as a combined danger and imply government incompetence to deal with them. To save the empire and family honour, John, having 'a chance to do something really important', infiltrates Zurof's compound and tower to send a radio message, 'the plum pudding is hot', which only Clive can explain, turning Grandfather's family story into a decoding device to save the nation and the empire. But the Office orders Clive to guide bombers to the compound, giving him a chance to save his reputation and career, while also putting him in the position of possibly killing his brother. John survives the bombs and Clive rescues him. Suddenly the film cuts to Mother opening the mansion doors to greet the returning imperial foursome with flowers, then to the family motto over the door, and finally to Clive, Helen, John and Phyllis in Grandfather's study redoing the map flags accompanied by ceremonial music.

Thresholds are important as metaphors for coming and going between metropole and colony. Family members leave and return through the door of their home. Clive asks to carry Helen over the threshold as they leave Africa, and John carries Phyllis over the threshold of their African abode after their marriage. The sea can be interpreted as a threshold early in the film as it marks Clive's and Helen's return to London. Doors are momentously opened and closed – the doors of the living room are closed by the rebellious John and opened by the chastened Phyllis. John crosses the threshold of Grandfather's study, where he will have his mind changed. Clive, bearing disappointing news, opens the dining-room door to an anxiously awaiting family. The British commissioner is denied access to Zurof's scientific expedition trailer, then let in. Thresholds mark disappointment, achievement, marriage and imperial comings and goings, distinguishing between home and colony and between home and Colonial Office in London, while in Africa home and office share a building. Imperial service and the British home overlap and intersect on micro and macro levels, sometimes joined, sometimes complementary, sometimes oppositional.

Thresholds mark overlaps and contrasts among three sites. The family home is a refuge *and* an incubator for civil servants *and* an archive of family-cum-British imperial-service history. At the Office, Clive's supervisor is a family friend but his superior insists home and work are incompatible. The Randolphs bring their family to Africa to domesticate imperial service, but the Home Office fails to grasp this, accusing Clive of dereliction of duty when he ministers to Helen. Clive then puts duty over family – taking the blame for attending his sick wife and agreeing to lead the bombers that endanger his brother. But the film does not entirely endorse this: John survives the bombing, and the brothers and their wives return to London presumably for good.

The editing that juxtaposes home, Colonial Office and Gold Coast also serves as a threshold, entering and leaving these three sites. The Gold Coast, of which we see almost nothing, represents the Victorian Africa of the European scramble, not the Africa of 1939 in which Gold Coast, Kenyan, Nigerian and Francophone Africans (Tunisia, Algeria, Chad) agitated for political representation and independence. In 1934 the Gold Coast Youth Conference, founded in 1930, sent a delegation to London's Colonial Office to petition for constitutional change. I. T. A. Wallace-Johnson (1895–1965) of Sierra Leone, who organised the first trade union in Nigeria in 1930, founded the Gold Coast West African Youth League (WAYL) in 1935, a group critical of imperialism; he was expelled from the Gold Coast in 1937 and arrested in 1939. In 1937–8 Gold Coast African cocoa planters, brokers and chiefs resisted monopolistic purchasing by expatriate British companies, refusing to sell cocoa (the 'hold up') until prices rose.[4] Similarly, youth movements sprang up, one in Nigeria was founded in 1933, and the Kikuyu Central Association formed in Kenya in the 1920s to protest British expropriation of agricultural land, while the British in Tanganyika

(Tanzania) attempted to coordinate and control indigenous political activity.[5] But the film submerges independence movements by barely showing Africans and instead depicting Zurof's machinations as the cause of problems. The film turns 1930s colonial agitation into a family romance, in which Africans are minimalised, appearing only to be chastised by Clive for their greed, or belittled when John picks a boy to be his servant.[6]

The Four Feathers, based on a 1902 novel by A. E. Mason (1865–1948),[7] was produced by pro-imperialist Alexander Korda and directed by his anti-imperialist brother Zoltan, both Hungarian refugees in Britain.[8] The Kordas created a film trilogy idealising empire: The Four Feathers; Sanders of the River (1935, Zoltan Korda) about twentieth-century Africa, with a sympathetic portrait of a British administrator; and Drums, which focused on the Northwest Punjab in the nineteenth century, heroised British military officers and demonised Muslims. This last film sparked riots in India and was condemned by the Indian press.[9]

Korda's translation of Mason's novel retains much of the original storyline: Harry Faversham (John Clements) disgraces himself by quitting the army, then redeems his manhood by suffering and heroism in the Sudan. But the novel is set during the first expedition to Egypt and the Sudan in 1882–5, which failed to rescue General Charles Gordon, while the film centres on the 1895–8 campaign led in 1896 by Herbert Kitchener, which defeated the Sudanese. Korda exchanges the novel's failed military campaign for a successful one in order to heroise Britain's empire and appeal to an audience witnessing German aggression against Czechoslovakia and Poland.

The film is filled with orientalist stereotypes: a casbah café, cruel Sudanese, the native informant Karaga Pasha (Amid Taftazani), ethnographic content typical of 1930s empire films, and aerial shots that emphasise the epic scale of empire. The invented 'oriental' music by Miklós Rózsa accompanies the opening title:

> In 1885 the rebellious army of cruel dervishes enslaved and killed many thousands of defenceless natives in the Sudan, then laid siege to Khartoum. The scanty garrison's heroic commander, General Gordon appealed for help from England – but no help reached him.

Thus, the 1898 return of the British to the Sudan appears justified by dervish cruelty towards defenceless natives.

This film was an early colour film, receiving an Academy Award for colour cinematography, and this turn to colour induced a focus on spectacle that boosted its popularity, as did its themes of self-sacrifice and gallantry among colonial armies acting as a 'good' force to liberate peoples from tyranny. Korda's and Osmond Borradaile's African footage has been reused in other movies, including remakes of this one. Zoltan Korda shot action scenes where the battles really took place. A former cavalry officer, he knew how to move men and horses. The film, however, is not monolithically militarist: it pokes fun at the military bravado of ageing Sir John Burroughs (C. Aubrey Smith again) ('Those were the days when war was war, and men were men') and criticises the harsh masculinity of Harry Faversham's father. There are touches of black humour: a friend lost his leg in the war, which 'ruined his cricket'. There is plenty of heroic excess here, too – especially Faversham turning starved and diseased Sudanese prisoners into a para-army that helps win the war.

The film opens with fighting dervishes on horses, swords drawn against helpless fleeing civilians. Gordon's death appears in a montage ending with the fictional *London News* report on the fall of Khartoum and 'murder' of Gordon in 1885. Then the film cuts sharply to a country house and a carriage driving up, the start of an annual banquet of a regiment of ageing Crimean soldiers at the home of General Faversham (Allan Jeayes). He and Dr Sutton (Frederick Culley) discuss Gordon's death, which Faversham blames on Gordon's softness, 'he wasn't hard enough', noting, too, that for the first time in 100 years no Faversham was serving in the army, another explanation for Gordon's failure. Faversham worries about his fifteen-year-old son Harry, who reads poetry, 'Shelley of all people', saying that he hopes to lick Harry into shape, 'make him hard'.

At dinner Burroughs lays out the Battle of Balaclava on the dinner table, later reenacting it several times to everyone's amusement. He claims to have led the 68th into battle. But the most compelling dinner-party stories concern frightened soldiers punished for cowardice. Burroughs threatened one until he went into battle and died 'as he should … shot to pieces'. They recall Willington, who had a father killed at Inkerman, a grandfather blown up under Nelson, and an uncle scalped by Indians. Harry's father says, 'there is no place in England for a coward', for whom suicide is deemed a fitting end. When Harry leaves, he walks past portraits of his forbears, each in military dress, the last on a rearing white horse, recalling Jacques-Louis David's famous portrait of *Napoleon*. Dr Sutton follows Harry; 'I knew your mother, too', he tells him. Sutton is a gentle, caring man without machismo or bravado and seems to understand adolescent Harry's trepidation. Referencing Harry's mother, Sutton validates Harry's 'feminine' side.

The film then cuts to Harry marching with soldiers in redcoats, as his North Surrey regiment prepares to join Kitchener. Hearing the news, all raise their helmets and cheer except Harry, who appears frightened. His friend John Durrance (Ralph Richardson) notes that Harry still reads poetry. Ethne Burroughs's (June Duprez) soldier brother Peter (Donald Gray) announces his sister's engagement to Harry and her debut is celebrated at the Burroughs' enormous country home with its grand ballroom.

Then Faversham suddenly resigns his commission, only taken to please his now-dead father. His commander, shocked to see a cowardly Faversham, accuses Harry of shirking his duty to both father and country. Then Harry in street clothes watches soldiers embark to cheering crowds and tenderly say goodbye to their families as the crowd sings 'Auld Lang Syne'.

The film cuts to Ethne's family manor house, where Harry reminds her that they had discussed the futility of going to war and that fact that it was a waste of time that they could otherwise spend together. He insists that at home he could save his estate and those neglected by his family, who preferred 'glory in India, glory in China, glory in Africa'. In this scene, a case is made for staying at home and the empire is characterised as a distraction from home duties.

A package arrives for Harry with three white feathers from his cohorts, including Ethne's brother and Durrance. Her father refuses to speak to Harry, who also recognises Ethne's disgust over his resignation. She explains that they were 'not born free … . We were born into a tradition, a code which we must obey, even if we don't

Empire and Film

believe ... because the pride and happiness of everyone surrounding us depends upon our obedience'. Harry takes her ostrich feather from her fan as his fourth feather.

The film cuts to soldiers in Kitchener's camp, including Harry's friends and the black corps of Sudanese soldiers. The Kitchener who invented the concentration camp in the Boer War is here presented as charming. Then back to London where Dr Sutton approaches Harry with an offer of help. Sutton agrees that duty to home should exert a stronger call than duty to African peasants, but Harry admits that stories told at his father's regiment banquet haunted him:

> my father despised me and fear turned to reality ... I am a coward, doctor .... To be a soldier and a coward is to be an imposter. I fought against it. I deceived myself .... The men who sent feathers knew me better.

Harry will leave for Egypt and contact the doctor within a year, if he is still alive.

Harry then sails on the Red Sea and visits Sutton's Arab doctor friend, requesting the disguise of a Senghali tribesman, branded and with his tongue supposedly torn out by the dervishes, so he can find Kitchener's troops. We watch the branding as the first test of his masculinity. The doctor calls him a brave man, but also calls the English a mad race, and tells Harry to be a coward and be happy, while giving him news of the whereabouts of Kitchener's regiment. Beautiful shots of the Nile are offset by native workers dragging boats and being whipped. The cruelty of Africans is what identifies them. Harry appears distinct, very white among anonymous black workers. Then the film jumps to Durrance's regiment amid locusts, desert, a hot sun and rocky terrain. Durrance loses his hat and goes sunblind. In a parched, barren, brown, dusty setting Harry and Durrance wander under circling buzzards. Then the film suddenly cuts to evening on the terrace of Ethne's home and the arrival of Dr Sutton, who has not heard from Harry in a year and presumes him dead. They pass the pond's tamed and subdued tropical water lilies, signs of empire abruptly contrasted by a cut to the Nile's wild nature. In Africa the army doctor diagnoses Durrance as permanently blind.

Finally, to complete this sequence on Durrance's blindness – its absoluteness, its effect on his relationship with Ethne and ultimately his inadvertent revelation about Harry – the film returns to the terraced gardens of the Burroughs estate and horses leaping over hurdles, as the blind Durrance relearns the upper-class pleasures of the hunt and prepares to marry Ethne. During dinner, Durrance tells of a silent, solitary Arab who saved his life, then robbed him, which Sutton calls 'Eastern' hospitality. Durrance only had Ethne's letter, which he gives her, whereupon she is stricken to see the white feather Durrance had given to Harry inside, a sign that Harry was the silent Arab. As they speak, the camera captures portraits of sixteenth- and seventeenth-century ancestors who once served the empire.

The link to Harry continues with the film's return to Omdurman, where a crowd is taunting two Englishmen in a cage, a sharp comedown from the aristocratic life these two once enjoyed and to which the blind Durrance has returned. Disguised, Harry plays a flute on which is written, 'don't despair', a signal to the two men. During the overlong battle, the prisoners escape and help the British win the war.

In England Sutton tells Durrance that the German specialist cannot help him. Reading Braille, Durrance then recites Caliban's speech from *The Tempest*:

Be not afeard; the isle is full of noises,
Sounds and sweet airs, that give delight, and hurt not.
Sometimes a thousand twangling instruments
Will hum about mine ears; and sometime voices,
That, if I then had wak'd after long sleep,
Will make me sleep again: and then, in dreaming,
The clouds methought would open, and show riches
Ready to drop upon me; that, when I wak'd,
I cried to dream again. (III.ii.133–41)[10]

Why cite these lines spoken by the savage, sometimes cowardly Caliban, but in poetry, to signify that he possessed sensitivity and intellect too? Is the isle of Britain 'full of noises' to a blind Durrance whose hearing is now his most important sense? Is this speech a comment on waking imperial anxieties expressed in castrating war stories, Durrance's blindness, references to 'Fuzzy Wuzzies', the 'savage' abject Arab identity Harry takes on to save others? For Julia Kristeva, abjection is a border and an ambiguity.[11] Harry's body is a border between colonised subject and coloniser, 'savage' and 'civiliser', Africa as dirty ('Arab' Harry is filthy) and England as clean. Harry's body, like Caliban's, seems a border between civilisation and savagery, human and beast, and Africa and England, not a contact zone of cultural exchange, but rather an impermeable boundary of containment for both places.

Abject Harry serves alone, not through an institution, unlike the Randolph brothers. Outside the military that promulgated horror stories and a harsh masculinity, Harry can read his Shelley and, like Byron, fight tyranny without identifying himself as a British coloniser. He saves his friends by playing the abject savage, like Caliban, while carrying out heroic actions outside institutional imperial intentions. After all, the military could not protect Harry's cohorts from abjection in the Sudan, so severe that these scenes were censored when the film was shown in India to avoid showing white men as vulnerable.[12]

Harry's disguise as a lowly member of a speechless and branded Senghali tribe resonates with his being symbolically branded a coward. But the Senghali were branded for their rebellion, brutally subjugated but none the less resistant, although Faversham performs his Senghali identity as a weak, orientalised figure. Harry conflates this disguise with his British aristocratic identity, but it is by sacrificing his social and ethnic identities, that cowardly Harry can now perform heroic feats motivated by personal rather than national or imperial intentions. At home, the brand remains on his forehead, a mark of service and suffering outside the military order, as a payment for his return to a privileged life.

Abjection defines Harry, Clive and John: Harry's tortured body, Clive's disgraced dismissal and lost child, John's incompetence and later willingness to sacrifice himself. In *FF*, Harry 'goes native' through painful and painfully repetitious abjection in the film – branded, whipped, starved, imprisoned and tortured, unlike traditional travel narratives in which disguised Englishmen triumphantly infiltrate colonial cultures (e.g., Richard Burton's paradigmatic travels to Mecca and Medina in the 1850s). As native and as victim, he is feminised, an abjection he must experience to regain his masculinity. Defined as the sickness at one's own body, abjection may allude to these protagonists' awareness of the growing stigmatisation of imperialism, a colonialism from which they all retreat. Abject Africa is where they must redeem themselves through suffering, but as Europe's 'other', abject Africa is cast out from these films by erasure (*SNS*) or demonisation (*FF*), underscored by editing.

The film cuts to Harry back at the country home where Burroughs again complains about the soft army compared to his day. Burroughs is an ambiguous figure – he unflinchingly views death as the soldier's lot, while having himself survived, and he speaks the combined bravado and anxieties of imperial wars. He berates a younger generation as 'soft', but bores everyone with his story. Finally, Harry points out that Burroughs did not deliberately lead the Balaclava charge. His horse Caesar, startled by a bullet, reared and ran and the regiment followed, Burroughs leading the charge inadvertently, a 'magnificent mistake'. Correcting Burroughs is the deed that permits Faversham to give Ethne back her feather. It also allows him to become the family patriarch, replacing Burroughs. Thus, Faversham gains his masculinity in the imperial sphere, abjectly but independently of the military, and in the domestic sphere by gently correcting his blustering father-in-law, who epitomises imperial aggression.

What thematic device links the busy, often sudden editing back and forth between the Sudan and the country home? It is not thresholds and there is no mediating Colonial Office. The dining table structures the film, coming at the beginning and at the end and in decisive moments: old soldiers at their annual banquet at the Faversham estate, the final dinner with family and cohorts resolving all relationships, and the dinner when Ethne and Sutton discover the feather in Durrance's letter. Furthermore, this is an imperial table – Burroughs in his Balaclava story represents himself as an exotic tropical pineapple plucked from the cornucopian fruit bowl.

These dining scenes are subsumed into the larger trope of officers' imperial wealth: vast homes and gardens, tropical fruit and water lilies, and, above all, Ethne's stunning oversized dresses with broad shoulders and military-style jackets. Iconic close-ups of her from below exaggerate her size to fill the screen, making her a trophy, not a partner like Helen Randolph. In *SNS*, family displaced empire as a reason for service, allowing women to participate in empire as they soon would in the war. Ethne's iconic, eroticised femininity, mildly masculinised in oversized clothing and low shots, mark differences from and proximity to Faversham's poetry-reading, war-resisting, empire-questioning masculinity, as the film discards the harsh masculinity of Burroughs and Harry's fanatical father. His surrogate father, Dr Sutton, understands the feminine side and mediates between Harry and Ethne. He joins the family in the last dinner which contrasts sharply with the first banquet marked by hostility between father and son. Now Harry tones down Burroughs's bravado with a softer masculinity that *endures* rather than fights and can bear terrible suffering in order to help friends. Clearly, Harry and friends will enjoy luxury and well-stocked tables of imperial goods, including Ethne's tartan plaids.

These films never mention the imperial concerns – control of the Suez Canal, the scramble for Africa, access to India from Africa's east coast, trade, Africa's mineral resources – that required someone to stay in the colonies, as characters did in other empire films. But perhaps everyone needed to go home in 1939, as Britain braced itself for the war that would put some imperial issues aside, while drawing on colonised populations to defend Britain.[13] *FF* does not address anti-imperial Sudanese nationalism in the 1930s against Britain and Egypt. These events are disguised, sublimated or implied by inscribing the British Empire as the 'good' empire.[14] Both films represent Africa as an imperial possession and the 'white man's grave', a place of death, abjection and castrating blindness.

Anglo-American empire films presenting vast landscapes and lone heroes often appear nearly identical to the Western, a genre busy justifying America's internal colonial wars and genocide. But in 1939 imperial films were attacked in the US as war propaganda. Lawyer-turned-journalist John T. Flynn (1882–1964), 'an ancient foe of fascism, and chairman of the New York America First Committee', condemned Hollywood for not

> depicting the tyrannies and oppressions in India, where at this moment there are 20,000 India patriots in jail … . Think of the magnificent scenes in Technicolor that could be filmed along the banks of the Ganges, and think of the scenes in the jails and the courts that could provide magnificent glamour … no, what we get is 'Four Feathers' and numerous other pictures glorifying the magnificence, humanity and democracy of the British Empire.

Flynn claimed that Hollywood, like Hitler, used film as propaganda, deploying 'a furious, a feverish, a half-maniacal hatred that will turn our emotions into a raging volcano and deprive us of our reason', i.e., American isolationism.[15]

Unlike Kipling's poetic Cockney narrators, these protagonists have a stake in Britain in the form of their property, from which future generations of officers and civil servants will spring. How much audiences identified with such privileged families is unclear, though *FF* was very popular, boasting the adventure and spectacle that *SNS* lacked. Clive, John and Harry try to please parents (flower-giving Mrs Randolph; father substitute Sutton) and wives, but without hiding their vulnerabilities behind bravado. But whether institutional or independent, their imperial service none the less confirms the colonies' odiousness, dehumanises the indigenous and focuses on the return home. Helen's service in an African school is never displayed, denying viewers any sympathy with Africans, especially children, as antithetical to depictions of abject Africa.

Neither film foregrounds a civilising mission, a justification no longer convincing by 1939. The return home may comment on the realities of the threat at home, as Germany was moving across Europe and empire was becoming troublesome abroad. What was the purpose of empire, then? John argues: 'I may not like it … but I think I ought to find out about myself first.' In both films lone individuals, tested by empire, triumph outside of rather bumbling imperial institutions to which they refuse to submit. They are motivated by personal commitments – John to save Clive's and his own reputation, Harry to retrieve his reputation, save his friends and marry Ethne. Harry's service and suffering are both self-imposed by his personal mission and his Englishness – he could not 'be a coward and live', as the Arab doctor advised. John's and Harry's sufferings are self-imposed compensation for their initial reluctance to serve the state, what Freud called moral masochism, the need for punishment from outside forces (Harry's friends) or the superego (John's shame). Both men succeed through abjection outside the symbolic order of imperial fathers (Harry) or the Colonial Office (John). Interestingly, Harry's speechlessness puts him outside the symbolic order but, when he regains his speech, he returns home to become the new patriarch of that order.

These films not only suggest a contested view of imperial masculinity, but also a distinct view of empire. In other 1930s films a dangerous, fragile and potentially explosive empire is beset by native 'villains' threatening both British rule and 'good' natives. Civil servants and soldiers remain in the colonies to maintain order against these continually emerging threats and are denied domestic lives – Sanders goes to England to marry, but must return to Africa to quell a native uprising fuelled by European gunrunners, and marriage is humorously attacked in *Gunga Din*.

But in *FF* and *SNS* imperial service is synthesised with, but also diluted by, family responsibilities that, in the end, supersede imperial duties. While empire is ostensibly the purpose for their actions, the 'natives' are erased in *SNS* and demonised in *FF*, so that everyone can return home, echoing Harry's words that he could do more good at home than in Africa. Empire becomes a testing ground of masculine maturity, not an institution to safeguard trade, enrich Britain or spread British culture or religion. Without the narcissism of imperial buddy films (*Gunga Din*, *The Lives of a Bengal Lancer*), whose male bonds validate imperial service, or the justification of preparing natives for indirect rule (*Drums*, *Sanders of the River*), *SNS* and *FF* present imperial service as personally motivated, conflicted, cruel, masochistic and only properly rewarded by a triumphant reintegration into a lavish family home, to forever enjoy England's green richness far from Africa's deserts and jungles. Like boys' adventure stories or fairy tales, a young man is tested, commits a daring deed and returns as master of his domestic sphere. Like a bad dream, Africa is erased from imperial purpose or agency, and the male protagonists' idyllic 'imaginary landscape' of a well-to-do home permits them to 'mythically explore their quite specific dilemmas around identity' through a merely temporary presence in Africa.[16]

Thus, imperial service is a means to overcome Oedipal constraints (Harry's father replaced by Sutton; the Randolphs against the patriarchal Colonial Office) and return home as the patriarch (Harry corrects his father-in-law's story; the Randolphs succeed Grandfather). Masculine identity is performed and reclaimed in the empire, but its reward is a return home forever. Those who pit family against country (Colonial Office), duty against desire (Burroughs), a monolithic masculinity against one's own nature (Harry's father) are defeated by those with loyalties to people rather than to empire or abstract ideals. These films suggest a subtextual critique of empire and its bureaucracy in which abjection – Harry's beaten, mud-covered body, Clive's demotion or John's attempted self-sacrifice to save the family honour – can rearrange the imperial order. These two films imply that empire itself cannot be 'saved', that staying abroad was no longer feasible because colonial agitation founded on Enlightenment principles of representation and 'self-government could no longer be dismissed' in Africa or India, while imperial servants were needed at home to protect Britain in response to emerging resistance in the empire and the threat of possible colonisation by Germany at home.[17]

NOTES

1. Julie Codell, 'Imperial Masculinity, Mimicry and the New Woman in *Rhodes of Africa*', in T. Barringer, D. Fordham and G. Quilley (eds), *Art and the British Empire* (Manchester: Manchester University Press, 2007), pp. 254–66.
2. Zurof alludes to munitions dealer Basil Zaharoff, who supplied guns to both sides in the Boer War. See <movies.tvguide.com/sun-sets/119395>.
3. The *New York Times* vol. 26 (9 June 1939, p. 2) described 'the irrepressible Randolph family whose coat-of-arms must be inscribed with a stiff upper lip rampant on a field of whisky-sodas'. See also Kevin Dunn, 'Lights ... Camera ... Africa', *African Studies Review* vol. 39 no. 1 (April 1996), pp. 149–75.
4. See Rod Alence, 'The 1937–1938 Gold Coast Cocoa Crisis: The Political Economy of Commercial Stalemate', *African Economic History* vol. 19 (1990–1), pp. 77–104.
5. Assa Okoth, *A History of Africa: African Nationalism and the De-colonisation Process* (Nairobi: Heinemann Kenya, 1988), pp. 48ff.
6. On the scene of John picking a boy servant, see Julie Codell, 'Blackface, Faciality and Colony Nostalgia in 1930s Empire Films', in S. Ponzanesi and M. Waller (eds), *Postcolonial Cinemas: History, Aesthetics, Episteme* (London: Routledge, forthcoming).
7. This novel was remade into films many times: *Four Feathers* (1915, J. Searle Dawley); *The Four Feathers* (1921, René Plaissetty; 1929, several directors); *Storm over the Nile* (1955, Terence Young and Zoltan Korda), which used footage from the 1939 version; *The Four Feathers* (1977, Don Sharp), which also inserted 1939 scenes; and *The Four Feathers* (2002, Shekhar Kapur), which set the story during the 1885 Battle of Abu Klea, thirteen years before Omdurman, and a battle the British won but which they lose in the film.
8. Korda, knighted in 1942 for unofficial intelligence, escaped to Vienna in 1919 after the overthrow of the Béla Kun regime in Hungary and there formed Korda Productions with his wife Maria. He contracted with various production companies in Hollywood and Britain from 1927 to 1946 and always hired well-known Shakespearean or Hollywood actors. See James Chapman and Nicholas J. Cull, *Projecting Empire* (London: I. B. Tauris, 2009), pp. 15–32; Jeffrey Richards, 'Patriotism with Profit: British Imperial Cinema in the 1930s', in James Curran and Vincent Porter (eds), *British Cinema History* (London: Weidenfeld and Nicolson, 1983), pp. 245–56.
9. The film was attacked in the *Bombay Chronicle* vol. 8 (13 and 14 September 1938).
10. The quotation raises interesting questions: perhaps Caliban, a conceit as a savage poet, is called upon to stir audiences to the glories of British culture they must save from a new order of savages alluded to by whippings and forced labour? Are Europeans like Caliban waking from their collective dream into the nightmare of reality? Is the speech a comment on Empire or Germany's threat? These allusions are hinted at in this scene.
11. Julia Kristeva, *Powers of Horror*, trans. L. S. Roudiez (New York: Columbia University Press, 1982), pp. 9–10.
12. Priya Jaikumar, *Cinema at the End of Empire: A Politics of Transition in Britain and India* (Durham, NC: Duke University Press, 2006), p. 160, cites one censored scene when a 'native' spits into the prisoners' food trough.
13. By 1937, overt calls for military preparedness emerge in *Fire over England* and *Our Fighting Navy*. See Jeffrey Richards, *The Age of the Dream Palace: Cinema and Society in 1930s Britain* (London: Routledge and Kegan Paul, 1984), pp. 286–8.

14. See Prem Chowdhry, *Colonial India and the Making of Empire Cinema* (Manchester: Manchester University Press, 2000) and Jeffrey Richards, 'Boy's Own Empire', in John M. MacKenzie (ed.), *Imperialism and Popular Culture* (Manchester: Manchester University Press, 1986), pp. 140–64.

15. See Page A, Third Day, 'Film Monopoly Glorifies War, Inquiry Told', Washington, DC, *Times Herald*, 12 September, Book on the Senate Sub-Committee War Film Hearing. V. 1, August–15 October 1941, press clipping file published by Academy of Motion Picture Arts and Sciences, located in the David Selznick Collection (#3503/7), Harry Ransom Humanities Library, University of Texas, Austin. I wish to thank the Ransom Library for a Skaaren Film Fellowship to examine their film archives while researching empire films.

16. Griselda Pollock, *Looking Back to the Future* (London: Taylor & Francis, 2001), pp. 316–17.

17. M. W. Daly, 'Egypt and the Anglo-Egyptian Sudan', in A. Roberts (ed.), *Cambridge History of Africa*, vol. 7 (Cambridge: Cambridge University Press, 1986), p. 783.

AFRICAN EXPERIMENTS

▐▐

The Bantu Educational Kinema Experiment and the Political Economy of Community Development

Aaron Windel

The Bantu Educational Kinema Experiment (BEKE) was one of the earliest colonial film units to operate in Africa. Spearheaded by the Geneva-based International Missionary Council's (IMC) Department of Social and Industrial Research, the project was meant to be a field study in the logistics of shooting and displaying instructional films for rural African audiences. Led by a former British army officer and a recently retired education minister for Northern Rhodesia, the film unit toured Native Reserve areas of Tanganyika, Nyasaland (Malawi), Northern Rhodesia (Zambia), Kenya and Uganda, first recruiting and filming African actors and then later displaying the edited films in mobile cinemas.

The project drew from wells of ecumenical missionary activism, Colonial Office and individual colonial Government House support and American philanthropic money.[1] The Carnegie Corporation of New York was the principal sponsor, and the films created by the project were in keeping with the corporation's interwar goals of creating systems of instruction to reach rural, and largely illiterate, audiences in the American South, the Caribbean and Africa with practical lessons of agricultural development. In its short lifespan, the film unit shot more than thirty films. Most were didactic short films on topics of health and hygiene, animal husbandry and cooperative economics. Others advertised the institutions, infrastructures and personnel of colonial rule. The Post Office and the improving effects of the British tax were featured, and the wise agricultural officer was often a protagonist.

The film project had much in common with contemporary efforts by missionaries and colonial government to hone a pedagogy for what was considered at the time to be the unique 'African mind'. The Carnegie Corporation and the American Phelps Stokes Foundation were at the forefront of this movement of reform that sought to 'adapt' education to the presumed race-bound proclivities of black people. Already by the mid-1920s, the British Colonial Office had begun to reform its systems of 'native education' in Africa along the lines of the American model to account for racial differences in perception and cognition.[2] The African mind, reformers argued, flourished when occupied with agricultural work. Earlier efforts by missionaries to primarily teach English reading and writing (literary education) now raised suspicion in the central state.[3] Education in English letters might lead to improved livelihoods for some – for instance, in clerical jobs in the city. Social anthropologists who advised London, though, argued that a literary education tended to separate Africans from the rural source of their social structure. Interwar colonial education reformers insisted that the

African mind was rooted in the soil, and that native education should draw lessons from local places and rely on vernacular languages for instruction.[4]

Even so, indigenous forms of farming were considered backward and ill equipped to handle the modern requirements of social welfare and economy. There was overwhelming agreement in the Colonial Office, individual colonial government houses and even among missionaries that a fuller integration into the global cash economy was the only viable solution for rural uplift. 'Community development', which increasingly from the interwar period came to describe such reforms that at once sought to modernise African community life while affirming its agricultural purpose, embraced this new political economy. Reformers who pushed for community development argued that new methods of mass communication and public instruction needed to be deployed, and the dawn of a new age of electronic communication promised these in abundance. Education thus became the primary front in a campaign to transform African lives and to relate African rural labour to the desires of the Western consumer.

Film, and other forms of electronic communication like radio, were regarded by reformers as especially useful media for reaching the primarily illiterate audiences that were the targets of community development. The organisers of the Bantu Educational Kinema Experiment anticipated a future world of connectivity and the global synchronisation of cultivation and consumption that might improve the lives of Africa's poor. They were among the earliest twentieth-century mass-media promoters of 'development' as we recognise it today – that is, as an expertly supervised integration of rural lives into economic relationships that seek the political co-operation of global citizen-consumers and citizen-producers.

THE CRISIS OF CULTURE CHANGE

The Bantu Educational Kinema Experiment, like other interwar experiments in mass education, should be read as part of a larger colonial reform movement that used social-welfare initiatives with the overt goal of preventing radical social and political change in the midst of crisis. As educational director of the BEKE, George Chitty Latham was, more than anyone else, responsible for the content of the films. A career government administrator, Latham had gained a name for himself as a reformer. During his tenure as director of education, Latham transformed the Copper Belt territory's education system, implementing the recommendations of the 1924 American Phelps Stokes Commission to Africa to 'adapt' education to the proposed racial proclivities of Africans. Latham was part of the vanguard of interwar reformers who believed that colonial administration should aim at community development. He was convinced that Africans could only be co-beneficiaries of enlightened imperial rule if government could find ways to instruct Africans in their presumed natural roles as agriculturalists and disrupt the drift of African labourers from land reserves into employment on mines, European plantations and the clerical and service jobs of the city. These patterns of social change drew constant commentary from colonial critics and social anthropologists, and rapid social change increasingly came to be seen as the primary cause of political instability.

The administrative vocabulary influenced by social anthropology labelled the phenomenon 'culture change'.[5] When the traditional institutions of 'tribal life' changed, the argument followed, then the field was open to any number of dangerous political threats. Clear on the horizon for anthropologists, missionaries and administrators were nascent nationalist and pan-Africanist movements. In their search for solutions to perceived structural problems of indirect rule, reform-minded administrators worked to stem the tide of culture change by planning for a community-focused rural development system on African reserved land that would align African production to the global market with the assistance of European and American economic and agricultural expertise and give empire a positive moral force measurable in improved living standards.

Latham was among the chorus of critical voices decrying the effects of culture change for Africa. Community development, with reformed education as a first step, was necessary to prevent a complete dissolution of the relationship between the West and Africa. Shortly before joining the film project, he wrote in the academic journal *Africa* in 1934:

> Education in the West, especially in its teaching of history, has tended to inculcate and foster this spirit of nationalism. Whatever some people may think of the importance of 'national sovereignty,' it can hardly be disputed that for the benefit of the world at large and of the Africans themselves it is most desirable that the peoples of Africa should be brought to look on interdependence as the keynote of their relations with each other and with non-African nations. They have everything to gain by co-operating with western nations, provided we pursue an enlightened and liberal policy in regard to them. They have everything to lose if they become imbued with a spirit of hatred and non-co-operative nationalism.[6]

Latham was well known in the Colonial Office for leading an effort to reform native education in the Northern Rhodesian territory. Before the 1920s, education had been by and large a missionary concern, with literacy most prized, for the purpose of Bible reading and evangelism. 'Latham's scheme', as it was termed by the Colonial Office, focused instead on non-literary pedagogies. He set up a government Jeanes School, also funded by Carnegie, at Mazabuka where African teachers-in-training studied techniques of practical instruction in modern farming, hygiene and co-operative economics.[7] 'Teach by doing' was the Jeanes motto, and lessons using visual aids in the field – e.g. an agricultural officer's demonstration plot or a community garden – were preferred to books in the classroom.

While culture change was perceived as a problem throughout British Africa, Latham's Northern Rhodesia was its epicentre. In the early 1920s, it was discovered that the richest copper deposits in the world were on the British side of the Northern Rhodesian border with the Belgian Congo. This meant that a reliable supply of the most important component of the communications and electrical delivery systems expanding in Europe was located in a region increasingly considered a crisis zone in internal Colonial Office correspondence and in academic analyses. Mining operations in the region escalated, and labour was drawn from all over Central and East Africa. A reforming vision of political community began to take hold among influential missionary, state and philanthropic interests that accounted for global interconnection through modern technologies of communication over distance. 'Interdependence' and 'co-operation', as in Latham's quote above, became watchwords of the interwar period for administrators.

If culture change was the central problem for Africa, it was often argued that adapted education along Phelps Stokes and Carnegie lines was the solution. In practice, adaptation required the ceding of missionary turf in village education to state control; then the lessening of English-language instruction; and then the translation of uplifting lessons (always centred on farming, cash-crop marketing and hygiene) to the vernacular or to visual, non-literary forms of instruction. As the tribal institutions of indirect rule failed under the weight of culture change, reformers hoped that the village school and the co-operative would be there to fill the void. The cinema would be an important third pillar of community development.

The earliest community development initiatives that came out of this reform movement were attempts to forge new connections between Africa and Western centres of modernity. Reformers sought to create spaces for Africans to gather and feel themselves part of a community. But these sites of community should also connect them to sources of European instruction for modern agricultural production for market and life in the cash and credit nexus. The cinema, as was believed by many throughout the quasi-state development apparatus that yoked colonial government with missions and corporate philanthropic capital, was in a privileged position to speak to 'the African mind'. While the modern government school overseen by the Jeanes teacher and the government-supervised co-op would allow for the constant movement of knowledge about Africans from periphery to centre and back, the reforming film-makers of the BEKE imagined another layer of circulation that would deliver standardised messages (films produced for interchangeable soundtracks in various languages) to thousands of illiterate peasants at once. The films might then circulate to other, often quite different, groups. The intelligence-gathering mission of the Bantu Educational Kinema Experiment was designed to ensure that the right films, with the right content, cut the proper way, would end up before the appropriate audiences. The problem of mediating instruction across differences among colonial subjects in Africa, a limitation of empire that had recommended indirect rule through local institutions in the first place, would be solved by a media form that could communicate above linguistic and cultural codes.

The International Missionary Council's film experiment was designed from the start as a venture to encounter methods of combating culture change. Indeed, the choice to set up their base of operations in Vugiri, Tanganyika Territory was strategic for addressing the problem of culture change, since it put the film crew near the midpoint of a circle that encompassed the crisis zones of the Copper Belt and the Kenyan White Highlands. These were the places where anthropologists argued African populations were changing most quickly due to contact with settlers and with industry. In Tanganyika Territory, the project aimed at the Tanga province, the railway strip to Dar-es-Salaam and the Mwanza, Bukoba and districts and as far south as the Mbeya area on the border of Nyasaland. In Kenya they were concerned with the central and western portions of the colony where white settlement had been spiking since the British Crown offered 999-year leases on fertile tracts in Gikuyuland. In Northern Rhodesia, they focused on the central and eastern portions – the Copper Belt and the railway zone. For Nyasaland, they would travel from Fort Jameson in Northern Rhodesia to Zomba along the railway line and then by steamer on Lake Nyasa to Mbeya and the border of Tanganyika.

CHRIST THE ANTHROPOLOGIST, AND THE EXPERIMENT ON THE GROUND

The BEKE emerged out of the International Missionary Council's highly publicised 1932 study of industrial life on the Copper Belt and the effects of the intensification of mining on 'native life'.[8] That 400-plus-page study of culture change, and the cinema experiment that became one of its key recommendations, was conducted by the IMC's department of social and industrial research. Headquartered in Geneva, the International Missionary Council was itself an ecumenical imitation of international government that received its most immediate inspiration from the League of Nations. Its goal was similar to that of the international Christian Youth Movement to which its leaders often also belonged – to 'win the world for Christ in this generation'. The missionaries-cum-social scientists-cum-bureaucrats of the IMC were convinced that the churches needed to address the social and economic bases of faith. J. Merle Davis headed up the research department and was the co-ordinator of the cinema experiment at its London base. He argued that Jesus Christ was himself a social anthropologist, and a 'practical' one at that since he used years of embedded fieldwork to hone his evangelism with an eye trained to see the social function of bad beliefs.[9] The problem for the church in the twentieth century, Merle Davis argued, was the same as that of the imperial state under indirect rule.

Rapid change in African life had attended industrial expansion. The drift of African labourers into European plantations and mines could create instability with the potential for violence. At the very least it led to worsening material conditions on the reserves. Merle Davis saw this process as far worse than lingering 'superstition', the erstwhile scourge for Christian missions in Africa. As loathsome as the 'witch doctor' may have been to the missionary in Africa, Merle Davis argued that African society depended on him for social cohesion and could not do without him until other connective tissue could be grafted onto African society.

The cinema, like co-operatives and like the expert-monitored village-school system, might provide this connective social tissue through a shared community leisure activity where the audience would be observed, as its title suggested, in an experiment. It was the missionary playing anthropologist all for the purpose of more effective government. Missionaries would reap rewards if the God of the Europeans helped them to heal rather than to hurt. Scientific knowledge could supplant witchcraft, but the process of cultural conversion would be gradual and would require that the benefits of science be available and apparent to Africans.[10]

Latham was joined in the field by retired Major Leslie Alan Notcutt, a former plantation manager from Kenya who had previously experimented with cinema as entertainment for workers on the settler farm and claimed that it increased worker contentment.[11] Though he was a far cry from a professional film-maker, he was J. Merle Davis's first choice for the job. According to Merle Davis, Notcutt offered indispensable knowledge of the technical and cultural sides of the project. In addition to his experience as a plantation manager and his acquaintance with 'African mentality', Notcutt was an electrical engineer of ten years' experience, and he had also experimented with sound-on-film attachment.[12]

From Vugiri, Tanganyika Territory, Latham and Notcutt launched expeditions to film their instructional scenarios. The film-makers tried to employ African actors and to shoot on location in recognisable village sites. They wanted the films to be both instructive and entertaining. Writing instructional scenarios was the easy part. It was in being entertaining that the film-makers seemed constantly thwarted. Early on in the project, Latham took a trip to Zanzibar to explore possibilities of musical scores for the films. He had hoped to interview and recruit renowned taarab soprano Siti binti Saad, though he was apparently unsuccessful.[13] It is doubtful that even the soprano's voice could have compensated for the generally dull content of the films, which tended to focus on didactic lessons on agricultural improvement, the virtues of European mine managers (this in the wake of the 1935 worker strikes and violent police reprisals on the Copper Belt!), and the systems of European financial infrastructure that might help create an interdependent and prosperous African peasantry that would rely on European markets and European supervision. The BEKE's greatest successes came when they deferred to African advisors. For instance, on the advice of an African assistant at the secretariat in Dar-es-Salaam, Martin Kayamba, they filmed dances that proved to be audience favourites like the popular 'Goma,' which was inspired by coastal and Zanzibari dances.[14]

The BEKE repertoire included films on crop rotation, seed selection, soil erosion and co-operative marketing as well as films advertising the colonial government's departments and services, such as the Post Office and the Post Office Savings Bank. One film showed the improving purpose of hut taxes for building modern infrastructure. Another film showed the benefit of co-operative credit and marketing societies when properly supervised by Europeans, and the film-makers travelled to Kilimanjaro to observe the Chagga co-operatives in action. While the film-makers were impressed by the technique of shading coffee with banana trees (a Chagga innovation), Latham and Notcutt were not usually interested in the African perspective on the project, unless it came through the forms of experiment and reporting they had contrived. When a group of students from Makerere College in Uganda suggested that European music be used rather than African sounds, dances and proverbs, Latham quickly dismissed the idea: 'Some sophistication must be discounted', he wrote in his diary. 'Probably these boys do not represent general opinion.'[15]

The BEKE also made films on hygiene and disease prevention. One of the three surviving BEKE films in the British Film Institute's collection is on the prevention of tropical hookworm – a parasite that thrived in the colonial situation in areas with concentrated populations, such as the reserves and large plantations. According to the East African Commission's Report of 1925, upwards of 80 per cent of Kenyans were afflicted by the worm. The commission, led by future Colonial Secretary William Ormsby-Gore, had argued that the only cure was prevention through propaganda.[16] The BEKE hookworm film adopted this approach to hookworm control, which also fulfilled J. Merle Davis's requirements that the films should show the benefits of Western science over superstition. Their ten-minute hookworm film opened with a man suffering from the disease and consulting an African doctor in Western dress. The

'Pit Latrines Will Prevent Infection Provided Everyone Has Them'. *Tropical Hookworm* (1936) was the twenty-second film produced by the BEKE and shot near their studio in Vugiri, Tanganyika Territory. It illustrates the didactic form of most BEKE films, demonstrating the step-by-step process of constructing a pit latrine. Text panels would have been read to audiences in a local vernacular language, either live or via gramophone recording. First, the latrine is dug using a box as a shovel. Then a wooden panel is placed over the pit and sticks are interlaced to form a frame. The privy is completed by attaching leaves to the frame

doctor in the first frames is seen tending to his own daily hygiene by brushing his teeth. The film-makers struggled to find a way of conveying the insights of Western medicine into the invisible causes of the hookworm disease. They included magnified images of the worm burrowing into intestines. The film ends with a detailed demonstration of how to construct sandals from used tyres and how to build a proper pit latrine.[17]

Though the disease was almost certainly worsened by the conditions of dense confinement in the spaces reserved for Africans, the BEKE film-makers pursued the political agenda typical of colonial cinema and instructed people in how to create sanitised spaces in spite of worsening conditions. Given more bodies in reduced living areas, health could only be preserved through creating spatial separations – in this case, the covered pit latrine. The conditions of terribly unequal distribution of land were papered over, and instead the film conveyed the message that African ignorance to the invisible causes of disease was solely to blame for poor health on the reserves.

At their base in Tanganyika Territory, Latham and Notcutt edited the films and engineered the soundtracks. They hired Africans to translate and record texts in multiple Central and East African languages. The films were then packed on a lorry along with a projector and collapsible screen and taken on tour. Latham did most of the travelling, writing letters to and sometimes even exchanging films by post with Notcutt at the base in Vugiri. With their touring exhibitions, the film-makers aimed at as broad an audience as possible and strove to make the films understandable to the illiterate peasant or miner. It was a delicate task, and one that they believed required deliberation about the racial, environmental and historical differences that represented the gulf between European civilisation and the social and cultural forms of African tribes. What was chiefly advertised was not a commodity as much as a promised future of peace, security, health and prosperity that co-operation with imperial government could provide.

'Simple Ways of Making Sandals from Old Tyres or Hides'. *Tropical Hookworm* (1936) focused more on prevention than treatment and made no effort to be entertaining. In addition to recommending a visit to a medical dispensary, eating cassava leaves and building latrines, the film demonstrated how to make sandals from discarded tyres and hides. After cutting a portion of a tyre and tracing the outline of his foot, a man cuts along a chalked line. Holes are driven through the rubber with an awl, and a fibre belt is drawn through to complete the sandal. The finished article is modelled for the camera and the man is shown smiling with delight

For all their attention to understanding 'African mentality', Latham's accounts of the screenings reveal that the film-makers were often at odds with their audiences and stymied in their efforts to get a handle on sometimes raucous crowds, whose members improvised their own roles in these real-life scenarios of surveillance, discipline, amusement and resistance.[18] For many in attendance, these film screenings would have been the first time they had seen the bizarre effects of light passing through moving film.[19] Audiences sometimes demanded second showings, while at other times, such as the screenings on mining compounds, the soundtracks were drowned out by the din of crowd noise that managers could not subdue. The colonial situation carried its own tensions. In Kenya, the films were all displayed outdoors at sites chosen strategically between city centres and the reserve areas. At any point walking to or from the cinema, people were liable to be stopped and asked to produce a native labourer registration card (*kipanda*) for inspection.[20] On the Copper Belt, miners would have gone from a system of subterranean labour surveillance that included frequent naked medical examinations – employed to establish bodily standards for labour recruitment – to a theatre where, as members of a film audience, they were part of a project that was even termed an 'experiment'. The spatial separations created in the mines and dormitories to prevent the spread of disease (once mine doctors began to understand the spread of common illnesses at the mines as something related to bodies in close proximity rather than the quality of air) were reinforced in films on hygiene practice like the BEKE hookworm film.

VISIONS OF A COMMUNICATING EMPIRE

Community development in its various forms was always concerned with creating infrastructures of connection between metropole and colony. The cinema experiment was no exception. Given the absence of electrical infrastructure in the places visited by the crew, the film-makers engineered mobile-cinema-display units. Notcutt anticipated a grid of these touring cinemas to be deployed in every district. Ideally, these units would be left behind for easy operation by trained Africans, who would also direct films under the auspices of a state agency akin to the nascent British Broadcasting Corporation, thus ensuring, as the BEKE letterhead stated, 'effective control' of the message. Notcutt wrote:

> The idea is that these cinemas would be run by a local committee of natives and Europeans, one European and two or three natives actively managing the cinema. The equipment is such that it can be entirely native operated and the European would not have to take any active part in the performances. There would be, say, a monthly change of talkie films (in the local language) and performances would be given at the main centres in the District. Admission would be charged for except in the case of schools. The admission money would pay for the operation of the cinema and contribute to the cost of the films.[21]

The system of production and exchange of expertly supervised film footage required that films be able to circulate among different crews in various states of production:

> By the end of the filming tour copies of the first films would have been received in the territory, and the last task would be to provide these with 'talkie' in the form of commentary prepared by the Field Producer and translated into as many languages as required.[22]

What was to be exchanged would be a combination of commercial films and films drawn from interchangeable stock footage collected by field film crews but processed in London. The development of this system would add to the profits of the British firms with a hand in the film industry. Thousands of mobile cinemas would need to be outfitted with cameras and projectors likely to be supplied through the BEKE's sources, the British corporations Cinex and Ensign. Recurring costs of such a system of instructional cinema would include hundreds of thousands of feet of 16mm celluloid (the limited BEKE experiment required 28,000 feet). The economic circulation involved here would mean the opening of a new market for the London-based Gaevert corporation, the BEKE's celluloid supplier. In addition to the costs of material, the insurance industry and the Royal Mail would profit from the process of moving the machine components and films.[23]

The roving film units, the BEKE directors hoped, would collect footage in six-to-eight-month tours, avoiding the rainy season when possible, and then send the footage to headquarters in London for skilled processing, printing and editing 'together with a completed scenario written up on standardised forms, and any notes for the editor which the producer might think necessary'. The London headquarters would be a combination of the BEKE advisory council (which already included such luminaries as former Nigeria governor Frederick Lugard and anthropologist C. G. Seligman, as well as Bronislaw Malinowski's student Audrey Richards) and an editing and scenario development organisation akin to the Empire Marketing Board. It would be a 'clearing house for the reception and circulation of new ideas', whereby 'the secret of success in one territory could be passed on to others' and common problems simplified 'for an executive having knowledge of it from all angles'. It would also be 'a clearing house for scenarios', and it was argued that more talent for scenario writing would be found in London, especially for story films. Finally, 'the rough edited film … would then be sent to some appointed official in the territory for inspection' and final cutting.[24] Notcutt reckoned the cheap mobile units could be manufactured in one day with proper training.

Notcutt was a systems man. His habit of using and repairing machines – of imagining ways of converting electricity into image and sound and synchronising languages with images – enabled him to visualise this network of display units that could transcend differences of place by making all the essential components modular and interchangeable. This was, after all, how machines in that period were repaired, and much time in Vugiri was spent waiting on parts to arrive by mail from London. His vision of educational development at the village level was likewise one of many parts being guided to fit together as a whole. Latham and Notcutt's experience in colonial education and plantation management had convinced them that work and consumption were the same everywhere, which allowed them to ignore the meanings of work or health that might be tied to place in Africa.

The image of an efficient system – a network of circulation that would allow for teaching different minds for the same forms of work and marketing – was an omnipresent feature of community development for Africa between the wars. Notcutt and Latham each saw their purpose in the experiment, and in the project of development more broadly, as that of strengthening the connective links that joined the advanced West to 'backward' Africa. In Latham's long career as a colonial reformer we see him constantly at work imagining the links that he could help forge. The village school would be a node in a network that would recursively filter knowledge about the field back to its expert metropolitan centre. In Northern Rhodesia, Latham ensured that this very modern version of village education and supervision was put in place. The cinema experiment would similarly speak to the African mind through a scientifically informed pedagogy designed to affirm lessons suited for a future of globally integrated farming and consumption and that embraced pedagogies that sidelined the teaching of English.

And yet instruction in English was more often exactly what Africans wanted from European education. It was easy for many Africans to see that the coming of Europeans – especially when their numbers began to increase exponentially as white settlement began in earnest after 1900 – meant that English was becoming the language of power and status. Rapid transformations in labour regimes and land tenure and tax systems made the quest for English fluency a matter of community self-defence. For instance, a tax on every hut, regardless of whether it was on African-owned land, was levied beginning in 1901 on for British East Africa. As the juridical and tax structures of indirect rule were rapidly developed in Central Africa with the opening of the Copper Belt, the need for English only increased.

Like other efforts to create community bulwarks against culture change and avenues of public instruction to guide them, the backers of the cinema experiment and the film-makers themselves were convinced that African economic practice must incorporate forms of exchange that would relate African agricultural production to Western consumers. The film-makers used the experiment to begin to test the pedagogical forms recommended by the American Phelps Stokes Commission and the Carnegie Corporation, which sought to preserve the uneven relationships of Africans to their white rulers. The American model for the Southern US 'Black Belt', was to be extended to Africa. The overarching vision of the globe embedded in the theory envisaged the US South, the Caribbean and Africa as bread baskets to supply the populations enjoying the machine modernity in full force in Europe and the North Atlantic world. It was a vision of development that also maintained a role for European advisors for perpetuity. Community developers argued that the crisis of culture change needed to be met with new institutions able to forge new, non-tribal community ties. Rural development required European expertise not only in the short term but as a permanent solution to perceived racial differences, which, by accident of evolution or creation, had made Africans natural cultivators and Europeans natural technical managers.

The culture-change thesis was compatible with the conviction among missionaries, philanthropists and state officials that to restore land alienated from Africans through European settlement and mining concessions was an untenable solution. The goals of trusteeship, administrators argued, could only be achieved through state-managed cash cropping (preferably through registered, and thus closely monitored, co-operatives) and the promotion of welfare systems that could mitigate empire's negative effects. Efforts to guide a co-operative movement formed part of the mainstream of community-development initiatives, and reformers liked to publicise the rare instances of success-ful African co-operatives – like the Chagga coffee co-operatives on Kilimanjaro in Tanganyika that were the subject of a BEKE film. As the BEKE displayed that film throughout the Central and East African territories in its mobile cinemas, it was reinforcing the message of agricultural officers who in the 1930s began to aggressively promote co-operative economics. The Jeanes Schools that the BEKE film unit visited in its tours of Northern Rhodesia and Kenya had model co-operative shops and co-operative community gardens to reinforce the lessons. Meanwhile, the Colonial Office sent experts in co-operative economics on tours of British Africa to study the feasibility of the co-operative model there and to advise colonial governments on legislation to control 'native co-operatives' as they emerged.[25]

But expert-driven community-development reforms between the wars in Africa aimed to instruct in better methods of cultivation on land that often could hardly bear fruit. The missionary and the reforming government official both ignored the problem of land and resource alienation for Africans. Instead, they understood the marketing problem for the peasant cultivator to be that he did not understand the difference between selling to a neighbour and selling to a distant market. They held instead that education, especially through its deployment in film, was something that could bridge distances and move knowledge from networked nodes of anthropological research (that itself bridged a knowledge route from the field to the metropole) and speak directly to the African mind and improve his condition.

CONCLUSION

Between the wars colonial administrators and their proto-NGO partners in missions and American corporate philanthropy responded to the League of Nation's call to take up the mantle of trusteeship and to govern Africa in the interests of its indigenous inhabitants. Their objective, however, was not nation building for independence but rather a deeper integration of African cultivators into systems of co-operative marketing and public instruction that could help preserve the essential character of extractive empire while defusing emergent political challenges. Reformers held a common conviction that politics and faith alike sprang from an economic base, that culture change was the root of colonial social ills, and that the crisis of culture threatened to undo the forms of government upon which British indirect rule relied. In order to salvage empire while also protecting the interests of Europeans, these reformers pursued a social-welfare agenda seeking to use public instruction in community building, health and hygiene and co-operative economics as the core of a social-welfare policy. The reformers saw societies as systems, and a global system that could ensure peace and prosperity required that people be integrated at the local and the global level. The sites of community government they sought to build were meant to achieve this integration, with education and propaganda as its vanguards.

The Bantu Educational Kinema Experiment can be counted among the 'best-laid schemes' of interwar propaganda, which, in the words of one Jeanes School principal, would be meaningless unless they could be 'chewed up and digested' by Africans.[26] The cinema was supposed to make this science of hoodwinking easier. Instead, the experiment proved a comedy of errors. Superior 35mm footage was too expensive for the project budget, which had to expend much of its funds on the salaries of the white producers. Two Europeans required a combined annual salary of £1,250 – more than a third of the annual budget, after the initial capital expenditure on equipment. The entire African staff – which included a clerk, a 'camera boy', a 'board boy' and booker, a porter, a mechanic, a driver and numerous actors – totalled less than £500 in annual wages. The project encountered technical and mechanical problems everywhere. In shooting a film showing the difference between violent, precolonial tax collecting and the efficient and improving system of the British, Notcutt and Latham had arranged with a chief to have an entire army of warriors stage a raid on a village that had failed to pay.[27] This would have no doubt been a thrilling montage had the chief not simply stood the film-makers up.

The lorry frequently broke down. Moving shots were impossible to stabilise on rough terrain. The poles that held up the display screen broke in high winds. The loudspeakers were always breaking down. And when everything seemed to be functioning properly, there was still the problem of voices and images being out of sync. The assumption was made early on that, due to the 'unsophisticated native audiences there is no necessity to use modern "talkie" methods, and the old system of synchronised gramophone records may be used'.[28] This was also a cost-saver since sound-on-film would require a prohibitive amount of celluloid and other production costs to be able to translate the films into different languages.[29] With gramophone sound, several records had to be produced in multiple languages, and it was impossible to synchronise voices in one language with lips speaking another. These limitations of the medium were especially frustrating for the film-makers because the imprecision was risible for audiences. Latham and Notcutt were bothered that, for all their attention to production, all of Merle Davis's planning, the applications for American money and negotiations with the Colonial Office and governments on the ground, the purchasing of equipment, the long passage from England, the hours of scriptwriting, and filming, and editing, the long hauls packed three to a seat (when an African was driving, that is, since when it was a white driver Africans had to sit in the trailer behind) – after all this, something so simple as an out-of-sync soundtrack could turn their serious instruction on health and hygiene into farce.

The Bantu Educational Kinema Experiment was an ambitious experiment in developing a public-information structure for the particular form of liberal imperialism suited for the era of trusteeship. But it is perhaps more significant for the glances it affords of a future form of 'third world' development, one that would steer international humanitarianism toward development agendas that went beyond the confines of national-imperial interest and helped map the 'developed' vs the 'developing' world in the later twentieth century. The project required a number of co-ordinated, multinational interests to come together. Here accidental collaborators – in the case of missionaries and government, for instance – became formal allies in managing the system failures as they saw them.

In his evaluation of the BEKE, Glenn Reynolds has argued that the discursive forces that defined imperial rule were in crisis and redefinition between the wars. Citing Edward Said's argument that colonial grammars call into existence a binary opposition between the movement of the coloniser and the stasis of the colonised, Reynolds writes that 'it was the ramifications of African labourers migrating from kraal to mine, with all the deterritorializations, porous borders, and flows of energy across the social field that this entailed, that precipitated the crisis within twentieth-century systems'.[30] I largely agree with Reynolds, and would only add that the interwar period also witnessed a reassertion of the difference between coloniser and colonised in terms of speed and stasis by mapping it onto a new material plane (electric and invisible though it may be). The fact that most Africans did not experience speed in the same way or with the same access to infrastructures that facilitated mobility had motivated the film-makers to go to the field in the first place. They hoped to address the collision of speed and stasis with a half-hearted attempt at bridging the gap without changing the basis of the uneven relationships of labour and ownership inherent in empire. The difference between movement and stasis was amplified and projected on the material plane where telecommunication in the twentieth century resided – the electromagnetic spectrum, where speed potentials measured near the speed of light. Civilisational differences could be measured then in terms of an abundance vs a lack of infrastructure, and since much of Africa's copper was being rapidly relocated to Europe and beyond, the convergence of citizen and subject would remain a distant fear. Compared to the world of telecommunications, where Latham, Notcutt and Merle Davis spent many of their waking hours defying distance by sending and receiving telegrams, listening to radio and even talking on the phone installed in their studio, the movement of African labourers from kraal to mine would have seemed reassuringly slow.

Yet, in promoting their vision of a future centralised, commercial and instructional cinema organisation, the film-makers had to look past the tremendous difficulties they in fact faced when it came to the infrastructures of global co-ordination. The problem for the BEKE was that the standard equipment for showing films in Europe was useless for Africa. European cities were already electrified, and this was not the case for the crisis areas of labour recruitment in Northern Rhodesia, Nyasaland, Tanganyika

Territory and Kenya Colony. Thus, Notcutt had to invent his own display units, which substituted a miniature, mobile 'power plant' (a diesel engine [or sometimes a hand-cranked 'Dynamo'], gramophone and screen) for the systems of electrical delivery available in the metropoles of Europe, the UK and the US. The BEKE failed to leave a working system to reach 'detribalizing areas' with instructional cinema in part because of the inability of the infrastructures of imperial communication to deliver on the speed it promised. By the 1930s, the difference between citizen and subject was becoming measurable in differences in speed and mobility, and J. Merle Davis would often point to the extraordinary length of journeys on foot for Africans compared to Europeans and to African purchases of bicycles as a signal of their progress. In fact, though, the film-makers could not operate at the speed that their vision of a connected globe required. Machine components could not be sent from England to Tanganyika Territory, built and deployed before the money for the project ran out. Notcutt sometimes spent weeks waiting on word from one or another European manufacturer about missing machine parts, and his cheap mobile displays were not produced beyond his original prototypes.

Individual schemes like the BEKE were often relative failures in their time. Still, the form of internationally collaborative development through strengthened circuits of commodity and knowledge exchange won out in the West in the twentieth century. Capitalism and the pursuit of national empires, the machine co-operators of the interwar period agreed, created dangerous ruptures in African life. But it was crucial that they believed in the permanence and utility of those transformations all the same. Whether they read the scene correctly or not, the political economy they espoused sought to make the uneven relationship between the West and Africa (technical managers vs. their students in rural economics) even more permanent and immune to political exigencies and African social movements. Latham argued that Africans could prosper, but only if they learned to co-operate with the West. Durable connections between distant communities needed to be built. The reformers' vision of the civilisation of the future was global and ecumenical. Between the wars, the distance between citizen and subject was beginning to be measured as a difference in lifestyles and in variable access to the machinery of modern life. The International Missionary Council understood this when it argued that the changing position of Africans relative to standards of living (in J. Merle Davis's words, the 'economic base' of the church) was the first step toward an effective mission throughout the colonial world. By the middle of the twentieth century, these standards would be measured in the availability of electricity, all-weather roads, communications systems and the innumerable electronic devices that came streaming off European and American conveyor belts. Electronic communications technologies are today more than ever the measure of Western civilisation relative to the global South.

Today it would seem that we have returned to community development as a philosophy around which to organise global relationships between rich and poor populations. For this it is worthwhile to revisit these early twentieth-century ideas. Today Western business leaders create 'partnerships' with African governments and international organisations press for the creation of small-scale financial links in the form of micro-finance between individuals in the West and aspiring 'entrepreneurs' in the global South. The United Nations, the great successor to the failed League of

Nations, declared 2005 to be 'the International Year of Microcredit', proclaiming the welfare benefits that will arrive once Western systems of value abstraction and transmission have taken root in new places.[31] Meanwhile, community developers have moved beyond the interwar vocabularies that introduced notions of 'international co-operation' and now speak of the 'international community' as if it were as alive and true as any other human community. Immense corporate philanthropies also still play their role. One journalist recently summed up efforts by the Gates Foundation to extend credit to the poor of Africa as the philosophy of 'Let them eat cash.' The same absurd logic of development pressed on the poor in the 1920s and 1930s – in which lack of money is mistaken for the lack of non-enclosed resources as the root cause of hunger – is alive and well today.[32]

NOTES

1. The film-makers published the results of their 'experiment' in L. A. Notcutt and G. C. Latham, *The African and the Cinema: An Account of the Bantu Educational Kinema Experiment during the Period March 1935 to May 1937* (London: Edinburgh House Press, 1937). The Colonial Office kept a file on the project, as did the Carnegie Corporation of New York (CCNY – now housed at Columbia University's Special Collections). Records of the International Missionary Council in Geneva (copies of which can also be found at the Yale Divinity School Library) contain the field notes, journals and correspondences of the crew. The cinema project has received attention in historical scholarship on Africa. See, for instance, Rosaleen Smyth's pioneering studies on film in Africa and film policy in the Colonial Office between the wars, especially Rosaleen Smyth, 'The Development of British Colonial Film Policy, 1927–1939, with Special Reference to East and Central Africa', *Journal of African History* vol. 20 no. 3 (1979), pp. 437–50. See also Smyth, 'The Feature Film in Tanzania', *African Affairs* vol. 88 no. 352 (July 1989), pp. 389–96. More recently, Glenn Reynolds has published several articles that discuss the experiment. Utilising the Kenya National Archive, Reynolds was able to reconstruct the ambivalent reception of the films by audiences and government at the district level. Reynolds has brought into view several aspects of the project that have gone unmentioned in previous studies, including the fact that Notcutt used young male actors to play female roles in the earliest films of the project. See Glenn Reynolds, 'The Bantu Educational Kinema Experiment and the Struggle for Hegemony in British East and Central Africa', *Historical Journal of Film, Radio, and Television* vol. 29 no. 1 (March 2009), pp. 57–78. Also, Reynolds, 'Image and Empire: Anglo-American Cinematic Interventions in Sub-Saharan Africa, 1921–1937', *South African Historical Journal* vol. 48 (May 2003), pp. 90–108.
2. The creation of an advisory committee to steer the decisions of Whitehall on matters relating to native education in the empire came on the heels of the 1924 Phelps Stokes tour of Africa. The recommendations of the American philanthropic commission were enshrined in the command paper that created the Advisory Committee on Education in Tropical Africa, the preamble of which stated that

    Education should be adapted to the mentality, aptitudes, occupations, and traditions of the various peoples, conserving as far as possible all sound and healthy elements in the fabric of their social life; adapting them where necessary to changed circumstances and progressive ideas, as an agent of natural growth and evolution.

See Command Paper 2374, London, HM Stationery Office, 1925. The committee would soon change its name to the Advisory Committee on Education in the Colonies (abbreviated ACEC in government documents) to reflect its empire-wide mandate to study and reform mass education.

3. In the 1920s, arguments from missionary leaders like J. H. Oldham yoked missions to a collaborative relationship with government and corporate philanthropy, recognising that missions must address the material conditions of poverty and economic marginalisation if the Gospel were ever to win hearts. The Colonial Office solidified the relationship by advancing programmes like the Jeanes Schools, which were funded by Carnegie, supervised by government and staffed by Scottish and Anglican missionaries.

4. An important front in the interwar debate over literary vs 'adapted' education was the question of the place of vernacular languages in colonial education. The Colonial Office solicited advice on the issue from missionaries, anthropologists and linguists operating in Africa. See 'The Place of the Vernacular in Native Education' (TNA, CO 822/4/17). See also Dietrich Westermann's 'The Linguistic Situation and Vernacular Literature in West Africa', *Africa: Journal of the International African Institute* vol. 2 no. 4 (October 1929), pp. 337–51. For book-length discussions of education and colonialism in Central and East Africa, see Carol Summers, *Colonial Lessons: Africans' Education in Southern Rhodesia, 1918–1940* (Portsmouth, NH: Heinemann, 2002); Derek Peterson, *Creative Writing: Translation, Bookkeeping, and the Work of Imagination in Colonial Kenya* (Portsmouth, NH: Heinemann, 2004); and John Anderson, *The Struggle for the School: The Interaction of Missionary, Colonial Government, and Nationalist Enterprise in the Development of Formal Education in Kenya* (London: Longman, 1970).

5. The most influential anthropologist in constructing the culture-change thesis was Bronislaw Malinowski. See Bronislaw Malinowski, 'Practical Anthropology', *Africa: Journal of the International African Institute* vol. 2 no. 1 (January 1929), pp. 22–38. For Malinowski's views on the political threats looming in areas of culture contact, see the posthumously published, 'The Pan-African Problem of Culture Contact', *American Journal of Sociology* vol. 48 no. 6 (May 1943), pp. 649–65.

6. Latham wrote this the same year he was recruited by J. Merle Davis to be one of the co-directors of the BEKE. Seee G. C. Latham, 'Indirect Rule and Education in East Africa', *Africa: Journal of the International African Institute* vol. 7 no. 4 (1934), pp. 423–30.

7. 'Proposed Establishment of a Jeanes School for Training Teachers [Northern Rhodesia]', 1928 (TNA, CO 795/23/6).

8. J. Merle Davis, *Modern Industry and the African* (London: MacMillan and Co., 1933). For Merle Davis's views on the mission of the church in the twentieth century, see J. Merle Davis and International Missionary Council, *New Buildings on Old Foundations: A Handbook on Stabilizing the Younger Churches in Their Environment* (New York: International Missionary Council, 1945)

9. Merle Davis wrote that 'The Gospel record reveals Jesus as a practical social Anthropologist. Jesus gained His introduction to anthropology by living for thirty years as a participant in the daily drama and tragedy of His people.' See Merle Davis and IMC, *New Buildings on Old Foundations*, pp. 48–9. The allusion was to Malinowski's 'Practical Anthropology'. Malinowski argued that anthropology should be useful to government in its practical

application on the reserves and that the anthropologist should be embedded in fieldwork. Malinowski, 'Practical Anthropology', pp. 22–38.

10. Merle Davis and IMC, *New Buildings on Old Foundations*, pp. 51–2.

11. Reynolds, 'The Bantu Educational Kinema Experiment and the Struggle for Hegemony in British East Africa', p. 60.

12. Notcutt's experience with sound on film proved unnecessary since the project opted for cheaper sound on disc that also suited its plans to produce multiple language tracks.

13. 'Latham's Journal, June 13, 1935' (IMC, 263129). Laura Fair has written of the musical culture of Zanzibar and of Siti binti Saad's translations of local struggle into song. See *Pastimes and Politics: Culture, Community, and Identity in Post-abolition Urban Zanzibar, 1890–1945* (Athens: Ohio University Press, 2001), pp. 169–225.

14. 'Latham's Journal, June 14, 1935'. See Reynolds, 'The Bantu Educational Kinema Experiment and the Struggle for Hegemony in British East Africa', pp. 66–7 for further discussion of these interviews and the film-makers' reception of advice from Africans.

15. 'Latham's Journal, June 28, 1935'.

16. *Report of the East Africa Commission Presented by the Secretary of State for the Colonies to Parliament by Command of His Majesty, April, 1925* (London: His Majesty's Stationery Office, 1925), p. 55. For discussion of *ankylostomiasis* (hookworm) as a plantation problem and the British Empire as a vector for its spread, see Soma Hewa, *Colonialism, Tropical Disease, and Imperial Medicine: Rockefeller Philanthropy in Sri Lanka* (Lanham, MD: University Press of America, 1995), pp. 47–67.

17. While the prevention of disease was the stated goal of imperial government between the wars, hookworm propaganda films were the speciality of American philanthropic endeavours in Africa and the rural US South. James Burns shows this for the case of the Rockefeller Foundation in this volume.

18. One of the expert interpreters of 'African mentality' for the BEKE in East Africa was J. W. C. Dougall, former principal of the flagship Jeanes School in Kabete, Kenya. Dougall was a supporter of the American model of adapted education and led the 1923–4 Phelps Stokes Commissions to Africa. During his time in Kenya, Dougall used his Jeanes School as a site of scholarship on the African mind, hosting a Carnegie-sponsored psychologist to conduct the first intelligence quotient examinations on African children and producing his own scholarship on pedagogy and African perception. See, for instance, J. W. C. Dougall, 'Characteristics of African Thought', *Africa: Journal of the International African Institute* vol. 5 no. 1 (July 1932), pp. 249–65. The Carnegie psychologist was Richard Oliver. Richard A. C. Oliver, 'Mental Tests in the Study of the African', *Africa: Journal of the International African Institute* vol. 7 no.1 (January 1934), pp. 40–6.

19. It is difficult to gauge what members of these audiences really thought of these films from the notes of Latham and Notcutt. Clearly they were sometimes entertaining, but it is also clear that audiences found their production value to be low. At least some in the audience, especially in urban centres like the mining towns of the Copper Belt, would have seen Hollywood productions. For a study of African reception, interpretation and use of film in a similar context, see James Burns, *Flickering Shadows: Cinema and Identity in Colonial Zimbabwe* (Athens: Ohio University Press, 2002).

20. As Bruce Berman has shown, the cards provided near-perfect tracking of labour deserters from white farms, and the data accumulated in their processing and review could be used to gauge the efficacy of labour recruitment and to hone policies designed by the Kenyan

government to encourage wage labour. Between the wars, the total number of Africans in wage labour for Kenya settlers fluctuated between 20 and 30 per cent of the total population. The majority of these worked on white farms or in domestic service. Berman notes, '2364 of 2790 reported deserters were traced and prosecuted' in the first year of the registration system's full implementation (1919–20). See Bruce Berman, *Control and Crisis in Colonial Kenya: The Dialectic of Domination* (Athens: Ohio University Press, 1990), pp. 147–57.

21. 'Notcutt's Memo: "Experimental District Native Cinema"' (IMC, 263128).
22. Notcutt and Latham, *The African and the Cinema*, p. 189.
23. Ibid., Appendix E.
24. Ibid., p. 189.
25. The Colonial Office's primary advisor on co-operation was C. F. Strickland, formerly the Co-operatives Registrar for the Punjab, another hotspot of anti-colonial politics between the wars. For Strickland's views on co-operation, see Claude Francis Strickland, *Co-operation for Africa* (Oxford: Oxford University Press, 1934).
26. T. Benson, 'The Jeanes School and the Education of the East African Native', *Journal of the Royal African Society* vol. 35 no. 141.
27. The chief is not named in the source, but he was probably a Chagga chief since the film was planned for Northern Tanganyika near Kilimanjaro. See Notcutt and Latham, *The African and the Cinema*, p. 35.
28. J. Merle Davis, 'An International Study of the Cinema' (BEKE Grant Files, CCNY Box 186/18). In fact, as Vincent Bouchard has explained, the narration was often done live by a hired narrator speaking the local language. For uncertain reasons, the BEKE film-makers extracted all reference to these interlopers from their published accounts of the experiment. See Vincent Bouchard, 'Nigeria Health Propaganda and the Bantu Educational Kinema Experiment: Colonial Film Unit's Precursors?', presented at the conference 'Colonial Film: Moving Images of the British Empire', Birkbeck College, London, 7–9 July 2010. My best guess is that the film-makers wanted to present the notion to readers and potential supporters and financial backers that this could all be done with machines and thus be self-sustaining – automatic even.
29. 'Interim Report of BEKE' [Received by Carnegie, 11 May 1936] (CCNY Box 186/18). The most frequent language used was Swahili (44 times), but records were made in African languages that were common in Tanganyika, Nyasaland and Kenya, including in Chibemba (16), Nyanja (17), Tumbuka (1), Sukume (6), Gikuyu (8) and Luo (3). In the Copper Belt, speakers of all these languages would likely have been present at the film showing at the mines. Especially later in the project when funds looked uncertain, decisions about where to send the display unit centred on the language question. Areas with more diversity of dialect, and thus more use of Swahili, were privileged over others. This is how the film-makers decided to display at Moshi (site of the Kilimanjaro Native Co-operative Union) rather than Mwanza, as Notcutt preferred. See 'Notcutt to Latham, October 22, 1936' (IMC, 261328).
30. Reynolds, 'Image and Empire', p. 92.
31. The G8 Conference and the World Bank have both thrown their weight behind micro-finance, and the UN claims that micro-loans are important in plans to meet its Millennium Development Goals. The UN micro-finance campaign is overseen by the United Nations Capital Development Fund, and the initiative has its own website: <http://www.yearof

microcredit.org>. Among the corporate partners of the UN initiative are titans of finance capital, Citigroup and Visa.

32. Frederick Kaufman, 'Let Them Eat Cash: Can Bill Gates Turn Hunger into Profit?', *Harper's Magazine*, June 2009. Meanwhile, the Microsoft Corporation exercises its political muscle and legal prowess to ensure that low-power, low-cost laptops donated to poor children will run its proprietary software system, Windows. See Steve Stecklow and James Bandler, 'A Little Laptop with Big Ambitions: How a Computer for the Poor Got Stomped by Tech Giants', *Wall Street Journal*, 24 November 2007.

12

Colonialism, Visuality and the Cinema: Revisiting the Bantu Educational Kinema Experiment

Aboubakar Sanogo

Colonialism is an order of the visible. It is an enterprise that seeks to order and consists in ordering the visible world in a particular way, a mode of arrangement of the visible around the principle of *dominatio*. This explains its relationship to the image. Indeed colonialism's purchase on the visible world is predicated on chunking the visible into images, into manageable images (of self, alterity, the world). As a result, colonialism is obsessed with the image. This obsession often translates into different modes of self-positioning with regard to the image, ranging across a spectrum from profound aversion to open embrace, from genuine and even at times ontological fear to pompous and shameless display. These modes of positioning in turn enable attitudes not only of accumulation and multiplication of the image (the phenomenon of the plethora), but also of concealment, which are wedded to a desire to subject the image, to domesticate it, indeed to police it.

Colonialism's dialectic relationship with the image makes its encounter and engagement with the moving image a compelling object of research. Indeed the cinema, arguably the ultimate technology of the visible, also happens to rely on a chunking of the visible world into images, which it in turn sends back to the world as a flow that emulates the visible world. It appears thus that both colonialism and the cinema seem, at first sight, to share analogous modes of operation.

This essay will offer a case study of the ways in which the mechanisms of colonialism and those of the cinema became imbricated in a project to produce a colonial order of the visible. The study situates itself in the context of the largest colonial empire of modern times, the British Empire. For such an oversized empire, the question of how to image itself in relation to the world, to other empires and to image the millions of souls spread out across the four corners of the earth was a project in and of itself. For colonialism wished nothing better than to see its regime of images coincide with the visible world, indeed to reorder the visible world. From the perspective of colonial power, an alliance with cinema was therefore deemed necessary, indeed indispensable.

The Bantu Educational Kinema Experiment (BEKE) of the 1930s was one of the ways in which the British colonial apparatus sought to engage with the cinema in its East and Central African colonies. It was a project initiated by the International Missionary Council, supported by the Colonial Office, funded by the Carnegie Corporation and other mining interests operating on the continent. The 'experiment' lasted between 1935 and 1937. Its avowed ambitions were nothing short of introducing film to Africa, making films for Africans, studying their reactions to films, transforming their habits and attitudes to labour, faith, health and agriculture and proposing a template for future British initiatives in the cinema.

It shall be the task of this article to take a closer look at this project, to make visible some aspects of the imbrications of the mechanisms of colonialism and those of the cinema. This will be done in two phases, one consisting in an examination of the historical and discursive conditions of possibility of the BEKE, and the other in a close-up on the experiment itself.

HISTORICAL AND DISCURSIVE CONDITIONS OF POSSIBILITY OF THE BEKE

Any examination of the BEKE must pass through the filter of some of the anterior experiences in cinema undertaken in Africa by Britain. A brief historical account of British cinematic involvement in Africa combined with an analysis of the centrality of the educational paradigm as structuring the relationship between the colonial state and the cinema is necessary. This paradigm was formed also in the seemingly external realms of the church, anthropology and philanthropy, and these contexts would inform the use of cinema by the colonial state.

Early British filmic involvement in Africa

The cinema came into being when Britain and other European countries were engaged in a concerted and merciless assault on the four corners of the African continent. Like France, with the Lumière brothers and others, Britain was in Africa in the first five years of the existence of the cinema. British cinematic presence was evident in Africa as early as 1896 and took several forms. On the initiative of individual production companies seeking to legitimise the new apparatus, operators/cameramen were sent to Africa to film events ranging from war, to state visits, to daily life. At times cinema was used to promote the colonisation and exploitation of the continent, along with encouraging massive immigration to the colonies.[1]

Film historians propose that World War I marked, for most countries, the realisation by various state apparatuses of the importance of cinema for propaganda efforts, and thus the official beginning of governmental thinking about possible involvement in the business both of making films in the colonies and of regulating cinematic activities.[2] The attempt at systematising the intervention of the British imperial state in cinema in the colonies gathered pace in the post-war moment. This moment of heightened state awareness coincided and was partly fuelled by the rise to power of the Conservative Party, historically interested in the cinema as well. The Conservative Party was involved in making films to rally its troops. Moreover, the party was committed to private economic interests, already involved in the cinema, and also called for the intervention of the state in the field.[3] In that sense, the coming together of economic and political-party interests made possible the mainstreaming of a colonial agenda with cinematic implications, which the British state would in turn endorse.

By the 1920s, and especially toward the end of the decade, the British state became proactive with regard to cinema, not only in the colonies, but also in the metropole itself. Indeed, debates regarding the status of cinema in the colonies were often wedded to general discussions pertaining to cinema in Britain itself. An important milestone was the passing of the British Cinematograph Films Act in 1927, which sought to react to the increased domination of the British market by Hollywood films by imposing upon exhibitors quotas of British films to be shown domestically.[4] The Act also sought to extend these to the Dominions (Canada, Australia, New Zealand and South Africa) and India (where an Indian Cinematograph Committee was created the same year) although without much success.[5]

The Colonial Office was also committed to drawing the implications of this Act for the British colonies in Africa and elsewhere by convening its very first conference in 1927 and setting up in 1929 a Colonial Films Committee to discuss three axes of priority: the circulation of British films in Africa, the control of films already circulating in Africa and the production of educational cinema for the supposed benefit of Africans.[6] In other words, the colonial state defined for itself a tripodic approach to the cinema: repression, profit and pedagogy.

To a large extent, each of these attitudes toward the moving image was informed by apprehension. The desire for profit, which partly drove the Cinematograph Films Act and its future implementation in African colonies, was the result of pressure from film lobbies in Britain, which felt a loss of grip on both their domestic market and on that of the empire. This sense of loss was augmented by political anxiety that the sun had finally found a way to begin to set on the British Empire, with the rise of the United States as a new geopolitical power, matched by the rise and projection of its film industry across the globe. At stake thus in the circulation of British films in the empire was an attempt to impose preferential treatment on British film production, faced with the Hollywood onslaught. The empire was seen as potentially providing a wide market, which, if devoted to British and empire films, would constitute a counterweight to the ambitious Hollywood hegemon.

At the same time, there was mounting anxiety with regard to the effects of the cinema on the colonised peoples.[7] This anxiety stemmed from a desire on the part of the colonial apparatus to see, have and use the cinema as an extension of the ways in which the empire sought to project itself. Indeed one of the sources of the hegemony of colonialism upon the colonised rested not only on the fact that the colonial conquest had been a 'shock and awe' campaign with tremendous implications on the colonised's representation of the coloniser as well as the coloniser's own self-representation and projection, but also on the fact that the vast majority of the colonised had never visited the colonising countries. As a result, the encounter between the colonised and the colonisers was largely mediated by the image the coloniser wished to project of himself. Thus while the coloniser had relatively unfettered access to the culture, wealth and land of the colonised, the reverse was profoundly mediated by the coloniser. It is in that sense that the cinema, especially in its commercial version, was regarded as a threat to colonial normativity because, through its representation of the mundane, the daily, the ordinary in the lives of colonisers, along with the stuff that drama is made of, i.e. cupidity, jealousy, envy, lust, weakness, fear, cowardice, treachery, the cinema projected almost a counter-image to the dominant colonial self-image of perfection, selflessness, might, righteousness, loyalty and higher morality. There was therefore the need on the part of the coloniser to establish strict censorship rules that would withhold from the view of the colonised those unwitting counter-images.

The last leg of the intervention of the colonial state in the management of cinema in the colonies of Africa entailed a proactive and to some extent 'corrective' to the commercial cinema through the actualisation of an educational cinema, of which the BEKE would become for a time one of the most accomplished forms.

The colonial state in the whirlwind and fever of educational cinema: the debates, the actors and the institutions

It must be remembered that colonialism saw itself as a pedagogic project intended to completely overhaul the ways of the colonised. In that regard, the problem of education occupied a central place in the entire colonial dispositif. In the British context, colonial governments included departments of so-called native education, which actualised colonial state policies on the question. It is thus not surprising that the question of the educational potential of cinema would attract special attention from the colonial state, as it could add images in motion to the arsenal of colonialism. The debates that took place in Britain and at the international level were both informed by colonialism and had implications for the nature and character of educational cinema in the colonies. The fact that the notion of educational cinema would be the principal, the dominant currency used by the British colonial state to intervene in the production of a colonial visible is symptomatic of the wide-ranging consequences of these debates. The BEKE must be read as one such consequence. It is time to briefly examine these debates in Britain and internationally.

The question of the ability of cinema to impart knowledge has haunted the medium since its advent. In some ways, the repressive attitude of the colonial state with regard to cinema was premised on a certain 'effect theory' of the medium. In the process of imparting knowledge, this theory ran, cinema may also have an effect on the behaviour and demeanour of its spectators. In the British context, some of these debates on the pedagogic potential of cinema date back at least to the late teens. Rachael Low traces them back to 1917 with the establishment of the Cinema Commission of Enquiry headed by Professors Spearman and Burt, who published the results of their research in 1925 under the title *The Cinema in Education*. Spearman and Burt sought to assess the feasibility of the introduction of films in schools.[8] This study seems to have opened a floodgate to other studies and experiments, which produced even more reports, arguably creating something of a structure of feeling in Britain with regard to educational cinema during what may be termed the decades of educational cinema (1920s–30s). Among them, the study on the ability of the cinema to teach history produced *The Report on the Value of Film in the Teaching of History* in 1931, whereas the Middlesex Experiment, exploring the significance of sound film for pedagogy, yielded the same year a report entitled *Sound Film in School*.[9] More important for the BEKE was the report of the Commission on Education and Cultural Films entitled *The Film in National Life*, published in 1932, which recommended among other things the creation of the British Film Institute.[10] The report also prescribed a role to cinema in the empire and functioned as legitimising discourse for the BEKE.[11]

The British debates resonated with an international context also concerned with harnessing the powers of the new medium to foster international co-operation in the aftermath of the war that was supposed to end all wars. The founding in 1919 of the League of Nations, the predecessor of the United Nations, was the institutional manifestation of this desire to put an end to war, especially at the global level. It was felt that, alongside diplomatic, political and economic means of feasibility, culture ought to play a central role in the preservation of peace, hence the importance of the latest and potentially more potent cultural form of the time, cinema. Zoë Druick has aptly demonstrated the multiple ways in which the League's International Institute of Intellectual Cooperation facilitated and spearheaded debates on both formal and informal, children's and adult education through cinema via conferences, the creation in 1928 of an International Educational Cinematography Institute and the publication of the multilingual *International Review of Educational Cinematography* from 1924 to 1934.[12]

The League of Nations was also, of course, led by the major colonial powers involved in Africa, and was thus arguably an intercolonial clearing house where knowledge and information was exchanged with regard to filming the colonies. In other words, international debates around the educational status of cinema helped inform larger debates on the status of cinema in the colonial context, and the place of the pedagogic in that configuration. One of the key reference documents for the BEKE was none other than the report of the International Educational Cinematography Institute entitled *The Social Aspects of the Cinema*.[13]

Far away from the metropole, a number of individual film experiments also took place in the colonies in the interwar years, which would inform discussions as well as create some of the conditions of possibility for the existence of the BEKE. Some of the most significant include those of William Sellers, Julian Huxley and Dr A. Paterson, all agents of the colonial state. We will briefly examine each in turn.

Although William Sellers would go on to lead the Colonial Film Unit upon the demise of the BEKE, his experimentation with film in Africa predates the existence of the BEKE. As a medical officer in the service of the colonial government of Nigeria in the late 20s, Sellers was among the first to use cinema for the purpose of education in Africa. He directed a film entitled *Anti-plague Operation in Lagos* (1929, 1937) to explain the ways in which rats could spread plague.[14] He made about fifteen films related to his health campaigns, observed the reactions of Nigerian peasants to cinema and was instrumental in creating the theoretical figure of the visually impaired, illiterate African peasant who would define much of British colonial film policy in Africa.

In 1929, Julian Huxley, a noted biologist and eugenicist (who would go on to become the first Director General of the United Nations Educational, Scientific and Cultural Organisation [UNESCO]), was sent on mission to Uganda, Kenya, Tanganyika and Zanzibar by the Colonial Office Advisory Committee on Native Education to 'advise upon certain aspects of native education'.[15] Huxley brought along some films and a projector and screened films made by the Empire Marketing Board to various educational institutions (mission schools, teacher-training schools, elementary schools, Makerere College, etc.). The films were about growing cotton in Nigeria, the growth process of a plant and life in deep water. Audience response essays following the screenings convinced Huxley that there was a place in Africa for educational cinema.

While in Kenya, Huxley met Paterson, deputy director of the department of medical and health services, who made a film chronicle of his odyssey fighting hookworms, which involved treating 49,000 people and digging 9,000 latrines.[16] For colonialism, the hookworm was no small foe, as it stood in the way of the productive potential of its colonised subjects, for 'you cannot be very efficient or energetic if dozens of hookworms are clinging on to your internal surfaces, steadily sucking your blood'.[17] Upon seeing Paterson's films, Huxley concluded that 'this will become a very important use of the cinema – the recording of special activities of Government Departments for demonstration and propaganda purposes'.[18]

The colonial state itself also had a more direct purchase on the problem of educational cinema in the colonies. This was negotiated through conferences, committees and proposals for experiments focused specifically on the colonies. Educational cinema was first discussed at the imperial education conference of 1923. This conference, organised by the Imperial Studies Institute of the Royal Colonial Institute, established a Cinematograph Committee, also known as the Gorell Committee, which sought to study the relationship between the cinema and education and issued the *Report on the Use and Value of the Cinematograph in Education* in 1924.[19]

The 1927 Colonial Office Conference of Governors (the very first) was the watershed event during which the problem of educational cinema in the colonies was at the forefront of debate.[20] The intervention of Hanns Vischer, secretary of the Advisory Committee of Native Education on Tropical Africa was central in articulating the different dimensions of the issue.[21] At the general level, Vischer used a comparative approach by examining the status of educational cinema in other colonising countries (France, Italy, Germany), concluding that Great Britain lagged behind others. Underscoring the desirability of the use of cinema both in formal and general education, for children as well as adults, he stressed the notion that, given the paucity of textbooks in African classrooms, cinema could prove even more important as an educational tool. For this, he advocated the creation of an organisational framework to co-ordinate for various colonial governments the selection, re-editing and circulation of already made educational films 'deemed suitable for Africans'. The Federation of British Industries also intervened at the conference, affirming the value of cinema as an instrument of education, and advocating the compilation of a catalogue of educational films already in existence.[22]

Following this conference, a Colonial Films Committee was set up by the Secretary of State for the Colonies to look into film-related matters in the colonies, including educational cinema. Its report was read at the second Colonial Office Conference of 1930.[23] Following the conference, various experiments were proposed, including one from inside the Colonial Office itself, put forward by R. V. Vernon and involving such major British anthropologists as Myers, Seligman and Malinowski. Another plan was proposed by Dr Paterson and endorsed by the British Film Institute Dominions, India and Colonies Panel.[24] None of these experiments saw the light of day due to funding problems. The door was now open for the BEKE to be actualised as the latter had managed to secure funding from none other than the Carnegie Corporation.

The educational impulse of the BEKE was also wedded to three important discursive frameworks, indispensable not only in bringing the experiment into the field of colonial visuality, but also belonging to the mechanisms that underwrite colonial visuality itself. These are the missionary, anthropological and philanthropic discourses.

The missionary, anthropological and philanthropic background

It may surprise the reader that the first state-sanctioned British film project to take place in Africa was initiated and sponsored by missionaries. Yet, it is important to remember the function of missionary discourse in the advent and preservation of colonialism. Part of the genius of this discourse was its ability to create by fiat, long before leaving Europe, an entire continent of heathens whom the missionary was supposed to save from the eternal damnation that would result from their godlessness. Indeed, the conditions making the missionary presence in Africa possible rested on the discursive *tour de force* of inventing a benighted race awaiting Christian enlightenment. This was literally a project of visuality, resting on metaphors of darkness and light.

Once this was done, what was left was simply to apply the additive principle, i.e. to modulate various aspects of the discourse to fit new needs. Thus, missionaries often paved the way, indeed performed the preliminary reconnaissance through exploratory mapping that made the military conquest of the continent possible. In some cases, they theorised and advocated the advent of colonialism and indeed provided the spiritual legitimation to bolster colonialism's earthly pursuits.[25]

The BEKE was born from the application of this additive principle, for religious conversion itself was a pre-cinematic educational project. It ushered in a regime of mediation, in which missionaries positioned themselves as intermediaries between Africans and God, and thus as educators in the ways of believing in God. This was naturally a potentially endless project, given the immensity of the continent. But missionary action did not stop with proselytism. It also entailed the management of the lives of the new converts – who also in the meantime had become colonised subjects – including their recreation time, their relationship to modern life and their negotiation with the past.

Such was the impetus of the research project led by the initiator of the BEKE, John Merle Davis, who, in his capacity as director of the department of social and industrial research of the International Missionary Council, headed a 1932 commission of enquiry in Northern Rhodesia and Belgian Congo 'to study the effects of the heavy industries of the Copper Belt upon native African life'.[26] In his report, Merle Davis highlighted 'the barrenness of Christian Native social life due to the general banning of heathen social and recreational activities',[27] along with

the undermining of the social fabric of the African tribe occasioned by the pace at which contact with Western industrial life is moving, one feature of this process is the ever widening gap between the outlook and ways of life of the industrialized Native living in towns and mine locations and those of his in the village.[28]

Having identified a new missionary frontier, the International Missionary Council proposed the wherewithal to transcend it.[29] For this, Merle Davis identified cinema 'as an aid to mission work'.[30] He thus defined the project of the BEKE as follows:

> It aims to be an auxiliary of the Church in its task of building a Christian society for the African. It proposes to place a new instrument of education in the hands of the missionary, to adapt it to native mentality and needs and to put it within the reach of the missionary educator. It aims to promote a permanent supply of useful films for the mission programme. Finally its purpose is to enrich the entertainment and recreational life of the New Christian native community.[31]

The BEKE is hereby placed within a larger proselytising impulse. It is not really a cinema for Africans, but a cinema for the missionary, indeed a missionary cinema. It seeks to auxiliarise the cinema and make it an instrument for the propagation of the Christian faith within the overdetermined context of colonialism. Faithful to its discursive structure, it posits the premise of differential mental abilities between Africans and Europeans, and thus seeks to adapt cinema to the 'mentality' and 'needs' of Africans. In doing so, the BEKE weds the missionary episteme with the colonial episteme, indeed places them in the proverbial 'missionary position'.

Alongside missionaries were anthropologists. The BEKE also locates anthropology at its very core, to offer scholarly legitimacy to the project by creating the figure of the anthropologist as script reader, film critic and implicitly censor, in addition to that of 'the expert' in African cultures. Merle Davis wrote:

> The experiment is essentially an undertaking in the field of Anthropology. Anthropologists are invited to assist by criticizing scenario synopses submitted to them and by viewing and criticizing the actual films. They will be able to prevent mistakes and help integrate the whole experiment with the latest developments in practical anthropology. Both anthropologists at home and those on the field could give invaluable help in these ways.[32]

Thus, the BEKE appealed to the very discipline which, in the days of colonialism, made alterity visible through the manufacture of concepts like race, tribe, clan and of the hierarchised classifications of mankind that informed all spheres of life. In other words, anthropology assisted in fabricating the concepts that helped install a colonial regime of visibility, providing the vocabulary used to designate (i.e. render visible) the objects of colonial desire.

Finally, the BEKE would not be possible without a certain philanthropic impulse that went beyond the actual funding of the project. This impulse helped shape not only the BEKE itself, but other educational projects undertaken by British colonialism in the interwar years as demonstrated in this volume by Aaron Windel and James Burns.[33] American business *qua* philanthropy was present in the British colonial sphere as early as 1920, with the making and distribution by the Rockefeller Foundation of *Unhooking the Hookworm* (1920), which set the paradigm for a major genre of colonial non-fiction film, the medical-health film.

More important however is the endorsement by British colonial authorities in the early 1920s of a pedagogic project spearheaded by the Phelps Stokes Foundation and the Carnegie Corporation. This articulated a certain ontology of the 'African mind', which was seen as coextensive, indeed deeply wedded to the soil, a notion derived from the treatment of African slaves and their descendants in the agricultural fields of the American South. Thus, just as African Americans 'naturally' belonged to the soil, so did their African brethren who remained on the continent. It is possible to see here a coming together of the heritage of the episteme of American slavery and domestic colonialism with that of imperial Britain, which, only two centuries earlier, had ruled the American colonies.

The production of colonial visuality, as exemplified by the BEKE, was conditioned, premised, made possible by the articulation of an array of discursive fields, ranging from education to filmic specificity, from missionary to anthropological and philanthropic discourses, and porosity between public and private spheres. Colonialism has proven to be congenitally and chronically incapable of keeping apart the private and the public, the academic and the non-academic, the state and the church. The membership of the Board of Advisors of the BEKE is testimony to this. Chairmanship of the board went to Lord Frederick Lugard, infamous empire builder, former colonial governor of Nigeria and Hong Kong and theoretician of imperialism. On the board were two representatives of the British Film Institute, three representatives of religious institutions (including John Merle Davis), one representative of the Royal Anthropological Institute, two representatives of the University of London's Institute of Education, a member of the British Social Hygiene Council, a member of the Geographical Association, a representative of Rhodesian Copper Mines and a representative from a private film company, Gaumont-British Instructional.[34]

CLOSE-UP ON THE EXPERIMENT

The idea for the BEKE gained momentum after the interests of two individuals coincided: that of John Merle Davis of the International Missionary Council, and of retired Major Leslie Alan Notcutt, a sisal plantation owner in East Africa, who 'thought that an estate cinema might be an effective method to help maintain a contented labour force'.[35] The two men were introduced in 1933 by Hanns Vischer of the Colonial Office. Davis requested from Notcutt an estimate for a two-year experiment of 'educational films for Africans', which the latter produced. The Carnegie Corporation expanded the project into an experiment 'with the production and exhibition of cultural, recreational and educational films for Bantu people' and furnished the bulk of the funding for the project ($55,000 dollars).[36]

The experiment was launched two years after the initial Davis–Notcutt meeting. Being a cinematic and educational project, the experiment was run by both Major Notcutt, who was named field director (i.e. the film person), and G. C. Latham, education director, in his capacity as specialist in 'native education'. They gathered a technical crew made of an electric and sound engineer (G. C. Gardner), a cinematographer (Captain C. F. Cooley), a projectionist (P. D. Woodall) and an accountant (Mrs Notcutt). The team benefited from technical counselling from the BBC, the Imperial College of Science and Technology and the Cinephotography Department of the Polytechnic School.[37]

For its film studio, the BEKE secured from the governor of Tanganyika the lease on an old sanatorium in Vugiri, seventy-seven miles from the nearest port of Tanga. It was now time to verify whether cinema could, among other things, 'help the adult African understand and adapt himself to new conditions invading and threatening to overwhelm him'; 'reinforce the ordinary methods of the classroom and the lecture hall'; 'conserve what is best in African traditions and culture by representing these in their proper setting as stages in racial development and as an inheritance to be cherished with pride'; and, in the last instance, 'provide recreation and entertainment'.[38]

To implement this ambitious project, the BEKE architects formulated a number of research questions, which they organised into three categories: the psychological, the technical and the economic. On the 'psychological' front (to some extent cognitive as well), the BEKE was interested to find out, given 'the African's state of development' (i.e. the slowness of his mental processes), how much he would be able to comprehend in a film screening session two and a half hours' long. It was thus important to assess the ability of Africans to 'understand' the 'educational idea behind the instructional film in the forms of a story'. Positing itself as a transformative cinema, the BEKE sought to produce effects on the very bodies of Africans by eliciting action on the basis of what was seen on screen. Seeking to somewhat account for some form of change, the BEKE also sought to pinpoint what would 'interest, amuse and stir the emotions' of Africans based on classic colonial classification, i.e. 'the educated, the partially detribalized and the primitive villager'.[39]

To answer these various questions, the BEKE developed a commensurate mode of film practice, through technical choices, aesthetic decisions and modes of exhibition. From a technical standpoint, the BEKE is the product of two moments: the rise of the 16mm film and the demise of the sound-on-disc technology. The 16mm film, officially launched in 1923 (a decade before the BEKE), was immediately positioned as an 'other' to the standard industry 35mm film, emphasising cost reduction, portability, an alternative distribution circuit antithetical to the dominant commercial system, with profound implications for domesticity and indeed wider access to the technology.[40] These elements were crucial to the very feasibility of the BEKE. The sound-on-disc film, which was increasingly being replaced in the early 1930s, was also, by virtue of affordability, preferred to the new sound-on-film technology. In other words, the BEKE had no problem embracing old technology. But the reasons were not only financial. Indeed, although 'film technicians with whom we have discussed the matter have, almost without exception, strongly criticized our proposal to revert to sound on disc', the BEKE retorted that, in addition to costs, 'its disadvantages are of relatively little importance for the type of audience'.[41] Thus, the BEKE reified the colonial premise of time lag between the coloniser and the colonised by inscribing it in its very choice of filming equipment.

The BEKE exposed 18,200 feet of negative film and 48,000 feet of positive film with a total yield, in the course of two years, of thirty-five short films as well as rushes for a few others.[42] Throughout the process, its aesthetic choices (casting, directing, cinematography, narrative) filmically inscribed colonialism. At the level of casting, for instance, although some of its methods may be deemed reminiscent or perhaps anticipatory of a neo-realist approach, an essentialising approach was evident in the choice and direction of professional actors.[43] Thus, they considered that, with Khalil bin Ali, one of their actors, 'the only trouble [was] that his ambition was to act in the European style', while the policy on the set was that 'we tried to avoid showing native actors European ideas on acting when we came to a scene which called for drama'.[44]

The BEKE also inscribed colonial ideas in its choices in cinematography. Devising what it termed 'simple' cinematography, it displayed a notoriously high degree of tolerance for amateurishness at the level of the quality of photography. Indeed the account of the experiment is replete with reports of poor cinematography. Thus, for the one-reeler entitled *First Farce* (1935) (an attempt at slapstick comedy), 'on the whole ... the film was marred by poor cinematography'.[45] Yet, Major Notcutt offered a rebuttal, devising the axiom according to which 'the impression gained from my previous experience [is] that natives are not critical of photographic quality'. Thus, in relation to lighting, 'one can spend a long time getting the lighting right for an attractive picture, but we rarely attempted this because we found that native audiences require, at present, nothing beyond a clear picture'.[46]

The narrative dimensions of the films were not immune from similar problems. The BEKE solicited narrative ideas from various quarters, from anthropologists to agents of colonial administration, but never from Africans themselves. They attempted to convince Africans to participate in the colonial order by creating the following narrative formula: a binaristic narrative, often based on the premise of the before and after, deploying excessively didactic repetition by reformulating at the end of the film the lesson to be taken, always pitting Africa versus Europe, with the European approach to organising the world always carrying the day.

In its very first film, *Post Office Savings Bank* (1935), it contrasts the way in which two Africans handle their salaries, which they receive from working on a plantation. While one buries his money in the floor of his hut, the other one takes his straight to the colonial Post Office Bank. Naturally, the one who does not must be punished, and thus his money is stolen by a thief who had observed him burying his money through a crack in the wall. In the end, the money is recovered and deposited safely in the bank. The film predictably fails to account for the fact that, the potential benefits of banking aside, this represented the colonial banking system taking charge of the revenues of the colonised. Likewise, the third BEKE film, *Tax* (1935), also sought to promote the hegemony of the colonial tax system over the colonised, by drawing out 'radical differences' between the precolonial and colonial modes of taxation. The film represented the precolonial era as one in which tributes were paid to chiefs who raided villages that refused to pay. While under colonial rule, taxes are shown as being used for the provision of services such as medical attention, education, emergency funds for famine and literally, 'maintenance of order and peace'.[47]

Another film idea (possibly never made or part of the reels that were never edited but none the less symptomatic of the BEKE approach) entitled *Poultry Keeping* is worth our attention. The story sought to 'show how a native can keep fowls in a village for profit'. Two enclosures are contrasted, one dirty, the second clean and well kept. We are told that the second one is well kept and prosperous because the owner has been 'imitating the white man' while the other refuses to do so on account that 'the spirits of their fathers don't like to see their customs change or it will bring evil upon the village'.[48] The catalysing event involves the announcement that the 'District

Commissioner is coming to collect taxes'.[49] The village is in pandemonium, with terrorised farmers wondering 'where the tax money might be found'. The farmers resort to contracting debts and resign themselves to improving their poultry. Here the repressive approach prevails over the supposed educational dimension of the film. Indeed, narrative transformation is predicated on the presence of the 'man on the ground',' i.e. the official representative at the village level of colonial power.

A better perspective may be gained from reminding the reader that part of the perversion of the colonial system consisted in the fact that Africans were constrained to pay, via taxes, for the costs of their own colonisation. These taxes paid for the maintenance and running of the colonial administration. Kwame Nkrumah makes this clear:

> There is a belief that the British Government contributed to the costs of administration and public services in their colonies. This is a fallacy. Each colony raised its own budget out of taxes and revenue, and the first charge upon it was the salaries of the European officials of the administration.[50]

Clearly, improvements in poultry raising and other aspects of the BEKE instructional/educational cinema project were not for the benefit of Africans, but rather meant to keep the colony running. Not surprisingly, within a year into the experiment, the BEKE had become integrated into the propaganda machinery of the various colonial governments of East and Central Africa and was only making commissioned films. Thus, BEKE titles, including *Improved Agriculture*, *Coffee under Banana Shade*, *High Yields from Selected Plants*, *Coffee Marketing*, *Farm Implements* or *Agricultural Education at Bukalasa* (all 1937), unwittingly made visible the place assigned to African economies in the world economy by colonialism, by casting them exclusively as producers and exporters of raw materials with decisions about them sanctioned by Europeans.

The exhibition dimension of the BEKE project consisted in the encounter between the project and East and Central African audiences, whose complexity had been condensed into the figure of the illiterate African peasant mentally challenged by a cinematic medium to which s/he had not been exposed to. The entire BEKE edifice rested on this quasi-ontological argument, premised on a biologisation, indeed a racialisation of visual literacy. Indeed one of the feats of the BEKE was its 'success' in conflating illiteracy in the English language with visual illiteracy *vis-à-vis* the cinema. This, they had already inscribed in the films themselves as demonstrated above. It was now time to test the validity of this 'new cinema' with African audiences, in order to possibly fine-tune it.

And so, the exhibition stage of the experiment was launched, relying on the mobile cinema. Touring began 4 September 1935, with a crew comprised of two Europeans, Peter Woodall as projectionist and G. C. Latham, the education director and four Africans (Jackson, the driver-mechanic, two servants, Hamedi and Mulishu and Alphonse, 'a hefty but brainless youth with an insatiable appetite').[51] They travelled across East and Central Africa with 'a two-ton Ford lorry with the cinema unit engine mounted on a trailer bouncing behind'.[52]

The films were screened in seventy districts, cities and mines and sixteen mission stations across five colonies (Tanganyika Territory, Northern Rhodesia, Nyasaland,

Kenya and Uganda). According to the BEKE, these mostly outdoors screenings were well attended, sometimes with crowds of about 3,000 to 5,000 people. Given that the audiences were reportedly seeing films for the very first time, the BEKE can hardly claim that the huge crowds validated its brand of cinema. Instead, one may propose such motivations as the desire for communal gathering around the cinema as a recreational object, the need to compensate for the recreational repressions enforced by the administration and the church (forcing the converts to renounce supposed heathen practices), but also the techniques used by BEKE to attract audiences, which included Swahili songs, missionary choirs, folk stories and the music of Paul Robeson.[53]

After the screenings, the BEKE collected responses from the audiences through such intermediaries as government officials, missionaries, anthropologists and educated Africans.[54] Up until this phase, the BEKE largely exercised control of the experiment in terms of its framing. Yet the question of the transitive/transparent relationship between its work and its desired audience remains open. The final part of this essay will be devoted to exploring the extent to which the experiment was thwarted or subverted by the colonised.

From the standpoint of reception, several of the BEKE films were criticised by the supposedly illiterate peasants on several accounts. Taking some of the films offered as examples above, it was found in the case of *Post Office Savings Bank* that the narrative resolution of the case of the thief as initially filmed by the BEKE was too cruel, too implausible. Indeed, in the first version of the film, the thief had fallen from a tree and died. This the illiterate peasants considered too drastic a retribution and they instead proposed that the thief be taken to court or to the chief, hereby displaying familiarity with such representational notions as realism, which they opposed to the melodramatic and rather 'excessive' impulse of the BEKE architects.

For the film *Tax*, the obvious non-verisimilitude of the portrayal of the taxation system and of the representation of the chief may account for its lack of success and the fact that it was not often shown. Indeed, African peasants were well aware of the fact that 'their impression that their tax money goes into the pockets of local administrative officers' was not a product of their imagination, demonstrated by the above Kwame Nkrumah quote.[55] Indeed these supposedly illiterate peasants proved extremely literate in the ways of colonialism, which they experienced firsthand, as it inscribed itself on their very bodies. The objectionable nature of the representation of their chief as cruel and uncaring, while the colonial system was portrayed as a Santa Claus of taxation, was also resisted, including by the chief himself, who 'failed to keep his promise to produce large numbers of warriors and other requirements'.[56]

Objections to the BEKE project were not limited to narratological questions in which illiterates sometimes proved more sophisticated than the directors themselves. They also related simply to the quality of the films. For, although the BEKE claimed success for many of their screenings (thus downplaying their limitations), it is important to look at other reception problems faced by a cinema with a high degree of tolerance for imperfection, indeed one with an ideological inscription of amateurish-ness, technological ruggedness, narrative and photographic legerdemain, if not plain incompetence. Many accounts of the fact demonstrate that audiences often found the films too crude and too boring.[57] At times, as if verbal expressions of discontent *vis-à-vis* the BEKE project were not enough, open hostility to the experiment was expressed through sabotage:

> At Mwanza, we stayed in a spare house at the central African School as the guests of the headmaster, Mr. Cutler and his wife. The following night we showed at the school and the cable connecting the projector-box to the engine was cut – the only time such a thing happened. We never discovered who was responsible.[58]

One of the noticeable aspects of the BEKE as part of its unique contribution to the production of the colonial real, the colonial visible, was the way in which it sought to time the relationship between Africans and cinema. Through the film-makers' writings, it is possible to abstract a desire for a cinema of incrementalism both ideologically and filmically. Ideologically, this entailed the desire to slow down Africans' embrace of modernity. Hence the argument that modernity is coming at too fast a pace for Africans, that values are being lost that need to be preserved, that they should constitute themselves into mediators between the old and the new in Africa. To do so, they created the figure of the illiterate and visually impaired African peasant as representative of a certain essence of Africa, who should be the object of filmic intervention in the form of educational cinema. Thus, although they mention their interest in 'semi-detribalized' and urban Africans, their main object of interpellation was the so-called illiterate peasant. This figure of the essential African, or rather this essentially fictional figure of Africans was brought into the field of the visible as a result of a denial. For it involved pushing outside the boundaries of visibility the domestic multi-secular, precolonial traditions of literacy, including several centuries of Islamic literacy (especially in this part of the continent facing the Indian Ocean, the royal route to Asia), centuries-old interactions with India, Japan or China, as well as evolving political, historical and cultural dynamics in Africa itself.

The cinematic implication of this was that commercial cinema, a faster-paced cinema, was positioned as the bad object that the 'essential' African spectator should be protected from. This in turn made it possible to position the BEKE's own brand of 'educational cinema', with its principles of 'slowed-down' cinema, emphasising the rural over the urban, in such a way as to condition rural audiences before they became 'spoilt'. The BEKE even imagined a taste-formation filmic diet, which would consist in first introducing the proverbial illiterate peasants to BEKE educational film to a point of saturation to such an extent that they would be 'weaned off' 'unsuitable' commercial films before even being exposed to them.

For the Africans who fell outside the ontological figure of illiteracy, i.e. educated and upper-class Africans, the BEKE co-opted, dismissed or simply ignored them. The co-opted ones would play such roles as collecting audience responses or that of the *benshi*, who would introduce every screening.[59] The second group represented the antithesis of the figure propagated by the BEKE, and thus were often quick to see through and deconstruct the BEKE imposture. Indeed the various screenings the BEKE organised in the cities were mostly failures, for the Natives there are in the habit of seeing films, most of which are comics of the Charlie Chaplin variety, or thrillers. They have become accustomed to go to the cinema to be amused and ... were not prepared to appreciate or pay for quite so much educational matter.[60]

Finally, the BEKE in its exhibition circuit encountered Africans who had already made films:

At Iganga, the Saza Chief of Kamuli, named William Wilberforce Kajiumbula Nadiope, who had seen our films the previous night, brought some of his own locally taken films, which we showed with our programme. Parts were quite good and parts were very bad ... .[61]

The concluding sentence of the quote demonstrates how the dogmatic adherence to a (colonial) visual regime can in fact foreclose the possibility of seeing, accepting, acknowledging and accounting for the new and the unexpected. For how else could the BEKE personnel be blindfolded to the unfolding of film history in front of their very eyes? Not only did this encounter demonstrate beyond doubt that Africans did not wait for the BEKE to come and introduce them to film-making, but that in the very area that they constructed as filmically impaired, a lone individual, Chief William Wilberforce, had actually directed films. Thus, instead of a *tabula rasa cinematographica*, the BEKE came face to face with one of the pioneers of African cinema. And thus in spite of themselves, thanks to their own account, it is possible to add William Wilberforce Kajiumbula Nadiope to the list of pioneering figures of African cinema, who made films at least two decades before the likes of Paulin Soumanou Vieyra and Ousmane Sembene.

With this, the BEKE had come full circle. Having come to East and Central Africa in search of a visually impaired audience that had never been exposed to cinema, they found instead not only a critical culture of spectatorship, but also an existing film-making practice.[62]

CONCLUSION

The BEKE proved itself to be an instrument devoted to the preservation and stabilisation of colonial normativity. It did so not only by using colonialism's mechanisms of the production of the visible for self-validation and legitimation, but also by using its own mode of film practice to provide its unique contribution to the construction of the colonial visible. The BEKE performed its process of reordering of the field of cinema, first by creating a bad object (commercial cinema), which it construed as its nemesis, and then by conjuring the figure of the visually illiterate African peasant whom it could turn into an object of both film practice and discourse within the context of colonialism. This produced a system characterised by a technical and aesthetic reification of the colonial order of the visible that simultaneously made it possible for the BEKE to push beyond or below the pale, beyond the threshold of the visible, the possibility of other film viewing (cinephilia) and making practices (the existence of an amateur cinema in Africa). Interestingly enough, the BEKE's own amateurish film practice was responsible for its ultimate demise at the very hands of the colonial apparatus it sought to serve. Indeed, in spite of the multitude of recommendations proposed by the architects of the BEKE at the end of the experiment in 1937, the project folded. The *monstrum informe ingens horrendum* had its head cut off and was laid to rest.[63]

But it is common knowledge that in spite of its claim and will to educate the colonised, colonialism itself is a bad student, indeed a poor learner. And thus instead of burying the monster once and for all, they chose to resurrect it two years later in the form of the Colonial Film Unit, reactivating many of the BEKE's features. This of course is another story, but one which would keep alive the much larger debate at stake, i.e. the ability of language, discourse and the image to produce the real and the visible.[64] At stake indeed is the question of the articulation of discourse and the image to produce the real, and whether their deconstruction could open up space for other reals, other visibles.

NOTES

1. For examples of British colonial films, see <www.colonialfilm.org.uk>. On early British film in Africa, see Guido Convents, 'Africa: Britain', in Richard Abel (ed.), *Encyclopedia of Early Cinema* (New York: Routledge, 2005), p. 12.
2. For a more comprehensive analysis of this, see Lee Grieveson, 'The Cinema and the (Common) Wealth of Nations', in this volume.
3. See also ibid.
4. Sarah Street offers precise figures regarding this increasing domination: 'Up to 1927, the majority of films exhibited in Britain had been American. In 1914, 25% of films shown were British ... by 1925, it was only 5%.' See Sarah Street, 'British Film and the National Interest, 1927–39', in Robert Murphy (ed.), *The British Cinema Book* (London: BFI, 2001), p. 28.
5. Priya Jaikumar, 'More than Morality: The Indian Cinematograph Interviews (1927)', *Moving Image* vol. 3 no. 1 (2003), pp. 83–109.
6. Rosaleen Smyth, 'The Development of British Colonial Film Policy, 1927–1939 with Special Reference to East and Central Africa', *Journal of African History* vol. 20 no. 3 (1979), pp. 437–50.
7. Several personalities expressed apprehension about the potential 'effect' of cinema on the colonised, referred to as subject races, from King George V to the Secretary of State for the Colonies. See L. A. Notcutt and G. C. Latham, *The African and the Cinema: An Account of the Bantu Educational Kinema Experiment during the Period March 1935 to May 1937* (London: Edinburgh House Press, 1937), p. 246 and Rosaleen Smyth, 'The Development of British Colonial Film Policy, 1927–1939', p. 438.
8. Rachael Low, 'The Educational Film', *The History of the British Film (1919–1929)* (London: Allen, 1971), p. 9.
9. Ibid., pp. 10–12.
10. Ibid., p. 12.
11. See Notcutt and Latham, *The African and the Cinema*, pp. 244–7.
12. Zoë Druick, 'Reaching the Multimillions', in Lee Grieveson and Haidee Wasson (eds), *Inventing Film Studies* (Durham, NC: Duke University Press, 2008), pp. 66–92.
13. Notcutt and Latham, *The African and the Cinema*, p. 22. Merle Davis adds to the international dimension of the BEKE in admitting that, in the process of doing groundwork

for the experiment, he consulted not only the International Educational Cinematography Institute in Rome, but also the Motion Picture Research Council of America, the Harvard University Film Foundation and Yale University Historical Films. Elsewhere in this volume, Aaron Windel further demonstrates that the International Missionary Council saw itself as a religious version of the League of Nations. See Aaron Windel, 'The Bantu Educational Kinema Experiment and the Political Economy of Community Development', this volume.

14. James M. Burns, *Flickering Shadows: Cinema and Identity in Colonial Zimbabwe* (Athens: Ohio University Press, 2002), p. 39.
15. Julian Huxley, *Africa View* (London: Chatto, 1931), p. 1.
16. Ibid., p. 160.
17. Ibid.
18. Ibid., p. 161.
19. Low, *The History of the British Film*, p. 53.
20. It is important to distinguish between imperial and Colonial Office conferences. The first included only the Dominions (Canada, Australia, New Zealand, South Africa) and India, while the latter included the rest of the colonies.
21. See Great Britain. Parliament. House of Commons. Colonial Office Conference, 1927. Appendices to the summary of proceedings [electronic resource]. Cambridge [England]: Proquest LLC, 2007, Annex 1, pp. 248–55.
22. Great Britain, 'Colonial Office Conference', pp. 255–61. Also see Grieveson 'The Cinema and the (Common) Wealth of Nations' for more specific analysis of the larger role of the Federation of British Industries in shaping debates on empire cinema.
23. Great Britain. Parliament. House of Commons. Colonial Office Conference, 1930. Summary of proceedings [electronic resource]. Cambridge [England]: Proquest LLC, 2007, Annex 1, pp. 35–40.
24. Rosaleen Smyth, 'The Development of British Colonial Film Policy, 1927–1939', pp. 441–2.
25. This was brilliantly demonstrated in Jean-Marie Teno's film *The Colonial Misunderstanding* (2005).
26. J. Merle Davis, 'Foreword', in L. A. Notcutt and G. C. Latham, *The African and the Cinema*, p. 9.
27. J. Merle Davis, *Modern Industry and the African: An Enquiry into the Effect of the Copper Mines of Central Africa upon Native Society and the Work of Christian Missions* (London: Frank Cass & Co. Ltd., 1967).
28. Notcutt and Latham, *The African and the Cinema*, p. 9.
29. This is indeed part of what constitutes the discursive structure of the production of colonial visuality: first a process of creating/inventing/clearing out a space of intervention; and second, proposing the means of intervention.
30. Merle Davis was very much inspired by the work of American missionaries with the cinema, particularly with Reverend Ray E. Philips, who organised a missionary film circuit serving 200 centres from South Africa to Southern and Northern Rhodesia. See Merle Davis, *Modern Industry and the African*, p. 325.
31. J. Merle Davis, *The Bantu Educational Kinema Experiment: Origin and History* (London: International Missionary Council), p. 2.
32. Merle Davis, *Modern Industry and the African*, p. 5.
33. See in this volume, Windel, 'The Bantu Educational Kinema Experiment and the Political Economy of Community Development' and James Burns, 'American Philanthropy and

Colonial Film-making: The Rockefeller Foundation, the Carnegie Corporation and the Birth of Colonial Cinema'.

34. Notcutt and Latham, *The African and the Cinema*, p. 210.
35. Ibid., p. 24.
36. Ibid., p. 25.
37. Ibid., p. 27.
38. Ibid., pp. 27–8.
39. Ibid., p. 28.
40. Haidee Wasson, 'Electric Homes! Automatic Movies! Efficient Entertainment!: 16mm and Cinema's Domestication in the 1920s', *Cinema Journal* vol. 48 no. 4 (Summer 2009), pp. 1–21.
41. Notcutt and Latham, *The African and the Cinema*, pp. 216–17.
42. Ibid., p. 31. There are at present only three BEKE films in the possession of the BFI's National Film Archive in London.
43. Dixit Notcutt: 'The selection of a male cast is mainly a matter of finding Natives who, in real life, approximate to the characters one wishes to portray. They will act what they are themselves with complete naturalness' (ibid., p. 144).
44. Ibid., pp. 143–4.
45. Ibid., pp. 39–40.
46. Ibid., p. 135.
47. Ibid., p. 35.
48. Merle Davis, *Modern Industry and the African*, p. 6.
49. Ibid., p. 7.
50. Kwame Nkrumah, *Africa Must Unite* (London: Panaf Books, 1963), pp. 22–3.
51. Notcutt and Latham, *The African and the Cinema*, p. 74.
52. Ibid., p. 75.
53. Ibid., p. 171.
54. Dixit Latham:

> At all displays, I endeavored to arrange for competent European observers to be present and to report to me later on the reactions of the Africans to the films. In this way, a vast amount of useful information was accumulated. Officials, missionaries, anthropologists and educated Africans were the chief contributors. Their reports were based partly on their own impressions and partly on the questioning of natives after the display. (Ibid., p. 77)

55. Ibid., p. 35.
56. Ibid.
57. Dixit Latham:

> The town Natives of Nairobi and Dar-Es-Salaam found our programs too educational. The main reason for this, no doubt, was that many of them were regular cinema goers, and were accustomed to a proportion of definitely funny films which they did not get in our programmes. Also these Natives were accustomed to professional films made primarily to entertain. They found our pictures inferior in quality and less entertaining in subject matter. (Ibid., p. 114)

58. Ibid., p. 89.
59. 'We found it useful ... to find someone (usually a local official, missionary or educated African) to give through a microphone in the local language a brief explanation of each film before it was shown' (ibid., p. 172).
60. Following a screening at the elite Makerere College, the BEKE was forced to acknowledge that 'for sophisticated audiences such as we had that night, films of better quality are really necessary' (ibid., p. 94).
61. Ibid.
62. As a consequence, at the end of the experiment, the BEKE had to acknowledge the obvious, albeit in an understated tone, namely, that 'the moving picture is understood by quite unsophisticated Natives which astonished people who have experienced their comparatively inability to recognize still pictures' (ibid., p. 183).
63. It was R. V. Vernon, a representative of the Colonial Office in the Colonial Films Committee, who appropriately referred to the BEKE as an 'immense, formless and frightful monster' (Vernon, cited in Smyth, 'The Development of British Colonial Film Policy, 1927–1939', p. 442.
64. It is a story taken up by Tom Rice and Rosaleen Smyth in Lee Grieveson and Colin MacCabe (eds), *Film and the End of Empire* (London: British Film Institute, 2011).

13

'Of great use at meetings': The Film-making Principles of the London Missionary Society

Francis Gooding

The congregation files out of a simple whitewashed church in a suburb of Lobatse, a southeastern town in the Bechuanaland Protectorate. Good Christians no doubt, they had chosen the vicar's sermon over the other form of public address offered on Sundays: political speech-making in the town square, featuring representatives of the 'People's Democratic Party'. It is a decision that one might perhaps expect any observing missionary to applaud: the verities of the one true God placed before the vicissitudes of politics, especially a politics advocating the dangerous jujus of independence and self-determination.

The sequence occurs near the start of the London Missionary Society (LMS) film *The Desert Shall Rejoice* (R. O. Latham; date uncertain, probably early 1960s), and it is indeed used to draw a direct equivalence between the dangers of superstitious traditional beliefs and those of modern politics. The commentary has already described Bechuanaland as a 'country at war', and the Sunday-morning clash of interests between church and politics – Bechuanaland was well on its way to independence by the time the film was made – is a second front, the first being the battle to wean the people off the harmful ministrations of the witch doctor in favour of Christian faith and modern medicine. The formal comparison itself is an artless demonstration of the conventional colonial principle that saw only some forms of modernisation as suitable for African colonial subjects (e.g. medicine, schooling), while others were deemed corrupting or dangerous (e.g. political awareness, urbanisation). Certainly the distributors of the film saw it in these terms, and apparently without either nuance or basic political awareness – despite Bechuanaland having achieved independence as Botswana in 1966, the Congregational Council for World Mission's 1968 *Audio Visual Aids Catalogue* describes the sequence as an illustration of 'the temptations posed by superstition and political fanaticism'.[1]

But unusually, and in contradistinction to both the catalogue summary and the film's own broad implication, the film commentary itself hesitates: there is no suggestion that the church-goers have made the wrong choice exactly, but it might be that the sermon has not served them well in these changing times. They have probably heard only a straightforward devotional sermon; better perhaps would have been one that taught 'Christian responsibility in social and political matters'.

However subtly made, it is an extraordinary admission – a missionary-produced film lamenting that the church may not be guiding its flock with sufficient focus in political and societal matters. It immediately marks *The Desert Shall Rejoice* out as an unusual film, especially when compared to most London Missionary Society productions. No doubt, it is still a very conservative picture in many regards, and the early characterisation of Bechuanaland as a 'spiritual desert', afflicted by ignorance, superstition and want, is of typical missionary-film stamp. But by indicating both that Africans might have a stake in some sort of political process and that the church might have a duty to foster political awareness, Latham starts pushing his film into fairly radical territory for the genre. Instead of eliding or completely ignoring contemporary issues in favour of presenting a backward and anonymous African mission field, the film actively, if circumspectly, begins to comprehend and present Africans as agents (and not merely as *patients*, in both the medical and philosophical sense of the term). They are not just the passive recipients of education and healthcare common in missionary films, but instead are presented as being at least potentially active and engaged in determining their own destinies, and that of their country. 'The devotional is important', continues the commentary, 'but so is the other [the social and political], especially now', going to on to assert that one of the contemporary tasks of the church in Bechuanaland is to help the 'African Christian bring to his politics Christian standards, Christian insight, Christian concern'. This may seem a very conservative aim, and it is connected to a more conventional message that there are not enough qualified missionaries and ministers in Bechuanaland, but it is the acknowledgment of any politics at all that is surprising. To get a sense of quite how unusual that message is for a missionary film, it is useful to examine some more standard London Missionary Society fare, and put the production of missionary films by the LMS in some historical context.

Though a prolific and relatively early producer of films, the LMS was by no means the first religious group to begin a programme of film-making within the British Empire – the Salvation Army, which had started experimenting with film in the 1890s, had made thirteen films in India by 1904,[2] and the Mill Hill Missionaries were making films in Uganda and other parts of the empire by the early 1920s (some elements of *Mill Hill Sheds Light on the Dark Places of the Earth: Uganda*, for instance, appear to date from 1920).[3] Though not actually an LMS film, Wetherell's famous *Livingstone* (1925) was one of the earliest popular films with a missionary theme, and does of course feature the LMS's most celebrated missionary as its protagonist; in return for some screening rights, the LMS contributed £200 to its production.[4]

Nevertheless the LMS was to become an enthusiastic adopter of film, and it seems that a closely considered policy toward film and an active film-making programme had been put in place during the mid-1930s. Judging from articles published in the LMS magazine the *Chronicle*, this increased focus on film-making seems to have been spurred by a combination of two factors – on the one hand, experiments and projects in the UK that looked toward developing an educational cinema, and on the other, the missionary-inspired Bantu Educational Kinema Experiment (BEKE) that was undertaken in East Africa between 1935–7. This latter project, a landmark in the development of British colonial cinema and an acknowledged precursor to the Colonial Film Unit, had some significant links to the LMS, and was itself born of an earlier missionary endeavour, the International Missionary Council's (IMC) 1932 commission of enquiry into social and working conditions among Africans living in the expanding mining communities of the Northern Rhodesian Copper Belt. The network of links between these different projects is worth exploring.

The IMC commission of enquiry was undertaken in order to make a straight-forward assessment concerning the future direction of missionary work in Africa. Social change had accelerated with the spread of industrialisation across the continent, and the missions were determined to keep step with the changing conditions faced by their flocks. 'Alien influences' were 'shaking the foundations of Bantu life', and the church was concerned to respond: where should it 'lend its influence, where put the emphasis of its activities and toward what goal direct the life of the people'?[5] Industrial exploitation of Northern Rhodesia's copper wealth had started in earnest during the 1920s, and by the dawn of the 1930s the Copper Belt mines were employing tens of thousands of workers.[6] However, the relative remoteness of Northern Rhodesia was no insulation against the Depression: numerous mines were forced to close, and the large Roan and Nkana mines could only operate at one-half capacity through 1932–3.[7] The already precarious existence of the African mineworker was made all the more difficult by these changes, and it was against the backdrop of the insecurity brought by the Depression that the IMC sent its commission to investigate life on the Copper Belt.

Funded by the Carnegie Corporation and the Phelps Stokes Foundation, the six-person commission was led by the director of the IMC's department of social and industrial research, John Merle Davis; the commission's other members consisted of three academics drawn from universities in the US, UK and South Africa and two missionaries working in Southern Africa. One of the missionaries, Mabel Shaw, was the principal of the LMS Livingstone Memorial Girls' School, in Mbereshi, Northern Rhodesia.[8] The commission spent six months in Africa during 1932, travelling to remote recruitment areas, visiting large mines, viewing missions and government posts. The result was the publication in 1933 of a long report, *Modern Industry and the African*,[9] whose condescending but serious analysis of all aspects of African life on the Copper Belt culminates in a series of 'recommendations' designed as a programme of practical guidance for the various missions working in the area. Of direct relevance in the present connection are both the commission's views on film, and its broad overall assessment of the problems facing Copper Belt Africans.

On the latter issue, the central finding of the commission was fairly straight-forward: the coming of mechanised heavy industry to remote areas, and the spontaneous establishment of large, industry-localised conurbations populated by a combination of rural migrant workers and urbanised residents, was dramatically transforming the life and outlook of Africans in both the Copper Belt mining areas proper and in the rural areas that functioned as labour reservoirs. For 'the African' it was, in the commission's view, a time of dramatic change ('The African is on the move'),[10] a change understood principally as a form of Westernisation epitomised by the loosening of ties to rural life and the adoption of certain European mores. The process was also a major concern for colonial administrations in Africa, for whom the development of an urban, increasingly politicised and 'detribalised' African proletariat was a serious worry, particularly as the principle of indirect rule was predicated on the stability of traditional social structures.

Naturally, this was considered an alarming situation by the missions: the raw material of evangelisation in Southern and Central Africa, the rural African peasant, was changing before their eyes, and missionary societies felt that they had been caught on the hop:

Now … the outside world has come to Africa and the people are exposed to the complex of forces political, economic, social and moral that is modern life, they are making their own interpretation of the White man's culture. The human material with which missions deal is changing so rapidly that their old methods are inadequate. Modern missions faced with the sophisticated Native who has 'seen the world' on the mines are much in the position of the hen that hatched a brood of ducklings.[11]

In response to this new situation *vis-à-vis* their 'human material', the commission urged that missions rise to the challenge and use their influence and position to assist 'the African' during the confusing change from one condition to the next: it was a time of 'tutelage and transition', during which the church should help rudderless Africans 'span the gulf between savagery and civilisation'.[12]

Despite the prejudiced and patronising tone, *Modern Industry and the African* was, as Frederick Cooper has pointed out,[13] actually considerably more engaged and intelligent in its conclusions than the reports of any official body had been at that date. Indeed, central government had paid precious little attention to events on the Copper Belt, as administrative control of the large concentrations of people in the mining districts was largely left to the mining companies.[14] Merle Davis's report presented a coherent critical overview of the situation based in the recognition that the rapid processes of industrialisation and urbanisation that had taken place were irreversible and had led to fundamental social shifts that could not be ignored. The missions would have to work with the situation as it stood, and needed to find a new attitude and *modus operandi*. The 'summary of recommendations' at the end of *Modern Industry* attempted to outline the new missionary challenge in a rapidly modernising African context, and the fundamental vision of the report is important in establishing tropes that are clearly visible in LMS films into the 1960s.

The central message was that missions must provide, in partnership with the mines, a combination of relevant moral guidance, healthcare, education and social instruction for African workers in the mining towns and compounds. The mineworkers were seen to be entering on a new way of life, and the missions should be there to help them understand its complexities. As contract mine work began to redefine the relation between country and town, and temporary migration to compounds increasingly gave way to the development of urban areas with permanent residents, the missions were no longer serving rural peasants, but wage-employed townspeople, and not only that, but townspeople whose 'towns' were frequently bereft of governmental administrative and social structures. All Protestant missions were recommended to unite in the common aim of helping to establish the shared social life that would come to 'serve as the foundation for urban Native society'.[15]

Central to this general aim to provide guidance was the customary missionary emphasis on education. Here the IMC commission touches directly on film, and in *Modern Industry*'s sections on the cinema are found passages that not only are a precursor to the BEKE, but also give an early sense of missionary film exhibition in African mission fields.

The main educational problem identified by the commission was not the education of children so much as the pressing need to educate adults:

If the growing Native communities in urban and mining districts are to be helped toward intelligent adjustments to the new order, it must come through the enlightenment of the adults rather than by waiting for the generation of children now in school to come to maturity.[16]

One problem here was widespread illiteracy, and the commission recommended two remedies to the difficulty of educating an illiterate population in the basics of modern life. The first, drawn from the example of the USSR, was the picture poster, which the commission warmly recommends, as the Soviet model had in its estimation given 'millions of illiterate people ... something of an understanding of the advocated advantages of the modern and Soviet way of life over the old'.[17]

The second was the cinema, and here the commission seems extremely impressed with its educational potential, noting that it 'goes far toward meeting the problem of the illiteracy of the adult', is suitable for teaching outside and to mass audiences ('several thousand Natives can get the benefit of its instruction together'), and is suited to 'the African's capacity for noting details, and for remembering and describing them':

> It is suited to the African by teaching through life and action. It deals with the concrete ... .
> Fundamental principles may be woven into the picture story. It maintains a freshness and
> vigour and rivets the interest as no other form of instruction.

The text goes on to list at some length those subjects that might be taught using film: 'hygiene, sanitation, Government administration, religious and moral instruction, economics, agriculture, art, child nurture, land utilisation, trade and commerce, geography, travel, natural science, physics, biology, physiology, astronomy, etc. etc.'.[18]

'A moving-picture outfit with suitable films', the report continues, 'could profitably form a part of the equipment of every African mission, and would have special value for those missions whose people are being influenced by the copper belt.'[19] In this context, attention is drawn to the Rev. Ray E. Phillips of the American Congregational Board, whose mobile-cinema service had 'for a number of years' extended 'social welfare' through film to over fifty mines on the Rand, and who had recently expanded his circuit to take in over 200 venues in missions, schools and industries in South Africa, and as far afield as the Rhodesias.[20]

The most historically significant elements of these passages concerning the cinema are no doubt the suggestions that a broad programme of film-making and exhibition, bringing together missions, mines and government, would be desirable. The commission was also clearly abreast of metropolitan developments in this area, and was already concerned that films of dubious morality might corrupt susceptible Africans. The relevant section, which is revised in short at Recommendation 62 of the 'summary of recommendations',[21] is worth quoting at length. *Modern Industry and the African* was a signally important missionary publication, and here within it can be seen the idea for a government-overseen and -financed film project for African audiences – the germ of the BEKE:

> The great expense of producing films and the difficulty of planning subjects thoroughly suited
> to the African, and the further difficulty of organising an adequate supply, point to the

necessity of joint action and financing. An impossible program for a single mission might be carried out through the pooling of the resources of a dozen mission societies in co-operation with Government or large industries … . The possibilities of the constructive use of the cinema in relation to the indigenous peoples of the British colonies are being studied by the Colonial Office. This is obviously a field in which extensive experiment and testing must be carried out under expert leadership. Missions should follow closely these developments and be prepared to co-operate with Government and industries in giving practical effect to any serious efforts in this direction. Unless prompt measures are taken to enter the Central African field with wholesome films, the commercial exploitation of the Native will proceed with a type of picture that caters to his worst instincts and depicts an unreal and corrupt European civilisation. Missions should be the among the first to throw the weight of their influence against such a development and study the problem of providing the African with sound and constructive pictures.[22]

How these attitudes relate to later LMS productions is more complex, and here the focus must shift briefly to the BEKE, and to the LMS connections and responses to it.

The Bantu Educational Kinema Experiment of 1935–7 was the first carefully orchestrated attempt to produce films for African audiences, and may be seen as the direct forerunner of the Ministry of Information's Colonial Film Unit, which was subsequently established in 1939 (the Colonial Film Unit, like the BEKE, began by making films with an African audience in mind; its initial aim was to bolster African support for the war effort). As one of the crucial official interventions into cinema in the empire, the development and productions of the BEKE have already received significant scholarly attention,[23] but it is worth reiterating how closely it was tied to missionary concerns, to the IMC commission in particular, and also to the LMS.

In execution, the BEKE remained 'under the auspices' of the IMC's department of social and industrial research, and according to the final 1937 report, the 'experiment was under the direction of Mr. [John] Merle Davis'.[24] Numerous missionary and Christian voices were present on the advisory council, alongside representatives of both officialdom and of various secular interests.[25] Among the missionaries on the council was A. M. Chirgwin, who was at this time the general secretary of the LMS. Chirgwin had been the LMS foreign secretary to the Southern Fields from 1929–32, and the missions on the Copper Belt were thus his direct professional concern during the period of the original IMC commission. The final report on the project, *The African and the Cinema*, was published in 1937: the foreword was penned by Merle Davis, and in the opening sentence he fixes the beginnings of the project in the findings of the IMC commission, and goes on to unequivocally assert its fundamentally missionary nature ('The experiment is an example of a new strategy that is being used in the programme of foreign missions … the experiment is a missionary project').[26] As well as coming from the Colonial Office, and from the governments of Tanganyika, Uganda and Kenya, the funding for the experiment, as for the IMC commission, came in part from the Carnegie Corporation of New York, with major Copper Belt mining companies also providing monies.

What is clear from these shared elements is that in many significant organisa-tional, funding and intellectual aspects, the BEKE can be seen to emerge from the IMC commission. And with the general secretary of the LMS sitting on the advisory council, it is no surprise that the LMS took a close interest. The beginnings of the experiment were reported in the June 1935 issue of the *Chronicle*, in a short article entitled 'African Films for Africa', and the February 1936 issue carried an update on the project, detailing the films that had been produced.[27] An increasing amount of references to film in subsequent issues makes it clear that from around this date film and its uses become an active concern of the society: from the possibilities suggested in the IMC report, and through the attempt to realise these possibilities in the BEKE, the LMS establishes that cinema must have an important place in its future activity.

The *Chronicle* for November 1936 carried a substantial article on film and film-making, 'Films in Britain', written by Howard Diamond, the LMS assistant treasurer.[28] As the most engaged meditation on film up to this point in the magazine, the article effectively articulates the considered LMS position on the medium, and sets up a contextual lens through which subsequent LMS productions can be viewed. 'There is an important movement on foot just now in the film world', writes Diamond, '… a movement among people who take films seriously and who know that they can be used for education and instruction as well as for entertainment.' He goes on to note recent developments in the educational use of film in schools, before mentioning that '[m]any churches, and certainly all the Missionary Societies, are fully alive to the possibilities inherent in this new method of education'. J. Arthur Rank's Religious Film Society production company and the Missionary Film Committee are both singled out as being active in the field.[29]

Quite in keeping with the BEKE and the IMC findings, the emphasis of the article is placed on the educative potential of film, and this should be seen in light of the flurry of research into educational film at the end of the 1920s in Britain, which saw the move toward using film as a teaching tool gather momentum in the early 1930s. The journal *Educational Film Review* had been founded in 1935, and the early years of the decade had seen a great number of enquiries, committees, books and papers all devoted to the educative potential of film. Diamond mentions the fact that 'Glasgow teachers' had recently made 'a number of educational films' and this reference is possibly to the 1933 'Glasgow Experiment', undertaken by the Corporation of Glasgow Education Department, which had tried to establish whether film was a significant aid to information retention.[30] Diamond explicitly identifies LMS productions as a vital part of these contemporary developments in British educational film – the LMS is 'right in the van of this movement [sic]' – and makes the perhaps unlikely boast that the society offers 'a programme which, for real interest and news value, leaves the studios far behind'.

This discovery of the educative potential of film is clearly the motivation for the IMC report's advocation of film as a teaching tool in the mission field, and the possibility for mass education via cinema was the guiding principle of the BEKE, as we have seen. But here there is a difference. The real significance of Diamond's article on film is not so much that it sets out the LMS position, but that it betrays an important shift of emphasis in relation to audience. It certainly seems that the BEKE, with its foundation in missionary concerns, and its basis in a missionary investigation undertaken in areas where the LMS was deeply embedded, functioned to catalyse LMS attitudes toward the cinema. However, rather than directing this important new development toward enhancing LMS work in the mission field – as one might expect, given that this was the entire thrust of the IMC findings, and the premise of the BEKE – the LMS instead sought to address a home audience, which it conceived of in terms of recent developments in British educational and schools cinema. This has some very important repercussions for LMS film-making.

The actual production capacities of the LMS at this time constituted two cameras, which were rotated from mission to mission around the world. These cameras, Diamond writes, were 'constantly at work sending new material home to London', where it was then 'made ready for film showings all around the country'.[31] It was, at this stage, a cottage industry at best, occupying an uneasy place between amateur and professional production. The films were toured around the country using equipment of 'the very latest design', complete with 'sound-amplification equipment' to allow for music and spoken commentaries (nevertheless, most LMS films of this period are intertitled). Although most audiences would have been drawn from church-goers, there is some indication that the films were shown elsewhere, and the June 1937 *Chronicle*, for example, carries a report on a screening, hosted by Rev. H. D. Cotton, of LMS films of Papua at the Royal Geographical Society.[32]

From autumn 1938, the LMS kept a film library and ran a hire service 'from which any Church or Sunday School or other group of people having their own Projector (16 mm. silent) may hire films from the LMS to show in their own hall'.[33] They were not alone in this. Rank's Religious Films Ltd had started hiring Christian productions out at around the same time, and other missionary societies would soon follow. A 1946 guide to religious film, published by the Church of England Films Commission, lists numerous religious and secular suppliers of such material, including the National Film Library. Three missionary societies are listed as film distributors – the LMS, the Church Missionary Society and the Universities Mission to Central Africa.[34] The same guide includes reviews of various missionary film productions by these societies, by the Religious Film Society and by the British and Foreign Bible Society (LMS films mentioned in the booklet include the 1930s productions *Tiger Kloof*, 30s–40s, *Scenes in Mailu*, 1930s, *Kasoma*, 1938 and *All Aboard The Tamate*, 1930s). The reviews are almost all critical, with the LMS productions repeatedly described as suffering from poor photography; the reviewer notes that this is a regular problem with missionary films.

Film screenings organised by the LMS seem to have been integrated into religious education sessions. R. O. Latham, maker of *The Desert Shall Rejoice*, himself authored a booklet on missionary teaching entitled *Practical Programmes*, which contains guidance on film screenings – his suggestions indicate films were often presented as part of a fully planned session, with questions and answers about the film's themes. Such sessions were to be bookended by prayers.[35] The LMS also ran regular, church-wide educational programmes that focused intensively on particular areas of LMS activity – 1951, for instance, saw the worldwide launch of the 'Introducing Papua' programme, which involved the distribution of prepared books, plays, 'pageants', phonograph records and films, including the film *Papua Patchwork* (1951).[36] The worldwide rollout of such programmes does indicate some field audience, but in this context such an audience is clearly conceived of as part of the missionary fold, not part of the raw field of evangelisation.

As is clear from this brief survey of evidence, the LMS film audience was primarily a British one. Film footage was sent home from missions to be cut in London, LMS films entered British lending libraries, where they were orientated toward the religious films' audience. The conceptual emphasis is on education. But what was this audience being educated in? Here we must look at the content of the films themselves, and from them a very simple answer is evident: the central subject of LMS missionary films is almost without exception the work of the missions. They do not seek as a rule to evangelise their audience, but instead show the progress of evangelisation elsewhere.

Very often they are little more than travelogues. Early LMS films of Western Samoa or Papua, for instance *Here and There in Samoa*, *Samoa Sidelights*, or *Port Moresby*, all produced during the 1930s, are often presented in this style, featuring scenes of journeys, panoramic landscapes and shots taken from cars or boats. They hardly examine missionary work. Other titles simply hope to show the good work the missions are doing, whether in healthcare, education or Christian duty: the numerous LMS films of the Neyyoor mission hospital in South India, the many films of the LMS *John Williams* ships that plied the Pacific islands. Films such as *Coral Islands Minister* (1974), *Build a Hospital (Mbereshi)* (1950s) and *Tiger Kloof* all fit into this category. Films such as these principally raise awareness about the society's activity in the mission field, and rarely pretend to any further value.

This perhaps stems in part from another central aim – sometimes implicit but often explicit – common to many missionary films, not merely those of the LMS: revenue generation. For, despite the emphasis on what is called 'education', the majority of films made by missionary societies do not, and perhaps do not really intend to, educate their audience in detail about anything other than the work of the mission itself. LMS films begin with accounts of Chalmers or a picture of Livingstone; they are educating their audience principally about the good works of missionaries, not about the worlds in which these missionaries have worked. Those worlds and their inhabitants often remain dark, backsliding and stricken with illness.

The real subject is always the hardworking missionary, a sort of metaphysical district officer. It is the missionary who brings spiritual, moral and bodily improvement to the needy and for that greater work to take place there must be resources. This is certainly the final message of even untypical films such as *The Desert Shall Rejoice*. Many missionary productions from all missionary groups end with an appeal for funds, and this practical requirement for donations from the congregation was acknowledged as part and parcel of the film-making programme. Missions largely relied, then as now, on donations for their survival, and films provided a good occasion: a notification of the new LMS film *Pacific Schooner* (1938) appeared in the *Chronicle* with the advice that the film 'will be of great use at meetings for the distribution of New Year Offering Cards'.[37]

However, despite this determined turn away from the mission field and toward the metropolitan congregation, the main attitude of the IMC report (and thus something resembling the underlying rationale for the BEKE) is reflected in several LMS films from the late 1930s onwards. The manner in which the arguments and conclusions of the IMC commission are manifested in these films is decisive to an understanding of how the LMS imagined their audience. For these ideas, so important to the genesis of LMS film, do not appear as motivating principles, orchestrating the purposes and defining the content of the films that they animate: instead they return in weakened form as explanatory cinematic narrative or documentary logic. Instead of furthering mission work, they are employed as a way of explaining to viewers the necessity and objects of mission work.

It is a strange result: the IMC commission reported that the task of missionaries would be aided by the cinema, a recommendation that eventually fed into the foundational premise of the BEKE. The LMS vocally concurred, and began to produce films in earnest – but turned the screen to face a home audience, presenting not the 'educational' films that would apparently assist the Copper Belt worker or the missionary in the field, but distorted renderings of the IMC conclusions about the Copper Belt, for people watching in British schools and church halls. In this baffling house of mirrors, what were once presented as the reasons for producing films are themselves reproduced in limited and distorted replica form for the edification of pious British audiences, rather than actually being concretely acted upon.

In films such as *Kasoma* or especially *Christianity and Copper* (1956), the observations of the IMC commission are reduced either to a narrative device, or to a method of theatrically staging footage from the mission field. In *Kasoma*, the practical desires of the Copper Belt missions, and the IMC-inspired analysis of their role, are presented in dramatised form. Returnees to a rural village bring news of the modern world after their time at the minefields of the Copper Belt, prompting the eponymous protagonist to leave the security of tribal life for the dangers and possibilities of the mines, and it is here that he encounters missionaries who guide him through danger and from whom he learns to read and write.

In *Christianity and Copper*, the role of the missions in the lives of Copper Belt inhabitants is explained, and the film gives an account of life in the mining districts. The people themselves are presented as confused and endangered, menaced by 'Westernisation', and without a landmark to guide them through 'this turmoil of a life'. Even the local market is a danger to them: in their villages, the women would work the land, but here, able to purchase goods they would normally grow, they are prey to the menace of empty hours. 'They are untrained in the ways of using leisure time', the narrator informs us; thankfully, missionaries are on hand to answer 'this great need' with handicrafts. In this case it is a dressmaking class, and we are witness to a toddler being dressed up in a newly cut smock. This sequence, and the language employed, are directly illustrative of conclusions that can be found in *Modern Industry*: 'The sudden transition from the busy life of the village to the unaccustomed leisure of the mine location calls for the training of the women in home industries and handicrafts.'[38]

The men are more of a problem. Many modern comestibles are 'unknown' to them, and they are 'quite unfamiliar with the use of tinned foodstuffs', so even the 'good nourishing diet' provided by the company – some bowls of what appears to be roughly cut offal and fat, swarming with flies in the open air – is confusing. They are prone to 'undesirable pastimes', principally drink: 'kaffir beer – an extremely potent and harmful beverage' is the tipple of choice, swilled down from jerry cans at 'illicit parties' (the 'party' shown does not appear especially illicit, as it is taking place in broad daylight, in a gazebo, in the centre of the mining compound). Their degeneration signified by their choice of Western clothes, daytime drinkers lounging on a patch of grass even force their baby to drink beer from a bottle. (This scene appears to be staged or semi-staged, and a fair amount of mugging for the camera is evident among the revellers.)

'All of this symbolises the new problem of Westernism which has been added to the existing problem of primitive paganism', we are told. The church is the answer to these problems, and the scene cuts to a shot of a ringing bell, and then of the bell-ringer. 'A new sense of purpose' can be instilled by the Christian message, and by the missionary work that will forge a 'new community based on higher values, to make of them new people'.

In this film in particular, the transformation of the IMC commission's conclusions from a call to action to a vulgar *post facto* justification of missionary activity is total. The date, too, is of interest when assessing what exact purpose is being served by this depiction of the mission's 'human material'. By 1956, the confused herd of mineworkers offered up to the spectator by the film, so helpless in the face of modernity as to be incapable even of coping with the challenge of tinned food, were in actual fact fully unionised and involved in running industrial disputes with the mine bosses. Such disputes, official or otherwise, had been ongoing since the mid-1930s, when riots in 1935 had thrown the Copper Belt into turmoil. White mineworkers had unionised in 1936; after intervention by the Colonial Office in 1946, African workers had been granted the right to unionise, and the African Mineworkers Union was formed on the Copper Belt in 1949.[39] The LMS was actually prepared to articulate progressive and informed views on the labour situation in the mines: a full fifteen years before *Christianity and Copper* was produced, an article had been published in the *Chronicle* discussing the Copper Belt riots of 1940.[40] The author examines in critical detail government reports and judgments, and argues that African mineworkers must be allowed to have organised industrial representation. The same article also presents a coherent moral and political rejection of the colour bar, which warns against its adoption in Northern Rhodesia. By comparison, *Christianity and Copper*'s commentary can only profess to finding the colour bar in Northern Rhodesia a 'baffling' problem.

The theoretical armature that structures this film is visible elsewhere too, for the specificities of the Copper Belt are actually unnecessary. The basic formula, once discovered, proved to be of broad application – reduced to the crude and robust principle that missionary work assists confused primitives with the transition to civilisation, the once specific recommendation that the cinema be employed to educate the illiterate in areas experiencing rapid industrial modernisation becomes an easily deployed mechanism for explicating and justifying the overall missionary project to potential donors and volunteers. In its most crystalline and evangelical variant, the theme appears as the straightforward assertion that the life of people in places such as Papua is simply 'disintegrating', and that the work of the missions is necessary to steer the locals out of pagan degradation into a salvation that is presented as being virtually coterminous with an encroaching but vague modernity. In the case of a film like *Papua Patchwork*, it is clear that even the narrative pretext that describes a missionary-aided movement from savagery to civilisation is itself a diaphanous veil, loosely thrown over a much more traditional missionary object of desire: the sheer Christian joy of converting people who are initially presented to the audience as stone-age cannibals.[41]

Only in exceptional cases, such as *The Desert Shall Rejoice*, is there any hint of a more complex or nuanced picture; for the most part there is a notable absence of any attempt toward historical detail beyond some basics about the history of the local mission itself. Also generally lacking is any directly evangelical religious message. Neither of these facts is surprising: it simply is not the aim of LMS films either to present complex accounts, or to evangelise their principal audiences, who were already

Christian. What religious significance they may have held for a British audience generally appears to consist in the example they provide of faith in action and extension, rather than any direct evangelical message, with a reciprocal show of faith demanded from the audience in the form of the financial contribution. They were morally strengthening, educative (about missionary work at least), furnished their audience with information and with examples of faith at work, and they did not pretend to more. In fact, despite the distant locations and exotic concerns, the films are decidedly self-absorbed (and this is perhaps only a metonymic fragment of the fundamental missionary narcissism that seeks to remake the distant and alien in the image of the pious European Christian).

What LMS films *do* show, however, and what makes them important and problematic documents of empire, is evidence about how the LMS wished to represent itself to audiences that were essentially private, insofar as they would frequently have consisted of people drawn from a particular social group already connected at some level with either missionary societies or the church. In a very literal sense, and quite unlike missionaries in the field, the films preach to the converted, and can be understood to reflect the prejudices and presuppositions of their audience, and to represent these prejudices and presuppositions in the manner most likely to produce the desired audience responses of support, volunteers and donations. That the films sometimes present accounts more basic and reactionary than published LMS analyses, as in the case of *Christianity and Copper*, should be understood as stemming at least in part from this basic utilitarian function. Missionary-society pictures were rather blunt propaganda tools – aids to 'education' that doubled as revenue-generating devices. The films speak of missionary work, to friends and supporters of missionary work, and they do not seek to muddy the clear waters of Christian charity with difficult ideas or troublesome facts.

Missionary societies such as the LMS were entrenched in imperial territory, and often profoundly implicated in the imperial project. Their cinematic missives to the faithful at home came from deep within the empire and went, without secular official oversight, directly to audiences being asked to applaud, assist with and pay for what they saw. While the films may not give an accurate representation of their ostensible subjects – it may well be that they do not even give an accurate picture of missionary work – they do hold up a faithful mirror to the expectations and prejudices of this audience, and to that extent they are documents that shed light on a different dark and poorly understood place, the imaginary empire of the metropole. Dreamt of in church halls and Sunday schools, this exotic fantasy world of sick, semi-clad heathens and fearful Africans may well be dismissed as little more than an ugly caricature, but as such it is only the crudest measure of a much more general alienation from colonial realities. More than missionary practice or priorities in the field, it is perhaps this profound metropolitan ignorance that glimmers as the true lodestar by whose wan light the course of missionary film-making was set.

FILMOGRAPHY

Africa Today (Missionary Film Committee, 1927); *All Aboard The Tamate* (LMS, probably 1930s); *Build a Hospital (Mbereshi)* (LMS, probably 1950s); *Christianity and*

Copper (LMS, 1956); *Coral Islands Minister* (LMS, 1974); *The Desert Shall Rejoice* (LMS, 1960s); *Here and There in Samoa* (LMS, probably 1930s); *Kasoma* (LMS, 1938); *Livingstone* (Hero Films, 1925); *Mill Hill Sheds Light on the Dark Places of the Earth: Uganda* (Mill Hill Missionary Society, c. 1922?); *Pacific Schooner* (LMS, 1938); *Papua Patchwork* (LMS, 1951); *Port Moresby* (LMS, probably 1930s); *Samoa Sidelights* (LMS, probably 1930s), *Scenes in Mailu* (LMS, probably 1930s); *Tiger Kloof* (LMS, probably 1930s or early 1940s).

NOTES

1. Congregational Council for World Mission (CCWM), *Audio Visual Aids Catalogue 1968*, p. 4. The CCWM was the successor organisation to the LMS.
2. Dean Rapp, 'The British Salvation Army, the Early Film Industry and Urban Working-class Adolescents, 1897–1918', *Twentieth Century British History* vol. 7 no. 2 (1996) pp. 157–88; p. 171.
3. Francis Gooding, '*Mill Hill Sheds Light on the Dark Places of the Earth: Uganda*', Colonial Film: Moving Images of the British Empire, <www.colonialfilm.org.uk/node/3802>.
4. Tom Rice, '*Livingstone*', Colonial Film: Moving Images of the British Empire, <www.colonialfilm.org.uk/node/1844>.
5. J. Merle Davis, *Modern Industry and the African: An Enquiry into the Effect of the Copper Mines of Central Africa upon Native Society and the Work of Christian Missions* (London: Macmillan and Co., 1933), p. vii.
6. Robert I. Rotberg, 'Introduction to the Second Edition', in J. Merle Davis, *Modern Industry and the African*, 2nd edn (London: Frank Cass and Co. Ltd, 1967 [1933]) pp. vii–xxiv; p. xi.
7. Elena L. Berger, *Labour, Race and Colonial Rule: The Copperbelt from 1924 to Independence* (Oxford: Clarendon, 1974), p. 20; L. J. Butler, *Copper Empire: Mining and the Colonial State in Northern Rhodesia, c. 1930–64* (Basingstoke: Palgrave Macmillan, 2007), p. 19.
8. J. Merle Davis, *Modern Industry and the African*, 1st edn, p. v; Shaw's participation is one of the several links joining the IMC commission, and subsequently the BEKE, to the LMS.
9. Merle Davis, *Modern Industry and the African*, 1933.
10. Ibid., p. 9.
11. Ibid.
12. Ibid.
13. Frederick Cooper, *Decolonization and African Society: The Labor Question in French and British Africa* (Cambridge: Cambridge University Press, 1996), pp. 53–4.
14. Berger, *Labour, Race and Colonial Rule*, pp. 27–8.
15. Merle Davis, *Modern Industry and the African*, p. 379. Protestant missions did eventually take the advice to work together, forming a 'United Mission to the Copper Belt' group in 1935, after the mines had experienced an episode of serious industrial unrest.
16. Ibid., p. 322.
17. Ibid., p. 323.
18. All quotations ibid., p. 324.
19. Ibid.
20. Ibid., p. 325.
21. Ibid., p. 390.
22. Ibid., pp. 324–6.

23. Glenn Reynolds, 'The Bantu Educational Kinema Experiment and the Struggle for
    Hegemony in British East and Central Africa, 1935–1937', *Historical Journal of Film, Radio
    and Television* vol. 29 no. 1 (2009), pp. 57–78; Tom Rice, 'Bekefilm', Colonial Film: Moving
    Images of the British Empire, 2010 <www.colonialfilm.org.uk/production-company/beke-
    film>; Rosaleen Smyth, 'The Development of British Colonial Film Policy, 1927–1939, with
    Special Reference to East and Central Africa', *Journal of African History* vol. 20 no. 3 (1979),
    pp. 437–50. See also the essays by Aaron Windel and Aboubakar Sanogo in this volume.
24. L. A. Notcutt, and G. C. Latham, *The African and the Cinema: An Account of the Bantu
    Educational Kinema Experiment during the Period March 1935 to May 1937* (London:
    Edinburgh House Press, 1937), p. 25.
25. Smyth, 'The Development of British Colonial Film Policy, 1927–1939', p. 443; Notcutt and
    Latham, *The African and the Cinema*, pp. 209–10.
26. Ibid., pp. 9, 10.
27. 'African Films for Africa', *Chronicle: A Magazine of World Enterprise*, June 1935 (London:
    London Missionary Society), p. 135; *Chronicle: A Magazine of World Enterprise*, February
    1936 (London: London Missionary Society), p. 38.
28. Howard Diamond, 'Films in Britain', *Chronicle: A Magazine of World Enterprise*, November
    1936 (London: London Missionary Society), p. 254.
29. The Missionary Film Committee had been formed by several Protestant missionary societies
    in the late 1920s. Its secretary, T. H. Baxter, had made a feature-length missionary film
    entitled *Africa Today* in 1927, and he would also sit on the advisory council of the BEKE;
    Roberts notes that Baxter had also made an earlier film in India. See Andrew D. Roberts,
    'African on Film to 1940', *History in Africa* vol. 14 (1987), pp. 189–227; 201.
30. See Rachael Low, *The History of British Film 1929–39: Documentary and Educational Films
    of the 1930s* (London: Routledge, 1997 [1979]), pp. 7–47; Jeffrey Richards, *The Age of the
    Dream Palace: Cinema and Society in Britain, 1930–1939* (London: Routledge and Kegan Paul,
    1984), pp. 48–9.
31. Diamond, 'Films in Britain'.
32. *Chronicle: A Magazine of World Enterprise*, July 1937 (London: London Missionary Society),
    p. 148.
33. *Chronicle: A Magazine of World Enterprise*, September 1938 (London: London Missionary
    Society), p. 213.
34. *The Church's Guide to Films for Religious Use* (London: Church of England Films Commission,
    1946), p. 54.
35. R. O. Latham, *Practical Programmes: Ideas and Suggestions for Missionary Occasions* (London:
    London Missionary Society, 1959), p. 35.
36. *Survey 1952: A Review of the Work of the London Missionary Society for the Year 1951/52*
    (London: Livingstone Press, 1952), p. 26.
37. *Chronicle: A Magazine of World Enterprise*, December 1938 (London: London Missionary
    Society), p. 268.
38. Merle Davis, *Modern Industry and the African*, p. 309.
39. Berger, *Labour, Race and Colonial Rule*, pp. 90–3 and *passim*.
40. T. Cocker-Brown, 'The Copper Belt Riots', *Chronicle: A Magazine of World Enterprise*, June
    1941 (London: London Missionary Society), p. 65.
41. See Francis Gooding, '*Papua Patchwork*', Colonial Film: Moving Images of the British Empire,
    <www.colonialfilm.org.uk/node/4913>.

14

Paul Robeson and the Cinema of Empire

Charles Musser

Paul Robeson worked in film for more than three decades – beginning in 1924 with Oscar Micheaux's *Body and Soul* and concluding in 1958 with the concert film *Brücke über den Ozean* [Bridge over the Ocean]; however, his period of most intensive involvement in motion pictures was limited to 1933–7, when he was based in England and appeared in eight feature-length films (two shot in the United States). Five focused on Britain's empire in Africa: *Sanders of the River* (1935), *Song of Freedom* (1936), *My Song Goes Forth* (1937), *King Solomon's Mines* (1937) and *Jericho* (1937). These were high-profile projects in which he played prominent roles. Given this intensive involvement, it is not hard to argue that Paul Robeson's career as a performer must crucially engage his complex involvement with Britain's colonialist cinema during this period, just as any broad exploration of British colonialist cinema in the 1930s must consider his role.

Robeson's initial interest in Africa was indebted to the Harlem Renaissance and involved a reconnection with his ancestral roots and a new sense of Negro identity. Africa – not America – was 'the true home of the negro', he remarked.[1] Increasingly his concerns were motivated and informed by his experiences as a London-based American expatriate from the late 1920s until his return to the US in 1939. In 1930, Robeson was already expressing a desire to visit Africa and to study its cultures, to gather together 'songs sung there that have been with the race for centuries' and 'bring them back and sing them ... here'.[2] This interview, which appeared in the Kingston *Daily Gleaner* (Jamaica), suggests how Robeson was also thinking more broadly in terms of the African diaspora or black Atlantic. Africa was integral to Robeson's construction of identity, and it is in this light that his decision to play African leaders on stage and screen can be understood. While interested in African art – particularly music and sculpture – he was also concerned with issues of black leadership, masculinity and political independence, all of which confront the realities of British colonialism directly or indirectly.

Although Paul Robeson was routinely identified as the pre-eminent black dramatic actor of the 1930s, most biographers have expressed serious reservations about his films, seeing his pictures as a noteworthy *but* generally embarrassing aspect of his prodigious career as an actor, singer, political activist and public figure. Robeson's films were often criticised for their ideological shortcomings, particularly in regard to their representations of race because his demeaning portrayals of black characters tended to reinforce negative stereotypes. From an artistic perspective, critics have often seen their production values as second rate, the scripts and stories as hokey. Robeson himself often expressed such critical attitudes. In 1938, he denounced *Sanders of the River* as 'a total loss' while subsequent films were 'the same story': 'an idea that attracted me, a result in which I wasn't interested'.[3] The actor's auto-critiques encouraged subsequent scholars to dismiss his films without pondering either their place or function in Robeson's overall artistic production or their complex intervention in the larger cultural and political realm. The irony has been that those who generally claim great admiration for Robeson, denigrate one of the most important phases in his career.

Robeson's own remarks must be understood strategically. First, Robeson was taking a forward-looking approach to his work, which often meant distancing himself from past pictures because he was working on new projects that held greater promise. Second, his criticisms were a means to negotiate an array of expectations from often conflicting constituencies: British and American, white and black as well as industry personnel, radical commentators and diverse audiences. In many respects, Paul Robeson, Jr offers a useful assessment of his father's work, evaluating Paul Sr's choices as those of an artist who well understood the practical aspects of building a career. He quotes an interview in which his father defended his appearance in *Sanders of the River*, and then added: 'To say that I had no right to appear in *Sanders of the River* is to say I shouldn't have appeared in *Emperor Jones* – that I shouldn't have accepted the role in *Show Boat*.'[4] In fact, many commentators come close to saying precisely that.[5] We should resist the temptation to see Robeson as a simple, even foolish victim of a white racist, capitalist system: he had agency and knew how to use it. Although Robeson operated within a system that was deeply antagonistic, it also possessed internal contradictions and fissures.

By embracing a number of approaches, we can usefully resituate and re-evaluate Robeson's achievements. For starters, these films should not be viewed and finally judged as isolated self-sufficient works of art in the Kantian mode. Nor do these films have self-evident, fixed meanings. They need to be understood not only historically but intertextually, not only generically but in relation to source materials from which they were adapted or appropriated elements. They functioned within different cultural formations in multifaceted ways. And what we as historians and commentators have to say about these films – again how we approach them – will have much to say about their cultural value and utility for today.

These films also need to be evaluated as much as process as product. To fully appreciate Robeson's involvement in these British films of Africa, it is not enough to focus on Robeson's construction of an affirmative black identity that stood in opposition to the racism and racial stereotypes with which he and others had to contend. Nor is it enough to see ways in which they seek (successfully or unsuccessfully) to engage British imperial conceptions of colonial rule in Africa. One also has to understand the terms of his interactions within a broader cosmopolitan culture, particularly his embrace of 'conviviality' as Paul Gilroy has employed the term. As Gilroy remarked,

> There is another quite different idea of cosmopolitanism to be explored here. Its value to the politics of multiculturalism lies in its refusal of state-centeredness and in its attractive

vernacular style … . This cosmopolitan attachment finds civic and ethical value in the process of exposure to otherness. It glories in the ordinary virtues and ironies – listening, looking, discretion, friendship – that can be cultivated when mundane encounters with difference become rewarding. The self-knowledge that can be acquired through the proximity to strangers is certainly precious but is no longer the primary issue. We might consider how to cultivate the capacity to act morally and justly not just in the face of otherness – imploring or hostile – but in response to the xenophobia and violence that threaten to engulf, purify or erase it.[6]

The underground conviviality that Gilroy embraces in present-day Great Britain was already being practised by Robeson in the 1930s. Indeed, Robeson often seems naive or wishy-washy when it comes to the politics of representation if his politics of conviviality are not taken into account. Inevitably there is a creative tension – often a contradiction – between these two dynamics. His cosmopolitan conviviality, often aligned with an integrationist impulse, can seem to compromise Robeson's efforts as a race man to revitalise black culture, often aligned with black cultural nationalism.[7] Conviviality was also part of Robeson's politics of representation – what initially attracted him to any creative undertaking – and a central component of his Utopian impulse.

SANDERS OF THE RIVER

Robeson's mid-1930s film work also needs to be grounded in the British film industry, which was going through a speculative bubble that made many of his films possible even as it shaped the parameters of what Robeson was able to achieve. The runaway success of Alexander Korda's *The Private Life of Henry VIII* (1933), starring Charles Laughton, who won an Oscar for his performance, launched a period of optimism and ready financing for British film productions.[8] Robeson rode the resulting wave of opportunities, which came crashing down by late 1936. Before it was over, he had played an African tribal chief or king in four films – and starred in each of them. By working with Korda on the first of these, *Sanders of the River*, Robeson associated himself with the British film industry's newly pre-eminent producer. The picture, which opened on Tuesday, 2 April 1935, at London's Leicester Square Theatre, was enthusiastically received by the British press and public. *The Times* noted approvingly that

> The tale of the struggle of an English District Commissioner (Mr. Leslie Banks) in alliance with a loyal tribe led by Mr. Robeson, to preserve peace and order among the fierce and superstitious people of the Congo is a vigorous narrative that may enthrall men and children alike.[9]

John Gammie of *Film Weekly* likewise found this 'story of British rule in Africa' to be 'a film of exceptional Interest'.[10] Historian Jeffrey Richards has focused on its ground-breaking position as the first in a series of British-made films that lionised the British Empire. Such films demonstrate, he argues, that British working-class culture of the

1930s, embraced the British Empire much more than has been generally recognised.[11] Indeed, with the rise of Hitler and an unstable world, this film reaffirmed the cherished belief in a *pax Britannica*, that 'a strong British Empire is an invaluable contribution to world peace'.[12]

Most scholarship that has looked at the film through the figure of Paul Robeson has taken a more critical, anti-colonial, 'pro-native' perspective and characterised *Sanders* as the most problematic picture of his entire oeuvre. Kneeling before Sanders (Leslie Banks) near the beginning of the picture, Bosambo (Paul Robeson) is little more than an obsequious servant of the British Crown. Soon after the film's release, rumours swirled, some saying that Robeson was fooled by Korda, others that he was naively unaware of what he was doing, and still others that his wife Eslanda had masterminded a Faustian bargain with the British imperialists.[13] In an interview he gave a few months after *Sanders of the River* was released, an African American newspaper reported:

> The much-criticised film, 'Sanders of the River,' Mr Robeson stated, was not originally planned as an empire-building epic. The first scenes were shot in Africa fully a year before he assumed his role, he said and the film was intended as just another Edgar Wallace thriller. The imperialist angle was placed in the plot during the last five days of shooting, the actor reported, when Korda (London Film Productions) decided to follow the lead of Hollywood and at the same time tie the venture up with the king's jubilee.[14]

This was an explanation picked up by Marie Seton in her biography, which she augmented with the fact that Robeson declined to sing after the film's opening-night screening as a form of protest. Whether the script was changed at the last minute (the change in the film's title from *Bosambo* to *Sanders of the River* makes this plausible) or Robeson's failure to sing was out of pique or for other reasons has been impossible to determine definitively.

For all the film's shortfalls, it is worth considering *Sanders of the River* as a historical intervention. Here was a large-budget spectacle by a prestigious producer, which starred a black actor with a storyline that paired him romantically with a magnetic black woman. And it was a huge *success*, launching Robeson's career as a movie star in Great Britain. This created a new kind of relationship between Robeson and the film industry as well as between Robeson and moviegoers of different classes and ethnicities. Robeson made this clear:

> The picture was such a great success, financially, he revealed, that Korda has decided to film the life of King Christophe with Mr. Robeson in the title role. After this picture is completed, he said, he feels sure that he can persuade Korda to present the life of Menelik II on the screen.
>
> 'That would really be worthwhile,' the actor stated. 'And of course it would have to be done in England or Europe. Could you imagine a black king being treated seriously in Hollywood?'[15]

King Christophe – Henri Christophe –was a key leader of the Haitian revolution. Menelik II was the Emperor of Ethiopia who defeated the Italian army in 1896 at the battle of Adwa. In 1935, Italy was once again invading that member state of the League of Nations. Neither project came to fruition, not surprising given their radical political potential and the fact that Korda was well known for embracing numerous picture ideas, most of which never reached screen. Here are two obviously anti-imperialist, anti-colonial projects, which Robeson was pursuing in the immediate wake of his newly achieved star status. It is worth pondering how Robeson could have possibly imagined Bosambo sharing company with these two historical figures.

Our understanding of *Sanders of the River* as well as Robeson's involvement in the film can be enriched by an examination of the numerous Sanders and Bosambo short stories written by Edgar Wallace, which merit more discerning attention than they have yet received. Not unlike Alexander Korda, language-in-education scholar Brian Street has offered a reductive view. Analysing the stories for their racist assumptions, he suggests that 'Wallace's hero, Sanders ... believes that the native has no memory.'[16] Wallace's stories, however, are frequently contradictory and perhaps succeed best because they are comically absurd. They are also complexly balanced. Although Africans may generally be naive, superstitious, uncivilised and ridiculous; an array of British and American missionaries, businessmen and government employees are little different. For instance, there is Sir George Carsley, a famous British professor whom the British government sent to study tropical diseases. In fact, he fakes his death and becomes a witch doctor responsible for large-scale poisonings in Sanders's district – using cyanide of potassium. Sandi (Sanders) has to track him down as he would a marauding chief. Or there is the reporter George Tackle – the son of a newspaper publisher – who comes to Sandi's district determined to verify tales of government torture and abuse of the natives. As it turned out there were four districts named 'Lukati' in West Africa and he went to the wrong one. This is only one way in which Tackle, who almost gets himself killed, proves comically clueless.

And then there is Bosambo. In Wallace's stories, Bosambo is Sanders's alter ego, his African *doppelgänger*. They are co-dependent. Bosambo is a trickster figure – not the obedient Uncle Tom of the Korda film.[17] In the introductory story 'Bosambo of Monrovia', Bosambo promises obedience to Sandi, claiming he always wanted to be a chief under the British. And yet at that very moment he is stealing the commissioner's field glasses. Smart and wily, he uses Sanders to his own advantage as much as vice versa. In 'The Wood of Devils', he tells Sanders, 'Master ... all that you order me to do, that I did.'[18] But he followed these orders very much in his own way. Afterwards, when reporting to Sanders, he forgets to mention the vast wealth of ivory that he found:

What else did you find?' asked Sanders.
'Nothing, master,' said Bosambo, looking him straight in the eye.
'That is probably a lie!' said Sanders.
Bosambo thought of the ivory buried beneath the floor of his hut and did not contradict him. (p. 205)

But then Sanders is often a trickster figure himself.

In the process of adaptation (or rather appropriation since the story 'Kongo Raid' on which the film was often said to be based was merely an early working title for the film),[19] Korda repeatedly indulged in what Budd Schulberg's Sammy Glick called 'the old switcheroo'. While Bosambo rescues Sanders from certain death in the first volume of Wallace's stories, *Sanders of the River* (1911), it is Sanders who rescues Bosambo in the movie. Here is Wallace's description of Sanders:

> Heroes should be tall and handsome, with flashing eyes; Sanders was not so tall, was yellow of face, moreover had grey hair. Heroes should also be of gentle address, full of soft phrases, for such tender women who come over their horizon; Sanders was a dispassionate man who swore on the slightest provocation, and had no use for women any way. (p. 118)

The Kordas' Sanders looks and acts like a conventional hero – indeed has an off-screen love affair. *Film Weekly*'s John Gammie celebrated him as the heroic embodiment of the British Empire:

> Without bombast or patriotic exaggeration, [the film] explains and illustrates the tremendous task of a British Commissioner on whose courage, wisdom and integrity the peace and safety of thousands of square miles of uncivilized territory depend. He must command the respect of the native chiefs. He must settle disputes and quell uprisings without costing his Government too much money.
>
> It is a testimonial to the ability and personality of Leslie Banks, as well as an incalculable asset to the picture, that he portrays this superman with admirable authority and complete conviction.[20]

While Sanders speaks the King's English in the movie, he is uncomfortable speaking English in Wallace's stories – preferring local languages instead. In fact, Wallace suggests, Sanders survives and prospers because he thinks like a native. This thinking is intuitive and not based on superior education.

Bosambo is paired with Sanders in Wallace's stories – one of Wallace's later books was titled *Bosambo of the River* – but, as Jeffrey Richards points out, in Korda's film he is paired with and opposite the bizarre and brutal 'bad African chief' King Mofolaba (Tony Wane). Such discrepancies were noted by contemporaneous reviewers. 'Wallace fans tell me', James Agate of the *Tatler* wrote, 'that the film has ruined the book in turning the character of Bosambo into pure hero, instead of leaving him as an impudent, semi-comic ex-convict.'[21] A consideration of Wallace's stories suggests another reason for Robeson's interest in the project and how he was subsequently 'fooled'. The Bosambo that he imagined came from reading Wallace's stories; moreover, in the fragmentary way in which films are created – isolated scenes shot out of order with some scenes cut or reshaped in the editing, it is not always easy to determine the end results in advance. He had not expected this trickster figure to be reimagined as a servile subject. Both Sanders and Bosambo had been turned into cardboard 'positive images' of British Empire.

Korda's *Sanders of the River* should also be compared to Wallace's short stories in terms of their respective diegetic worlds – of time and place. Wallace's stories are set in a semi-mythic, comic world that is ostensibly colonial West Africa of the late 1890s and early 1900s. In their endless, non-progressive temporal repetitions and contradictions, the stories construct a somewhat absurdist time that is ludic, 'timeless', and nonlinear. Select chiefs are imprisoned or executed, only to be casually recycled and subsequently 'chopped'.

Although the Korda film contains its own temporal ambiguities, its spatio-temporal constructions are ultimately much more linear and concrete. In the process of making Sanders a more respectable civil servant, the Kordas transposed Wallace's stories to the 1930s as Sandi flies to Bosambo's rescue in an airplane. In a revealing article on Alexander Korda in *Film Weekly*, Leonard Wallace reported, 'Sanders of the River was originally conceived as "Wings Over the Jungle," with Alfred Hitchcock mentioned as director.'[22] Osa and Martin Johnson had also been making a much publicised film with the working title 'Wings over Africa' in 1933–4 (released as *Baboona* in early 1935): aerial shots of Africa and the novelty of safari by plane were all the rage.[23] To take advantage of their spectacular footage, the Kordas anachronistically resituated Wallace's mythico-comic world of 1895/1910 in 1934/5. This parachrony contributes significantly to the picture's reactionary character in that the film refuses to acknowledge that much had changed in Nigeria during the intervening thirty years. Institutions of higher education had been started.[24] The Nigerian Legislative Council was instituted in 1923 and the Nigerian National Democratic Party was formed to participate in the resulting elections. In 1934, a more radical, anti-colonial political organisation was formed – the Lagos Youth Movement, which became the Nigerian Youth Movement in 1936.[25] Labour unions existed; and the Depression had negatively impacted on African life, making taxes more onerous.[26] *Sanders of the River* was made as if such developments did not, could not, exist. British spectators were allowed to imagine an unchanging empire where natives are always primitive savages and the British heroic civil servants.[27] In this regard, Gilroy's characterisation of England's postcolonial melancholia – the nation's refusal to confront its loss of empire – is already inscribed in this film. Nigeria embodies the unchanging primitive – forever in need of colonial oversight.

The casting of Robeson and Nina Mae McKinney in *Sanders of the Rivers* also bears closer scrutiny, building on the insights of my colleague Terri Francis in her study of Josephine Baker.[28] Baker appeared in *Princess Tam Tam* in the same year that Robeson and McKinney appeared in *Sanders of the River*. Baker plays Alwina, a shepherdess and free spirit in North Africa (Tunisia). These African American actors of the New Negro Renaissance – international stars who had based themselves in England and France respectively – were convenient mediating figures. They were African Americans who played Africans even though they had never actually been to Africa. On the one hand, this enabled these actors to avoid American roles, which almost inevitably involved all-too-familiar degrading racial stereotypes. Yet as Americans rather than native Africans and colonial subjects, these Negro stars enabled the British and French to finesse their politics of race and empire.

As American stars, Robeson and McKinney also helped to provide London Films with an opening to the American market. Korda's picture enjoyed a broad release in first-run American theatres: opening at New York City's Rivoli Theater on 26 June, at Los Angeles' Four Star Theater on 23 August, and at Chicago's State-Lake Theater on 25 October 1935.[29] Robeson was featured over Leslie Banks.[30] McKinney, whose only previous starring film role was in King Vidor's *Hallelujah* (1929), was then enjoying top billing in London as a blues singer: she co-starred and was listed third. They supplied the on-screen romance that ensured Robeson's centrality to the film. These American casting choices arguably undermined the realism of *Sanders* (and subsequent films as well), creating a pastiche – a pastiche also evident in the occasional use of rearscreen projection and the awkward efforts to integrate scenes of the principals with the second-unit photography shot in Africa itself.

Sanders of the River must also be examined in relation to *The Emperor Jones* (1934), and here Robeson proves to be a pivotally rich figure since the O'Neill play is unexpectedly linked to Wallace's stories of Sanders and Bosambo. The interplay between the two film adaptations only enriches the connection, creating a Gordian knot. It is hard to imagine that Robeson, Korda and others did not see their uncanny similarities. Bosambo and Jones are both escaped convicts; each is an outsider who comes to a black community and uses his wits to take over and become chief or emperor. Eugene O'Neill signals his debt to the Wallace stories, I would argue, in his choice of names – specifically in their first letters. Bosambo becomes Brutus while Sanders becomes Smithers. Indeed, Wallace's Sanders is arguably closer to the Smithers of *The Emperor Jones*, with his Cockney accent, than he is to the character played by Leslie Banks.[31] While Wallace's stories of Bosambo are played as comedy, O'Neill turned them into tragedy. Wallace's comic stasis produces an unchanging diegetic world, which inexorably unravels in *The Emperor Jones*. The Kordas, in contrast, chose to turn Wallace's ludic narratives into romantic drama.

Robeson had played Brutus in the 1925 London theatrical production of O'Neill's *The Emperor Jones*, but this and other stage performances generated little interest from the British film industry. This changed with the British release of the film version. The picture debuted at the Marble Arch Pavilion in London's Piccadilly Circus on 18 March 1934, to generally enthusiastic reviews, with Robeson making a strong impression. C. A. Lejeune praised 'Paul Robeson's magnificent gestures, stormy face, and voice like a bass-viol'.[32] R. H. of the *Guardian* enthused,

> *The Emperor Jones* is more than a photographed version of O'Neill's play, and Robeson is not content with repeating a theatrical performance. He not only dominates the screen, as might be expected, but seems freer and fuller, a giant rejoicing in his strength. The part calls for a development of character from youthful mischief to deliberate self-seeking, and the star's performance is such that one forgets, in watching the film, the personality of the actor who is giving it life.[33]

After interviewing Robeson, one journalist reported, 'his work in *Emperor Jones* ... resulted in his being selected for the starring role in *Sanders of the River*, which received much praise from dramatic critics; and his work in that production was responsible for his present part in *Showboat* [sic]'.[34]

Dudley Murphy's film *The Emperor Jones* brought Robeson to the attention of Alexander Korda. Shortly before his director-brother Zoltan returned from Africa with location footage for a film then entitled 'Kongo Raid' – destined to be an adaptation of Wallace's first collection of stories – *The Emperor Jones* was being screened for the trade in London, with Robeson's acting garnering enthusiastic comment.[35] Soon attached to Korda's project as its star, Robeson clearly shaped the project in important ways – as the change in working title from 'Kongo Raid' to 'Bosambo' (as Robeson was in rehearsals) would suggest.[36] When the Korda film was released in the US, a critic for the *Chicago Defender* noticed their uncanny parallels:

The Emperor Jones is the production one most easily remembers while watching the final reel of *Sanders of the River*. There is a sameness to the two pictures that almost bespeaks plagiarism and one wonders if the success of the former instigated the arrival of the latter film.[37]

If the play *The Emperor Jones* was inspired by Wallace's short stories, Korda's film was influenced by Murphy's film. Again, we might speculate as to the meaning that British moviegoers might have taken from the O'Neill film both on its own and then as paired with *Sanders of the River*. On this small Caribbean isle, the local native population had a system of independent but autocratic and self-destructive rule, which kept its people trapped in desperate poverty. Enlightened British colonialism must have seemed to be a superior alternative.

If the subversive potentials of *Sanders of the River* were dissipated, the film none the less fostered Robeson's cosmopolitan conviviality. Working on the set put him in touch with Africans and West Indians in ways that generated long-term connections within London's fragmented black community. Music afforded a similar opportunity. When the making of *Sanders* was still in its early stages, he was tremendously excited by the recordings that director Zoltan Korda had made in Africa: 'these records of Korda's have much more melody than I've ever heard come out of Africa', he exclaimed.[38] Yet he was also ecstatic to discern important similarities with Chinese, Celtic and other musical traditions. 'I'm not trying to postulate a common origin between these various races, but I think it is quite possibly the result of a common element of centuries of serfdom; at any rate, a common way of looking at life.'[39] Robeson used music as a means to further overcome barriers that separated peoples as his musical repertoire became increasingly international and multicultural.

Although Robeson publicly oscillated between condemning his role in *Sanders of the River* and affirming it (he continued to sing 'The Canoe Song' from *Sanders of the River* throughout the 1930s), his choice of future projects clearly indicates his determination to revise the film's identities, actions and ideologies. On the stage, the actor briefly took the role of an independent African chieftain in *Basalik*, a play that debuted 7 April – less than a week after the premiere of *Sanders*.[40] During the course of this drama, which was written specifically for Robeson, he rescues the local populace from the corrupt British governor. That *Basalik*'s name starts with B, like Bosambo – and for that matter Brutus – underscores the ways that plays and films were working off each other. On a small, intimate scale it undid the role he had just performed in the film – offering a rejection of the film's colonialist ideology. He also played L'Overture in C. L. R. James's play *Toussaint L'Ouverture* (March 1936). These performances were widely reported in the UK though much less so in the US. Their politics – shaped in part by his visits to the Soviet Union, which had begun in 1934 –were part of his British persona in ways that did not hold for his American profile. They also functioned as important sites of conviviality with members of the left theatre and London's eclectic black community. One of the novice actors in the play *Stevedore* was Robert Adams, born in British Guiana. A law student and wrestler, he had had a bit part in *Sanders of the River* and eventually became the leading black actor in England after Robeson's departure.[41]

One constructive way to evaluate Robeson's involvement in *Sanders of the River* is not as an isolated text but as part of a series of films and plays in which the star played black leaders, often African chiefs. These roles were balanced by a second series of off-castings in which Robeson played dockworkers, as in the play *Stevedore*, a 'vivid dramatization of the battle of black dockworkers in New Orleans to unionize and fight racial oppression'.[42] This London production of an American play ran in May 1935 – just before Paul and his business-manager wife Eslanda entered into negotiations with Carl Laemmle, Jr on the film version of *Show Boat* (1936), in which he also appears briefly as a dockworker.[43] At the beginning of *Song of Freedom*, released in September 1936, his character is also a dockworker. Such repetitions are not the result of an impoverished palate but a self-conscious engagement with prior texts – as *Song of Freedom* makes evident.

SONG OF FREEDOM

Song of Freedom (1936) was made by Hammer Productions: its chairman was comedian, theatre owner and insurgent producer Will Hammer (the stage name for William Hinds). Although Hammer made a brief on-screen appearance in *Song of Freedom*, the film's actual producer was Henry Fraser Passmore, a former art director and assistant producer. It was made in association with British Lion, a modest company originally formed to make feature films utilising Edgar Wallace's storytelling talents. To woo Robeson and his new box-office clout, Passmore allowed the star to retain creative control, including final cut over the film. The resulting picture was a response to and reworking of *Sanders of the River* and *Show Boat*. It is not just by chance that the film's title also starts with 'S': all three films can be seen as part of Robeson's 'S' trilogy. The actor plays John Zinga: the first two letters of his first name are the same as Joe – which was his character's name in *Show Boat*. Although he again plays a singing dockworker as in *Show Boat*, he does not play a lazybones. He is not only highly energetic, his singing is recognised inside the diegetic world of the film. Initially he sings at a local pub, a centre for this working-class community where transracial conviviality flourishes. This scene, pleasurable in its display of fellowship, contrasted with the real state of blacks then living in Britain's port cities where racial hostilities ran high.[44] The pub functions as an idealised space though one that in some ways resembled London's Harlem-style nightclubs where racial interactions were common and more relaxed – and with which Robeson was more familiar.

Zinga, discovered by an impresario, soon becomes an opera star and eventually performs the role of a black emperor: a backhanded reference to the opera *The Emperor Jones*, which had just been performed at the Metropolitan Opera in New York with the white actor Lawrence Tibbett in blackface. But it also references *Show Boat*, in which Joe is a supernumerary strutting outside the theatre in his military uniform (evoking, of course, Robeson's role in the play and film *The Emperor Jones*). Like Joe, John has a wife. In contrast to Aunt Jemima (Hattie McDaniels), she is a non-Mammy character who appreciates her husband – played by the elegant but down-to-earth Elizabeth Welch.[45]

The reworking of *Sanders of the River* is even more central to *Song of Freedom*. This 'song of freedom' might be contrasted to the song of adoring loyalty that Robeson had sung in that colonialist film. There is no Sandi here. It is Zinga, the descendant of former kings, who is the vehicle for bringing Western medicine and civilisation to the desperate island of Casanga. The story itself was sometimes said to be based on *The*

Kingdom of the Zinga, a novel by Claude Williams and Dorothy Holloway. This is no more real than the story 'Kongo Raid'. The story source was provided by Claude Wallace, who was no relation to Edgar Wallace but, in fact, the uncle of Robeson's friend and early biographer Marie Seton. Major Claude Wallace had spent years in Africa and led the romantic life of empire, which he details in his book *From Jungle to Jutland* (1932). He tried to start a coconut plantation on the small island of Casanga off the African coast. He failed as the island was purportedly cursed by the horrific activities of Queen Zinga in the mid-1600s. According to Major Wallace, 'it is said that she used to have a daily orgy of sacrifice, killing off between ten and twenty people each time'.[46] Among the people she murdered was her brother, from whom John Zinga is a fictional descendant. Claude Wallace had been responsible for the authentic look of the sets for *Sanders of the River* while his co-writer – Holloway – was the story editor for Korda's London Films. Again these ongoing associations suggest a more friendly and sustained relationship to that earlier project than one of angry rejection.

As with *Sanders of the River*, the climactic scene in *Song of Freedom* occurs as the Robeson character and his wife are tied to the stake and about to be brutally executed. While Sandi rescues Bosambo, John Zinga rescues himself (and his wife) by singing the chief's song, which suddenly comes back to him. Zinga becomes the new tribal king, saving his people from superstition and poverty as he moves back and forth between his new African home and the European concert tours that generate the income needed to turn the isle into an earthly paradise. Here again, a Utopian relationship between Africa and Europe is imagined, one free of colonial dynamics.

Song of Freedom opened at the Plaza Theatre in Piccadilly Circus on 19 September 1936 – three months after the London premiere of *Show Boat*. It generated a mixed reaction in the British press. *Film Weekly* felt the story was 'attractively told and provides excellent material for Paul Robeson's magnificent singing and sincere acting'.[47] John Milford compared the picture to *Sanders of the River* and *Show Boat*, declaring that 'Paul Robeson comes into his own' as 'we have him in a story after his own heart'.[48] While noting the film's various gestures to *Sanders of the River*, C. A. Lejeune was less kind in the *Observer*. 'The eminent coloured singer, one knows, is a loyal child of the people, but this constant preoccupation with the sweated torso and the wriggling witch doctor might seem to carry the back-to-the-land movement too far.'[49]

Despite its many intertextual references, *Song of Freedom* should also be framed in a larger cultural and cinematic context. The picture was made in the immediate wake of Jean Renoir's *Le Crime de M. Lange* (released in January 1936). Although any direct inspiration seems unlikely, the writer Amédée Lange (René LeFèvre) and the singer Zinga take on the central moral and economic responsibilities in both dramas. Lange's stories about the cowboy Arizona Jim enable the bankrupt publishing house to reinvent itself as a thriving working-class collective. Then he takes on the responsibility for killing Batala (Jules Berry), the nefarious publisher who has resurfaced to reclaim the business he had abused and destroyed. In *Song of Freedom* John's singing is not only a key source of working-class and elite conviviality among the races, it saves Zinga's life and proves his identity so that he can become king. Singing likewise provides the funds that make possible the transformation of the backwards isle into an earthly paradise. The hokey quality of Robeson's Africa sets might even be rescued by a comparison to the naive sets for the movie version of Arizona Jim in Renoir's film – for Robeson's relationship to Africa was in truth little different than that of Lange's to the American West. In both films, art and artists have privileged and unrealistically important roles. Likewise, in the alternate world constructed by *Song of Freedom*, colonialism is never an issue but is strangely absent.

MY SONG GOES FORTH

Robeson also took greater control of his image and films by becoming involved in *My Song Goes Forth*, a five-reel documentary about modern-day South Africa, directed by Joseph Best.[50] Best had been making feature-length films about Great Britain's overseas empire since the 1920s. While the four-reel core of the documentary is not without interest, Paul Robeson's remarkable one-reel prologue is what makes this film distinctive. Paul Robeson at least partially funded the prologue, which he effectively produced and directed – with important contributions from his wife Eslanda, who visited Africa midway through the attenuated post-production process. (Best had initially approached Robeson, footage in hand, hoping he would sing a song for the film, which would make it more commercial.) The nine-minute prologue, dominated by Robeson's on-screen performance, was the result. This reel of film is probably the only instance of film-making where Robeson had near-total control. It is also one of the few instances in which we can gain a sense of what it might have been like to have an intimate conversation with Robeson.

Robeson's utopic impulse, which guided all his work as a performer, is fully evident in the prologue, which embodies his principles of conviviality. He charms his audience with a talk that is much more intimate than a lecture. He confides and engages the viewer with a smile as if speaking on a one-to-one basis. Addressing the listener directly ('when you are shown pictures ...'), he makes his own stake in the declarations explicit. In short, he addresses the listener as if s/he was an acquaintance introduced by a mutual friend. This is in sharp contrast to the subsequent four reels of Joseph Best's film, which maintain a sense of formal distance connected to the educational authority of an expert and British elitism. And yet, for all its problems, the main section of *My Song Goes Forth* depicts modern South Africa and problematises many elements of the apartheid system that were then in the process of consolidation. As the film opened at London's Studio One Theatre on 6 April 1937, the *Manchester Guardian* remarked, so it is 'by reason of the unvarnished picture this film gives of the conditions under which both educated and uneducated natives live that we can understand and applaud Mr. Robeson's participation'.[51] Robeson's move from the realm of fiction to what Bill Nichols calls the discourse of sobriety was part of his evolution as a political figure.[52] Government organisations took notice of 'this recent film ... in which Paul Robeson appeared'.[53] South Africa House had heard that it was to be the first of 'a series of films which would be in the nature of "pro-native" propaganda' and contacted the Secretary of State, which alerted the Colonial Office.[54] The Colonial Office assured the Secretary of State, 'If any film is produced which is thought to be objectionable the Colonial Office would consider the question of making semi-official representations to the Board of Censors.'[55]

KING SOLOMON'S MINES

Following *Sanders of the River*, fiction films of imperial adventure became popular and the British film industry eagerly courted Robeson when they needed someone to play native African royalty. In the early 1930s British Gaumont was the largest and most successful vertically integrated British film company: for Robeson a starring role in one of its films was a logical step as he built his new film career. In the immediate aftermath of *Sanders of the River*, he was scheduled to appear in British Gaumont's empire film *Rhodes of Africa* (1936) as Lobengula, the last king of the Matabeles. He was able to void that commitment in order to appear in *Show Boat*,[56] but agreeing to play Umbopa in a subsequent British Gaumont adaptation of H. Rider Haggard's 1885 novel *King Solomon's Mines* was the likely *quid pro quo* of this arrangement. That Michael Balcon and British Gaumont were substantially invested in this picture is evident in the supporting cast, which included the recently knighted Cedric Hardwicke and Roland Young, who was about to receive an Academy Award for his supporting performance in *Topper* (1937). It was directed by Robert Stevenson, who had developed a strong reputation and would later receive an Oscar nomination for directing *Mary Poppins* (1964).

Haggard's book and the film adaptation contain many of the story elements one finds in *Sanders of the River* and *Song of Freedom*. Umbopa (Robeson) is a disenfranchised king who helps the British adventurers reach King Solomon's diamond mines but in the process is also returned to his rightful throne. Unlike *Sanders*, *King Solomon's Mines* remains a period piece, avoiding the unfortunate parachrony of the Korda film. Likewise, the Kukuana are a free and noble people living completely independently of colonial rule, ensuring that the Robeson character avoided the obsequiousness of the Bosambo role. Despite these attractive elements, *King Solomon's Mines* received mixed reviews when it opened at the Gaumont Haymarket Theatre on 26 July 1937 – less than three months after *My Song Goes Forth*. *The Times* reviewer hemmed and hawed, concluding 'in general, there is very little about which one can definitely complain. Yet there is something lacking, though the film makes reasonable entertainment.'[57] The film's departure from the classic novel undermined many of the book's best features while offering little in its place, disappointing Graham Greene and many viewers. At the same time, Greene considered the film 'seeable'.[58] Indeed, Rachael Low indicates the film was 'liked by the public'.[59] Certainly, Haggard's story was one of the foundational texts of the empire genre, and its influence can be felt in all four of Robeson's fiction films of empire.

Some of the discrepancies between novel and film suggest ways that Robeson once again encountered 'an idea that attracted me, a result in which I wasn't interested'. The novel unfolds around the actions of four characters: the narrator and 'white hunter' Allan Quatermain (Cedric Hardwicke), the wealthy English gentleman Sir Henry Curtis (John Loder), retired naval officer Commander John Good (Roland Young) (living on a meagre half-pay salary), and Umbopa, a mysterious African who proved the lost king of the remote Kukuana people. In some sense the story is about their camaraderie – one in which Sir Curtis and Umbopa share a special bond due to their aristocratic lineages. A noteworthy conviviality among the male characters evolves over the course of the novel. However, the film introduces two new characters that change the novel's homosocial dynamic. One of them – Kathleen O'Brien – becomes the love interest for Sir Henry Curtis. Curtis, played by John Loder, and Kathleen, played by Stevenson's wife Anna Lee, become the story's new centre and marginalise Umbopa's friendship with Curtis, in which race had offered little impediment. Moreover, Haggard's novel offered a nascent romance between John Good and a Kukuana woman whom he had helped to save. While never consummated, this interracial attraction was also banished from the film. Interactions across races were reduced, in contrast to sustained efforts in this regard with *Song of Freedom*.

Stevenson's film posed a number of constraints on Robeson. In *Sanders* and *Song of Freedom*, Robeson played the romantic lead, a factor that kept the black star at the centre of both films. Although he was still given top billing in *King Solomon's Mines*, it did not necessarily match his actual prominence in the picture (or on the posters). This is ultimately linked to the problem of 'positive images'. Robeson's character of Umbopa faces an impossible tension between the actions of a good black man – one who saves his white comrades and makes possible the success of their adventure – and a virile, independent black man. By being good to Allan Quatermain, Captain Good and Sir Henry Curtis, which is merited on the basis of personal relations and mutual aid, Umbopa sustains and fosters the machinery of empire, which will reduce native leaders to obedient factotums. This is even more pronounced in the film since the novel was written when parts of Africa were still beyond colonial control. By 1937, with the Italian occupation of Ethiopia, all of Africa was under imperial rule. Moreover, the homosocial conviviality of the novel functions in a separate space that could not credibly exist in 1930s commercial cinema except as a boyish fantasy. Robeson's character thus facilitates white plunder and white romance even as the actor portrays a now desexualised black man, who sings his way through the narrative of adventure. As a result of such changes, the adaptation suffers from a shift in genre and tone, becoming a modified and somewhat awkward musical.

JERICHO AKA *DARK SANDS*

Jericho, like *Song of Freedom*, was made by a small British company that relied heavily on Robeson's stardom for its commercial viability. One beneficiary of the British film industry's post-1933 bubble was Max Schach, a Central European cineaste and Korda wannabe. Schach started a number of film companies, including Buckingham Film Productions in February 1936. Although company executives announced their intention to make three super productions a year, the only film that Buckingham managed to complete was *Jericho*, with American producer Walter Futter and American director Thornton Freeland.[60] Freeland, who had directed *Flying down to Rio* for RKO in 1933, had moved to London in the mid-1930s and was directing films for the British industry. Futter's involvement is more puzzling. He was the producer and mastermind behind the safari documentary *Africa Speaks!* (1930), which was promoted as 'the first talking picture' made in Africa –though sync sound inserts were shot in California.[61] Praised by the *New York Times* and other American newspapers, it encountered protests in Europe due to its demeaning depictions of native Africans.[62] Futter subsequently produced *India Speaks* (1933) and a number of low-budget independent Westerns in the mid-1930s before landing this job. Perhaps he had convinced investors that he knew both Africa and the American market.

The last of Robeson's roles as an African king, *Jericho* is often considered the most successful when it comes to dealing with black themes.[63] Like Brutus Jones, Jericho Jackson is an escaped convict – but in this case one unjustly convicted. A heroic soldier during World War I, he accidentally kills a white officer who had panicked and was preventing his men from escaping a sinking ship torpedoed by the enemy. Jericho is convicted of murder, faces execution, but escapes from prison. He flees to North Africa, where he uses his skills as a former medical student to do good (recalling *Song of Freedom*). He soon marries the chief of a nomadic Tuareg tribe – played by the charming Kouka, a real-life Sudanese princess, whose looks in some respects recall Josephine Baker in *Princess Tam Tam*. Soon Jericho becomes the tribal chief.

Jericho opened at the New Gallery Theatre on 1 November 1937, a mere three months after *King Solomon's Mines* (*Africa Speaks!* had played at the same theatre barely six years before). Reviews were mixed. The *Guardian* called it 'one of his most successful pictures', but the review was extremely brief.[64] 'It is always a pleasure to hear Mr. Robeson sing whether on sand-dunes or off them', remarked *The Times*, 'but he is an actor too good to be thrown away on Jericho.'[65] Although *Jericho* does lack a degree of gravitas, it would seem to have justified Robeson's persistence in the genre. Western knowledge is used to benefit rather than conquer and exploit African people. Jericho helps both whites and blacks – though in saving whites he faces the prejudicial application of the law. He is once again the romantic centre of the film – paired with an appealing young 'discovery'. Nevertheless, even though its production provided Robeson with the opportunity to briefly visit Africa and see the Egyptian pyramids, the performer did not take the film very seriously nor was he particularly happy with it.[66] Why was Robeson's attitude so unenthusiastic? There would seem to be a variety of likely explanations. First, Robeson always found it difficult to work with American producers and directors. Given Futter's previous films (specifically *Africa Speaks!*), a degree of disinvestment must have been inevitable. In many respects, Futter embodied everything that Robeson opposed. Second, while the money was almost certainly appealing for Robeson, these roles as African chieftains had become overly familiar (for Robeson and his fans). Third, if the role of Jericho was less problematic than that of Bosambo, Robeson's own sense of his role as an artist and political figure was changing even more quickly. The films could not keep up.

As Robeson moved in a more political direction, he looked beyond the commercial film industry for opportunities to address his interests and concerns with Africa. Documentary was one means – a mode he would continue to embrace throughout the remainder of his career. The production of *Jericho* coincided with the completion and release of *My Song Goes Forth*, and we should remember that Robeson envisioned this as the first in a series of documentaries on Africa and colonialism. More importantly Robeson's political involvement with Africa found a direct outlet through the International Committee on African Affairs.[67] The organisation was founded by African American Max Yergan in January 1937, shortly after returning from his post as YMCA secretary in South Africa; its purpose was 'to effect a change in the economic and political structure of the colonies of South Africa and the adjacent territories'.[68] Eslanda Robeson had spent a significant amount of time with Yergan during her trip to

Africa in 1936, so it is not entirely surprising that her husband became a prominent member of the committee. In April 1937, Yergan travelled to England and France where he met the actor and activist. Soon after he declared,

> I know of no person more constructively effective in the international life of peoples of African descent than Paul Robeson. He has given me several hours of his busy time during the last week in London. He is a power in many ways, and as we talked and planned together I became increasingly aware of the significance of his membership on the International Committee on African Affairs.[69]

Robeson became a key Europe-based member of the committee – along with French African/Guyanese author Rene Maran and Leonard Barnes. Moreover, like others on the left, Robeson was becoming increasingly concerned about the rise of fascism and the Spanish Civil War; as a result, fiction film-making became less of a priority.

In mid-1941, not long after Robeson returned to the US, the International Committee on African Affairs changed its name to the Council on African Affairs, and Robeson became its chairman. During World War II it had significant influence on American foreign policy *vis-à-vis* colonialism and Africa, reinforcing the United States' anti-colonial foreign-policy positions. By then Robeson had left fiction films of empire far behind him – indeed they had become embarrassments that were best forgotten. At best, given his activist anti-colonial stance, they were traces of a former self he had long outgrown and left behind.

Robeson's films of Africa left him with a complex legacy. Although most of his films may seem overtly supportive of Great Britain's faith in its empire and a *pax Britannica*, a more nuanced assessment suggests that this characterisation is only strictly true for *Sanders of the River*. If we remember that Nigeria's own anti-colonial movement – the Lagos Youth Movement, which soon became the Nigerian Youth Movement – was only established in 1934/6, then Robeson's rapid political evolution might be seen as consistent with a larger political development. And yet, given that the sole African territory within the US sphere of influence was Liberia, a more or less independent nation that held tremendous symbolic importance for Americans of African descent, anti-colonialism was an established fact in the United States. Here the British and American contexts diverged quite radically, and we can see how difficult it was for Robeson and the films in which he appeared to address these diverse audiences. What did it mean for an exemplary American to kneel down before an official of the British Empire – even if he was only acting and even if (or rather, especially because) he was black. If racial politics in the US were in a painful state, white and black Americans alike shared strong anti-colonial attitudes – a product of the country's own history as a British colony liberated through revolution.

Conflicting assumptions by diverging audiences were further echoed by distinctions between the work Robeson did with the leading British producers/film companies such as London Films or British Gaumont and those smaller efforts over which he had more control – this second category not only including films such as *Song of Freedom* and the prologue to *My Song Goes Forth* but various stage productions. The first group of films established his stardom, and one must acknowledge the novel force of a black moviestar who was consistently given top billing over long-established, highly regarded British actors who were knighted and won Oscars. (Robeson's character of Bosambo may have bowed before Sanders but Leslie Banks and others deferred to Robeson when it came to star billing.) This was its own radical form of decolonisation: the inversion of established racial, cultural and political orderings. The second group of films and plays might have exhibited a more radical political orientation but they received less distribution and less media coverage, particularly in the US. Of course, movie stardom (along with radio) was also a crucial means for Robeson to connect with the British working class. (Among other things, Robeson made a point of giving live concerts in British cinemas during the 1930s.) Making films on African subjects was also a way to learn about Africa as well as about the politics of representation and colonialism. Robeson's evolution from starring in *Sanders of the River* to chairing the Council on African Affairs may have been less a question of personal intellectual advancement and more one of method – from movie-making to heading a nongovernmental organisation. And yet, his work in the cinema (1935–7) provided a platform for launching his more radical and explicitly anti-colonial political efforts just a short time later (1937–45).

NOTES

1. T. Thompson, 'Paul Robeson Speaks about Art and the Negro', *Millgate*, December 1930, in Philip S. Foner (ed.), *Paul Robeson Speaks: Writings, Speeches, Interviews, 1918–1974* (New York: Brunner/Mazel, 1978), p. 79.
2. G. G. G., 'True Negro Culture Will Come', *Daily Gleaner*, 15 November 1930, p. 35.
3. 'Paul Robeson Tells Us Why', *Cine-Technician*, September–October 1938, pp. 74–5, in Foner, *Paul Robeson Speaks*, p. 121.
4. Paul Robeson, Jr, *The Undiscovered Paul Robeson: An Artist's Journey, 1898–1939* (New York: John Wiley & Sons, 2001), p. 231. Robeson's quotation can be found in 'Robeson, Home Again, Defends Cinema Role', *Philadelphia Tribune*, 10 October 1935, p. 13.
5. Marie Seton, Robeson's friend and biographer, dismissively criticised his best-known efforts: *The Emperor Jones, Sanders of the River, Show Boat* and *King Solomon's Mines*; skipped over others: *Big Fella* (1937) and *Tales of Manhattan* (1942); had nice things to say about *Song of Freedom* and (briefly) *Jericho* but concluded that *Proud Valley* (1940) 'was the one film which did honour to him'. See *Paul Robeson* (London: Dennis Dobson, 1958), p. 105. Thirty years later, in one of the earliest sustained examinations of Robeson's film work, Anatol I. Schlosser sought to offer a balanced assessment, laying out the mixed reactions to *The Emperor Jones*, while quickly dismissing his appearance in *Sanders of the River* and *Show Boat*. Schlosser argued that in *Big Fella*, Robeson at last 'found a role that gave him greater scope for his acting than his previous British pictures', though this promise was not sustained with *Jericho*. *Proud Valley* was his greatest achievement, while *Tales of Manhattan* represented a setback. See Anatol Schlosser, 'Paul Robeson in Film: An Iconoclast's Quest for a Role', in *Freedomways* (eds), *Paul Robeson: The Great Forerunner* (New York: Dodd, Mead & Company, 1978), pp. 72–93. In his extensive, in-depth biography, Martin Duberman avoided evaluations of Robeson's films, treating them from an historical perspective in terms of their production history and reception – a subtle if significant change. See Martin Duberman, *Paul Robeson* (New York: Knopf, 1988). As Mark Reid has noted, 'many critics

chastise Robeson for the stereotypical film roles he performed, but the same critics have not extended their criticism to the systematic realities that determined his roles in American and British cinema'. See '*Freedom* and Jericho', in Jeffrey C. Stewart (ed.), *Paul Robeson: Artist and Citizen* (New Brunswick, NJ: Rutgers University Press, 1998), p. 166.

6. Paul Gilroy, *Postcolonial Melancholia* (New York: Columbia University Press, 2005), p. 67.
7. Hazel Carby, *Race Men: The W. E. B. DuBois Lectures* (Cambridge, MA: Harvard University Press, 1998), pp. 45–86.
8. Rachael Low, *The History of the British Film, 1929–1939: Film Making in 1930s Britain* (London: George Allen & Unwin, 1985), pp. 198–206.
9. 'Entertainments', *The Times*, 3 April 1935, p. 12.
10. John Gammie, 'Sanders of the River', *Film Weekly*, 12 April 1935, p. 31.
11. Jeffrey Richards, 'Boys Own Empire: Feature Films and Imperialism in the 1930s', in John M. MacKenzie (ed.), *Imperialism and Popular Culture* (Manchester: Manchester University Press, 1986), pp. 140–64; Anthony Aldgate and Jeffrey Richards, *Best of British: Cinema and Society from 1930 to the Present* (London: I. B. Tauris, 1999), pp. 19–36.
12. 'Traditions of Empire', *The Times*, 10 June 1936, p. 18.
13. 'An Actor Cannot Eat His Ideals', *Baltimore Afro-American*, 12 October 1935, p. 9.
14. Ibid.
15. Ibid.
16. Brian V. Street, *The Savage in Literature: Representations of 'Primitive' Society in English Fiction, 1858–1920* (London: Routledge & Kegan Paul, 1975), p. 73.
17. Robeson's character was immediately labelled an Uncle Tom by Tom Wells in the Marcus Garvey newspaper, *Liberator*. See 'An Actor Cannot Eat His Ideals', p. 9.
18. Edgar Wallace, *Sanders of the Rivers* (1911; Garden City, NY: Doubleday, Doran & Co., 1930), p. 204. Page numbers henceforth in the text.
19. C. A. L., 'Big African Negro Film', *Observer*, 29 July 1934, p. 12.
20. John Gammie, 'What – and What Not – to See', *Film Weekly*, 12 April 1935, p. 31.
21. James Agate, *Around Cinema* (Amsterdam: Home & Van Thal, 1948), p. 118. Andre Sennwald makes the same basic point in his *New York Times* review (27 June 1935, p. 16).
22. Leonard Wallace, 'Korda's Castles in the Air', *Film Weekly*, 20 June 1936, p. 9.
23. 'Wings over Africa', *New York Times*, 20 January 1935, p. X4; Andre Sennwald, 'The Screen', *New York Times*, 23 January 1935, p. 21.
24. Barbara Bush, *Imperialism, Race and Resistance: Africa and Britain, 1919–1945* (London: Routledge, 1999), pp. 97–8.
25. 'The Legislative Council', <www.onlinenigeria.com/independence/?blurb=634>.
26. Bush, *Imperialism, Race and Resistance*, pp. 105–10.
27. In an article 'Impressions of West Africa', published in the *Manchester Guardian* on 7 January 1935, Charles Roden Buxton complained that British rule 'does not take enough account of the educated African as opposed to the primitive African' (p. 9). Such a criticism was certainly applicable to the film *Sanders of the River*.
28. Terri Francis, 'The Audacious Josephine Baker: Stardom, Cinema and Paris', in Darlene Clark Hine *et al.* (eds), *Black Europe and the African Diaspora* (Urbana: University of Illinois Press, 2009), pp. 238–59.
29. Mae Tinée, 'Film of White Rule in Africa Is Achievement', *Chicago Daily Tribune*, 26 October 1935, p. 17.
30. '"Little Africa" in London', *Manchester Guardian*, 10 October 1934, p. 20.

31. One should always be cautious in asserting textual appropriations (as opposed to noting intriguing parallels). O'Neill's appropriation outlined above is quite basic but there are other parallels that are worth noting even if their influence on O'Neill would be harder to assert. These include a somewhat similar sequence of visions and the use of the word 'nigger'.

32. C. A. Lejeune, 'The Emperor Jones', *Observer*, 18 March 1934, p. 23.

33. R. H., '"The Emperor Jones" Paul Robeson's Film', *Manchester Guardian*, 19 March 1934, p. 18.

34. '"Showboat" the Same Old Thing; Robeson Hopes for True Role', *Baltimore Afro-American*, 11 January 1936, p. 5.

35. 'Emperor Jones', *Kinematograph Weekly*, 1 February 1934, p. 24; 'Kongo Raid', *Kinematograph Weekly*, 22 February 1934, p. 33.

36. C. A. L., 'Big African Negro Film', p. 12.

37. Rob Roy, '"Sanders of the River" Is Tuneful Plagiarism', *Chicago Defender*, 16 November 1935, p. 9.

38. C. A. L., 'Big African Negro Film', p. 12.

39. Ibid.

40. 'Mr. Paul Robeson's New Part', *The Times*, 4 April 1935, p. 12; 'Basalik', *The Times*, 8 April 1935, p. 12.

41. 'Robert Adams (actor)', wikipedia.

42. S. T. Boyle and A. Bunie, *Paul Robeson: The Years of Promise and Achievement* (Amherst: University of Massachusetts Press, 2001), p. 329.

43. Ibid., p. 332.

44. Bush, *Imperialism, Race and Resistance*, pp. 209–11.

45. Stephen Bourne, *Elisabeth Welch: Soft Lights and Sweet Music* (Lanham, MD: Scarecrow Press, 2005). Welch's first name is spelt with a 'z' in the film credits.

46. Claude Wallace, *From Jungle to Jutland* (London: Nisbet & Co., 1932), p. 299.

47. 'Song of Freedom', *Film Weekly*, 6 March 1937, p. 34.

48. John Milford, 'Song of Freedom',' *Film Pictorial*, 6 March 1937, p. 22.

49. C. A. Lejeune, 'Films of the Week', *Observer*, 20 September 1936, p. 18.

50. For a close examination of *My Song Goes Forth*, see Charles Musser, 'Presenting "a True Idea of the African of To-day": Two Documentary Forays by Paul and Eslanda Robeson', *Film History* vol. 18 no. 4 (2006), pp. 412–39.

51. R. H., 'My Song Goes Forth', *Manchester Guardian*, 6 April 1937, p. 8.

52. Bill Nichols, *Representing Reality: Issues and Concepts in Documentary* (Bloomington: Indiana University Press, 1991).

53. E. J. H. to Sir E. Garding and H. Tait, 15 March 1937, C0 323/1421/2, Public Records Office, National Archives (UK). My thanks to James M. Burns for bringing this correspondence to my attention.

54. Ibid.

55. H. Tait, 'Copy of Minutes', 22 March 1937, C0 323/1421/2, Public Records Office, National Archives (UK).

56. 'An Actor Cannot Eat His Ideals', p. 9. The role was played by Ndaniso Kumala.

57. 'New Films in London', *The Times*, 26 July 1937, p. 10.

58. Graham Greene, 'Tribute to Harpo', *Night and Day*, 12 August 1937, in David Parkinson (ed.), *The Graham Greene Reader: Mornings in the Dark* (Manchester: Carcanet Press, 1993), pp. 212–13.

59. Low, *The History of the British Film, 1929–1939*, p. 142.

60. Ibid., pp. 198–206.
61. Edward Bernds, *Mr. Bernds Goes to Hollywood: My Early Life and Career in Sound Recording at Columbia with Frank Capra and Others* (Lanham, MD: Scarecrow Press, 1999), pp. 137–9.
62. Mordaunt Hall, 'Sounds in the Jungle', *New York Times*, 30 September 1930, p. 23; 'The Wrong Sort of Realism', *Manchester Guardian*, 31 January 1931, p. 10. This protest against the motion-picture depiction of an African's on-screen death was taken up by many British critics as well as left-wing French and German journalists.
63. See, for instance, Chris Norton, 'The Paul Robeson Centennial Collection: Jericho', *Images 5*, <www.imagesjournal.com/issue05/reviews/robeson-jericho.htm>.
64. 'British Films', *Manchester Guardian*, 30 October 1937, p. 16.
65. 'New Gallery', *The Times*, 1 November 1937, p. 12.
66. Boyle and Bunie, *Paul Robeson*, pp. 369–71.
67. Hollis R. Lynch, *Black American Radicals and the Liberation of Africa: The Council on African American Affairs, 1937–1955* (Ithaca, NY: Africana Studies and Research Center, Cornell University, 1978); Penny M. von Eschen, *Race against Empire: Black Americans and Anticolonialism, 1937–1957* (Ithaca, NY: Cornell University Press, 1997).
68. 'Yergan Faces Bitter Fight in his Planning to Redeem Africans', *New York Amsterdam News*, 13 February 1937, p. 6.
69. Max Yergan, 'A Committee on Africa Affairs is Organized', *Chicago Defender*, 29 May 1927, p. 24.

Index

Notes
Colonies are indexed under their colonial names, not those of the present independent nations (e.g. Gold Coast not Ghana).

Page numbers in **bold** denote extended/detailed treatment; those in *italic* refer to illustrations.

Great Depression (1930s)
81–2
The Great Recovery (1934) 82
The Great War (TV, 1964) 39
Greene, Graham 139,
148*n42*, 273
Greville Brothers 117–18,
121, 131*n29*
Grierson, John 11, **93–100**,
112*n144*, 112*n146*,
135–6, 144–5
'Further Notes on Cinema
Production' 95
'Notes for English
Producers' 93–4
theory of film 93–4
Griffith, D. W. 31*n8*
Grigg, Sir Edward, Governor
62, 68*n40*
Guggisberg, Sir Gordon 117
Gunga Din (1939) 190, 201

Haggard, H. Rider, *King
Solomon's Mines* 273–4
Hamedi (BEKE assistant)
238
Hammer, Will 270
*Handbook for Geography
Teachers* 170, 172, 173,
184*n13*
Hansen, Miriam Bratu
188*n57*
Harcourt, Lewis 56
Hardwicke, Cedric 273
Harlem Renaissance 261
Harlow, Vincent 68*n56*
Harmsworth, Alfred *see*
Northcliffe, Lord
Harvey, David 73, 101*n5*,
151, 152
Hathaway, Henry 189–90
Hays, Will/Hays Code (1934)
5, 85
Heffernan, Michael 154
Heidegger, Martin 173–4,
186*n27*
Henri Christophe of Haiti
264–5
Hepworth, Barbara 141
Hepworth, Cecil 28

Here and There in Samoa
(1930s) 255, 259
Heroes of Gallipoli (1920) 39
Hesketh Bell, Sir Henry 63
*High Yields from Selected
Plants* (1937) 238
Highways of Empire 116–17
Higson, Andrew 109*n92*
A Himalayan Town: Katmandu
(1937) 168
Hirst, Paul 2–3
historiography, links with
cinema 181–2
Hitchcock, Alfred 267
Hoare, Sir Samuel 154, 157
Hobsbawm, Eric 31*n1*,
103*n20*
Holloway, Dorothy 271
Hong Kong
return to China (1997) 3
hookworm *see Tropical
Hookworm*; *Unhooking the
Hookworm*
Hoover, Herbert 106*n70*
Hopkins, Tony, Professor
102–3*n15*
Horne, Sir Robert 89
Hughes, Deborah L. 116
Hull, Cordell 112–13*n155*
Huxley, Julian 132*n48*, 231–2

Imperial Agricultural
Committee 95
Imperial Airways 9, 135,
137–42, 144, 154–6, 161
imperial and international
communications 157
Imperial Cinematograph
Corporation 84
imperial conference (1926)
130*n21*
see also Balfour Declaration
Imperial Relations Trust 99
Imperial War Museum 2, 4,
7, 35, **36–8**, 39
curatorial staff/policy 40–1
Import Duties Act 1932 76,
102*n14*
Improved Agriculture (1937)
238

India 97, **167–82**
cartographic
standardisation 179–80
famine (1943) 6, 7
films of governors/royalty
29–30, 33*n37*, 42
independence 6–7
involvement of troops in
World War I 37, **41–4**
'Mutiny' (1857) 43–4
showings of British films
229
India Division **41–4**
India Speaks (1933) 274
'Indian Town Studies' series
168–71, 177–80, 182,
183*n2*
affinities with map-making
170–1, 178–9
non-dramatic presentation
169
use of cartographic symbols
178–9
use of voiceover 170
Industrial Britain (1933) 144
Information Films of India 5
Innis, Harold 30, 33*n39*
International Civil Aviation
Organisation (ICAO)
141, 144
International Committee
(later Council) on African
Affairs 275–6
International Educational
Cinematography Institute
231
International Health Board
56–7, 65–6
International Institute of
Intellectual Cooperation
231
International Missionary
Council 207, 210, 211,
220, 227, 233–4, 248–9
interracial relationships, ban
on depictions 90

Jackson (BEKE
driver/mechanic) 238
Jaikumar, Priya 125